# ABSOLUTE
# BEGINNER'S
# GUIDE

to

# Programming

Greg Perry

800 East 96th Street,
Indianapolis, Indiana 46240

# Absolute Beginner's Guide to Programming, Second Edition

International Standard Book Number: 0-7897-2905-9

Library of Congress Catalog Card Number: 2002113848

Printed in the United States of America

First Printing: December 2002
Reprinted with corrections: November 2003

05   04        7   6   5

## Trademarks

## Warning and Disclaimer

**Executive Editor**
Candace Hall

**Development Editor**
Mark Cierzniak

**Managing Editor**
Thomas F. Hayes

**Project Editor**
Sheila Schroeder

**Copy Editor**
Gene Redding

**Indexer**
Kelly Castell

**Proofreader**
Juli Cook

**Technical Editor**
Betsy Stern Hill

**Team Coordinator**
Cindy Teeters

**Interior Designer**
Anne Jones

**Cover Designer**
Anne Jones

# Contents at a Glance

Introduction, 1

**Part I    Prelude to Programming, 3**

  1    Computers Are Tools, 5

  2    Anatomy of a Program, 21

**Part II   Fundamentals of
            Programming, 39**

  3    Programming Languages: The Early
       Years, 41

  4    Programming Languages: Modern
       Day, 61

**Part III  Hands-on Programming, 75**

  5    Your First Language:
       Visual Basic, 77

  6    Input and Output, 89

  7    Data Processing with
       Visual Basic, 109

  8    Working with Data, 125

  9    Having Fun with Visual Basic, 143

  10   Advanced Visual Basic
       Programming, 159

  11   Online Visual Basic
       Programming, 179

**Part IV   Programming in Various
            Environments, 195**

  12   Program Algorithms, 197

  13   Programming with C, 211

  14   Programming with C++, 227

  15   Macro, Batch, and Scripting
       Languages, 243

  16   Internet Programming
       Concepts, 259

  17   HTML Programming, 273

  18   Dynamic HTML, 285

  19   Introduction to XML, 295

  20   Java Programming, 305

  21   JavaScript, 323

**Part V    The Business of
            Programming, 333**

  22   The Importance of
       Maintenance, 335

  23   Distributing Your Applications, 357

  24   The Programming Business, 373

  25   Your Programming Future, 389

       Index, 399

# Table of Contents

**Introduction   1**

Who Should Read This Book?   **1**

Conventions Used in This Book   **1**

## I Prelude to Programming

### 1 Computers Are Tools   5

Computers and Programming   **6**

What a Computer Does   **6**

Common Misconceptions   **7**
   Myth 1: "Only Math Experts Can Program Computers"   **8**
   Myth 2: "Computer Programs Make Mistakes"   **8**
   Myth 3: "Programming Is Difficult"   **9**

Ease-of-Use Matters to Programmers   **9**

People and Computers   **10**

It Takes More than a Computer   **10**
   The Hardware   **11**
   The Software   **12**
   The People   **13**
   The Data   **13**
   The Procedures   **14**

A Quick Overview   **14**
   The First Generation   **14**
   The Second Generation   **15**
   The Third Generation   **15**

Networking It All   **16**

Today's Computers   **17**

Types of Computers   **17**
   Supercomputers   **17**
   Mainframes   **18**
   Minicomputers   **19**
   Microcomputers   **19**

Summary   **20**

### 2 Anatomy of a Program   21

The Programmer's Life   **22**

The Need for Programs   **22**

Programs, Programs, Everywhere   **24**

Programs As Directions   **24**
   Art or Science?   **26**
   Speak the Language   **27**

The Language Translator   **29**

Accuracy Is Everything   **30**

The Need for Design   **31**
   Step 1: Define the Output   **33**
   Step 2: Develop the Logic   **36**
   Step 3: Write the Program   **36**

The Program Language   **36**

Summary   **37**

## II Fundamentals of Programming

### 3 Programming Languages: The Early Years   41

Storage of Programs and Data   **42**

Binary Arithmetic   **44**

The First Programs   **47**

Enter the Keyboard   **48**

Getting Closer to English   **50**
　The FORTRAN Language   **50**
　The Business of COBOL   **52**

Other Languages Through the Years   **55**

Summary   **59**

**4  Programming Languages: Modern Day   61**

Pascal's Importance and Demise   **62**

The C Programming Language   **63**
　The Success of C   **64**
　C++: A Better C   **65**

C++'s Impact on Modern Languages   **65**

Hypertext and Scripting Languages   **66**

The BASICs   **66**
　The Early BASICs   **67**
　Graphical Programming with Visual Basic   **71**

Which Language Is Best?   **72**

Summary   **73**

**III  Hands-On Programming**

**5  Your First Language: Visual Basic   77**

A Visual Basic Quick Start   **78**

Your First Visual Basic Program   **78**

Learning the Visual Basic Environment   **80**
　Visual Basic Programming Steps   **80**
　Working in Visual Basic   **81**

The Visual Basic Screen   **82**
　The Menu Bar and the Toolbar   **82**
　Looking at the Form Window   **83**

The Toolbox Provides the Controls   **84**
　The Form Layout Window   **86**
　The Project Explorer Window   **86**
　The Properties Window   **87**

Help Is Close By   **87**

Summary   **87**

**6  Input and Output   89**

A Quick Windows Program Analysis   **90**

Controlling Events   **91**

Application Specifics   **91**

The Interface Controls   **92**
　Placing Controls   **92**
　Setting Properties   **93**

Walking Through an Application's Development   **96**

Other Controls   **99**

Document with Remarks   **101**

Message and Input Boxes   **103**
　Using Message Boxes   **104**
　Using Input Boxes   **107**

Summary   **108**

**7  Data Processing with Visual Basic   109**

Adding Code   **110**

The Basics of Visual Basic Data   **111**
　Data Types   **111**
　Specifying Values   **112**
　Variables Hold Data   **114**
　Putting Data in Variables   **117**

Expressions and Math Operators   **119**

Comparison Operators   **122**

Summary   **124**

8 **Working with Data** 125

Making Decisions in Code 126

Using `Else` 127

Other Forms of Decision Making 129

Nesting `If...Else` Statements 131

Selecting with `Select Case` 131

Looping in Visual Basic 135
The `Do While` Loop 135
The `Do Until` Loop 137
The `For` Loop 139

Summary 141

9 **Having Fun with Visual Basic** 143

Using Shapes 144

An Aside About Controls 145

The Line Control 145

Mastering the Shape Control 147

A Sample Shape Application 150

The Picture Box Control 154
Picture Box Control Setup 155
Picture Box File Types 156

Summary 157

10 **Advanced Visual Basic Programming** 159

Application: Interest Calculation 160
Getting Ready to Write 160
Creating the Application 161
Hotkeys and Target Controls 163
A Detour: Understanding Focus at Runtime 163
Tab Order 165

Adding the Form's Labels and Text Boxes 165
Putting on the First Label and Text Box Set 166
Completing the Controls and Learning About Control Arrays 166

Adding Code 171
The Calculation Code 171
The `Unload` Statement 174
Error Checking 174

Summary 178

11 **Online Visual Basic Programming** 179

Introducing Visual Basic Wizards 180

Using the Wizard for the Internet 184
Working the Wizard 184
Default URL 185
Creating an Internet-Aware Application 185
Trying the Application 187

Sampling the Internet Controls 188

A Preview of Advanced Issues 190
ActiveX Documents 191
HTML and VBScript 191

Summary 192

IV **Programming in Various Environments**

12 **Program Algorithms** 197

Counters and Accumulators 198

Swapping Values 200

Sorting 201

Nested Loops 203

Searching Arrays **204**
   The Sequential Search **205**
   The Binary Search **206**

A Brief Introduction to Data Structures **208**
   Data Structures Help Group Data **208**
   Referencing Data Structure Items **209**

Summary **210**

**13 Programming with C**   211

Introducing C **212**

Analyzing a C Program **214**

Using the `main()` Function's Format **214**

Using the `#include` Statement **215**

C Data **215**

C Comments **216**

Declaring Variables **217**

C Functions **217**
   Using Built-In Functions **217**
   The `printf()` Output Function **218**
   The `scanf()` Input Function **220**
   Writing General Program Functions **222**

C Operators **224**

C Control Statements **224**

Summary **226**

**14 Programming with C++**   227

Learning C++ **228**

Object Terminology **228**

Fundamental Differences Between C and C++ **229**
   Comments **229**
   Name Differences **230**
   I/O Differences **230**

Introducing Objects **231**
   Defining Classes **233**
   Declaring Object Variables **234**
   Accessing Members **235**
   Adding Behavior to Objects **235**
   Working with Class Scope **238**

Benefits of OOP **239**

Summary **241**

**15 Macro, Batch, and Scripting Languages**   243

Batch: The One That Started Everything **244**
   Batch File Usage **244**
   Reviewing the Batch Language **246**

Macro Languages **248**
   The Need for Macros **248**
   Using a Keyboard Macro **249**

Visual Basic for Applications (VBA) **251**

Scripting in Windows **254**

Summary **257**

**16 Internet Programming Concepts**   259

Internet Programming Considerations **260**
   Internet Connections **260**
   Internet Communications **262**

The Need for Simple Navigation **262**

HTML Programming **264**

ActiveX Controls **266**

Scripting in Internet Applications **267**

ASP and .NET Technologies **268**

Summary **271**

**17  HTML Programming**  273

Understanding HTML  **274**

Simple HTML  **276**

Simple HTML Text Formatting  **277**

Simple HTML Graphics  **280**

Using Hyperlinks  **282**

E-mail HyperLinks  **283**

Summary  **284**

**18  DHTML Programming**  285

Introducing DHTML  **286**

A Sample DHTML Page  **287**

The Technology Behind DHTML  **289**

The Microsoft and Netscape Battle  **290**

The Rollover Effect  **290**

Summary  **293**

**19  Introduction to XML**  295

XML and Its Impact  **296**

Multiple Platforms  **297**

A Complete XML Example  **298**
Using Well-Formed XML Code  **298**
Validating XML Code  **300**
Defining the DTD  **301**

Summary  **304**

**20  Java Programming**  305

Introducing Java  **306**

Java Provides Executable Content  **307**

Multiplatform Executable Content  **309**

The Java Usage Summary  **310**

The Security Issue  **311**

Give Java a Spin  **312**

Visual J++: A Sample Java System  **312**

The Java Language Specifics  **314**
The Language Format  **314**
Java Details  **315**
Understanding the Code  **316**

Exception Handling  **318**
Setting Up Exceptions  **319**
Using try and catch  **320**

Summary  **321**

**21  JavaScript**  323

What JavaScript Can Do for You  **324**

Reviewing JavaScript's Objects  **326**

JavaScript's Events and Handlers  **328**

JavaScript's Language Is Complete  **331**

Summary  **331**

**V  The Business of Programming**

**22  The Importance of Maintenance**  335

Flowcharts  **336**
Flowchart Symbols  **336**
The Rules of Flowcharting  **338**
A Real-World Flowchart  **339**

Pseudocode  **342**

Introduction to Structured
Programming **344**
   Structured Programming
   Techniques **344**
   Structuring Problems **345**
   The Constructs of Structured
   Programming **347**

Structured Programming Techniques **347**
   Sequence **347**
   Decision (Selection) **348**
   Looping **349**

Proper Testing Is Vital **352**
   Desk Checking **352**
   Beta Testing **352**
   Parallel Testing **353**

Debugging **353**

Summary **356**

**23 Distributing Your Applications 357**

Issues Surrounding Software
Distribution **358**

Distribution Used to Be Easy **358**

Windows Application Distribution **359**
   Your First Step: Compilation **359**

Deploying Your Application **361**

After Generating the Setup **367**
   Remember the Networks **367**
   Uninstalling the Application **368**

More Helpful Tools **368**
   Profilers **368**
   Version Controllers **369**
   Resource Editors **370**

Summary **371**

**24 The Programming Business 373**

Data Processing and Other
Departments **374**

Paying for the Data Processing
Department **376**
   Understanding the Overhead
   Approach **376**
   Understanding the Chargeback
   Approach **377**
   The Contract Programmer's Role **377**

Computer Jobs **378**

Job Titles **379**
   Degrees and Certificates **380**
   Certification **381**
   Data Entry **381**
   Types of Programmers **382**
   Analysis and Design Staff **384**
   Internet and Network-Related Jobs **385**
   Management Possibilities **385**

Consulting **387**

Summary **387**

**25 Your Programming Future 389**

Will Programming Go Away? **390**
   Tools Go Out of Style, Programming Does
   Not **390**
   The Changing Technology Requires
   Changing Programmers **391**

Training Never Stops **391**
   Industry Periodicals **392**
   Books **392**
   The Classroom and the Web **394**

From Beginner to Guru **396**

Summary **397**

**Index 399**

# About the Author

**Greg Perry** has personally taught thousands of people how to program in the classroom and lectures, as well as impacted the computer world through the sale of more than two million computer books internationally.

He has been a programmer and trainer for the past 20 years. He received an undergraduate degree in computer science, followed by a master's degree in corporate finance. After working as a supervisor of financial systems for a Fortune 500 company, he turned to teaching at the college level, where he remained until he began to write full-time and lecture at programming conferences.

Some of his other book titles include *Sams Teach Yourself Visual Basic 6 in 21 Days*, *C by Example*, and several books in the *24 Hours* series, including *Sams Teach Yourself PCs in 24 Hours*, *Sams Teach Yourself Office in 24 Hours*, and *Sams Teach Yourself Windows Millennium in 24 Hours*. He has also written articles for several magazines, including *PC World* and *Data Training*. He is fluent in several computer languages and speaks a little Italian as well.

# Dedication

*"This book is for a man who has been a true friend to my family and to me. Thanks, Darrell Creamer, for being such a great pal."*

# Acknowledgments

Jenny Watson gave me the opportunity to revise the first edition of this book. I am extremely grateful for her trust and the encouragement of all at Que Publishing.

Thanks to my development editor, Mark Cierzniak, who shaped my work into a book. Talking to a beginning audience without talking *down* to the audience is not easy.

In addition, Betsy Stern-Hill's technical edits removed some earlier problems.

I want to thank the copy editor, Gene Redding, who cared enough about the reader to put clear writing before everything else.

The other editors and staff who worked closely with this text all deserve vacations now.

My favorite people—my beautiful bride Jayne, my parents Glen and Bettye Perry—keep me wanting to be the best I can. Thanks so much to all of you.

# We Want to Hear from You!

As the reader of this book, *you* are our most important critic and commentator. We value your opinion and want to know what we're doing right, what we could do better, what areas you'd like to see us publish in, and any other words of wisdom you're willing to pass our way.

As an executive editor for Que, I welcome your comments. You can email or write me directly to let me know what you did or didn't like about this book—as well as what we can do to make our books better.

Please note that I cannot help you with technical problems related to the *topic* of this book. We do have a User Services group, however, where I will forward specific technical questions related to the book.

When you write, please be sure to include this book's title and author as well as your name, email address, and phone number. I will carefully review your comments and share them with the author and editors who worked on the book.

Email:      feedback@samspublishing.com or feedback@quepublishing.com

Mail:       Candace Hall
            Executive Editor
            Que Publishing
            800 East 96th Street
            Indianapolis, IN 46240 USA

For more information about this book or another Que title, visit our Web site at www.quepublishing.com. Type the ISBN (excluding hyphens) or the title of a book in the Search field to find the page you're looking for.

# INTRODUCTION

You will learn how companies program and how to become a needed resource in a programming position. You will learn about programming job titles and what to expect if you want to write programs for others.

## Who Should Read This Book?

The title of this book says it all. If you have never programmed a computer and if your VCR's timer throws you into fits, take three sighs of relief! This book was written for *you*.

This book is aimed at three different groups of people:

- Individuals with no programming experience but who want an introduction to it.
- Companies that want to train nonprogramming computer users for programming careers.
- Schools that want to promote good coding design and style and that want to offer an overview of the life of a programmer, both for introductory language classes and for systems analysis and design classes.

## Conventions Used in This Book

The following typographic conventions are used in this book:

- Code lines, variables, and any text you see on the screen appear in a `computer typeface`.
- New terms appear in *italic*.

Within each chapter, you will encounter several icons that help you pinpoint the current topic's direction:

**note**

Notes bring a particular topic to your attention when further thought is warranted.

**tip**

Tips are an insight into a certain topic that provide an immediate way of doing something.

**caution**

Warnings focus your attention on a problem or side effect that can occur in a specific situation. Warnings can help you work around problems.

# PART i

# PRELUDE TO PROGRAMMING

1  Computers Are Tools . . . . . . . . . . . . . .5

2  Anatomy of a Program . . . . . . . . . . . .21

## IN THIS CHAPTER

- Computers and Programming
- What a Computer Does
- Common Misconceptions
- Ease-of-Use Matters to Programmers
- People and Computers
- It Takes More than a Computer
- A Quick Overview
- Networking It All
- Today's Computers
- Types of Computers

1

# COMPUTERS ARE TOOLS

Computers are tools that help people get their work done. They are special tools because, unlike a hammer or saw, a computer is multi-functional. When a computer needs to perform a specific job, a program directs the computer and tells it exactly what to do and how to do it.

The highlights of this chapter include the following:

- At its most basic level, a computer program turns raw data into meaningful information.

- Fortunately, no math skills are required to program computers!

- A computer information system requires more than just hardware to be useful.

- Networked, distributed computing adds challenges for programmers.

- Computer hardware changes rapidly; networked computers are becoming a standard programming platform.

# Computers and Programming

The book you now hold promises you one thing above all else: to respect your ability to think and learn but not to teach above your head. This book shows that you don't have to be a wizard to become a proficient (or even an expert) programmer. Without programs, computers would be nothing more than big calculators, and people write programs. Thanks to programs, computers become tools that help achieve goals.

Although the computer industry seems to have been around a long time, it is actually one of the newest in existence. Medicine, mathematics, and engineering all date back to the early ages, but the first real computer was invented in the 1940s. As a new programmer, you need to understand the trends of the industry to know where it is heading, because some obvious trends still appear that have been around since the very first computer. The trend, as you probably know, is toward smaller, cheaper, and faster computers that often are loosely networked in a worldwide information system called the Internet.

# What a Computer Does

From a programmer's viewpoint, at its simplest level a computer processes data into meaningful information. You may not have considered the difference between the words "data" and "information" before, but there is a tremendous difference to a computer professional.

*Data* (plural for *datum*, although most use *data* for both singular and plural) consists of raw facts and figures. *Information*, on the other hand, is processed data. Information has meaning; data, in its raw form, does not. Figure 1.1 shows the fundamental data processing model. Notice that data goes into the computer, the computer processes that data, and meaningful information is the result.

**FIGURE 1.1**

Data becomes more meaningful as processed information.

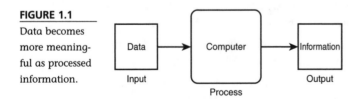

Data by itself is not useful to people who need to make decisions with it. For example, a company's president does not need a report of detailed payroll amounts for 1,500 employees to study payroll trends. Instead, the company president needs more meaningful information, such as the total payroll per department, the payroll increases over the same time the previous year, or the average payroll per employee compared to other companies in the same business. A computer with the right program can rapidly produce the information that the president needs from the raw payroll data.

The program is the driving force behind any job that any computer does. A *program* is a list of detailed instructions that tells the computer what to do. The computer cannot do anything without a program. It is the job of the programmer to write programs that direct the computer to take raw data and transform that data into meaningful information for the end user, such as the company president in the preceding example.

Modern-day programs produce information in many formats. Programs play music, talk to other computers over the phone lines, and control external devices. Output sent to the screen and printer still makes up the majority of today's program output.

Learning to program computers takes a while, but programming is rewarding, both financially and personally. Computer programming offers the advantage of instant feedback—you see the results of your work as soon as you run a program. The Fortune 500 companies may or may not beat down your door for your skills after you master the skills presented in this single book, but this book directs your programming path and explains what you can expect from programming as no other book does.

# Common Misconceptions

People seem to either love computers or hate them. Typically, a person's dislike for computers directly reflects a lack of knowledge. Despite worldwide use of computers, many people still know very little about them. To those people, computers and the programs that drive them are nothing more than magic boxes that mere mortals need not understand.

People need to understand that a computer is nothing more than a dumb machine that "knows" absolutely nothing. A computer is a slave that waits on your every command and acts out your instructions exactly as you give them. Sometimes the program instructions are incorrect. If they are, the computer goes right ahead and attempts them anyway.

Computers are not only useful tools; they are required tools. Most businesses, schools, and banks would have to close their doors if computers disappeared. There is simply too much information moving from point to point to handle the numerous transactions manually. Consider how difficult and dangerous it would be to navigate airplanes around major airports without computerized assistance. Computers perform needed analysis for business, produce bulk mailing letters for charities, forecast the weather, improve air traffic control, and keep children entertained while teaching them math, science, and reading skills.

The next three sections attack three popular computer programming myths.

## Myth 1: "Only Math Experts Can Program Computers"

Thank goodness this is a myth and not reality—thousands of people would be out of work (including this author). Computers would be elitist machines used by engineers and scientists; the casual user could not master them. Computers would still be beneficial in some areas, but they would not provide the benefits that so many people can enjoy.

Not only can you be poor at math, you don't have to like math or even have the desire to learn math. The computer does math for you; that's one of its jobs. There are countless expert computer programmers in the world who do not know the square root of 64. It turns out that, as you become a better programmer, you may find your math skills improving. Developing programming skills tends to improve your thinking on the left side of your brain (where psychologists believe that math and numeric skills reside).

## Myth 2: "Computer Programs Make Mistakes"

You might have heard the adage, "To err is human, but to *really* foul things up takes a computer!" This might be accurate, but only in that a computer is so very fast that it duplicates a person's mistakes rapidly.

Computers do not make mistakes—people make mistakes. If you have heard a bank teller tell you that $24 was incorrectly deleted from your savings account because "the computer made a mistake," the teller probably has no idea what really happened. Before computers were invented, banks kept their records on ledger cards. When a teller found a mistake, do you think the teller said, "The ledger card made a mistake"? Absolutely not. People program computers, people run them, and people enter the data that the computer processes.

The odds of a computer randomly fouling up a customer's bank balance are minute. Computers simply do not make random mistakes unless they are programmed incorrectly. Computers are finite machines; when given the same input, they always produce the same output. That is, computers always do the same things under the same conditions.

When a computer malfunctions, it does not make a simple mistake; rather, it *really* messes things up. When a computer fails, it typically breaks down completely, or a disk drive breaks, or the power goes out. Whatever happens, computers go all out when they have problems. The good news is that computers rarely have problems; they usually work.

## Myth 3: "Programming Is Difficult"

Computers are getting easier to use every day. Chances are good that you use a computer when you drive a car, watch television, or use your microwave. Did you know you were using a computer? The makers of computers have found ways to integrate computers into your everyday life to monitor and correct problems that might otherwise occur.

Of course, if you are reading this book, you want to learn enough about computers to write your own programs. Writing computer programs takes more work than using a microwave oven's computerized timer functions (notice that I did not say it takes smarter people). The work, however, primarily involves getting down to the computer's level and learning what it expects.

Not only are computers getting easier to use every day, but you have better opportunities to learn about them than ever before. Internet-based classes, educational television, and community colleges are loaded with training material for programming computers.

# Ease-of-Use Matters to Programmers

When computer manufacturers make computers easier to use, more people will buy them, more people will use them, and computers will help more people do their jobs better. It will be your job as a computer programmer to develop programs that are simple to use.

Despite all the popular programs in use by business today, there is still a vast number of programs that organizations and individuals need that haven't been created. The transactions of business are too complex and change too rapidly for current programs to fill all computer users' needs. The programmer's world changes constantly, so the newness of programming never fades.

Look in your Sunday newspaper's help-wanted professional section. You'll find that there is a severe shortage of computer programmers. Amid the requests for Java programmers, C++ programmers, Internet programmers, systems analysts, senior systems analysts, object-oriented programmers, systems programmers, and application programmers, you may find yourself lost in a sea of uncertainty and TLAs (three-letter acronyms) that might, at first, seem hopeless. Do not fret; this book helps direct you toward areas of programming that might be right for you.

Chapter 24, "The Programming Business," explores computer jobs and describes what each type of programming job is all about. If you are just starting out, you probably won't be able to go to work as the most senior-level programmer, but you will be surprised at the salary your programming skills can bring you.

# People and Computers

People and computers can work together very well. A person cannot total a list of 100 numbers in the blink of an eye, but a computer can. A person cannot print 1,000 names and addresses sorted by ZIP Code in under a minute, but a computer can. People get bored doing the same job over and over, but computers never get bored. Computers can perform varied tasks, from graphic art to scientific calculations, whereas people are often really good at only a handful of different tasks.

The computer, however, is no match for a human being. People can think, whereas a computer can only blindly perform instructions line by line. Where do those instructions come from? They come from people who write the programs of instructions. People have insight into problems that computers can never achieve. People are intuitive and creative. People think. People can deal with ambiguities far better than the most powerful computer in the world can. No computer yet can understand a large vocabulary of human speech. Computers stumble between different accents and speaking patterns. Computers have no sense of the world around them except for some very limited devices that people attach to them.

# It Takes More than a Computer

Many people today buy a computer thinking that all of their problems are solved, only to find that the computer offers little or no help at all. Perhaps more computer buyers should be taught that the computer by itself is useless. As a programmer, it is incumbent upon you to teach others that a computer is useless but a computer information system is useful. It is a computer information system that most people need when they purchase a computer, but it is just a computer that they usually end up with.

A computer information system is more than just a computer. Buyers of computers are not satisfied by the promise of computing unless they learn that a successful computer information system always consists of the following five components:

- Hardware
- Software
- People

■ Data

■ Procedures

The following sections look at each component of a computer information system and show you why all five components must be in place before a computer purchase is successful.

## The Hardware

Hardware has been described as the parts of the computer you can kick. Although it is a sloppy definition, it does make the point that *hardware* is the collection of physical components that make up the computer. The screen, printer, and system unit are hardware components. An analogy to a stereo system is useful here. Your stereo hardware is the tuner, amplifier, tape deck, and CD player. Just as a stereo owner does not consider audio tapes and CDs to be part of the hardware, neither do computer owners consider CD-ROMs and programs to be hardware components. They fall into the category of *software*.

The falling prices of computers in the last few years have allowed more and more people to buy and use computers, but the falling prices have also led to many people buying a computer and then asking, "What now?" As mentioned in the previous section, a successful computer installation requires more than hardware alone. Business owners often face a dilemma: Hardware is extremely affordable, but the hardware is just one-fifth of the equation that makes up a successful computer information system. When an accountant or attorney buys a $1,000 computer and gets it to the office, it is sad to note that the hardware is the least-expensive component of the computer information system.

Figure 1.2 shows a graph that illustrates this point. You can see that time is going to the right and dollars is going up the left side of the graph. As time goes by, the cost of hardware steadily becomes cheaper. Today, you can buy more computing power than ever before. It seems that a computer is obsolete almost as soon as you buy it, because another one takes its place that does a lot more for less money.

**tip**

The cost of your computer hardware is analogous to the cost of your entertainment system. At first you might think you pay much more for your system than for your CDs and tapes (including rentals), but if you had a fire tonight and could save only either your stereo equipment or your CDs and tapes, which would you choose? Almost anyone would save his CDs and tapes; those are much harder to replace and much more costly than the actual equipment. You can replace your equipment today, but it could take another lifetime to replace all your tapes and CDs.

**FIGURE 1.2**

Hardware is going down in price while the cost of other computer information system components is going up.

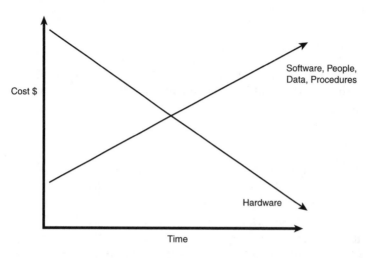

## The Software

Although individual software (another term for the programs on computers) packages are going down in price, companies and private computer owners invest more and more in software every year. Not only do people purchase new software as it comes out, they also update older versions of programs they bought before. The Internet allows companies to take orders on their Web sites. Software that used to work in a non-online environment must now be made to work over the Internet.

Businesses and individuals must factor in the cost of software when making decisions regarding the cost of a computer. Whereas an individual usually buys a computer and is done with hardware purchasing for a while, software purchasing never seems to end. Software changes rapidly. As a future programmer, this is welcome news because this means you have a chance for a secure career. For the uninformed computer purchaser, the cost of software can be staggering.

---

**YOU RARELY OWN SOFTWARE**

When you buy a video, you do not own the movie; you have purchased only the right to watch the movie. You legally cannot alter it, copy it, or give away copies of it, and most importantly, you cannot sell copies.

The same is true for software that you buy. When you purchase software, you most often purchase a *software license*. If a company wants to buy a word processing program for 100 employees, legally it must purchase 100 copies of the program, or at least buy a site license that allows the company to use the software on more than one machine. The license for individual software grants you permission to use the software on one computer at any one time.

---

## The People

When a company buys a computer, whether it's a desktop computer or a huge mainframe computer that fills an entire room, it must consider the cost of the people who will be a part of the computer information system. There will be costs associated with training, programming, and using the computer. There will have to be backup personnel trained to take over the computer chores if someone else leaves. And as with software, the cost of personnel does not quit; it is an ongoing process. Often, a computer information system can save a company money in efficiency and processing power, but the company may have to hire additional staff, and people are expensive.

## The Data

Look back at Figure 1.1 for a moment and consider this: It is vital that the data going into the computer be as accurate as possible. If bad data comes in, almost assuredly bad information goes out. This is known as *GIGO*, or *garbage-in, garbage-out*. The programmer must constantly be on the lookout for better ways to get data so that it is accurate. The program cannot always determine if the data is bad.

When a company computerizes its payroll, someone must enter the weekly payroll figures, direct the payroll processing programs, and be there to put the checks in the printer. The payroll data that was previously recorded by hand and sent to an accountant must now be accurately entered into the computer.

Some larger companies have complete staffs of 20 or more people whose full-time job is to sit in front of a computer and enter data. Large companies have massive amounts of data. Computers can process that data, but only when it is entered properly and accurately. Oil companies must account for every drop of oil they refine and sell, accounts payable and accounts receivable must be updated every period, and records must be filed. The entry of this kind of data is intrinsic to its processing and is a cost that must be factored into the price of a successful computer information system.

**note**

A company's data entry department not only enters the data needed for its data processing, but it enters it twice. Typically, this is done by two different people. Because of the garbage-in, garbage-out factor, companies help ensure that their data is accurate with double entry. After two different people enter the same data, a computer program compares the data for discrepancies. Although errors can still creep in, the chances are slim that any will.

## The Procedures

Data processing procedures must be put into place soon after a computer is installed. These procedures generally include everything the user of the computer does on a daily basis to process the data needed.

Backup disks of all data should be made each night and taken offsite (the backups would not be much use if a fire destroyed both the computer files and the backup disks sitting next to the computer). Safeguards should be built into every program you write to make unauthorized use more difficult.

Data privacy should also be maintained. Although most employees are honest, important company figures such as payroll amounts should be guarded. Don't let employees have direct access to their payroll files, and make sure the person who runs the payroll programs knows the importance of privacy.

# A Quick Overview

The following sections take you on a journey through the young roots of the computer industry. A different approach is taken from that of a lot of historical computing textbooks. Instead of concentrating on the facts and dates, the patterns of the evolving computer are presented with an emphasis on the three distinct periods of computers: first-generation, second-generation, and third-generation computers.

## The First Generation

The early computers were huge. They were known as *first-generation* computers. The first-generation computers, developed in the late 1940s, were tube based. If you have ever looked inside an old television set, you may have seen components that look like little light bulbs. These are tubes—also known as vacuum tubes—and they were the storage and computing mechanisms used in the early computers.

First-generation computers were so massive that they took up several rooms—almost an entire building. Actually, the computers took up much of the space, and the gigantic air conditioning needed to keep the huge machines cool took the rest. Large power plants were needed to supply the power to the thousands of tubes inside those machines.

First-generation computers were incredibly powerful—not quite as powerful as today's solar-powered pocket calculators, but for their time, they were a needed invention. Until electronic computers came along, there was simply no way to compute and process large amounts of data.

First-generation computers were so massive and took so much energy to run that only one organization, the United States government, had the funds to buy them and keep them running. The military used these early computers for their calculations and projections.

The cost, size, and energy requirements kept first-generation computers out of the hands of most organizations. It was not until the second generation came along that more people began using them and learning about computing possibilities.

## The Second Generation

First-generation computers were replaced by the second generation in the late 1950s. Second-generation computers used transistors. If you have ever seen the inside of a transistor radio, you may have seen the little colored parts, some of which are transistors. Transistors were the smaller replacements for vacuum tubes in electronic computers, immediately increasing computers' power, decreasing their size, and lowering their cost. Hundreds of transistors fit in the space of a single vacuum tube. Transistors also are much more reliable than tubes. If a transistor works the first time power is supplied to it, it will usually work for 20 years or more.

Transistors take much less power to use and run much cooler than vacuum tubes. Also, instead of taking up an entire building, second-generation computers took only a large room or two. What was even more important than their size was that businesses and schools could afford them. The cost of first-generation computers kept people away from them.

The 1960s saw unbelievable growth in large computer use and jobs. More companies got into the computer business, science fiction stories and movies were produced that showed these computing machines in both good and bad light, and everybody knew that the computer was here to stay.

## The Third Generation

In the 1960s, NASA decided it wanted to send people to the moon. Imagine that! There was a problem, however. The lightning-fast calculation of

**tip**

Because more organizations could afford computers, more people had access to computers. A synergy took place, because not only was the hardware being fine-tuned by leaps and bounds, but advances in software were also taking place at unbelievable rates.

It was primarily during the second generation of computers that programming languages, many of which you will learn about in this book, were developed.

a computer was needed during the flight. Computers had to be in control of a lot of the operations.

Some NASA genius developed a component, still used today, called the *integrated circuit* (*IC*). An integrated circuit (also called a *chip*) is about the size of a matchbook and black in color and has silver connections that usually run along two sides, making the IC look like a high-tech black beetle. Whereas the transistor replaced vacuum tubes one-for-one, integrated circuits replaced thousands of transistors. The entire circuitry of a second-generation computer could be squeezed into the space of a matchbook. Computers instantly got dramatically smaller, NASA got to the moon and back with onboard computers, we got desktop computers, computing devices such as calculators were available to every person, and the third-generation computers were born and have thrived ever since.

An integrated circuit is an almost magical device. Its designers use laser tools to install and connect the thousands of miniature components onto its wafer body. Some integrated circuits are also known as *microprocessors*. Because of the microprocessor's widespread use in today's desktop computers, the term *microcomputer* was coined and the name stuck, although *PC* (for personal computer) is most commonly used now.

# Networking It All

The Internet is not an entity but a collection of loosely networked computers connected via phone lines and other types of connections. Instead of centralized computing, today's world requires decentralized computing with a central mainframe and attached keyboards and screens.

**note**

The term "machine" is used in the computer industry to mean "computer." Unlike most other devices called machines, computers have relatively few moving parts. Printers and disk drives have moving parts, but there are few others.

Computers now span the globe and communicate among themselves. Computers now share processing power (called *distributing the processing*).

A programmer's job is made more exciting by distributed computing, but at the same time, more challenges await programmers. The online world of programming requires not only a mastery of logic and computer languages but also expertise in security and an understanding of how an application can be run across a network of computers.

# Today's Computers

The future of computer technology seems likely to repeat the previous 50 years. It appears that more and more computing power will be squeezed into smaller, more reliable, faster, and cheaper boxes. More and more people will use computers for more and more tasks, and computers will be networked to other computers.

What this means to the programmer is twofold. First, as more people use computers, more programmers are needed to write the programs for the computers. Second, as computers get more powerful and faster, older uses of computers (and therefore, older programs) have to be updated to take advantage of the new hardware.

# Types of Computers

Computers come in all shapes and sizes, but they fall within four broad categories: supercomputers, mainframes, minicomputers, and microcomputers. Before delving into the hardware specifics, it will be helpful to define what the four types of computers are all about.

Most computers today are designed to be multi-user computers. Even though a computer can perform only one instruction at a time, it does it so fast that more than one person can share the computer, and each person can think he is the only person on that computer at the time.

## tip

How fast is fast enough? Will there be a day when computers do not have to go any faster? Have we already reached that point?

Think about this for a moment: If computers were several times faster than today's machines, forecasters could predict the weather with much more accuracy than today. "So what?" you might still ask. Think about how many lives could be saved if the exact pattern and severity of every hurricane, tornado, and flood could be tracked weeks in advance. The advantages of working until computers are fast enough to predict the weather perfectly can be calculated in human lives. Completely accurate weather prediction is just one of many areas in which computers much faster than today's versions would benefit society, along with space exploration, statistics, economic policy planning, and scientific research.

## Supercomputers

The most expensive and fastest computers in existence are supercomputers. Supercomputers are so fast that they are best used for scientific applications where heavy mathematical calculations must be swift. The expense of supercomputers and their lack of availability (there are only a few hundred in existence) cause most businesses to turn to the other kinds of computers.

The name most associated with supercomputers is the Cray Research Company, the largest (and first) maker of supercomputers. Founded by the late Seymour Cray, it is the company best known for supercomputers.

Analysts measure the speed of supercomputers in *teraflops*; one teraflop equals one trillion calculations per second. The storage required by many corporations that use supercomputers today runs as high as a *petabyte* (one million gigabytes of storage). Supercomputers appear in many configurations, from a traditional single large box to *Beowulf clusters*, thousands of smaller computers (such as high-speed PCs) that run in parallel to achieve lightning speed.

## caution

PCs will never be fast enough to replace mainframes completely. As desktop computers become faster and more powerful, larger computers become faster and more powerful, too. The largest computers of today, called *supercomputers*, are four times as fast as the supercomputers of two years ago.

---

**WANT YOUR OWN SUPERCOMPUTER?**

You can have your own supercomputer without spending a million dollars! Build more raw computing power than your banker has and your small business loan should be easier to get!

Go to `http://www.beowulf.org/` and `http://www.beowulf-underground.org` for information on the hardware and software you'll need. Most of the software is free, and you can use old PCs that aren't fast enough to run today's games.

---

# Mainframes

Mainframe computers are the cornerstone of modern-day business data processing. When heavy processing and several thousand users must be handled at once, a mainframe is the primary choice for businesses.

Mainframe computers require large staffs of maintenance personnel, operators, programmers, and data entry clerks. They run around the clock, and any *downtime* (machine failure) is costly to the companies that rely on them. Mainframe computers require a large room or two to house because of their large system units and the numerous storage devices attached to them. These rooms are often environmentally controlled, being cooled to keep the computer running at a comfortable level, and the air is filtered to keep as much dust out of the system as possible.

Some companies have two or more mainframe computers connected to each other and also networked to PCs and the Internet. The smaller computers offload some of the workload from the mainframe, leaving the mainframe to handle the more calculation-intensive tasks.

# Minicomputers

The minicomputer isn't seen much these days due to the low cost and high power of microcomputers. Minis generally are multiuser computers that can handle up to 200 users connected by screens and keyboards.

During the 1970s and 1980s, the minicomputer filled a niche that PCs were not capable of filling at the time. Mainframes were out of reach to a lot of companies, and the PC was not powerful enough for serious multiuser business data processing. The minicomputer was able to handle the invoicing and accounting processing for small businesses.

# Microcomputers

The microcomputer is the smallest, least expensive, and most popular computer in existence today. Often called a *desktop computer*, *PC*, or *personal computer*, the microcomputer has seen a tremendous growth in popularity since the late 1970s, and its fast-paced growth seems to be continuing into the future.

PCs are taken very seriously in the world of business. "A PC on every desktop" seems to be the objective of today's management. Laptops are small enough to fit in a briefcase, and fewer business travelers are without their PCs. It is also common in most homes to see at least one microcomputer, something almost unheard of a decade ago.

**tip**

Small, handheld wireless devices are introducing even greater challenges to tomorrow's programmers. The small size and wireless technology require special handling of programs because of limited memory and data that often comes from a source far outside the device itself.

Powerful and advanced programs require considerable computer memory and disk storage. The more advanced a program is, the more space is required to store and execute that program. Fortunately, the cost of memory and disk storage has dropped rapidly, and PCs contain enough resources now to handle advanced applications that required far larger and more costly computing hardware just a few years ago.

# Summary

You now have an understanding of what computers do and how they are used. Many people who are unaccustomed to computers have fears that are not justifiable. You can now help alleviate those fears that are based on computer myths and show them where computers help streamline what we do today.

Now that you know where the computer industry has been, you will have a good idea of where it is heading. The computers of tomorrow will be faster, cheaper, more networked, and smaller than today's, and more people will be needed to program them.

- You now understand that computers are not magic; they are only machines that perform the tasks they are given.

- The computer is a tool to help you and others do more efficient work than you could do without it.

- At its most fundamental level, the computer takes input data, processes it, and turns it into meaningful information.

- To use a computer successfully, people must understand that a computer information system is more than just the hardware. To be successful, the hardware, software, people, data, and procedures must be in place.

- Without programs, and therefore without programmers who create them, a computer can do nothing.

## IN THIS CHAPTER

- The Programmer's Life
- The Need for Programs
- Programs, Programs, Everywhere
- Programs as Directions
- The Language Translator
- Accuracy Is Everything
- The Need for Design
- The Program Language

# 2

# ANATOMY OF A PROGRAM

Before delving into the specifics of programming languages, this chapter attempts to explain what a program really is. A firm grasp of this chapter's material is a prerequisite for moving on to specific programming languages later in this book.

The highlights of this chapter include the following:

- In spite of the wide availability of computer programs, many companies produce their own.
- Perhaps the most difficult part of programming is breaking the problem into detailed steps the computer can follow.
- Two kinds of programming errors exist: syntax and logic errors.
- Top-down design enables a programming staff to keep the primary goal of the program in focus.
- The more upfront design you do as a programmer, the faster you will write an accurate program.

# The Programmer's Life

Programmers often feel a creative rush that artists and skilled craftspeople get while honing their projects. Writing a program, however, can be tedious. It is often a detailed task, and ample frustration comes with the territory. If you are not a details person, don't fret—the tedium of programming does not really translate into the same tedium that other types of jobs generate. The computer's quick feedback on your mistakes often provides a sense of accomplishment that keeps you programming until you get it right.

A programmer learns to develop patience early in his programming career. He learns that proper design is critical to a successful program. Perhaps you have heard the term *systems analysis and design*. This is the name given to the practice of analyzing the problem to be programmed and then designing the program from that analysis. Complete books and college courses have been written about systems analysis and design. This chapter attempts to cover the highlights of systems analysis and design, letting you see what mainstream computer programmers go through before writing programs.

# The Need for Programs

When an individual or a company needs a program, there are three ways to obtain it:

- They can buy one that's already written.
- They can buy one and modify it.
- They can write their own.

Table 2.1 lists advantages and disadvantages of each option. The first two options are much quicker than the third and also much less expensive.

**Table 2.1**    Three Methods to Obtain Software

| Option | Advantages and Disadvantages |
| --- | --- |
| Buy one | *Advantage*: The program can be obtained quickly and inexpensively. |
| | *Disadvantage*: The program may not be exactly what you need. |
| Buy and modify one | *Advantage*: A usable program that does what is needed can be obtained fairly quickly. Also, the program is relatively inexpensive, depending on the changes needed. |
| | *Disadvantage*: It isn't always possible to modify the program. |
| Write one | *Advantage*: The program (after proper design and debugging) does exactly what you want it to do. |
| | *Disadvantage*: This option is very expensive and takes a lot longer than the other options. |

Most PC users choose the first option because most programs are fairly inexpensive. Because companies such as Microsoft sell so many of the same versions of programs, they can do so at fairly low prices. The average user is not going to write his own operating system or word processing program. Today, many programs are available for purchase directly on the Internet—buy the program, download the program, and you can be using it immediately.

Companies do not always choose the first option. They spend years distinguishing themselves from other companies through the products and services they develop. When a company computerizes its recordkeeping, it is vital that the programs mimic the data flow the company had before computerization. The company should not have to change the way it does business just so it can use the programs it buys. Purchased programs have to be generic so that their developers can sell them to multiple customers.

The second option might then seem like the smartest, but it is chosen least often. If a company could buy a program that was already written, it would have a framework to adapt to its specific needs. The problem is that software is rarely sold; rather, it is licensed. When you buy a program, you do not own it; you own only the right to use it. Legally you cannot change it, sell it, or copy it (except for backup purposes). Not only are there legalities involved, but sometimes you cannot physically change the software, either. As you will learn later in this chapter, after a program is written, it is translated to a compressed format that programmers can no longer modify.

Therefore, although it is expensive and time-consuming to write programs from scratch, most businesses prefer to do so, keeping large programming departments on hand to handle the load. A company's data processing staff might spend a full year writing a program that is similar to but not exactly like one the company could buy. Despite the cost and effort involved, it is worth it to the company not to have to conform to a program it buys from someone else.

**tip**

Some companies have found that they can sell programs they develop to other firms doing similar business, thereby recapturing some of their development costs.

**note**

Companies never write every program they use. For example, a company might use the Microsoft Office suite for its word processing and spreadsheet capabilities, but create programs for more specialized needs.

# Programs, Programs, Everywhere

Why aren't all the programs needed already written? Surf to any Internet software site or walk into any computer store today and you'll see hundreds of programs for sale. There are programs for everything: word processing, accounting, drawing, playing games, designing homes, and planning trip itineraries. It seems as if any program you could ever need is within reach. Because computers have been around for 50 years, you would think we'd be about done with all the programming anyone would need for a long time.

If all the programs needed were already written, you would not see the large listings of "Programmer Wanted" ads in today's newspapers. The fact is, the world is changing every day, and businesses and people must change with it. Programs written 10 years ago are not up to today's practices. They were written on computers much slower and more limited than today's machines. As hardware advances are made, the software must advance with it.

# Programs As Directions

Your computer is a blind and dumb machine waiting for you to give it instructions. When you do, it follows the instructions without second-guessing them. If you tell it to do something incorrectly, it does its best to do so. To repeat, a program is a list of detailed instructions that the computer carries out.

Detail is vital to making a machine follow out your orders. Programming is not difficult; what is difficult is breaking the computer's job into simple and detailed steps that assume nothing.

To get an idea of the thinking involved in programming, think about how you would describe starting a car to someone from the past. Suppose a cowboy named Heath from the Old West appears at your doorstep, bewildered by the sights around him. After getting over the future shock, Heath wants to adapt to this new world. Before learning to drive a car, Heath must learn to start it. Once he is comfortable doing that, you will teach him to drive. Unlike a 16-year-old learning to drive, Heath has not grown up seeing adults starting cars, so he really needs to master this process before going any further. Being the busy programmer you are, you leave him the following set of instructions:

1. Use this key.

2. Start the car.

How far would Heath get? Not very far. You gave correct instructions for starting a car, but you assumed too much knowledge on his part. You must remember that he knows nothing about these contraptions called automobiles and that he is relying on you to give him instructions that he can understand. Instead of assuming so much, these might be better instructions:

1. Attached is the key to the car. You need it to start the car.

2. With the key in hand, go to the car door that is closest to the front door of the house.

3. Under the door's handle, you will see a round silver dollar–size metal part in which you can insert the key (with its rough side pointing down).

4. After sticking the key into the hole as far as it goes, turn it to the right until you hear a click.

5. Turn the key back to the left until it faces the same way as it did when you inserted it and remove the key.

6. Open the door and get into the car. Be sure to sit in front of the round wheel on the left side of the front seat.

7. Close the door.

8. On the right side of the column holding the big round wheel (called a *steering wheel*), you will see a slot into which you can put the key.

Are you beginning to get the idea? This list of eight items is very detailed, and Heath hasn't even started the car yet. You still have to describe the gas pedal that he must press while he turns the key (in the correct direction, of course), and you don't want to assume that Heath will turn off the car when he is done practicing, so you have to give him those directions as well.

If you are beginning to think this car-starting analogy is going a little too far, consider what you must do to tell a nonthinking piece of electronic equipment to perform your company's payroll. A payroll program cannot consist of only the following steps:

1. Get the payroll data.

2. Calculate the payroll and taxes.

3. Print the checks.

## tip

A typical payroll program might contain 20,000 or more lines of instructions. Don't let this deter you, however. Most companies' large programming projects are written by teams of programmers; you will have plenty of help if you ever write such programs for a living. Also, new programming techniques and programming environments for today's computer languages make programming much easier than ever before, even for the individual programmer working alone.

To the computer, these instructions lack thousands of details that you might take for granted. It is the detailing of the program's instructions that provides the tedium and occasional frustration of programming. Programming computers isn't difficult, but breaking down real-world problems into lots of detailed steps that a computer can understand is hard.

There are many design tools that help you take large problems and break them down into detailed components that translate into programming elements. Throughout this book, you'll see some methods programmers use to get to a program's details.

## Art or Science?

A debate that you often see in computer literature is whether programming is an art or a science. Throughout the years, advances have been made in programming that, if followed, improve a program's accuracy, readability, and maintainability (the process of changing the program later to perform a different or additional set of tasks). Two of the most important advances in programming are based more on philosophy than engineering. They are *structured programming* and *object-oriented programming*. This book explores these two programming advances in the chapters that follow. Both offer ways that a programmer can write a program to make it better.

There are many ways to write even the smallest and simplest programs. Just as authors write differently and musicians play differently, each programmer has his own style. Therefore, you would think that programming is more of an art than a science. You would be closer to being correct than those few who argue that programming is more of a science.

Nevertheless, as advances are made in programming approaches such as structured programming and object-oriented programming, you should see a shift in thinking. With the proliferation of computers in today's world, there is a move in process to train tomorrow's programmers. Some of the biggest proponents of moving from the artistic approach to a more scientific approach are the companies paying the programmers. Companies need to react quickly to changing business conditions, and they need programs written as quickly and as accurately as possible. As advances in computer programming are discovered, more companies are going to adopt policies that require their programmers to use more scientific and proven methods of writing better programs.

**caution**

Not only are the programming instructions themselves important, but so is their order. When writing a program, you must think through the exact order necessary to perform the job at hand. The computer executes a program in the order that your commands dictate. You cannot print bills before calculating how much the customers owe.

## Speak the Language

The instructions you give in your programs must be in a language the computer understands. At its lowest level, a computer is nothing more than thousands of switches, flipping on and off lightning fast. A switch can have only two states: on or off.

If it were up to your computer, you would have to give it instructions using switches that represent on and off states of electricity. In fact, that is exactly the way the early computers were programmed. A panel of switches, such as the one shown in Figure 2.1, had to be used to enter all programs and data.

**FIGURE 2.1**

A panel of switches programmed early computers.

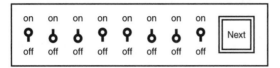

The on and off states of electricity are represented as 1s (ones) and 0s (zeros) at the computer's lowest level. You can control what your computer does if you know the correct pattern of 1s and 0s required to give it a command. Of course, programming in 1s and 0s is not much better than the switch panel, so there has to be a better way.

Spoken languages are too ambiguous for computers. The human brain can decipher sentences intuitively, something a nonthinking machine cannot do. Inroads are being made into *artificial intelligence*, which is the science of programming computers so they can learn on their own. It also includes programming them to understand a spoken language such as English. Despite recent advancements, artificial intelligence is many years away (if it is even possible for computers to understand simple English).

Consider the sentence "Time flies like an arrow."

Your mind has no trouble understanding the parts of this sentence. You know that it is an analogy, and the parts of speech make total sense to you. "Time" is a noun that performs an action, it "flies," and it does so "like an arrow." If you teach the computer to accept these descriptions of this sentence, it will work fine until it runs into something like "Fruit flies like an orange."

Think about this for a moment. Again, you have no problem understanding this sentence, even though it is completely different in every way from the other one. The computer taught to decipher the first sentence, however, is going to throw its cables up in frustration at the second sentence because none of the parts of the sentence are the same. The word "flies" is now a noun and not an action verb. The phrase "like an orange" is no longer a description of the action, but rather both the verb (like) and the object receiving the action (an orange). As you can see from these two sentences alone, understanding simple sentences that most people take for granted poses a tremendous problem for programmers trying to teach a computer to understand English.

Therefore, computers and people are at opposite ends of the spectrum. People want to speak their own language, but so do computers that understand only 1s and 0s. There has to be some kind of go-between, so programming languages were created to appease both the computer and the person programming the computer. Programming languages use words similar to those that people use, but they have a highly specific *syntax* (ordering, grammar, and spelling) that allows little room for the ambiguity so prevalent in spoken languages. The computer can translate a programming language down to its machine language of 1s and 0s; the human programmer can learn, remember, and use the programming languages more effectively than 1s and 0s because they are similar to spoken languages.

> **tip**
>
> Learning a foreign language is much more difficult than learning a programming language. Most of a programming language is made up of words you already know, such as *while*, *if*, *then*, *for*, *let*, and so on. The computer's strict nature dictates very specific uses of these words, but the similarity of the words' meanings to their English usage makes programming languages easy for you to learn and remember.

Over the years since the first computer language was invented, hundreds of programming languages have been written, but there are a handful that have dominated the rest. The following is a list of several programming languages that gained more than obscure notoriety through the years:

| | | |
|---|---|---|
| Machine Language * | Assembler * | Algol |
| PL/I * | PROLOG * | LISP |
| COBOL * | Forth | RPG * |
| Java * | Pascal * | HTML * |
| SNOBOL | Ada * | C * |
| C++ * | XML * | FORTRAN * |
| SmallTalk | BASIC * | Visual Basic * |
| APL * | | |

The languages marked with an asterisk (*) achieved dominance either through sheer numbers of users or within a specific area of expertise. For example, PROLOG was rarely used outside the artificial intelligence field but was the language of choice there in the early years.

Each programming language has its own dialects. BASIC is tremendously popular in all of the following varieties:

> GW-BASIC
>
> QuickBasic
>
> QBasic
>
> BASICA
>
> Visual Basic

Before you finish this book, you will be writing complete Windows programs in Visual Basic. Chapters 5 through 11 teach you Visual Basic (today's most popular version of the original BASIC language) and show you how to write programs that do what you want them to do.

There are lots of reasons why so many programming languages exist. Different people have different preferences, some languages are better than others depending on the tasks, and some people have access to only one or two of the languages.

**note**

The program that you write is called a *source program* (or *source code*). Throughout this book, when you see the term *source program*, that text is referring to your program before it is compiled into machine-readable code.

## The Language Translator

Your computer cannot actually understand BASIC, C, Java, or any of the other programming languages. "Wait!" you might yell. "The previous section explained that computer languages are important because the computer cannot understand English, or any other language that people speak, because there is too much

**tip**

Once compiled, a program cannot be changed easily. When you buy a program that is already written, the chances are good that it is compiled. You can run it, but you cannot see the source program itself. This security helps to protect the integrity of the code that the program designers worked hard to produce.

ambiguity in speech." Even so, the computer cannot understand C++ either, but it is easy for a program to translate C++ to the actual 1s and 0s that the computer *does* understand. A *compiler* takes programs written in high-level programming languages and translates them into a form readable by the computer.

# Accuracy Is Everything

You now are well aware that the computer is a machine that does not deal well with ambiguity. A programmer's plague is the errors that show up in code. Programmers must ensure that they do not write programs that contain errors, and this is not always easy.

A program error is known as a *bug*. When breaking the programming problem into detailed instructions, programmers often leave things out or code the wrong thing. When the program runs, errors creep up due to the bugs in the code.

*Debugging* is the process a programmer goes through to exterminate the bugs from a program. As a programmer writes a program, he often runs the program in its unfinished state (as much as can be run) to catch as many bugs as possible and keep them out of the finished program. Often the majority of the bugs can be found only after the program is completely written.

Beginning programmers often fail to realize how easy it is for bugs to creep into code. When you begin to write your first programs, expect to have to correct some problems. Nobody writes a perfect program every time.

There are two categories of computer bugs: syntax errors and logic errors. To learn the difference, take a few moments to find the two errors in the following statement:

> *There are two errrors in this sentence.*

**note**

The term *bug* has an interesting origin. The late naval admiral Grace Hopper, one of the early pioneers of computer hardware and software (she helped write the first COBOL compiler), was working on a military computer system in the early 1950s. While printing a report, the printer stopped working. Admiral Hopper and her co-workers set out to find the problem.

After spending lots of time without finding any problems in the program or data, Admiral Hopper looked in the printer and noticed that a moth had lodged itself in the wires of the printer, keeping the printer from operating properly. As soon as the bug (get it?) was removed, the printer worked perfectly.

The first error is obvious. The word "errrors" is misspelled. It should be "errors." The second problem is much more difficult to find. The second problem with the statement is that the entire premise of the statement is incorrect. There is only one error in the statement, and that error is the misspelled word "errrors." Therefore, the statement itself is in error.

This problem demonstrates the difference between a syntax error and a logic error. The syntax error is much easier to find. Syntax errors commonly are misspelled commands and grammatical problems with the way you used the programming language. Logic errors occur when your program is syntactically correct but you told it to do something that is not what should really be done.

Compilers and interpreters locate your program's syntax errors when you try to compile or run it. This is another reason why syntax errors are easier to spot: Your computer tells you where they are. When a computer runs into a syntax error, it halts and refuses to analyze the program further until you correct the syntax error. Figure 2.2 shows a Visual Basic program that stopped compiling because of a syntax error.

**FIGURE 2.2**

The Visual Basic compiler stops and tells you the exact line where the error occurred.

Suppose you're writing a program to print invoices for your company's accounts receivable. Because of an error, the computer prints all the invoices with a balance due of negative $1,000. In other words, according to the invoice, every customer has a $1,000 credit. Your computer did its job, following your program's instructions. The program obviously contained no syntax errors because it ran without stopping. The logic errors, however, kept it from working properly.

Extensive testing is critical. The programmer wants to get all the errors out so the program will work correctly when the user finally uses it. The larger the program, the more difficult this is. Exterminating program bugs is just part of the job programmers tackle daily.

# The Need for Design

When a builder begins to build a house, he doesn't pick up a hammer and begin on the kitchen's frame. The house must be properly designed before anything can happen. The builder must first find out what the purchaser of the house wants. Once the plans for the house are drawn, the builder must plan the resources needed to build the house. The builder must file the proper permits, get financing, gather the materials, and gather the workers. The builder must also decide on some kind of timeframe and determine a proper schedule for completing each part of the building (the roof cannot go up before the foundation).

The more effort the builder puts into these preliminary requirements, the faster the house can actually be built. The problem with building a house before it is properly designed is that the eventual owners may want changes made after it is too late to change them. It is very difficult to add a bathroom in the middle of two bedrooms after the house is completed.

A program must also be designed before it is written. You should not go to the keyboard and start typing instructions into the program before designing it.

Thanks to computer technology, a computer program is easier to modify than a house. If you leave out a routine that a user wants, you can add it later more easily than a builder can add a room to a finished house. Nevertheless, adding something to a program is never as easy as designing the program correctly the first time.

Program maintenance is one of the most time-consuming parts of the programming process. Programs are continually updated to reflect new user needs. If the program is not designed properly before it is written, the user will not want the program until it does exactly what he wants it to do.

Computer consultants learn early to get the user's acceptance and even his signature on a program's design before the programming begins. If both the user and the programmers agree on what to do, there is little room for argument when the final program is presented. Companies with internal data processing departments also require that their programming staff come to a written agreement with the user who wants them to write a program. Company resources are limited; there is no time to add something later that should have been in the system all along.

> **caution**
>
> Because computer programs must be extremely detailed, you have to follow some tried and tested procedures for breaking down problems into their components. This chapter shows you how to do this. Only after you understand that a program's details are critical can you begin to write programs with any success.

There are three steps you should perform when you have a program to write:

1. Define the output.
2. Develop the logic to get to that output.
3. Write the program.

Notice that writing the program is the last step. Remember that constructing the house is the last stage of building a house; proper planning is critical before construction can start.

# Step 1: Define the Output

Before beginning a program, you must have a firm idea of what the program should produce. Remember that in the fundamental model of programming, the output is the last thing produced, but it is the first thing you must design. Just as a builder must know what the house should look like before beginning to build it, a programmer must know what the output is going to be before writing the program.

A program's output consists of more than just printed information. Anything that the program produces and the user sees is considered output that you must define. You must know what every screen in the program should look like and what will be on every page of every report, invoice, and paycheck generated by programs.

The output definition is more than a preliminary output design. It gives you insight into what data elements the program should track, compute, and produce. Defining the output also helps you gather all the input you need to produce the output.

The output definition consists of many pages of details. You must be able to specify all the details of a problem before you know what output you need.

## Top-Down Program Design

The most important design tool available is top-down design. *Top-down design* is the process of taking the overall problem and breaking it down more and more until you finalize all the details.

The problem with top-down design is that programmers tend not to use it. They tend to design from the opposite direction (called *bottom-up design*). When you ignore top-down design, you impose a heavy burden on yourself to remember every detail that will be needed. You do not have to worry about the details if you follow a strict top-down design process because the process takes care of producing the details.

Top-down design is not just for programming problems. You can apply it to any part of your life that you must plan in detail. Perhaps the most detailed event that a person can plan is a

**tip**

One of the keys to top-down design is that it forces you to put off the details until later. Top-down design forces you to think in terms of the overall problem for as long as possible. Top-down design keeps you focused. If you use bottom-up design, it is too easy to lose sight of the forest for the trees. You get to the details too fast and lose sight of your program's primary objectives.

wedding. The way not to plan a wedding is to worry about the details first, but this is the way most people plan them. They start thinking about the dresses, the organist, the flowers, and the nuts to serve at the reception. The biggest problem with trying to cover all these details from the beginning is that you lose sight of so much; it is too easy to forget a detail until it is too late. The details of bottom-up design get in your way.

## Steps for Top-Down Design

Here is the three-step process necessary for top-down design:

1. Determine the overall goal.

2. Break that goal into two, three, four, or more detailed parts. Too many more parts make you leave out things.

3. Put off the details as long as possible. Repeat step 2 until you cannot reasonably break down the problem any further.

What is the overall goal of a wedding? "Have a wedding" is about as general as it can get. Now that you know where you're heading, begin breaking down the overall goal into two or three details. For instance, what about the colors of the wedding, what about the guest list, what about paying the minister…oops, too many details. The idea of top-down design is to put off the details for as long as possible. When you find yourself breaking the current problem into more than two to four parts, you are rushing the top-down design. You can break down "have a wedding" into the following two components: the ceremony and the reception.

The next step is to take those components and do the same for each of them. What makes up the ceremony is the people and the location. The reception includes the food, the people, and the location. The ceremony's people include the guests, the wedding party, and the workers (minister, organist, and so on, but those details come a little later).

The top-down design naturally produces a triangular result, the first part of which appears in Figure 2.3. There are a lot of details left to put in, but that is just the point; you should put off the details as long as possible. The details fall out on their own as you divide the tasks into more parts.

Eventually you will have several pages of details that cannot be broken down any further. For instance, you'll probably end up with the details of the reception food, such as peanuts for snacking. (If you start out listing those details, however, you probably will forget many of them.)

What if you were assigned the task of writing a payroll program for a company? What would that payroll program require? You might begin to list the payroll program's details, such as this:

1. Print payroll checks

2. Calculate federal taxes

3. Calculate state taxes

**FIGURE 2.3**

The early part of planning a wedding using top-down design.

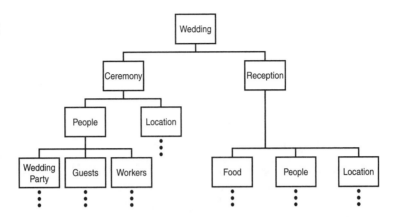

What is wrong with this approach? If you said that the details were coming too early, you are correct. The perfect place to start is at the top. The most general goal of a payroll program might be to "perform the payroll." Despite this obvious statement, the overall goal keeps other details out of this program (no general ledger processing will be included, unless part of the payroll system updates a general ledger file) and keeps you focused on the problem at hand.

Consider Figure 2.4. This might be the first page of the payroll program's top-down design. Any payroll program has to include some mechanism for entering, deleting, and changing employee information such as address, city, state, ZIP Code, number of exemptions, and so on. What other details about the employees do you need? At this point, don't ask. The design is not ready for all those details.

**FIGURE 2.4**

The first page of the payroll program's top-down design.

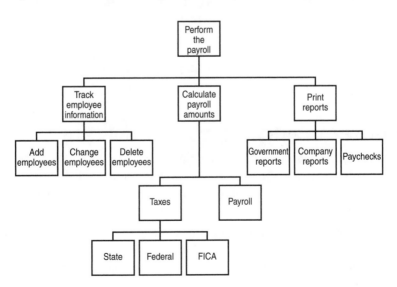

There is a long way to go before you finish with the design. You must keep breaking down each of the components until the details finally appear. Only after you have all the details ready can you begin to decide what the program is going to produce.

What do you do with all the details of the design and output definition? You must move them into some kind of time-order logic that your program can follow to produce the details.

## Step 2: Develop the Logic

Once you and the user agree to the goals and output of the program, the rest is up to you. It is now your job to take that output definition and decide how to make a computer produce the output. You have taken the overall problem and broken it down into detailed instructions that the computer can carry out. This does not mean that you are ready to write the program—quite the contrary. You are now ready to develop the logic that produces that output.

The output definition goes a long way toward describing what the program is supposed to do. Now you must decide how to accomplish the job. You must order the details that you have so that they operate in a time-ordered fashion. You must also decide which decisions your program must make and the actions produced by each of those decisions.

## Step 3: Write the Program

Now for the big finale! Once the output is defined and the logic determined to get that output, you must go to the computer and generate the code—the programming language statements—you need to get there. This means that you must learn a programming language first. Writing the program takes the longest to learn. Once you learn to program, however, the actual programming process takes less time than the design if your design is accurate and complete. The nature of programming requires that you learn some new skills.

# The Program Language

One important step has been left out of this book so far. That is the step of learning the language itself. The rest of this book is devoted to describing the various programming languages available. It also introduces you to a popular programming language named Visual Basic.

Most programming books jump right in and start teaching a language in the first chapter. There is nothing wrong with this approach, but somewhere along the way you need to learn to design programs, and that is the purpose of this book. At this point, you have a good grasp of programming fundamentals, and you understand more about what professional programmers do in their programming environments.

# Summary

There are several ways to get programs for computers, but to really make computers do what you want, you have to write the programs yourself. Programs direct the processing of data. You have to learn a programming language before you can write a program that the computer will understand. Too often, programmers rush to the keyboard without thinking through the logic. The result of a badly designed program is lots of bugs and later maintenance.

- Most companies find they have to write programs they need. This explains the large programming staffs many companies hire.
- Programming languages enable communication between the low-level computer's 1s and 0s and the high-level human programmer who speaks in ambiguous speech.
- A bug is a program error.
- You must design a program before writing it. Proper design ensures a quicker programming process and fewer errors.

# PART

# FUNDAMENTALS OF PROGRAMMING

3 Programming Languages: The Early
Years . . . . . . . . . . . . . . . . . . . . . . . . .41

4 Programming Languages: Modern
Day . . . . . . . . . . . . . . . . . . . . . . . . .61

## IN THIS CHAPTER

- Storage of Programs and Data
- Binary Arithmetic
- The First Programs
- Enter the Keyboard
- Getting Closer to English
- Other Languages Through the Years

**3**

# PROGRAMMING LANGUAGES: THE EARLY YEARS

With this chapter, you can step into the ranks of the few, the proud, the people of tomorrow, by developing an understanding of several programming languages. This chapter focuses on the earlier programming languages, some of which are still in use today. You will learn how programming languages began and how they have evolved over the years.

The highlights of this chapter include the following:

- As you type keys on your keyboard, your computer accepts binary values that represent data.
- The ASCII code defines the binary patterns for each character the computer represents.

- The earliest computers were programmed using wires.
- FORTRAN and COBOL were the languages of choice for science and business for many years.
- ADA was the government's language of choice for many years.

# Storage of Programs and Data

While typing at your keyboard, what do you think happens when you press the keys? Does a letter A go somewhere inside the computer's memory when you press the A key? It must, or else the computer could never remember your program's contents. The computer does store the A, but not in the format you might expect. The computer stores only a representation of the letter A. For all intents, the A is in memory, but it does not look like you think it should.

Remember that your computer is nothing more than thousands of switches turning electricity on and off. Each character in your computer is represented by a combination of on and off switches.

> **tip**
>
> The reason it takes eight switches is that if there were fewer, there wouldn't be enough combinations of on and off states to represent all the characters possible (uppercase, lowercase, digits, and special characters such as %, ^, and *).

Programmers generally refer to an on switch as a 1 (one) and an off switch as a 0 (zero). Since these switches have only two values, programmers call the 0s and 1s *binary digits*, or *bits* for short. There is a total of eight bits for every character in your computer, and eight bits is known as a *byte*. Therefore, every character of storage takes eight bits to represent (eight on and off switches), and therefore, a character is a byte.

Years ago, somebody wrote the various combinations of eight 1s and 0s from 00000000 to 11111111 and assigned a unique character to each one. The table of characters was standardized and is known today as the *ASCII table* (pronounced askee, so if you don't know-ee, you can ASCII). Table 3.1 shows a partial listing of the ASCII table. ASCII stands for *American Standard Code for Information Interchange*.

**TABLE 3.1**    ASCII Values Represent Characters

| Character | ASCII Code | Decimal Equivalent |
|-----------|-----------|--------------------|
| Space | 00100000 | 32 |
| 0 | 00110000 | 48 |
| 1 | 00110001 | 49 |
| 2 | 00110010 | 50 |
| 3 | 00110011 | 51 |
| 9 | 00111001 | 57 |
| ? | 00111111 | 63 |
| A | 01000001 | 65 |
| B | 01000010 | 66 |
| C | 01000011 | 67 |
| a | 01100001 | 97 |
| b | 01100010 | 98 |

Each of the ASCII values has a corresponding decimal number associated with it. These values are shown at the right of the eight-bit values in Table 3.1. Therefore, even though the computer represents the character ? as 00111111 (two off switches with six on switches), you can refer, through programming, to that ASCII value as 63 and your computer will know you mean 00111111. One of the advantages of high-level programming languages is that they often let you use the easier (for people) decimal values, and the programming language converts the value to the eight-bit binary value used inside the computer.

Think back to the internal storage of single characters described earlier in this section. When you press the letter A, that A is not stored in your computer; rather, the ASCII value of the A is stored. As you can see from the ASCII values in the previous table, the letter A is represented as 01000001 (all of the eight switches except two are off in every byte of memory that holds a letter A).

**note**

As you can tell from the ASCII values in Table 3.1, every character in the computer, both uppercase and lowercase letters, and even the space, has its own unique ASCII value. The unique ASCII code is the only way the computer has to differentiate characters. Some mainframes use a similar system called the *EBCDIC table*, pronounced *eb-se-dik*.

As Figure 3.1 shows, when you press the letter A on your keyboard, the A does not go into memory, but the ASCII value of 01000001 does. The computer keeps that pattern of on and off switches in that memory location as long as the A is to remain there. As far as you are concerned, the A is in memory as the letter A, but now you know exactly what happens. If you print the program you just typed, and the computer is ready to print the character stored in that memory location, the computer's CPU sends the ASCII code for the A to the printer. Just before printing, the printer knows that it must make its output readable to people, so it looks up 01000001 in its own ASCII table and prints the A to paper. From the time the A left the keyboard until right before it printed, it was not an A at all, but just a combination of eight 1s and 0s that represents an A.

**tip**

The ASCII table is not very different from another type of coded table you may have heard of. Morse Code is a table of representations for letters of the alphabet.
Instead of 1s and 0s, the code uses combinations of dashes and dots to represent characters. The dashes and dots represent the length of radio signals people send or receive. The letters SOS are represented by DOT-DOT-DOT DASH-DASH-DASH DOT-DOT-DOT.

**FIGURE 3.1**
The A is not an A once it leaves the keyboard.

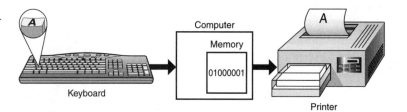

# Binary Arithmetic

At their lowest level, computers cannot subtract, multiply, or divide. Neither can calculators. The world's largest and fastest supercomputer can only add—that's it. It performs the addition at the bit level. Binary arithmetic is the only means by which any electronic digital computing machine can perform arithmetic.

Suppose you want the computer to add seven 6s together. If you asked the computer (through programming) to perform the calculation

6 + 6 + 6 + 6 + 6 + 6 + 6

the computer would zing the answer, 42, back to you before you could say *bit bucket*. The computer has no problem performing addition. The problems arise when you request that the computer perform another type of calculation, such as this one:

42 – 6 – 6 – 6 – 6 – 6 – 6 – 6

Because the computer can only add, it cannot do the subtraction. However, the computer can negate numbers. That is, the computer can take the negative of a number. Therefore, it can take the negative of 6 and represent (at the bit level) negative 6. Once it has done that, it can add –6 to 42 seven times. In effect, the internal calculation becomes this:

42 + (–6) + (–6) + (–6) + (–6) + (–6) + (–6) + (–6)

Adding seven –6s produces the correct result of 0. This may seem like a cop-out to you. After all, the computer is really subtracting, right? In reality, the computer is not subtracting. At its bit level, the computer can convert a number to its negative through a process known as *2's complement*. A number's 2's complement is the negative of its original value at the bit level. The computer has in its internal logic circuits the capability to convert a number to its 2's complement and then carry out the addition of negatives, thereby seemingly performing subtraction.

Once the computer can add and simulate subtraction, it can simulate multiplying and dividing. To multiply 6 times 7, the computer actually adds 6 together seven times and produces 42. Therefore

6 × 7

becomes this:

6 + 6 + 6 + 6 + 6 + 6 + 6

To divide 42 by 7, the computer subtracts 7 from 42 (well, it adds the *negative* of 7 to 42) until it reaches zero and counts the number of times (6) it took to reach zero, like this:

42 + (–7) + (–7) + (–7) + (–7) + (–7) + (–7)

The computer represents numbers in a manner similar to characters. As Table 3.2 shows, numbers are easy to represent at the binary level. Once numbers reach a certain limit (256 to be exact), the computer will use more than one byte to represent the number, taking as many memory locations as it needs to represent the number. After it is taught to add, subtract, multiply, and divide, the computer can then perform any math necessary as long as a program is supplied to direct it.

**TABLE 3.2**   All Numbers Can Be Represented as Binary Numbers

| Number | Binary Equivalent |
| --- | --- |
| 0 | 00000000 |
| 1 | 00000001 |
| 2 | 00000010 |
| 3 | 00000011 |
| 4 | 00000100 |

**TABLE 3.2** (continued)

| Number | Binary Equivalent |
| --- | --- |
| 5 | 00000101 |
| 6 | 00000110 |
| 7 | 00000111 |
| 8 | 00001000 |
| 9 | 00001001 |
| 10 | 00001010 |
| 11 | 00001011 |
| 12 | 00001100 |
| 13 | 00001101 |
| 14 | 00001110 |
| 15 | 00001111 |
| 16 | 00010000 |
| 17 | 00010001 |
| 18 | 00010010 |
| 19 | 00010011 |
| 20 | 00010100 |

To see an example of what goes on at the bit level, follow this example to see what happens when you ask the computer to subtract 65 from 65. The result should be zero and, as you can see from the following steps, that is exactly what the result is at the binary level.

1. Suppose you want the computer to calculate the following:

   65 – 65

2. The binary representation for 65 is 01000001, and the 2's complement for 65 is 10111111 (which is –65 in computerese). Therefore, you are requesting that the computer perform this calculation:

   01000001 + 10111111

**tip**

The first 255 binary numbers overlap the ASCII table values. That is, the binary representation for the letter A is 01000001, and the binary number for 65 is also 01000001. The computer knows by the context of how your programs use the memory location whether the value is the letter A or the number 65.

3. Because a binary number cannot have the digit 2 (there are only 0s and 1s in binary), the computer carries 1 anytime a calculation results in a value of 2; 1 + 1 equals 10 in binary. Although this can be confusing, you can make an analogy with decimal arithmetic. People work in a base 10 numbering system. (Binary is known as base 2.) There is no single digit to represent ten; we have to reuse two digits already used to form ten: 1 and 0. In base 10, 9 + 1 is 10. Therefore, the result of 1 + 1 in binary is 10 or "0 and carry 1 to the next column."

```
 01000001
+10111111
100000000
```

> **tip**
>
> The good thing about all this binary arithmetic is that you don't have to understand a bit of it (pun intended) to be an expert programmer. Nevertheless, the more you know about what is going on under the hood, the better you will understand how programming languages work and the faster you will master new ones by seeing similarities between them.

4. Because the answer should fit within the same number of bits as the two original numbers (at least for this example—your computer may use more bits to represent numbers), the ninth bit is discarded, leaving the zero result. This example shows that binary 65 plus binary negative 65 equals zero as it should.

# The First Programs

The earliest computers were not programmed in the same way as today's computers. It took much more effort. The early computers' memories held only data and not programs. The concept of programming those early computers was vastly different because the programs were hard-wired into the machine. The programs were physically wired by experts to generate and process the data. The first computer programmers had never heard of using a keyboard, editor, and compiler; the first programmers were hardware experts, not software experts.

Programming these computers was very difficult. To make a change, the hardware programmer had to reroute the wires that made the program do its thing. It wasn't long before a man by the name of John von Neumann invented the shared-program concept. He demonstrated that a program could be stored in memory along with the data. Once the programs were in memory and out of the wired hardware, the programs were much easier to change. John von Neumann's breakthrough was one of the most important and lasting advances in the entire computing history; we still use his shared-program concept in today's machines.

Those early programmers used the switch panel to enter programs into the computer's shared memory. Although it was fantastic for its time, programming these computers took a tremendous effort because they had to be programmed in the machine's native 1s and 0s. Therefore, the first few instructions to a computer might look like this:

```
01000110
11000100
10111011
00011101
```

Whenever a programmer wanted to add two numbers, move values in memory, or whatever, the programmer had to refer to a table that described the proper patterns of 1s and 0s for the desired instructions. Flipping the switches and programming the machine took hours, but it was a giant leap forward from hard-wired computer programming.

# Enter the Keyboard

Someone watching over the programming process got the brilliant, but today seemingly obvious, idea of attaching a keyboard to the computer. Instead of typing those 1s and 0s, the programmer could type names associated with each instruction in the machine language. Therefore, the previous few instructions might look something like this:

```
ADD A, 6
MOV A, OUT
LOAD B
SUB B, A
     :
```

These commands are cryptic, but they are a lot easier to remember than the 1s and 0s. The words are called *mnemonics*, which means the words are easy-to-remember abbreviations for the instructions. ADD A, 6 is a lot easier to remember when you need to add 6 to the value of a memory location named A than is 01000110.

Of course, the computer could not understand the mnemonics, but a translator program called an *assembler* was written to be the go-between for the programmer's mnemonics and the 1s and 0s to which they were translated. Figure 3.2 shows how the assembler acts as the go-between for the human programmer at the keyboard and the machine. A huge leap forward was made when the assembler language became the primary means by which programmers entered instructions into the computer. This second programming language (the first was the native 1s and 0s machine language) enabled much faster program development. The software revolution began just a few years after the computer hardware was born.

These first two programming languages—machine language and assembler language—are called *low-level* programming languages. The computer doesn't need to translate much to convert assembler language to machine language because each assembler instruction has a one-to-one correlation with a machine-language instruction (a machine-language instruction may take more than one byte of memory, though). Low-level languages are rarely used today due to the nature and efficiency of high-level programming languages (C++ and Visual Basic, for example).

Machine language programming is cryptic. Today's machine-level code is more powerful than before. For instance, there are machine-language instructions to perform multiplication and division, whereas computers of the first and second generation rarely had that power at the machine level. Programmers had to write machine language programs to perform such mathematical feats.

**note**

The keyboards used with the early computers were not attached to the machines as directly as they are today. Often, programmers would use a card-punch machine. These machines had keyboards, but the typing produced punched holes in computer cards. Then the cards were read into the computer's memory. You may have seen these punched cards, but they are rarely used today. Online terminals (screen and keyboard combinations) are much more efficient than card-punch machines, and you won't rearrange a thousand-line program on a terminal as easily as you would if you dropped a box of punched cards.

**FIGURE 3.2**

The assembler translates mnemonics into 1s and 0s.

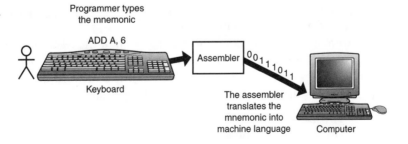

Programmer types the mnemonic

ADD A, 6

Keyboard

Assembler

The assembler translates the mnemonic into machine language

Computer

# Getting Closer to English

High-level programming languages evolved from the complexity of the low-level languages. Once assembler language was made available, more companies began using computers. With the beginning of widespread use of computers came the need to write more complex software applications to support those companies. The low-level machine and assembler languages were too inefficient for the quick turnaround that the companies needed. Therefore, high-level languages were developed to add one more layer between the programmer and the hardware. That extra layer meant that more work was required by the computer to translate a high-level language into machine language, but the programmers were free from the job of low-level coding. Two of the earliest high-level programming compilers were FORTRAN and COBOL.

## The FORTRAN Language

FORTRAN stands for *FORmula TRANslator*. As its name implies, it is used for mathematical and scientific applications. FORTRAN works very well with high-precision numbers and offers an excellent library of built-in trigonometric routines that aid the scientific developer.

Over the years, programmers have added to the FORTRAN language, giving it more character-manipulation capabilities. The early versions of FORTRAN existed to solve mathematical computations without much regard for the cosmetics of how the results looked. Later FORTRAN compilers work better with character data (often called *character string* data because strings of characters make up words and sentences) than the older versions did, but they still retain their mathematical capabilities.

It is not the goal of this book to teach you FORTRAN. FORTRAN is not regarded as a beginner's language (although it is not as difficult as many of the others; once you learn Visual Basic, you could pick up FORTRAN relatively easily). The FORTRAN program in Listing 3.1 is an example of a payroll computation that you can study.

**tip**

Until today's fast computers arrived on the scene, whenever a program's speed and low overhead were critical in the past, programmers often used assembler and machine language instead of a higher-level language such as COBOL (you'll learn about high-level languages throughout the rest of this and the next chapter). It is more difficult to learn a low-level language than a high-level language, and it takes longer to program in the low-level languages, but for some applications the assembler level is the only place to be.

Quite often, programmers would combine a high-level programming language such as C with some assembler language routines, speeding up the critical processes while keeping the more readable (and maintainable) high-level language for the majority of the program.

## LISTING 3.1   A Sample FORTRAN Program That Calculates Payroll

```
*
* Calculate payroll amounts and print the net pay
*
* Print a title
      WRITE(6,10)
   10 FORMAT(1H1, 2X, '** PAYROLL COMPUTATION **'//)
*
* Initialize overtime to 0
*
      TOVRTM = 0.0
*
* Get hours worked and other pay data from user
*
      WRITE(6, 20)
   20 FORMAT('WHAT WERE THE HOURS WORKED? ')
      READ(5, 21) HRS
   21 FORMAT(F4.1)
      WRITE(6, 22)
   22 FORMAT(/'WHAT IS THE HOURLY RATE? ')
      READ(5, 23) RATE
   23 FORMAT(F7.2)
      WRITE(6, 24)
   24 FORMAT(/'WHAT IS THE TAX RATE? ')
      READ(6, 25) TAXRTE
   25 FORMAT(F7.2)
*
* Calculate the results
*
* Overtime is left at 0.0 or is double pay
* depending on the hours the employee worked
      IF (HRS .LT. 40.0) GOTO 100
      TOVRTM = (HRS - 40.0) * RATE * 2.0
      GROSS = 40.0 * RATE
      GOTO 200
  100 GROSS = HRS * RATE
  200 GROSS = GROSS + TOVRTM
      TNET = GROSS * (1.0 - TAXRTE)
*
* PRINT THE RESULTS
*
```

## LISTING 3.1   (continued)

```
     WRITE(6, 300) HRS, RATE, TAXRTE, GROSS, TNET
300 FORMAT(//'Hours: ', F4.1, 2X, 'Rate: ', F7.2,
   1    2x, 'Tax rate: ', F7.2, 2x, 'Gross: $', F10.2,
   2    2x, 'Net: $', F10.2)
     END
```

Notice that FORTRAN is a high-level language, easier to read than its assembler language precursor shown earlier, but still not extremely obvious to nonprogrammers. Although you may not understand everything in the program, you can see some words you recognize, such as WRITE and FORMAT. You should begin to see that high-level programming languages are closer to spoken language than either the 1s and 0s or the mnemonics of the low-level languages.

FORTRAN is not known as a large language. It has relatively few commands (as opposed to COBOL and modern-day BASIC languages), although its compactness causes some confusion if you do not know the language. FORTRAN is not regarded as a self-documenting language, a sometimes-overused term applied to languages that offer some readability for nonprogrammers. Nevertheless, FORTRAN appears to have its foothold in the scientific community, and it will for some time. In fairness, FORTRAN has lost ground over the years to more modern languages, especially as today's languages support mathematical operations better than before.

## The Business of COBOL

The late Grace Hopper, the naval admiral who is credited with discovering the first computer bug (refer back to Chapter 3 for a refresher if you need it), is also known as the author of COBOL. In 1960, Admiral Hopper and her team of programmers decided they needed a language for the business side of computing (even the Navy has to meet a payroll and pay its bills). FORTRAN was taking care of the scientific side of things, but the FORTRAN language was never designed to handle business transactions. Programmers were also discovering that FORTRAN's cryptic nature slowed down programming maintenance chores as well.

**note**

All COBOL programs are separated into four divisions. The identification division describes the program. The environment division describes the computer system running the program. The data division describes the format of all data in the program. The procedure division contains the code that processes the data. See if you can find these four divisions in Listing 3.2.

Admiral Hopper's team developed COBOL, an acronym for COmmon Business Oriented Language. The COBOL design team's primary goal was to develop a self-documenting language that could process a large amount of business data such as inventory and personnel records. A sample of their achievement is shown in Listing 3.2. This is a program that performs the very same processing as its FORTRAN counterpart in Listing 3.1, but the COBOL listing is almost twice as long. Take a few minutes to peruse the listing and become familiar with the nature of COBOL.

## LISTING 3.2 A Sample COBOL Program That Calculates Payroll

```
IDENTIFICATION DIVISION.
PROGRAM-ID.     'PAYROLL'

ENVIRONMENT DIVISION.
INPUT-OUTPUT SECTION.
FILE-CONTROL.
   SELECT GET-DATA, ASSIGN TO KEYIN.
   SELECT OUT-DATA, ASSIGN TO DISPLAY.

DATA DIVISION.
FILE SECTION.
FD  GET-DATA
    LABEL RECORDS ARE OMITTED.
01  GET-REC.
    02 AMOUNT        PICTURE 9(5)V2.

FD  OUT-DATA
    LABEL RECORDS ARE OMITTED.
01  OUT-REC.
    02 FILLER        PICTURE X(80).

WORKING-STORAGE SECTION.
01  ARITHMETIC-DATA.
    02 TOT-OVR       PICTURE 9(5)V2 VALUE ZERO.
    02 HOURS         PICTURE 9(3)V1 VALUE ZERO.
    02 RATE          PICTURE 9(5)V2 VALUE ZERO.
    02 TAX-RATE      PICTURE 9(5)V2 VALUE ZERO.
    02 GROSS-PAY     PICTURE 9(5)V2 VALUE ZERO.
    02 NET-PAY       PICTURE 9(5)V2 VALUE ZERO.
01  OUT-LINE-1.
    02 FILLER        PICTURE X(28)
       VALUE 'What were the hours worked? '.
```

## LISTING 3.2    (continued)

```
    02 FILLER        PICTURE X(52) VALUE SPACES.
 01 OUT-LINE-2.
    02 FILLER        PICTURE X(25)
       VALUE 'What is the hourly rate? '.
    02 FILLER        PICTURE X(55) VALUE SPACES.
 01 OUT-LINE-3.
    02 FILLER        PICTURE X(22)
       VALUE 'What is the tax rate? '.
    02 FILLER        PICTURE X(58) VALUE SPACES.
 01 OUT-LINE-4.
    02 FILLER        PICTURE X(17)
       VALUE 'The gross pay is '
    02 OUT-GROSS     PICTURE $ZZ,ZZZ.99.
    02 FILLER        PICTURE X(53) VALUE SPACES.
 01 OUT-LINE-5.
    02 FILLER        PICTURE X(15)
       VALUE 'The net pay is '
    02 OUT-NET       PICTURE $ZZ,ZZZ.99.
    02 FILLER        PICTURE X(55) VALUE SPACES.

PROCEDURE DIVISION.
BEGIN.
    OPEN INPUT GET-DATA.
    OPEN OUTPUT OUT-DATA.

    MOVE OUT-LINE-1 TO OUT-REC.
    WRITE OUT-REC.
    READ GET-DATA.
    MOVE AMOUNT TO HOURS.

    MOVE OUT-LINE-2 TO OUT-REC.
    WRITE OUT-REC.
    READ GET-DATA.
    MOVE AMOUNT TO RATE.

    MOVE OUT-LINE-3 TO OUT-REC.
    WRITE OUT-REC.
    READ GET-DATA.
    MOVE AMOUNT TO TAX-RATE.
```

**LISTING 3.2**   (continued)

```
IF HOURS > 40.0
   THEN COMPUTE TOT-OVR = (40.0 - HOURS) * RATE * 2
        COMPUTE GROSS-PAY = 40.0 * RATE + TOT-OVR
ELSE
   COMPUTE GROSS-PAY = HOURS * RATE.
COMPUTE NET-PAY = GROSS-PAY * (1.0 - TAX-RATE).

MOVE GROSS-PAY TO OUT-GROSS.
MOVE OUT-LINE-4 TO OUT-REC.
WRITE OUT-REC.

MOVE NET-PAY TO OUT-NET.
MOVE OUT-LINE-5 TO OUT-REC.
WRITE OUT-REC.

CLOSE GET-DATA, OUT-DATA.
STOP RUN.
```

Admiral Hopper's crew wanted COBOL to be self-documenting so that nonprogrammers could understand what the program was attempting to do by looking at a program listing. Can you figure out what Listing 3.2 is doing just by reading the code? Don't feel bad if you can't; if you get lost in the program's silver-dollar words, don't be dismayed. Instead of being self-documenting, COBOL ended up being very wordy. There is so much that gets in the way of the working code that most people would probably agree (even COBOL fans, of whom there are many thousands) that COBOL does not achieve a self-documenting effect. Nevertheless, it shines as the world's premiere business language of choice, and it did for almost 40 years before the newer languages such as C++ and the Internet took over.

# Other Languages Through the Years

After FORTRAN and COBOL gained ground, there was no turning back the software industry. Languages began appearing all over the place. Companies would develop their own in-house programming languages that, supposedly, supported their environment better than the big two languages, FORTRAN and COBOL.

So many languages began appearing that the programming community started becoming fragmented, wallowing in the sheer number of possibilities, unable to decide which language was the best to use for any given project. At least, that was the scenario that IBM saw when it decided to create "the only programming language anyone would ever need." IBM saw (or tried to create, there is debate today, even among IBMers) a need for a programming language that did it all. The new language would be the best scientific language. It would be the best business language. It would solve any programmer's needs.

Therefore, IBM created the PL/I programming language to solve the problem of too many languages. PL/I stands for *Programming Language I*. IBM designed PL/I by taking the best of the COBOL language, the best of FORTRAN, and the best of some other programming languages of the time. The end result, at least in terms of sales, was never achieved; IBM never had the success with PL/I it had hoped for. Instead of being the only programming language anyone would ever need, PL/I became just another programming language among many.

The primary problem with PL/I was that it was too good; it was massive. IBM made use of the best of every programming language of the day, but in doing so, IBM created a huge language that required massive computing resources to run. During the 1960s, not enough businesses had enough computer power to devote 100% of the CPU's time to PL/I compiles. Also, PL/I took too long for programmers to learn. The language was so large that programmers rarely mastered it.

Listing 3.3 shows part of a PL/I program that performs the same routine as the FORTRAN and COBOL listings you saw earlier. In this example, the code looks more like its COBOL counterpart than FORTRAN, but much of PL/I differs from COBOL. The differences become more apparent as you begin programming scientific and other non-business applications.

## LISTING 3.3 A Sample PL/I Program That Performs Payroll Calculation

```
PAYROLL: PROCEDURE OPTIONS (MAIN);
DECLARE OVRTIM    FIXED DECIMAL (2);
DECLARE HOURS     FIXED DECIMAL (5,2);
DECLARE RATE      FIXED DECIMAL (9,2);
DECLARE TAXRATE   FIXED DECIMAL (9,2);
DECLARE GROSS     FIXED DECIMAL (9,2);
DECLARE NETPAY    FIXED DECIMAL (9,2);

BEGIN: GET LIST(HOURS, RATE, TAXRATE);
   IF HOURS > 40 THEN
      OVRTIM = (HOURS - 40) * RATE * 2
      GROSS = 40 * RATE
   ELSE
```

**LISTING 3.3**   (continued)

```
      OVRTIM = 0
      GROSS = HOURS * RATE;
   NETPAY = GROSS * (1 - TAXRATE);
   PUT LIST (OVRTIM, HOURS, RATE, TAXRATE, GROSS, NETPAY);
END PAYROLL
```

Perhaps another reason for PL/I's decline is that it was never ported to a microcomputer environment. Originally, the microcomputer did not have the memory or disk space for a language as large as PL/I. Although today's PCs would have no trouble running PL/I, other languages such as C and Pascal took hold in the PC arena before PL/I had a chance to.

Another programming language that has been around for many years is Report Program Generator (RPG). RPG exists in newer versions named RPG II and RPG III. As its name implies, RPG began as a report writer only. It was originally intended to be a language that nonprogrammers (shades of COBOL's ideals) could use to generate reports from data in disk files.

RPG is unlike most other programming languages. The languages you have seen so far are *procedural languages*. That is, they offer individual instructions that the computer follows in a sequential manner until the job is done. RPG does not have typical commands, and its logic is nonprocedural. (Some of the later versions of RPG do offer limited procedural capabilities.) An RPG program is one that is written using codes that follow strict column placements. Nonprogrammers, and even veteran programmers who are inexperienced in RPG, have a difficult time deciphering RPG programs. To make matters worse, there are several nonstandard versions of RPG in widespread use.

Listing 3.4 shows a sample RPG program. The placement of the codes must be exact. If you shift any line of the program to the right or left a few spaces, the program does not work. As you might imagine, an RPG program is difficult to follow and extremely difficult to get right the first time you write one.

**LISTING 3.4**   A Sample RPG Program Shows RPG's Cryptic Nature

```
F*    PAYROLL PROGRAM
FOUTP    IP  F    80          KEYBOARD
FINP     O   F    80          SCREEN
IREPORT  AA  01                   1    10RATE
I                                 8    30HOURS
I                                12    40TAXRATE
```

## LISTING 3.4    (continued)

```
C         *PY01      IFGT  '40'
C         OVTIM      MULT       RATE*2
C         OVTIM      MULT       HOURS
C                    END
C         *GROSS     IFLE  '40'
C         GROSS      MULT       RATE  *  HOURS
C                    END
OOUTP      H   100 1P
```

Programmers used RPG primarily on minicomputers. As you might recall from Chapter 2, in just a few short years the minicomputer has mostly gone the way of the dinosaur, and RPG went with it.

Two other programming languages, APL and ADA, have also been used a lot over the years. APL (which stands for *A Programming Language*) is a highly mathematical programming language developed by IBM. APL is a language as different from COBOL and FORTRAN as is RPG. An APL program consists of many strange symbols (housetops, curved arrows, triangles, and so forth) and requires special hardware to generate its symbols. Because of the hardware restriction and its slow speed compared to other programming languages (APL is almost always run in an interpreted mode and rarely compiled), it quickly lost favor even by those who were fans.

ADA, named after Lady Augusta Ada Byron (daughter of the poet Lord Byron and girlfriend of Charles Babbage, the father of computers), was used almost exclusively by the Department of Defense and other governmental contracts. The government thought it best to standardize on a programming language so that all of its programs would be consistent and governmental programmers would be familiar with the language of all in-house code. Experts viewed ADA as a mediocre programming language that is difficult to learn (keep in mind that the government put its blessing on ADA as the language of choice, and the government has never been known for being extremely efficient or logical). One wonders why the Department of Defense, which designed and wrote the first COBOL compiler years earlier, chose to use something besides COBOL when almost every company at the time had adopted COBOL and was having tremendous success using it.

Because the government standardized on the ADA programming language early (it was the Department of Defense that designed ADA in 1979), you had to know ADA to produce programs for the government. Today, other languages are accepted.

This completes the first discussion of programming languages. In the next chapter, you get a look at some of the newer programming languages (those developed within the last 20 years).

# Summary

Understanding the inner workings of your computer is a prerequisite for becoming a master programmer. Only after learning about what is under the hood can your programming skills blossom. Computer programming has come a long way since the early days of wiring panels and switches. High-level languages such as COBOL and FORTRAN offered a much easier approach to making computers do what you wanted them to do.

- Memory is little more than on and off switches.

- The pattern of bits that corresponds to a specific character is determined by the ASCII table.

- Once keyboards were attached to computers, many advances began. The earliest non-binary programming language was called *assembler language*. The assembler translates assembler coded mnemonics into 1s and 0s.

- High-level programming languages such as FORTRAN and COBOL provide a much easier programming environment because they are one step closer to spoken language and one step further from the machine's native binary code.

## IN THIS CHAPTER

- Pascal's Importance and Demise
- The C Programming Language
- C++'s Impact on Modern Languages
- Hypertext and Scripting Languages
- The BASICs
- Which Language Is Best?

4

# PROGRAMMING LANGUAGES: MODERN DAY

Programming languages have come a long way since the original COBOL compiler. With each new programming language comes the promise of faster learning and more maintainable code. Graphical User Interfaces (GUIs) such as Windows environments and the Internet have dramatically changed the way languages are used and have forced the entry of almost as many new languages in the past few years as were created in the first 35 years of computing. This chapter focuses on newer languages.

The highlights of this chapter include the following:

■ Pascal opened the door for more modern languages.

■ C is a very efficient programming language that set the stage for several more languages.

- The online world brings new challenges to programming languages and requires new kinds of languages.
- Visual Basic has its roots in BASIC, a beginner's language.
- Although Visual Basic is simple to learn, you can create powerful Windows programs with it.

# Pascal's Importance and Demise

In 1968, Niklaus Wirth wrote the first Pascal compiler. Pascal was named after the French mathematician Blaise Pascal. Pascal is a good general-purpose programming language, offering support for scientific work as well as business. Pascal's input/output capabilities are not as advanced as other programming languages used in business, such as COBOL, so it was never a contender for removing COBOL from its business perch. Nevertheless, when released, Pascal was a solid language that did its job well.

Pascal had a huge and fast rise in popularity in the 1970s. Its biggest advantage was that it was the first major language to support structured programming concepts that made for more maintainable programs. (Chapter 22, "The Importance of Maintenance," describes structured programming.) The structured programming ideology is integrated into the design of Pascal, meaning that Pascal programs are simpler to maintain than programs written in other languages of the day.

During the 1970s, it was thought that Pascal would become "the only programming language you would ever need." IBM had that same prediction for PL/I, a language you learned about in the previous chapter. As with PL/I, Pascal never achieved that lofty goal. Pascal's use seemed to shrink as quickly as it grew. The 1970s saw tremendous growth in Pascal, and the 1980s saw it decline.

Despite its demise in the 1980s, Pascal set the way for programming languages to support structured concepts, maintainable programs, and free-form use. Listing 4.1 shows a sample Pascal program listing. C and C++ can thank Pascal for their fundamental structures.

> **tip**
>
> Unlike FORTRAN and COBOL, Pascal (and all modern-day languages) is *free-form*. That means that you can put as many blank lines and spaces in the program (called *whitespace*) as you like to make the program more readable.

**LISTING 4.1**   A Pascal Program Is More Free-form than Other Languages

```
{ Typed constant arrays with records
  that hold people's statistics }
PROGRAM People;
USES Crt;
TYPE PersonTypes  = (Employee, Vendor, Customer);
     PersonString = STRING[9];
     PersonRecord = RECORD
                      Name:    PersonString;
                      Balance: WORD;
                    END;
   PersonNameArray = ARRAY[PersonTypes] OF PersonRecord;
CONST People: PersonNameArray =
               ((Name: 'Sally'; Balance: 323.56),
                (Name: 'Ted';   Balance:   0.00),
                (Name: 'John';  Balance: 1212.37));
VAR Person: PersonTypes;

{The primary output routine appears next }
BEGIN
   CLRSCR;
   WRITELN( '*** People in System ***'):
   WRITELN;
   FOR Person := Employee TO Customer DO
     WITH People[Person] DO
        BEGIN
           WRITELN( Name, ' has a balance of $',
                    Balance, '.');
           WRITELN;
        END;  {with}
END.  {People}
```

# The C Programming Language

C was developed at Bell Laboratories by two men named Brian Kernighan and Dennis Ritchie. In 1972, Bell Laboratories needed to write a new operating system. Until that point, most operating systems were written in assembler language because the high-level programming languages were not efficient enough, given the lack of computer power at that time. The problem with the low-level programming of assembler language is that the code is difficult to maintain. As the operating systems were updated, programmers dreaded the nightmares that updating assembler code brought.

Bell did not want its new operating system to be as difficult to maintain as previous ones were, but there was simply no high-level language at the time that was efficient enough to do the job. Therefore, they set out to write a new programming language, one that would be as easy to maintain as high-level programming languages tend to be, and one that was almost as efficient as assembler code.

Kernighan and Ritchie (known in the industry as simply K&R) made several attempts to find a way around this maintenance problem, finally coming up with the C programming language. C is referred to as a "high low-level language," meaning that it supports all the programming constructs of any high-level language, including structured programming constructs, but also compiles into extremely tight and efficient code that runs almost as fast as assembler language. The Bell labs ended up with an operating system that was efficient but still easy to maintain and update. As a bonus, it became one of the most popular languages of the 1980s and beyond.

**note**

The operating system that resulted from this endeavor was called Unix, which is still in use today and which inspired Linux, a popular PC operating system.

## The Success of C

C's popularity grew rapidly. Companies liked the idea of having more efficient programs. A C program might run up to 10 times faster than an equivalent COBOL program. As PCs grew in popularity, an efficient and small language became even more important to use.

The reason C is still important, despite its diminishing use, is that it is a foundation language for C++, Java, C#, and many other languages of today and tomorrow. C is easier.

**note**

Given C's importance as a foundation language, all of Chapter 13, "Programming with C," covers C programming fundamentals.

## C++: A Better C

C's successor, C++, quickly gained extensive support after its introduction. C++ is a newer version of C and was designed by a Swedish programmer named Bjarne Stroustrup in the early 1980s. C++ offers a few additional commands and operators but is mostly just another approach to programming in C.

The biggest reason for the current success of C++ is that it contains object-oriented programming capabilities. *Object-oriented programming* (*OOP*) is a different way of writing programs that helps programmers write programs more quickly and with fewer errors. OOP also helps speed the program maintenance process. Chapter 14, "Programming with C++," explains more about object-oriented programming and C++.

# C++'s Impact on Modern Languages

The popularity of the object-oriented power of C++ gave rise to many of the newer languages of today's Internet. One of the reasons the Java language (and its off-shoots such as JavaScript) is in widespread use is that C++ did not contain enough security support for online Web site programming, and yet the object-oriented nature of C++ made it a good candidate in other ways for programming the objects of the Internet. Sun Microsystems modified C++ to include enough security and took away some of C++'s more confusing aspects. (An example is *multiple inheritance*, which enables one programming object, such as a window, to be generated from a set of multiple parent windows of different characteristics; as you can see, such concepts are confusing even when described at a high level.)

It is certain that Java and other kinds of online Web page programming would look greatly different from the Java language that we have if it were not for C++. Surely, the Internet would still be popular today even if C and then C++ were never written. Web languages probably would center more around Pascal if C and C++ had not displaced Pascal as the primary language of the 1980s and 1990s.

## caution

Don't get the impression that a company develops a language just to have something new. Sometimes a company uses an alternative language because of licensing problems with another language. Microsoft does not use Java for that very reason, although Microsoft created a couple of Java-like languages called Visual J++ and C# (pronounced *C-sharp*). Most companies prefer to use a known language for a problem when that language will do the job.

# Hypertext and Scripting Languages

Some computer programmers are not programmers in the traditional sense in that they do not write standalone applications that perform specific tasks. Instead, they write the code behind Web pages. A Web page looks the way it does because the programmer has placed items and formatted text on the page using a language called *Hypertext Markup Language (HTML)*. HTML is a formatting language that determines how text, graphics, tables, and other information appear on a Web page. In addition, the true power of HTML comes from its capability to provide links between pieces of information. If you've clicked a hyperlink on a Web page to traverse to another Web page, you have used HTML. By the time you finish Chapter 17, "HTML Programming," you will understand the basics of HTML. HTML is relatively simple to learn, as you will see.

Another category of programming language that does not fit the strictest definition of a programming language is a scripting language. If you've ever used Microsoft Office, you may have developed a keyboard macro, which is a named list of keystrokes. When you execute a macro, the keystrokes inside the macro file execute as though you were at the keyboard pressing the keys. By combining several keystrokes into a single macro, you can automate repetitive tasks.

A scripting language, an offshoot of batch languages from mainframe and pre-Windows PC operating systems, is similar to keyboard macros in that it combines individual commands that control the operating environment into a list that becomes a program. The user can execute the entire list of commands by triggering the program's execution. You will learn more about scripting and batch languages in Chapter 15, "Macro, Batch, and Scripting Languages."

# The BASICs

This discussion on specific languages concludes with an explanation of BASIC to springboard your thoughts into the next chapter, which teaches you a modern-day version of BASIC called Visual Basic.

BASIC was originally developed at Dartmouth College for teaching beginners how to program. The FORTRAN programming language was a bit too complex for non-mathematical students to learn quickly enough to use it in their studies. John Kemeny and Thomas Kurtz, who taught at Dartmouth, used FORTRAN as a foundation for creating BASIC. BASIC stands for Beginner's All-purpose Symbolic Instruction Code, a name that is more foreboding than the language itself.

BASIC typically is run in an interpreted environment, although modern-day versions of BASIC are compiled. This allows beginners to concentrate on the programming language and not worry about the details of compiling a program. As with any interpreted language, interpreted BASIC programs run slower than compiled programs, so interpreted BASIC programs are not used much in business.

---

**INTERPRETED VERSUS COMPILED CODE**

When a language is interpreted, the computer analyzes each instruction as the program is executed, converts each instruction to machine language, and executes that instruction. If the program repeats a section of code, the interpreter must re-analyze and convert that section of code once again before executing it.

A compiled language, on the other hand, converts the entire source code file to machine language before the user runs the program. Only after every instruction is compiled into machine language does the program run. If a section of the compiled program is executed a second time, the compilation doesn't have to take place again as it would if the program were interpreted. Therefore, compiled programs run much faster than interpreted programs, although beginning programmers often find an interpreted environment easier to learn.

Most of today's languages are compiled. Script languages and HTML-based languages are still interpreted, however, because their source code is not typically large enough to require compilation, and the instant execution of the interpreted code works well for those file sizes.

---

## The Early BASICs

Over the years, BASIC has been distributed in many different forms. The original BASIC language had very little structure and a strict set of coding rules. It was thought that the strict rules would take away some of the ambiguity present in other programming languages and speed the beginner's learning of the language. Listing 4.2 shows a version of a program written in the original BASIC language. Each line required a line number. The common practice was to increment the line numbers by tens so that you could insert up to nine more lines between existing lines if you had to later.

**LISTING 4.2**   An Example of the Original BASIC Language

```
10  REM Letter-guessing game in BASIC
20  REM Generate a random number from 65 to 90
30  REM (ASCII 65 is A and ASCII 90 is Z)
40  NUM = (INT(RND * 26)) + 65
50  CA$ = CHR$(NUM)
60  CLS
```

## LISTING 4.2 (continued)

```
70  PRINT "*** Letter Guessing Game ***"
80  PRINT
90  PRINT "I am thinking of a letter..."
100 INPUT "What is your guess"; UG$
110 TR = TR + 1
120 IF (UG$ > CA$) THEN GOTO 150
130 IF (UG$ < CA$) THEN GOTO 180
140 GOTO 210
150 PRINT "Your guess was too high"
160 PRINT "Try again..."
170 GOTO 200
180 PRINT "Your guess was too low"
190 PRINT "Try again..."
200 GOTO 100
210 REM Here if guess was correct
220 PRINT "*** Congratulations!  You got it right!"
230 PRINT "It took you only"; TR; "tries to guess."
240 END
```

The output of this program appears below. Try to follow the program to see how the output was produced and answer these questions: Where is the program's remark? (A remark is a statement that comments the program. Remarks are ignored by BASIC when you run the program. Remarks are there for you to document the code so that someone looking through the program listing has a better idea what the program is supposed to do.) Where is the program's loop? What BASIC command produces output? If you cannot answer these questions, don't fret; the next chapter will teach the details of programming.

```
*** Letter Guessing Game ***

I am thinking of a letter...
What is your guess? A
Your guess was too low
Try again...
What is your guess? Z
Your guess was too high
Try again...
What is your guess? M
Your guess was too low
Try again...
```

```
What is your guess? V
Your guess was too high
Try again...
What is your guess? S
*** Congratulations!  You got it right! It took you only 5 tries to guess.
```

Although BASIC began as a language for beginners and is still quite useful for introducing programming, today's versions of BASIC provide a rich assortment of advanced programming elements. Here are a few of the names BASIC has had as it has evolved through the years:

- BASICA (for *BASIC Advanced* )
- GWBASIC (for *Gee Whiz BASIC* )
- Power BASIC
- Turbo BASIC
- QuickBASIC (a compiled version)
- QBasic (which began shipping with MS-DOS starting with DOS version 5.0)
- Visual Basic (a Windows programming environment)

Microsoft was one of the first companies to offer a compiled BASIC for PCs (QuickBASIC). Microsoft is the company that supplied QBasic (an interactive version of BASIC) in DOS 5.0 and later versions. Microsoft currently produces Visual Basic, a graphical programming tool with which you can write customized Windows programs.

One of the biggest changes Microsoft made in the BASIC language was when it introduced QuickBASIC, a compiled version of BASIC. With QuickBASIC, BASIC left the ranks of amateur programming languages and became a well-written, structured, compiled programming language that rivaled both Pascal and C.

Listing 4.3 shows a QuickBASIC version of the letter-guessing game you saw earlier in this chapter. Notice that there are no line numbers and that the program is free-form and easy to follow, features of which the rigid BASICs of old could not boast. QuickBASIC is almost C-like or Pascal-like in its appearance.

## LISTING 4.3    A QuickBASIC Version of the Letter-Guessing Game

```
' Newer BASIC allows the more succinct ' for a remark instead of REM
' A letter-guessing game

num = (INT(RND * 26)) + 65    ' Generate a random number from 65 to 90
                              ' (ASCII 65 is A and ASCII 90 is Z)
```

## Listing 4.3   (continued)

```
compAns$ = CHR$(num)      ' Converts the number to a letter
tries = 0

CLS    ' Clear the screen
PRINT "*** Letter guessing game ***"
PRINT
PRINT "I am thinking of a letter..."

DO
   INPUT "What is your guess"; userGuess$
   tries = tries + 1
   IF (userGuess$ > compAns$) THEN
      PRINT "Your guess was too high"
      PRINT "Try again..."
   ELSE
      IF (userGuess$ < compAns$) THEN
         PRINT "Your guess was too low"
         PRINT "Try again..."
      END IF
   END IF
LOOP WHILE (userGuess$ <> compAns$)    ' Quit when a match is found

' User got it right, announce it
PRINT "*** Congratulations!  You got it right!"
PRINT "It took you only"; tries; "tries to guess."
END
```

Microsoft won industry favor with its QuickBASIC compiler. Finally, there was a compiler for BASIC—and an integrated full-screen editor as well. Most BASIC versions before QuickBASIC included their own line editor or limited full-screen editor. Many people feel that Microsoft's integrated full-screen editor played as important a role in QuickBASIC's success as the improved language itself.

Microsoft helped ensure its leadership in the BASIC arena when it introduced QBasic, an interpreted version of BASIC that now comes supplied with every version of MS-DOS. QBasic was the language of choice for most beginning programmers for many years in the 1980s and 1990s. Fortunately, with Visual Basic, Microsoft maintained many of BASIC's advantages so that the language is more easily learned than other languages but is also powerful enough to produce advanced Windows programs.

# Graphical Programming with Visual Basic

Perhaps the most impressive programming language of all time is Visual Basic. Visual Basic combines a powerful but relatively simple programming language with a collection of graphical controls with which you build BASIC programs. Visual Basic is a Windows programming environment that you can use to write Windows programs. When you first start Visual Basic, you see the screen shown in Figure 4.1. As you can see from the screen, the term *visual* is an extremely accurate description.

Do not let the seeming complexity of the Visual Basic screen frighten you. As you learn more about Visual Basic, you'll better understand how the different parts of the screen fit together, and you'll learn ways to customize the screen to your preferences.

**FIGURE 4.1**

The opening screen of Visual Basic seems complex at first.

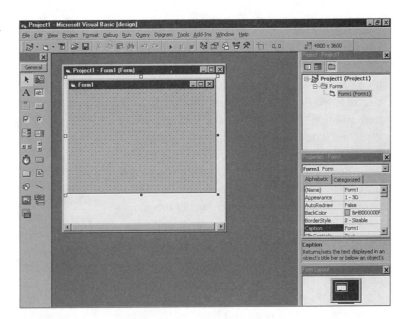

Windows programs are usually more difficult to write than programs for text-based environments. Windows programs are *event driven*. Unlike text-based procedural programs that perform a sequence of actions based on the user's expected input, a Windows program must be able to expect almost anything at any given time. For example, the user might press a key, move the mouse, press a mouse button, or select from a menu. If Windows programs were as procedural in nature as other programs are, the programs could respond to a mouse movement only when the program was ready, not when the user was ready. By being event driven, the program responds to events in any order that they happen.

A Windows program might be stopped at any time or temporarily put on hold while the user executes another Windows program. Because Windows programs run inside windows on the screen, the programs must be able to respond to resizing commands that the user might issue. A user might want to see a Visual Basic program run in a window at the top of the screen and see an animated graphing sequence at the bottom of the screen. Writing a Windows program from scratch was a nightmare until Visual Basic came along, especially for beginning programmers. Visual Basic takes care of all the petty details of the Windows application, enabling the user to resize the program's window, select from a menu, click with the mouse, or press a key. Visual Basic ensures that the proper event occurs when it is called for. The programmer only has to tell Visual Basic what he wants when certain events occur.

# Which Language Is Best?

The best programming language depends on the job you need to perform.

If you really want to know which language is the best to learn first, this book has already answered that question. Visual Basic is the best all-purpose Windows language for beginning programmers. The next chapter begins to develop your Visual Basic programming skills. Those who master an introductory language often move on to C++ and online programming environments of languages such as Java.

The languages you know often determine the language in which you program. If you are working on a rush project (as most data processing projects are), you won't have time to master a new language, so if C++ is all you know at the time, that is the language you will probably use.

It is hard to determine how many programming languages a good programmer should know. Some highly paid, highly skilled programmers know only a single language, but most know several. You will find that you prefer some programming languages over others, and you will become truly expert in only one or two, although you may learn several over the years.

**note**

Whatever happens in your computer education, plan to keep learning as long as you program. Computing is an exciting field to work in because there is always something new around the corner.

Less than 10 years ago, integrated programming environments such as Visual Basic would have amazed the programming community; today those environments are commonplace. Visual Basic would have been nothing less than magic before it was introduced in 1991; now beginners use such programming tools to create powerful Windows applications.

The language a company uses to write a particular application is determined by many factors. The company might license only one or two compilers. If so, their applications will be written using one of those compilers. Mainframe compilers can cost several thousand dollars, so it is difficult for companies to move around from language to language looking for the best one. Often, the language currently owned is made to work.

**note**

Companies generally prefer programming languages that are common over those that are more obscure. For instance, there is an object-oriented programming language called *Actor* that is a very good language, but only a handful of programmers know it. C++ is a much better choice if someone else might have to take care of program maintenance in the future.

# Summary

As programming languages mature, they become easier to use. Most of today's programming languages include integrated environments and offer support for structured programming. Today's graphical user interfaces such as Microsoft Windows require more complex programming tools, but easy-to-use languages such as Visual Basic are easing even beginning programmers into the graphical world of programming.

- Modern-day programming languages offer tremendous improvements over previous languages. They are more structured and offer integrated programming environments.

- Pascal was a good general-purpose programming language that boomed during the 1970s and declined in use in the 1980s.

- C, developed by Bell Laboratories, is a highly efficient, high low-level programming language. C is the foundation of many languages in use today.

- C++'s biggest improvement over its predecessor C is its capability to provide support for object-oriented programming (OOP).

- Visual Basic, a BASIC descendant, offers the best programming platform for beginners.

- The programming language you use depends on many factors. Most languages are best suited to certain kinds of programs. The language you select can depend on how scientific- or business-oriented your application is. Also, you must give consideration to how many other programmers know the language you select in case someone else has to maintain your programs later.

# PART III

# HANDS ON PROGRAMMING

5 Your First Language: Visual Basic . . . . . . .77

6 Input and Output . . . . . . . . . . . . . . . .89

7 Data Processing with Visual Basic . . . . .109

8 Working with Data . . . . . . . . . . . . . .125

9 Having Fun with Visual Basic . . . . . . . .143

10 Advanced Visual Basic Programming . . .159

11 Online Visual Basic Programming . . . . .179

- A Visual Basic Quick Start
- Your First Visual Basic Program
- Learning the Visual Basic Environment
- The Visual Basic Screen
- Help Is Close By

5

# YOUR FIRST LANGUAGE: VISUAL BASIC

One of the greatest features of Visual Basic is that programming in Visual Basic is fun. At first, Visual Basic seems confusing to newcomers. Part of that confusion comes from the busy screen that the newcomer sees when he starts Visual Basic for the first time. This chapter explains the common parts of the Visual Basic environment, including the contents, windows, and icons that appear on the screen. Before you are one-third of the way through this chapter, you will have created your first Visual Basic program.

The highlights of this chapter include the following:

- Visual Basic is a Windows program environment.
- With a few keystrokes and mouse clicks, you can create a working Windows program.
- The Form window is the background window where your application resides.

- The toolbox contains the controls you'll place on your application's screen.

- Controls, such as labels and command buttons, all have properties.

## A Visual Basic Quick Start

Remember that Visual Basic is as much a programming language as it is a collection of graphical controls with which you build programs. A Windows programming environment requires these graphical controls, such as menus, command buttons, scrolling lists, text boxes, and all the other Windows elements you interact with. From the moment you start Visual Basic, you have access to all the tools that you'll need to write programs from within that environment.

**note**

Several versions of Visual Basic exist. To keep figures relatively simple for this book, Visual Basic 6.0 Working Model is used. This is a learning version of Visual Basic that includes the full language but does not include all the advanced elements found in the full retail Visual Basic 6.0 Professional Edition. Check out Microsoft's Web site for the latest products related to Visual Basic and other programming languages at http://www.Microsoft.com/.

## Your First Visual Basic Program

The following example walks you through the creation of a fully functional Visual Basic program. You might not have access to a Visual Basic system, and you might never have used Windows. Even so, this example and the remaining chapters in this part give you a glimpse of Visual Basic.

To write a fully functional Visual Basic Windows program, all you have to do is start Visual Basic. Select Standard EXE from the Project window and then double-click the box in the center of the screen. You will see a window open up such as the one shown in Figure 5.1.

The window is Visual Basic's code window. The *code window* is where you type a program in the Visual Basic language. Click the window's right drop-down list box to display a list of choices. Select the MouseMove option. Notice that Visual Basic fills in some of the window for you. Visual Basic helps you create accurate code by entering some bookkeeping code for you.

This first program requires only one programming statement. Type `Print "I am programming!"`. The code appears in the code window as you type it. Now, simply press the F5 function key (F5 is a shortcut keystroke for running a Visual Basic program); you'll see the program run. (You can also select Run Start from the pull-down menu at the top of the screen to run the program.)

Click to open List.

**FIGURE 5.1**

You've now opened Visual Basic's *code window.*

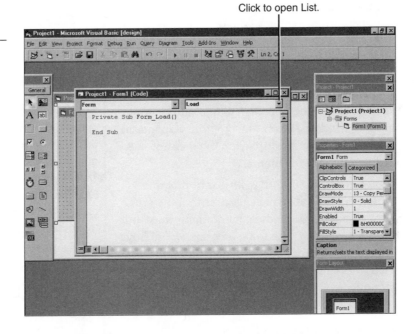

The Output window

**FIGURE 5.2**

This Visual Basic program was simple to produce.

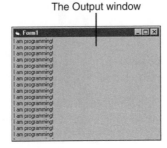

The program appears to do nothing. Only a blank, gray window appears on the screen. Move your mouse cursor to that blank window. When you do, the words `I am programming!` appear. As you move the mouse, the words keep appearing, filling up the window. The result of this Visual Basic program after moving the mouse several times in the output window is shown in Figure 5.2.

The reason the program is so amazing is that it took two mouse clicks, one programming statement, and the F5 key, and that was it. Visual Basic took care of the rest. Visual Basic displayed a window on the screen, but not just any window: a resizable window. With the mouse, you can expand the output window, shrink it, move it, and reduce it to a Windows icon with one mouse click. The normal Windows control menu is available by clicking on the box in the upper-left corner of the program's window. Finally, the program responds to the mouse event by displaying the message every time you move the mouse.

You have to admit that writing that program took very little effort. The result is that the program does not do a whole lot on the surface, but it is a beginning. The same program would have taken a couple of pages of code if you had written it using the C or C++ programming language.

## Learning the Visual Basic Environment

Mastering the Visual Basic environment—that is, learning its windows and controls—is the first step toward becoming a Visual Basic programming pro.

### Visual Basic Programming Steps

These are the basic steps you'll follow every time you write a Visual Basic program:

1. Start Visual Basic from within Windows.

2. Create a new project. A *project* is a collection of one or more Visual Basic programs that comprise an application. A project keeps an application's files together in one folder so that you can access them together. If you want to change a Visual Basic application that you have already written, you'll open that application's project and modify the files in the project.

**caution**

Visual Basic is not an object-oriented programming language. Nevertheless, Visual Basic does work with several objects at one time. The Windows environment, by its very nature, is an object-oriented environment. Therefore, as we program in Visual Basic, you'll be working with several objects such as Windows and menus and controls such as text boxes and scrollbars.

**tip**

The window where the program's results appear is called the *output window*. If you were to compile the Visual Basic program and save it to the disk, then execute the program from the Windows environment instead of from within the Visual Basic environment, this is the only window you would see. It would then be the program window.

3. Write the Visual Basic program. This involves creating the windows that serve as the program's output and can include all the standard Windows controls you've seen while using other Windows programs. These controls may be command buttons, list boxes, scrollbars, and menus.

4. Compile your Visual Basic program.

5. Test your Visual Basic program. Recompile the program and keep testing until the program operates accurately.

6. After it is tested, compile a final application that you can distribute to other users who may need to use the program.

7. Quit Visual Basic.

**tip**

To stop the program and return to the Visual Basic programming environment, close the output window by clicking the **X** in the upper-right corner.

## Working in Visual Basic

When you first start Visual Basic from the Windows Start menu, the New Project window appears (see Figure 5.3). Often, more elements appear than are seen in Figure 5.3. The number of items depends on the kind of Visual Basic programming environment you own. For example, if you own the Visual Basic Professional Enterprise Edition, icons will appear that enable you to add extra networking elements to your Visual Basic application.

**FIGURE 5.3**

The New Project window is where you specify the kind of Visual Basic program you want to write.

For all programs in this book, as well as for most programs that you write toward the beginning of your Visual Basic programming career, you'll select the Standard EXE icon as you did in the previous section. This tells Visual Basic that you want to create a simple, single-file Visual Basic application.

# The Visual Basic Screen

Figure 5.4 illustrates several of Visual Basic's screen elements. As you can see from the menu bar and toolbar, Visual Basic looks somewhat like other Windows programs. Many of Visual Basic's menu bar commands work just as they do in other applications such as Microsoft Word. For example, you can select **File**, **Open** and **Edit**, **Paste**.

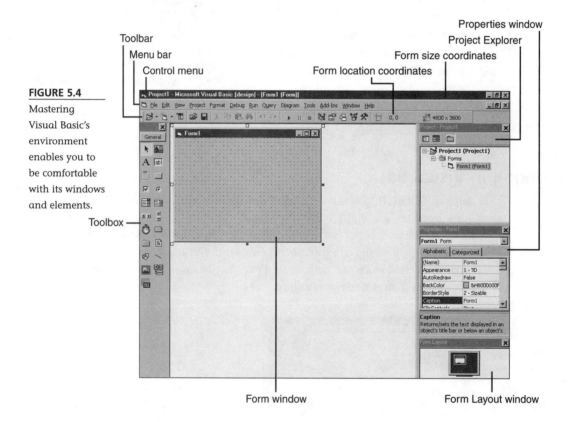

**FIGURE 5.4**

Mastering Visual Basic's environment enables you to be comfortable with its windows and elements.

## The Menu Bar and the Toolbar

The menu bar and the toolbar set in Visual Basic work as they do in other Windows programs. You can click or press a menu bar option's hotkey (for example, **Alt+F** displays the **File** menu) to see a list of menu options that provide commands, another level of menus, or dialog boxes. The toolbar provides single-button access to many common menu commands. Instead of selecting **Edit**, **Paste**, for example, you could click the **Paste** toolbar button. Select **View**, **Toolbars** to see a list of available toolbars. Each one that is currently showing will appear with a check mark by its name.

---

**VISUAL BASIC MEASUREMENTS**

Visual Basic uses twips to measure the size and location of forms and objects located on windows (called *forms*). A twip is 1/1,440 of an inch, the smallest screen measurement that you can specify. Twip values usually appear in pairs. The first location value describes the x coordinate (the number of twips from the left of the screen), and the second value describes the y coordinate (the number of twips from the top of the screen), with **0,0** indicating the upper-left corner of the screen.

The first size value describes the width of the form, and the second size value describes the height of the form. Therefore, the size coordinate pair **1000,3000** indicates that the Form window will be 1,000 twips wide and 3,000 twips tall when the program runs. The Form window is the primary window for the applications you write. When you run your programs, the program background is the Form window. The location and size coordinates describe the form's location and size when you run the application.

---

## Looking at the Form Window

The Form window is your primary work area, and it makes up the background of your application. If you write a Windows-based calculator with Visual Basic, the calculator's buttons all reside on the Form window. When someone runs the calculator, what appears is really just the application's Form window with components placed there and tied together with code.

You'll never see program code on the Form window. The Form window holds the program's interactive objects, such as command buttons, labels, text boxes, scrollbars, and other controls. The code appears elsewhere in the code window. The code window does not appear in Figure 5.5, but you can select **View**, **Code** to see it. A code window is little more than a text editor with which you write the programming statements that tie together the application's elements.

Consider the sample program running and the window seen in Figure 5.5. The window shows a simple dialog box with a few options, text boxes, and command buttons.

Form window

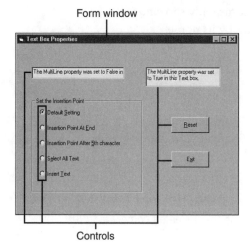

Controls

Creating the dialog box in Figure 5.5 was the result
of opening a Form window, adding some controls
(the items on the Form window that interact with
the user—sometimes called tools), and tying the
components together with some Visual Basic
code. An application might even require multiple
Form windows.

Compare Figure 5.6 with Figure 5.5. As you can
see, Figure 5.6 shows the same application in the
Visual Basic development environment. When
inside the development environment, an application is said to be in its *design-time state* as
opposed to its runtime state, which was shown in
Figure 5.5 during the program's execution. It is
during design time that you create, edit, and correct the application. When you run the
application, you can see the result of your work.

note

Visual Basic source
code comprises all the windows, the controls on those windows, and the code. Once it is
compiled, you cannot make
changes to the program.
Nevertheless, you can go back to
the compiled program's source
code and make the changes within
the Visual Basic development environment.

## The Toolbox Provides the Controls

The toolbox contains the controls that you place
on the Form window. All the controls in Figure 5.7
appear on the toolbox. In Chapter 6, "Input and Output," you will learn how to
place toolbox controls on the Form window. The toolbox never runs out of controls;
if you place a command button on the Form window, another is available in the
toolbox, ready to be placed.

Form window

**FIGURE 5.6**

The same dialog box, shown in Visual Basic's development environment.

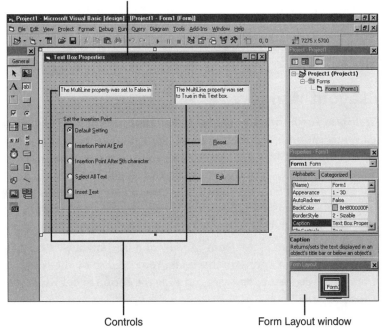

Controls

Form Layout window

**FIGURE 5.7**

Several controls appear on the toolbox.

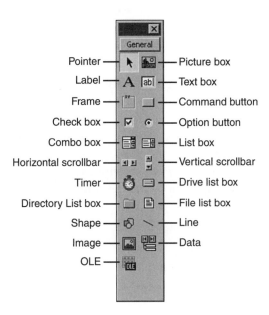

Pointer — Picture box

Label — Text box

Frame — Command button

Check box — Option button

Combo box — List box

Horizontal scrollbar — Vertical scrollbar

Timer — Drive list box

Directory List box — File list box

Shape — Line

Image — Data

OLE

Figure 5.7 names everything that appears on the standard toolbox window. These are standard controls that appear in all versions of Visual Basic. You can add controls to the toolbox as your needs grow, but these extra tools don't appear on the toolbox window until you add them through the **Project**, **Components** menu option.

## The Form Layout Window

The Form Layout window displays the initial position and relative size of the form currently shown in the Form window. For example, look back at Figure 5.6 to see the Form Layout window. The application shown is a multiple-form application. The Text Box Properties form is to have several forms. The Form Layout window always shows where the form appears in the current Form window. If you want the form to appear at a different location, you can move it inside the Form Layout window to the position at which it appears when the user runs the application.

To give more room to the Form window and its contents, we rarely show the Form Layout window in figures in this book. You can display the Form Layout window from the **View** menu, and you can hide the Form Layout window by clicking its **Close** button.

## The Project Explorer Window

The Project Explorer window, often called the project window, gives you a tree-structure view of all the application's files. You can expand and collapse branches in the view for more or less detail.

The Project Explorer window displays forms, modules (files that hold supporting code for the application), classes (advanced modules), and more. When you want to work with a particular part of the loaded application, double-click the component in the project window to bring that component into focus. In other words, if the Project Explorer window displays three forms and you need to edit one of the forms, locate and double-click the form name in the project window to activate that form in the Form window. Figure 5.8 shows a Project Explorer window that contains several kinds of files.

**FIGURE 5.8**

The Project Explorer window keeps track of the project's elements.

## The Properties Window

*A property* is a specific characteristic of a control. A different list of properties appears in the Properties window every time you click over a different Form window tool. The Properties window lists the properties (descriptive and functional information) of the form and its controls. The Properties window lists all the properties of the Form window's selected control.

# Help Is Close By

Visual Basic contains an extensive help system. When you want help with a control, window, tool, or command, press F1. Most versions of Visual Basic support a tremendous help resource called Books Online. When you select Books Online from the Help menu, Visual Basic displays a tree-structure view of books about Visual Basic that you can search and read. The online help extends to the Internet as well. If you have an Internet connection, you can browse the latest help topics by selecting Help, Microsoft on the Web.

# Summary

In this chapter, you created and ran your first Visual Basic program. Congratulations! Visual Basic does much of the bookkeeping work for you so that you can concentrate on your application's goals. Before you can be an effective Visual Basic programmer, you must understand the purpose for the windows that appear in Visual Basic. You now know that the Form window holds your application's elements and that the Form Layout window describes the location of your application's forms. You might not fully understand the purpose of these windows, but you're well on your way to mastering Visual Basic.

- You have now created your first Visual Basic application.
- You need only to press the **F5** key to compile and run a Visual Basic program.
- The Visual Basic development environment is busy, but the windows and toolbox provide the tools you need to create your applications.
- The controls in your Visual Basic application have properties. You will learn more about properties and controls in the next chapter.

## IN THIS CHAPTER

- A Quick Windows Program Analysis
- Controlling Events
- Application Specifics
- The Interface Controls
- Walking Through an Application's Development
- Other Controls
- Document with Remarks
- Message and Input Boxes

**6**

# INPUT AND OUTPUT

In this chapter, you're going to create your very first Visual Basic application from scratch. You will learn how to place controls onto a form and how to set up those controls, such as a command button, with characteristics that make them work for your specific application. Don't expect to become a Visual Basic guru by the end of this chapter; rather, enjoy the tour, and you'll pick up several pointers that you can use in your programming career.

The highlights of this chapter include the following:

- The graphical and multitasking nature of Windows programs requires that your program respond to events.

- You can place controls onto the Form window that serves as the background for your Visual Basic application window.

- The Properties window determines the characteristics of each of your application's controls.

- The code window contains the code that works in the background to tie your application together.
- Remarks help document your program.
- Message and input boxes display output and receive input.

# A Quick Windows Program Analysis

Developing effective Visual Basic programs requires an understanding of the way Windows programs work. You may recall from Chapter 4, "Programming Languages: Modern Day," that all Windows programs are event driven. That is, your Windows program must respond to events that can happen during the program's execution. At any time, the user may move the mouse, click the mouse, double-click the mouse, right-click the mouse, type on the keyboard, resize the program window, close the program, or start a completely different program and leave yours running in the background.

Before windowed environments became so popular, the program dictated what the user was to do next. It might ask a question and then not allow the user to do anything else (such as select from a menu) until that question was answered. If the user was presented with a menu, he had a choice of menu options but could not do anything else, such as enter data into a form. The program always guided the user and gave him choices only on occasion. This was the nature of the computer environment before windowed graphical interfaces.

The multitasking, multiwindowed environments changed everything. Today's Windows programs have no idea what might happen next. Programs offer choices that range from menu options to various controls at data entry locations. Windowed environments give the user far more flexibility in controlling program flow, but the burden is increased for the programmer.

The users of programs now can perform one of many tasks at any time inside a Windows program. The user has more freedom to do what he wants to do. The problem for the programmer is responding to the user's actions when so many actions are possible. Fortunately, Microsoft designed Windows to be elegant not only for the user but for the programmer as well. When virtually anything happens in the Windows environment, Windows generates something called an *event*. An event might be a key press, an internal clock tick, a menu selection, a mouse click, a mouse movement, or any of hundreds of others.

**note**

An event is something that happens during a program's execution, usually but not always due to a user action with the keyboard or mouse.

Before Windows, you would write one big program that guided the user through the execution of the code step by step. The program would take the user to a menu, ask him questions, and offer only a limited set of choices. In many ways, a Visual Basic program is nothing more than a collection of small routines. These routines, called *event procedures*, handle individual events. Only if an event occurs for which you've written an event procedure does that event procedure execute. You don't have to do anything special to execute the event procedure—just write the code. In other words, your program responds to events by supplying a matching event procedure, and your program ignores events if you haven't written an event procedure.

# Controlling Events

A control might be a text box, a command button, or a menu. Visual Basic supports many controls that you can put on a form, and these controls appear in the toolbox window.

Every control that you place on a form supports one or more events. For example, if you place a text box in the center of the Form window and run the program, you can click the text box, enter text in the text box, or ignore the text box. The text box control supports events that can recognize when you do anything to that control.

If you've written an event procedure for the text box event that occurs, your code's instructions will execute automatically as soon as the event occurs. Therefore, if you've written code to blank out the text box as soon as the user clicks the text box, and you've written another event procedure that fills the text box with Xs when the user double-clicks over that text box, which event procedure that executes and what happens to the text box are totally within the user's control.

# Application Specifics

If Visual Basic is loaded on your computer, start Visual Basic now. Select Standard EXE and click Open to open a new application. Before adding any code to a Visual Basic program, you must create the program window, with all its controls in the window. As you learn more about Visual Basic, you will be able to add code as you go, but for now the best way to learn Visual Basic is to place controls on the Form window.

When you place controls on the Form window, you must name the controls, position the controls, set control properties, adjust control sizes, and connect all event procedure code that goes with each control.

Although you can double-click the Form window's title bar to increase the Form window to full-screen size, your Form window then will be difficult to manage because of its large size. Therefore, the applications that you create in this book will require a relatively small Form window. By keeping the form size manageable, you can see the rest of the Visual Basic screen controls. Click and drag one edge of the Form window toward the lower-right corner of your screen until it is approximately 7215×6120 twips. You may recall from the previous chapter that the Form window's size appears at the right of the Visual Basic toolbar. You don't need to resize the Form window to exactly 7215×6120 twips, but come close to this size. You will learn how to specify exact measurements for values such as window sizes in the next section.

**tip**

One of the first things you will do when you create a new application is to increase the Form window size. The default size is small. Most applications appear either full-screen or in an initial window much larger than the Form window size that first appears.

# The Interface Controls

The controls you select for your application's form are important because the controls (also called *tools*) provide the application interface for your users. Users interact with applications by clicking the controls and entering text into them. Placing and sizing controls are perhaps the two most important tasks you can master now.

## Placing Controls

You can use either of these two methods for placing controls on a form:

- Double-click in the control on the toolbox window to place that control on the Form window. As Figure 6.1 shows, the control appears in the center of the Form window.

**FIGURE 6.1**
The command button appears in the center of the window when you double-click within the control.

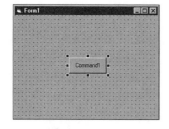

If a control already appears in the center of the window, Visual Basic places the new control directly on top of the existing one. You can drag the new control to a different location. The eight sizing handles (the small boxes that appear around a selected control) indicate that the control is selected. If several controls appear on the Form window, the selected control displays its sizing handles.

■ Another way to place a control is to click that control once on the toolbox to highlight it. If you then move the mouse cursor to the Form window, the mouse cursor turns into a crosshair, indicating that you can place the selected control anywhere on the form. Although a control appears in the center of the Form window automatically as soon as you double-click the control, a selected control appears only when you click and drag your mouse crosshair onto the Form window. The control appears when you release your mouse button.

The advantage of using this approach is that you don't have to move and resize the control after you've placed it. Figure 6.2 shows a command button placed with a double-click in the center of the form, as well as a new command button placed on the form by dragging the control. You can place the control exactly where and at the size you want when you drag it onto the form.

**FIGURE 6.2**

You can position and size a control immediately by dragging it onto your form.

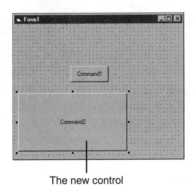

The new control

Of course, if you place a control onto your Form window by double-clicking it in the toolbox, you can drag the control to another part of the Form window or resize it by dragging its sizing handles.

## Setting Properties

As you add controls to the Form window, the Properties window updates to show the properties for the currently selected control. The selected control is usually one you last placed on the form. Visual Basic lets you see a control's properties in the Properties window by clicking the control or by selecting it from the Property window's drop-down list box, as shown in Figure 6.3.

**FIGURE 6.3**

The Properties window enables you to specify the properties of a selected control.

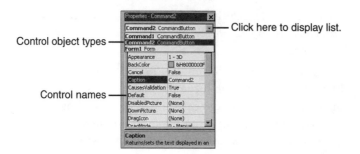

Control object types

Control names

Click here to display list.

Left, Top, Height, and Width are about the only properties you can set without accessing the Properties window. As you size and move the control into place, Visual Basic updates the Left, Top, Height, and Width properties according to the location and size at which you place the control on the form. These properties appear in twips. Left indicates how far from the form's left edge the control appears, Top indicates how far from the top of the form the control appears, and the Height and Width properties indicate the control's size.

Visual Basic assigns default names to all controls that you place on the form. Although it is okay to use these default names, you often refer to an object in Visual Basic code by its name. Therefore, it helps improve the readability of the code later if you name your objects when you place them onto the form. For example, a text box to hold the user's name could be called Text1, and you could refer to that name throughout your code. However, txtUserName would be easier to remember.

**note**

Click a blank area on the Form window and look at the Properties window. You will see that the name of the form is Form1, which is the default name for your first form. You can change the name of your form by changing the property in the Properties window.

Visual Basic considers the Name property so important that it appears at the top of the Properties window instead of alphabetically with the other control properties. To change the name of the control that was placed on the form, click the Name property and enter a new name. Visual Basic programmers often assign a prefix to the control, such as cmd for a command button, txt for a text box, or lbl for a label, to make clear by its name the type of control it is. Such a naming convention is not necessary but does help improve the maintenance of your code later.

Some properties require a selection from a drop-down list box. For example, Figure 6.4 shows a command button's `Visible` property's drop-down list box. The `Visible` property can be either `True` or `False`.

**FIGURE 6.4**

Some properties require that you select from a list box inside the Properties window.

If Visual Basic displays an ellipsis (...) when you click a property value inside the Properties window, a dialog box opens when you click the ellipsis. A `Font` property is more than just a style name or size. The control's property can take on all kinds of values. The dialog box that appears when you click the `Font` property's ellipsis enables you to select the font typeface, font size, and other characteristics.

Figure 6.5 shows the dialog box that appears in the Properties window. Select from this dialog box when you need to adjust the font characteristic for a property that has text, such as a command button's label.

**FIGURE 6.5**

Some properties require that you select from a dialog box.

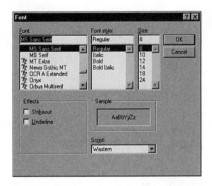

As you can see, placing a control requires much more involvement with property values than simply moving and sizing controls. You rarely if ever have to change all the properties of the control, because many of the default values work well for most applications. Nevertheless, many property values make the control unique to your specific application.

# Walking Through an Application's Development

You will now create a complete, fully functional but simple project from scratch. You'll learn how to assign controls and write code that will hook everything together using the Visual Basic language.

1. Create a new project by selecting **File**, **New Project** and choosing **Standard EXE**. Don't save any changes from earlier in this chapter if you were following along during the discussion of controls and their placement.

2. Change the form's Name property to frmFirst and change its Caption property to My First Application. The form's Caption property text will appear in the title bar when you run the application.

3. Expand the Form window to the property values Height 7380 and Width 7095. You can set these two property values yourself by changing them in the Properties window.

4. Click the **Label** control once. As you saw in the previous chapter, the **Label** control is the tool on the toolbox with the capital letter A. When you click the **Label** control once, Visual Basic shows it depressed on the toolbox.

5. Move the mouse pointer onto the Form window and drag a Label control toward the top of the Form window in the approximate location you see in Figure 6.6.

**FIGURE 6.6**

Place a label on your form at approximately the same size and position as this label.

6. Change the label's Name property to lblFirst. Change the label's Caption property to I am learning VB.

7. Click the label's Font property value to display the ellipsis. Click the ellipsis to display the dialog box for the label. Set the font size to 24 points and set the Bold property. As Figure 6.7 shows, the label's text is now large enough to read, but the text is not well centered within the label. Change the label's Alignment property to 2-Center, and Visual Basic immediately centers the text.

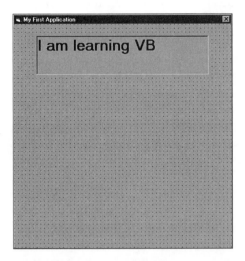

8. Change the label's BorderStyle property to 1-FixedSingle. This property adds a single-line 3D border around the label. You will see that the label's Height property is too large, so click the label to display its sizing handles and drag the top edge downward to center the text within the label.

9. Add a command button, but to do so, double-click the command button tool on the toolbox window. The command button appears in the middle of the form; leave it where it is. In this case, the default location and size values work well.

10. Change the command button's Name property to cmdExit. The Properties window will display the property values for the command button and not for the label you placed earlier, because the command button is selected. You can tell that the command button is selected by the eight sizing handles around it.

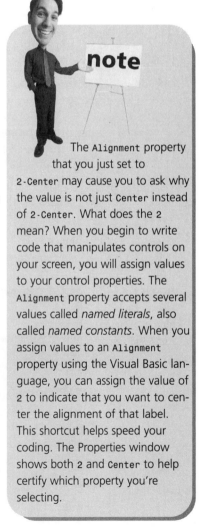

The Alignment property that you just set to 2-Center may cause you to ask why the value is not just Center instead of 2-Center. What does the 2 mean? When you begin to write code that manipulates controls on your screen, you will assign values to your control properties. The Alignment property accepts several values called *named literals*, also called *named constants*. When you assign values to an Alignment property using the Visual Basic language, you can assign the value of 2 to indicate that you want to center the alignment of that label. This shortcut helps speed your coding. The Properties window shows both 2 and Center to help certify which property you're selecting.

11. Change the Caption property to E&xit. Watch the command button as you type this text. The command button's caption becomes the text you type with one exception: The x is underlined. When you precede a letter in the name of a Caption property with an ampersand (&), Visual Basic uses that letter for the control's hotkey. Users of your application will be able to select the command button not only by clicking the mouse over it but also by pressing **Alt+X**, which is the hotkey on the keyboard.

12. The command button will be used to exit the program. When the user clicks the command button, your application should end. What happens when a user clicks a command button? A Click event occurs. Therefore, to respond to this event, you must write an event procedure for the command button. Visual Basic helps you do this. Double-click the form's command button now, and Visual Basic instantly opens the code window and displays the following outline code for the command button's Click event procedure:

```
Private Sub cmdExit_Click()


End Sub
```

You now need only to fill in the body of this event procedure. The name of the procedure, cmdExit_Click(), describes both the control and the event being processed by the code. Type **End** for the one-word body of the event procedure and close the code window by clicking the window's close button. End is the first Visual Basic programming language statement you have learned! End tells Visual Basic to terminate the running application, so the application will terminate when the user clicks this command button.

13. Press **F5** to compile and run your program. As shown in Figure 6.8, the form appears with the label and command button in place.

**FIGURE 6.8**

Your first running application works well.

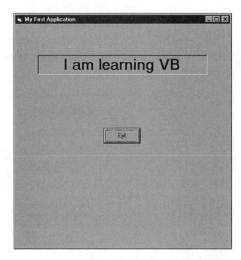

Stop your program by clicking the **Exit** command button. Visual Basic regains control. If you had compiled this program and saved the compiled version on disk, you could have run the compiled program from the **Windows Round** command or from a **Start Menu** icon if you assign the compiled file an icon. For this book, familiarizing yourself with the Visual Basic environment comes faster if you stay within the environment as we're doing now.

If you want to save your application, you will need to save all the files within the project. Remember that the project is a collection of all the files related to your application. In this case, the project will contain your Form window, the code that goes with the Exit command button, and the objects that appear on the Form window. To save the project, select **File**, **Save Project**. Visual Basic asks for the form's name with a Save File As dialog box; you can select a different drive or folder if you want. Within the project, you're able to name the form and save it by itself. Doing so is useful if you make changes to the form and not to the rest of the project.

# Other Controls

Now that you have created a simple Visual Basic application, you should experiment with other controls by placing them on a new form. All the familiar Windows controls, such as check boxes and list boxes, appear on the toolbox. Each tool has its own set of unique properties. For example, labels, which hold text on the window, have `Alignment`, `BorderStyle`, `Font`, size, and location properties such as those you saw in the previous section. In addition, you can set other properties for labels such as the background color, text color, and even add ToolTips to the labels.

**note**

A *ToolTip* is a great feature that helps your users and is easy to implement by typing text into the `ToolTipText` property of a control. Most Windows applications use ToolTips, and there's no reason your applications should not include them as well. Figure 6.9 shows a ToolTip that appears when you rest your mouse pointer over the Form Layout window toolbar button. Every control you place on a form can have a ToolTip, so specify ToolTips when you place all your controls on your form, especially if a control is somewhat ambiguous. For example, if your application requests information from your user such as name and address information, you may want to add a ToolTip that reads `You can leave this blank` to the second address line, telling the user that a second address line is not required if his address does not include a second line.

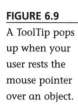

**FIGURE 6.9**

A ToolTip pops
up when your
user rests the
mouse pointer
over an object.

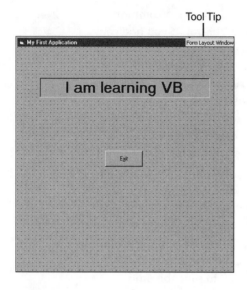

Table 6.1 lists all the standard tools that appear on the toolbox, with a brief description of each. Most of these controls will be familiar to anyone who has used Windows before.

## TABLE 6.1   Controls Found in Most Visual Basic Applications

| Control | Description |
| --- | --- |
| Pointer | Not actually a control that you place on a form. Instead, enables you to select controls and properties. |
| Label | Holds text that appears on the form. |
| Frame | A rectangular region on a form that holds other controls and groups the controls into a single set. |
| Check Box | Enables the user to choose one or more options on a form. |
| Combo Box | Holds a list of items to which the user can add items. |
| Horizontal Scroll Bar | Enables the user to scroll the window left and right to see information that will not fit within a single window. |
| Timer | Does not appear on the screen but works in the background, triggering one or more events at preset time intervals. |
| Directory list box | Enables the user to select from disk folders (also called directories). |
| Shape | Displays shapes such as circles and squares. |
| Image | Displays certain kinds of graphic images on the screen. |
| OLE | Refers to the placement of non–Visual Basic objects into a Visual Basic application (*object linking and embedding*). |

**TABLE 6.1** (continued)

| Control | Description |
| --- | --- |
| Picture Box | Displays certain kinds of graphics on the screen. Can display images that the Image control cannot display. |
| Text Box | Holds text that the user enters. |
| Command Button | Enables the user to select program options and control the execution of the program. |
| Option Button | Allows the user to select only one option from a list. |
| List Box | Enables the user to select from a scrolling list of values. |
| Vertical Scroll Bar | Enables the user to scroll the window up and down to see information that will not fit within a single window. |
| Drive List Box | Enables the user to select from a list of disk drives. |
| File List Box | Enables the user to select from a list of disk files. |
| Line | Draws lines on a form. |
| Data | Enables the user to track, view, and edit items within a large database of information. |

# Document with Remarks

A *remark* is a message that you put inside program code. Programmers concerned with maintenance or future modifications know that ample remarks help verify code. Visual Basic ignores remarks, and users don't see them because users don't see the program's code.

Programmers often add remarks to their programs for the following purposes:

- To state the programmer's name and the date that the program was written.
- To describe the overall goals of the program.
- To describe the goal of a particular procedure.
- To explain tricky or difficult statements so that others who modify the program later can understand the lines of code.

**tip**

Add remarks as you write your programs. Often, programmers say to themselves, "I'll finish the program and add remarks later." Trust me, the remarks never get added.

Even if you write programs for yourself and are the only one who will modify your programs, you should still add remarks to your programs.

Visual Basic supports two kinds of remarks:

- Those that begin with the Rem statement
- Those that begin with an apostrophe (')

The Rem statement is more limiting than the apostrophe and isn't as easy to use. Nevertheless, you'll run across programs that use Rem statements, so you should learn how it works. Here is the format of the Rem statement:

```
Rem The remark's text appears here
```

You can put anything you want in place of *The remark's text appears here*. The following is a section of a program that contains several remarks:

```
Private Sub cmdExit_Click()
   Rem Programmer Julie See, April 7, 2003
   Rem
   Rem This program supports the check-in and check-out
   Rem  process for a video-rental business.
   Rem
   Rem This event procedure executes when the user
   Rem  clicks on the Exit command button. When clicked,
   Rem  this event procedure closes the program's data
   Rem  files, prints an exception report, and
   Rem  and terminates the application.
```

**note** You will see throughout this book that the body of an event procedure is typically indented one or two spaces. Indent your remarks as well as the code in an event procedure. Doing so helps you keep track of where a procedure begins and ends.

After the final remark, the event procedure's code would begin. In place of the Rem statement, you can use an apostrophe to shorten the amount of typing you must do. The following lines show the apostrophe being used in place of Rem:

```
Private Sub cmdExit_Click()
   ' Programmer Julie See, April 7, 2003
   '
   ' This program supports the check-in and check-out
   '  process for a video-rental business.
   '
```

Visual Basic ignores all remark lines. When someone looks at your program code, however, he will know who the programmer is, the overall purpose of the program, the date it was written, and an overall description of each procedure if you've placed that information inside remarks. Remarks do not have to do with the beginning of procedure, but you can place them anywhere within a procedure between code lines.

The apostrophe remark has the advantage of being cleaner and capable of being used where the Rem cannot. You can place an apostrophe remark at the end of a line of code to clarify what the code does:

```
a = 3.14159 * r * r    ' Calculates a
➥circle's area
```

Without the remark, perhaps only a mathematician will understand the purpose of the statement. Later when the programmer makes changes to the program, he does not have to reinterpret the purpose of the calculation; he can simply read the remark.

## Message and Input Boxes

Sometimes your applications will need to display messages and ask questions of the user. Some messages and questions are best displayed from within a dialog box such as the one in Figure 6.10.

Such a dialog box pops up with a message or question when needed but stays out of the way and does not require extra controls on your form at other times.

For example, suppose you want to know if the user has prepared the printer for printing a report. The user has to turn on the printer, make sure it has paper, and see that the online light is on. Your program should not attempt to print until the user has performed these actions, or an error will occur. Therefore, when it is time to print, your application pauses to ask the user if the printer is ready. (Actually, when a message box asks a question, it is known as an *input box*.) Only after the user presses Enter at the input box does your program send the report to the printer.

**caution**

Do not use redundant remarks. A lot of code doesn't need remarks to explain its purpose. The following remark wastes your time and the time of anyone who maintains the program later:

```
Dim sngSales As Single    '
➥Declare a variable named
➥sngSales
```

**tip**

When you write programs, think about the future modifications that you and others might make. Write your programs clearly, using ample spacing and indentation, and add remarks that help explain complex sections of code.

**FIGURE 6.10**

**FIGURE 6.10**

A message box provides a handy way to tell your user something.

Input boxes such as the one in Figure 6.11 always give the user a place to respond with an answer. Note that there is more than one way for the user to respond to the input box in Figure 6.11. He can enter the name of the server and press **Enter** or he can click **OK**. The user can also click **Cancel** without entering the server name. Therefore, the program must be capable of reading the user's answer and responding to a Cancel command button. Responding to message box and input box command buttons is part of the processing that you will learn about in the next section.

**FIGURE 6.11**

Input boxes get user information.

## Using Message Boxes

You will use a function to indicate in your Visual Basic code that you want to display a message box or an input box. When you use such a function, the function name always ends with a pair of parentheses, similar to event procedures. The message box function is called `MsgBox()`, and the input box function is called `InputBox()`.

Always assign the function to an integer variable. The variable holds the return value and indicates which button the user clicked (such as **OK** or **Cancel**).

Here is the format of the `MsgBox()` function:

*IntVariable* = MsgBox( *strMsg* [, [*intType*] [, ➡*strTitle*]])

*strMsg* is a string and forms the text of the message displayed in the message box. *intType* is an optional numeric value that describes the options you want in the message box. Tables 6.2, 6.3, and 6.4 contain all the possible values you can use for

**note**

The message box function format accepts one required (*strMsg*) and two optional (*intType* and *strTitle*) values. Function values such as these are called *arguments*. Actually, `MsgBox()` accepts more arguments, but these are the most common.

the type of message box you want to display. If you want to use a value from two or more of the tables, add those values together.

**TABLE 6.2**   Values to Determine Which Buttons Appear in a Message Box

| Named Literal | Value | Description |
| --- | --- | --- |
| vbOKOnly | 0 | Displays the OK button. |
| vbOKCancel | 1 | Displays the OK and Cancel buttons. |
| vbAbortRetryIgnore | 2 | Displays the Abort, Retry, and Ignore buttons. |
| vbYesNoCancel | 3 | Displays the Yes, No, and Cancel buttons. |
| vbYesNo | 4 | Displays the Yes and No buttons. |
| vbRetryCancel | 5 | Displays the Retry and Cancel buttons. |

**TABLE 6.3**   Values to Select the Icon Displayed in a Message Box

| Named Literal | Value | Description |
| --- | --- | --- |
| vbCritical | 16 | Displays the Critical Message icon. |
| vbQuestion | 32 | Displays the Warning Query icon. |
| vbExclamation | 48 | Displays the Warning Message icon. |
| vbInformation | 64 | Displays the Information Message icon. |
| vbSystemModal | 4096 | Displays a System Modal dialog box. The user must acknowledge a System Modal dialog box before the application will continue. |

**TABLE 6.4**   Setting a Default Button

| Named Literal | Value | Description |
| --- | --- | --- |
| vbDefaultButton1 | 0 | The first button is the default. |
| vbDefaultButton2 | 256 | The second button is the default. |
| vbDefaultButton3 | 512 | The third button is the default. |

The named literals in the table help you document your MsgBox() function. Obviously, this

```
intPress = MsgBox("Are you ready for the report?", vbQuestion +
➥vbYesNoCancel, "Report Request")
```

is less confusing, even though it takes more typing, than this, even though both do the same thing:

```
intPress = MsgBox("Are you ready for the report?", 35, "Report Request")
```

Figure 6.12 shows the result of both statements. By adding two values from the tables, the statement requested the question mark icon and the Yes, No, and Cancel buttons.

**FIGURE 6.12**

Message boxes support several command buttons and icons.

The reason you assign MsgBox() functions to integers is so that you can tell which button the user presses. Suppose that the user clicks the Yes button in Figure 6.12. The program can then print the report. However, if the user clicks the No button, the program describes what the user needs to do to get ready for the report, such as loading the paper, turning on the printer, and so forth. If the user presses the Cancel button, the program knows that the user does not want the report printed.

Table 6.5 lists the seven possible MsgBox() return values. You can test for the integer or for a specific named literal return value.

**TABLE 6.5**  Possible MsgBox() Return Values

| Named Literal | Value | Description |
|---|---|---|
| vbOK | 1 | The user clicked the OK button. |
| vbCancel | 2 | The user clicked the Cancel button. |
| vbAbort | 3 | The user clicked the Abort button. |
| vbRetry | 4 | The user clicked the Retry button. |
| vbIgnore | 5 | The user clicked the Ignore button. |
| vbYes | 6 | The user clicked the Yes button. |
| vbNo | 7 | The user clicked the No button. |

You don't know quite enough to test for specific values with these return values. However, before the next chapter is finished, you will know how to determine what the user clicked from inside a message box.

## Using Input Boxes

The InputBox() function is simple to use because it acts much like the MsgBox() function. The InputBox() function receives answers that are more complete than MsgBox() can receive. Whereas MsgBox() returns one of seven values that indicate the user's command button press, the InputBox() function returns a string data value that holds an answer typed by the user.

The format of the InputBox() function is

```
strVariable = InputBox( strPrompt [, [strTitle] [, strDefault] [, intXpos,
➥intYpos]]])
```

*strPrompt* works a lot like the strMsg value in a MsgBox() function. The user sees *strPrompt* inside the input box displayed on the screen. *strDefault* is a default string value that Visual Basic displays for a default answer, and the user can accept the default answer or change it. The *intXpos* and *intYpos* values indicate the exact location where you want the input box to appear on the form. The *intXpos* value is the number of twips from the left edge of the Form window to the top edge of the input box. The *intYpos* value is the number of twips from the top edge of the Form window to the bottom edge of the input box. If you omit the *intXpos* and *intYpos* values, Visual Basic centers the message box on the form.

The following statement displays an input box that asks the user for a company name. The user enters a response to the prompt or clicks the Cancel command button to indicate that no answer is coming:

```
strCompName = InputBox("What is the name of the
➥company?", "Company Request", "XYZ, Inc.")
```

> **note**
>
> Input boxes always contain OK and Cancel command buttons. If the user clicks **OK** (or presses **Enter** to select OK by default), the answer in the input box is sent to the variable being assigned to the return value. If the user clicks Cancel, a null string ("") returns from the InputBox() function.

The default answer is an answer that automatically appears inside the input box answer area. The user can enter a new answer or simply click **OK** to accept the default value. Figure 6.13 shows the input box that appears when your Visual Basic code executes the statement just shown.

**FIGURE 6.13**

The InputBox()
function is used
to ask a ques-
tion.

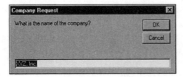

# Summary

This chapter showed you how to place controls onto a form and how to size and position those controls. After you place a control, you must set its properties so that it takes on the appearance and characteristics that your application requires. You experienced the creation of a simple Visual Basic program that included a Form window, controls, and code that you typed into a code window. In the next chapter, you will begin learning the specifics of the Visual Basic language, with which you can test for message and input box return values and execute the same section of your program several times.

■ Events drive Windows programs.

■ For simple, single-window applications, you will use the Standard EXE option when creating a new project.

■ You can place and size controls on a form.

■ The code window ties all your controls together into an application that does specific work.

■ The remark statement offers information for programmers and does not appear to users.

■ You can display messages and ask the user questions from within message and input boxes.

## IN THIS CHAPTER

- Adding Code
- The Basics of Visual Basic Data
- Expressions and Math Operators
- Comparison Operators

7

# DATA PROCESSING WITH VISUAL BASIC

In this chapter, you will learn the "meat and potatoes" of programming. Although Visual Basic will be the language of choice, almost every concept learned in this chapter can be applied to other programming languages. Therefore, when you master this chapter's information on data types, mathematical operators, and comparison operators, you will be prepared to learn the basics of virtually any programming language that exists.

The highlights of this chapter include the following:

- Data appears in many different forms.
- The way that your program processes data depends on the data type.

■ The mathematical operators enable you to perform calculations in Visual Basic.

■ The comparison operators enable you to compare one value to another so that your program can make decisions.

# Adding Code

If a Visual Basic application were simply composed of controls that you place on a form with characteristics that you set from the Properties window, Visual Basic programming would be easy. However, Visual Basic programming is more than controls placed on a form. As a matter of fact, the placement and setting of control properties are among the easiest aspects of Visual Basic programming. Through its graphical development environment, Visual Basic allows you to produce output from your application easily. Your Form window becomes your program's output because that is the window your user sees when he runs your program.

Keep in mind that a Visual Basic program consists of the following:

■ One or more forms

■ Controls on the forms

■ Code written in the Visual Basic programming language

Although you can create great-looking applications just by directing controls onto forms and setting properties, the applications don't really become useful until you add code to tie the controls together, to perform calculations, and to manipulate data when needed.

Consider an inventory program, for example. No control exists on the toolbar to calculate inventory accounting values; you must add the code to do such things. Even though Visual Basic is a general-purpose programming language, Microsoft could not put a control in the toolbox that would handle every specific task needed, so Microsoft chose to use generic tools you can build on using the Visual Basic language.

Before looking at specifics, take a moment to consider the location of the code in a Visual Basic application. You know that the code resides in the code window. A Visual Basic program's code is comprised of small event procedures that respond to events. As you saw in the previous chapter, the name of the event procedure shows which control that code goes with and which event will trigger that code's execution. A code window exists for every form in a Visual Basic application. Although the applications you create in this text will include single windows and therefore single code windows, advanced Visual Basic applications require multiple windows of output, and each of those Form windows comes with its own code window. The code window determines what happens when an event is triggered on the form that code window goes with.

# The Basics of Visual Basic Data

Before you can write programs in a programming language, you must understand how that language handles different kinds of data. Only when you're able to represent data properly can you learn commands that manipulate and process that data. Data is the cornerstone for learning the rest of the Visual Basic programming language. Although writing code that initializes data might not seem to be as much fun as working with graphic controls on the form, you'll soon see how the code ties in with the controls. After you learn to present and process data, you'll be able to work with controls in more powerful ways than without the language inside the code window.

## Data Types

Data falls into three broad categories:

- Numeric data that represents numbers and calculations
- String data that represents textual information such as names, addresses, and values that you would not use for calculations, such as Social Security numbers
- Special data that doesn't fall within the first two categories

Other data might fall into one of several special data type categories, such as a data item that represents whether or not a check box control is checked. (Check box data is represented in the Visual Basic language by the Boolean values of True and False. Table 7.1 explains the Boolean data type.)

Table 7.1 lists all the data types that Visual Basic supports. As you work with Visual Basic, you'll become familiar with all of these data types.

**TABLE 7.1**   Data Types Supported by Visual Basic

| Data Type | Description |
| --- | --- |
| Boolean | A data type that takes on one of two values: True or False. |
| Byte | Positive numeric values without decimals that range from 0 to 255. |
| Currency | Data that holds dollar amounts. Visual Basic keeps track of currency values to four decimal places to ensure that proper rounding occurs when working with money values. Visual Basic respects your Windows International settings and adjusts currency amounts according to your country's requirements. Never include a dollar sign when entering Currency values. |

**TABLE 7.1**   (continued)

| Data Type | Description |
| --- | --- |
| Date | Holds date and time values. |
| Decimal | A new data type not yet supported in Visual Basic except in a few advanced situations. The Decimal data type represents numbers to 28 decimal places of accuracy. |
| Double | Numeric values that are extremely large or extremely small and that require high precision for advanced mathematical calculations. The Double data type is also known as the *double-precision* data type. |
| Integer | Numeric values ranging from –32,768 to 32,767 with no decimal points or fractions. |
| Long | Integer values with a range beyond that of regular (and more efficient) Integer data values. Long data values can range from –2,147,483,648 to 2,147,483,647. Long data values consume more memory space than Integer values, and they are less efficient, slowing down your programs. The Long data type is often called a *long integer*. |
| Object | A special data type that holds and references objects such as controls and forms. |
| Single | Numeric values with decimal points and fractional values that do not require the precision (or high overhead) the Long data type requires. |
| String | Data that consists of 0 to 65,500 characters of alphanumeric data. *Alphanumeric* means that the data can be both alphabetic and numeric. String data values may also contain special characters such as &, *, #, and I. |
| Variant | Data of any data type, used for controls and for other data values for which the data type might be unknown. |

# Specifying Values

A *literal* is a value that does not change. You'll sprinkle literals throughout your programs. For example, if you need to annualize a monthly calculation, you'll surely multiply a value by 12 somewhere in the calculation, because 12 months appear in each year. Twelve is a literal and represents a Byte, an Integer, or a Long data type, depending on the context of the calculation and the accuracy required. If you multiply a monthly value by 12.0, the 12.0 is also a literal, but 12.0 must be a Single or Double data type because of the decimal point.

When typing numeric literal values, you don't have to concern yourself with the data type, because Visual Basic attaches the best data type for the calculation. However, if you specify data of other data types, you must predict the type your program is to expect and write code that works with that non-numeric data.

Quotation marks are required to designate a String literal, but the String literal doesn't actually contain the quotation marks. The following are literals that take the String data type:

```
"Que"          "123 E. Sycamore St."

"19380"        "%$##@$"

"[Adam]"       "Happy Birthday!"

" "
```

You must embed date and time literals, using the Date data type, inside pound signs (#). Depending on your international settings, you can specify the date or time in just about any valid date or time format, as follows:

```
#12-Mar-2003#    #10:04 PM#

#21:03:22#       #December 31, 2003#
```

A Boolean literal is always true or false, so any time you must store or retrieve a true or false value, Visual Basic uses the Boolean data type to hold the value. Option boxes and check box controls return their values in the Boolean data type. Many programmers use the Boolean data type to store two-value data such as yes/no and on/off values.

**note**

Data comes in all shapes and sizes these days. With multimedia, data can be audio or even a video clip. The Variant data type and the Object data type are helpful for describing data that is not numeric or alphabetic.

The last string in this list is called an *empty string* because the quotation marks are together without anything between them. Not even a space appears inside an empty string. Sometimes you'll use an empty string to represent data that is to be filled in by the user.

Although Visual Basic normally takes care of data types when you type numeric values in your program, you might need to ensure that it interprets a numeric literal as one of the specific data types. For example, you might type the literal 86 and need Visual Basic to store or display the value as a Long data type, even though 86 fits within a Byte or Integer data type.

You can use the data type suffix characters from Table 7.2 to override the default data type. The suffix characters let you specify the data type for numeric literals. Occasionally, Visual Basic will also use the data type suffix characters when displaying numeric information. Therefore, if you type 86#, Visual Basic treats it as a double-precision value. Without the # suffix, Visual Basic would treat the 86 as an integer.

**TABLE 7.2**   Data Type Suffix Characters

| Character | Data Type | Example |
|-----------|-----------|---------|
| & | Long | 86& |
| ! | Single | 86! |
| # | Double | 86# |
| @ | Currency | 86@ |

## Variables Hold Data

All your data cannot be literals. The information that your program's users enter in controls such as text boxes isn't literal data because the user can change it. In addition, your program has to have a place to hold information temporarily for calculations and for in-memory storage before sending the information to a disk file or to the printer. To hold data that might change due to calculations or state changes within the application, you must declare variables. A *variable* is a named location that holds data.

Unlike literals, variables can change. You can store a number in a variable early in the program and change that number later in the program. The variable acts like a box that holds a value. The data that you store in variables doesn't have to change, but often the program does change the contents of variables.

A program can have as many variables as you will use to hold data. Before you can use a variable, you must request that Visual Basic create one. First, declare the variable before using it. To declare a variable, you tell Visual Basic its name and data type.

**caution**

A variable can hold at most one data type.

After you declare a variable, it always retains its original data type. Therefore, a single-precision variable can hold only single-precision values. When you store an integer in a single-precision variable, Visual Basic converts the integer to a single-precision number before the number gets to the variable. Such data type conversions are common, and they typically don't cause many problems.

You must use the Dim statement to declare and define a variable. (Dim stands for *dimension* and has its roots, as with most Visual Basic commands, in the original

BASIC language.) `Dim` tells Visual Basic that the program will need to use a variable; the statement describes the data type and assigns a name.

When you learn a new statement in Visual Basic or any other programming language, you must learn the format for that statement. The format shows you the command and its options.

Here is the format for a `Dim` statement:

`Dim VarName As DataType`

When you see an italicized word inside a format, the italicized word is known as a *placeholder*. In this case, the words `Dim` and `As` are required, and you must fill in your own values for *VarName* and *DataType*. When Visual Basic executes the `Dim` statement at runtime, it creates a variable in memory and assigns it the name you give it in the *VarName* placeholder. *DataType* is one of the data types listed in Table 7.1.

`Dim` statements typically appear toward the top of an event procedure. You will see several examples throughout the next few chapters that show the location of `Dim`.

The following statement defines a variable named `curProductTotal`:

`Dim curProductTotal As Currency`

> **caution**
>
> Two variables cannot have the same name in the same code window. For example, you cannot declare two variables with the name `intNumber` in the same event procedure.

From the `Dim` statement, you know that the variable holds the Currency data type and that the variable's name is `curProductTotal`. Programmers often prefix a variable name with a three-letter abbreviation that indicates the variable's data type, but such a prefix is not required. Table 7.3 lists these common variable prefix values. Remember to use these prefixes at the beginning of variable names to remind yourself of the variable's data type. The prefix itself has no meaning to Visual Basic because the `Dim` statement is what informs Visual Basic of the variable's type.

## TABLE 7.3 Variable Name Prefixes

| Prefix | Data Type | Example |
|--------|-----------|---------|
| bln | Boolean | blnIsOverTime |
| byt | Byte | bytAge |
| cur | Currency | curHourlyPay |
| dte | Date | dteFirstBegan |
| dbl | Double | dblMicroMeasurement |

**TABLE 7.3**   (continued)

| Prefix | Data Type | Example |
|---|---|---|
| int | Integer | intCount |
| lng | Long | lngStarDistance |
| obj | Object | objSoundClip |
| sng | Single | sngYearSales |
| str | String | strLastName |
| vnt or var | Variant | vntControlValue |

The following statements define Integer, Single, and Double variables:

```
Dim intLength As Integer
Dim sngPrice As Single
Dim dblStructure As Double
```

If you want to run a program that stores the user's text box entry for a first name, you would define a string like this:

```
Dim strFirstName As String
```

You can get fancy when you define strings. This strFirstName string can hold any string from 0 to 65,500 characters long. In the next section, you learn how to store data in a String variable that you define with a Dim statement. The strFirstName string can hold data of virtually any size. You could store a small string such as "Joe" in strFirstName, and then a longer string, such as "Mercedes" in strFirstName because strFirstName is a variable-length string.

Sometimes you want to limit the amount of text that a string holds. For example, you might need to define a String variable to hold a name that you read from the disk file. Later, you'll display the contents in a label on a form. The form's label has a fixed length, however, assuming that the AutoSize property is set to True. Therefore, you want to keep the String variable at a reasonable length. The following Dim statement demonstrates how you can add the optional * *StringLength* option to your Dim statement when you want to define a fixed-length string. Replace *StringLength* with a value that represents the maximum length of the string like this:

```
Dim strTitle As String * 20
```

strTitle is the name of a String variable that can hold a string from 0 to 20 characters long. If the program attempts to store a String value that is longer than 20 characters in strTitle, Visual Basic truncates the string and stores only the first 20 characters.

When you declare Variant data, you add the `As Variant` qualifier to let Visual Basic know that the data type is unknown. Perhaps the data is coming from a text box and the user can enter either a number or a string. Instead of specifying `As Variant` inside the `Dim` statement, you can use this shortcut: Omit the `As Variant` descriptor when you define Variant variables. This `Dim` statement

```
Dim varValue As Variant
```

does exactly the same thing as this:

```
Dim varValue
```

A good rule of thumb is to make your code as explicit as possible, so use `As Variant` to clarify your code's intentions. If you begin calling a variable one name, you must stay with that name for the entire program. `curSale` is not the same variable name as `curSales`.

Visual Basic offers another shortcut when defining several variables. Instead of listing each variable definition on separate lines like this:

```
Dim A As Integer
Dim B As Double
Dim C As Integer
Dim D As String
Dim E As String
```

you can combine several definitions on a single line. Here's an example:

```
Dim A As Integer, C As Integer
Dim B As Double
Dim D As String, E As String
```

## Putting Data in Variables

So far you have learned how to define variables but not how to store data in them. Use the assignment statement when you want to put a data value into a variable. Here is the format for the assignment statement:

```
VarName = Expression
```

An *assignment statement* is a program statement that puts data into a control, a variable, or another object. In most cases, you'll use an assignment statement to store data into variables that will hold that data for later in the program. *VarName* is a variable name that you have defined using the `Dim` statement. *Expression* can be a literal, another variable, or a mathematical expression.

Suppose that you need to store a minimum age value of 18 in an Integer variable named `IntMinAge`. The following assignment statement does that:

```
intMinAge = 18
```

To store the temperature data type in a single-precision data type variable named sngTodayTemp, you could do this:

```
sngTodayTemp = 42.1
```

The data type of *Expression* must match the data type of the variable to which you are assigning it. In other words, the following statement is invalid because it would produce an error:

```
sngTodayTemp = "Forty-Two point One"
```

sngTodayTemp is a single-precision variable, so you cannot assign a string to it. However, Visual Basic often makes a quick conversion for you when the conversion is trivial. For example, it's possible to perform the following assignment even if you have defined dblMeasure to be a double-precision variable:

```
dblMeasure = 921.23
```

At first glance, it appears that 921.23 is a single-precision item because of its size. It is actually a Variant data value. Visual Basic assumes that all data literals are Variant unless you explicitly add a suffix character to the literal to make the constant a specific data type. Visual Basic can easily and safely convert the Variant value to double-precision. That's just what happens here, so the assignment works.

You can assign other variables to variables. Consider the following code:

```
Dim sngSales As Single, sngNewSales As Single
sngSales = 3945.42
sngNewSales = sngSales
```

When the third statement finishes, both sngSales and sngNewSales have the value 3945.42.

Feel free to assign variables to controls and controls to variables. For example, suppose that the user types the value 18.34 into a text box. Visual Basic instantly stores the value 18.34 in the text box's Text property. If the text box's Name property is txtFactor, the following statement stores the value of the text box in a variable named sngFactorVal:

```
sngFactorVal = txtFactor.Text
```

Notice that when you assign a control's property value to a variable (or to another control property value), you separate the control name from the property name with a period. txtFactor.Text refers to the Text property of the text box named txtFactor.

Suppose that you defined strTitle to be a String variable with a fixed length of 10, but the user types Mondays Always Feel Blue in the text box's Text property that you want to assign to strTitle. Visual Basic stores only the first 10 characters of the control's property value to strTitle and truncates the rest of the title. Therefore, strTitle holds only the string Mondays Al (strings don't hold the quotation marks).

You can make data appear on a form instantly from within the Visual Basic language by assigning the Text property of text boxes or the Caption property of labels and command buttons. No variables are required to do this. Suppose you put a command button named cmdPress on a form. The event procedure shown in Listing 7.1 changes the command button's Caption property and immediately places a new caption on the form (this occurs at runtime when the event procedure executes).

**LISTING 7.1** Placing a Caption on the Form

```
Private Sub cmdPress_Click()
  cmdPress.Caption = "Brush your teeth daily!"
End Sub
```

No matter what the command button's Caption property is set to at the start of the event procedure, when the user clicks the command button, the event procedure executes and the command button's caption changes to Brush your teeth daily!.

Some properties accept only a limited range of values. The possible values that you can select for a label's BorderStyle property in the Properties window are 0-None and 1-Fixed Single. To assign a border style directly in code, you can assign the style just 0 or 1. Never spell out the entire property when assigning limited values to these kinds of properties. Therefore, if your Form window contains a label named lblSinger, the program could put a border around the label with the following assignment statement:

```
lblSinger.BorderStyle = 1
```

# Expressions and Math Operators

You should learn Visual Basic's math operators so that you can calculate and assign expression results to variables when you code assignment statements that contain expressions. An *operator* is a symbol or word that does math and data manipulation.

**note**

You may recall that Visual Basic automatically creates the opening and closing lines of an event procedure. Therefore, you will never have to write the first or last line for a command button's Click event procedure. The Private keyword (supplied by Visual Basic) keeps the event procedure private so that code in other Form windows cannot access it. Except in rare circumstances, it is advantageous to keep code local, or private, to a code window and to the Form window the code goes with. Another name for procedure is *subroutine*, hence the name Sub. The final statement in an event procedure must be End Sub so that Visual Basic knows where one event procedure ends and another one begins.

Table 7.4 describes Visual Basic's primary math operators. Other operators exist, but those in Table 7.4 suffice for most of the programs you'll write. Look over the operators. You are already familiar with most of them because they look and act like their real-world counterparts.

**TABLE 7.4**   Primary Math Operators

| Operator | Example | Description |
|---|---|---|
| + | Net + Disc | Adds two values |
| - | Price - 4.25 | Subtracts one value from another |
| * | Total * Factor | Multiplies two values |
| / | Tax / Adjust | Divides one value by another value |
| ^ | Adjust ^ 3 | Raises a value to a power |
| & | Name1 & Name2 | Concatenates (merges) two strings |

Suppose that you want to store the difference between annual sales (stored in a variable named curAnnualSales) and cost of sales (stored in a variable named curCostOfSales) in a variable named curNetSales. Assuming that all three variables have been defined and initialized, the following assignment statement computes the correct value for curNetSales:

curNetSales = curAnnualSales - curCostOfSales

This tells Visual Basic to compute the value of the expression and store the result in the variable named curNetSales. Of course, you can store the result of this expression in the control's Caption or Text property as well.

If you want to raise a value by a power (multiply the value by itself a certain number of times), you can do so. The following code assigns 10,000 to lngValue; 10 raised to the fourth power (that is, 10 times 10 times 10 times 10) is 10,000:

intYears = 4
lngValue = 10 ^ intYears

No matter how complex the expression is, Visual Basic computes the entire result before it stores the result in the variable at the left of the equals symbol. In the following assignment statement, Visual Basic computes the result and stores the value in the variable named sngAns:

sngAns = 8 * sngFactor - sngPi + 12 * sngMonthlyAmts

Combining expressions often produces unintended results because Visual Basic computes mathematical results in a predetermined order. If one or more ^ operator appears in an expression, Visual Basic always calculates exponents first. Visual Basic then computes all multiplication and division—working from left to right—before any addition and subtraction.

Visual Basic assigns 13 to intResult in the following assignment:
```
intResult = 3 + 5 * 2
```

You might expect Visual Basic to assign 16 to intResult because 3 + 5 is 8 and 8×2 is 16. However, Visual Basic always computes multiplication and division before addition. Therefore, it first computes the value of 5×2, or 10, and then adds 3 to 10 to get 13. Then it assigns 13 to intResult.

If both multiplication and division appear in the same expression, Visual Basic calculates from left to right. For example, Visual Basic assigns 20 to the following expression:
```
intResult = 8 / 2 + 4 + 3 * 4
```

Visual Basic computes the division first because the division appears to the left of the multiplication. After Visual Basic does the division and the multiplication, it performs the addition and stores the final answer of 20 in intResult.

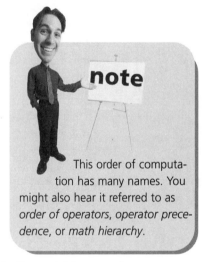

It is possible to override the operator precedence by using parentheses. Visual Basic always computes values inside any pair of parentheses before anything else in the expression, even if it means ignoring operator precedence. The following assignment statement stores 16 in intResult because the parentheses force Visual Basic to compute the addition before the multiplication:
```
intResult = (3 + 5) * 2
```

This order of computation has many names. You might also hear it referred to as *order of operators, operator precedence,* or *math hierarchy.*

The following expression stores the fifth root of 125 in the variable named sngRoot5:
```
sngRoot5 = 125 ^ (1/5)
```

As you can see from this expression, Visual Basic supports fractional exponents. Programmers who do not write scientific or advanced financial programs may never have a use for fractional exponents, but Visual Basic supports them in case you do.

To *concatenate* means to merge two strings together. One of Visual Basic's primary operators has nothing to do with math. The concatenation operator, &, joins one string to the end of another. Suppose the user enters his first name in a Label control named lblFirst and his last name in a Label control named lblLast. The following concatenation expression stores the full name in the String variable named strFullName:
```
strFullName = strFirstName & strLastName
```

There is a problem here, though, that might not be apparent at first. No space appears between the two names inside the `strFullName` variable after concatenation. The & operator doesn't automatically insert a space because you don't always want space inserted when you concatenate two strings. Therefore, you might have to concatenate a third string between the other two and make that string a literal that holds a single space:

```
strFullName = strFirstName & " " &
➥strLastName
```

> **tip**
>
> The plus sign also concatenates two strings if you use it in place of the &. Many programmers believe that the plus sign should be reserved only for mathematical operations and that the & should be used for string concatenation. Using the + on two different data types may be confusing.

# Comparison Operators

Visual Basic supports several operators that do not perform math. Instead, these *comparison operators* compare one data value to another. One value can be greater than, equal to, or less than the other value. With comparison operators, you can write programs that make decisions at runtime.

All comparison operators produce true or false results. In other words, the comparison is either true or the comparison is false. The rest of your code uses the result of this comparison to determine what to do next. For example, if a comparison returns a false value when determining whether an employee worked during a pay period, the rest of the program knows not to print a paycheck for the employee.

Table 7.5 describes the six comparison operators.

**TABLE 7.5** The Comparison Operators

| Operator | Example | Description |
|---|---|---|
| > | `lblSales.Caption > Goal` | The *greater than* operator returns true if the value on the left side of the > is numerically or alphabetically greater than the value on the right. |
| < | `Pay < 2000.00` | The *less than* operator returns true if the value on the left side of the < is numerically or alphabetically less than the value on the right. |
| = | `Age = Limit` | The *equal to* operator (or simply *equal* operator) returns true if the values on both sides of = are equal. |

**TABLE 7.5** (continued)

| Operator | Example | Description |
|----------|---------|-------------|
| >= | FirstName >= "Mike" | The *greater than or equal to* operator returns true if the value on the left side of >= is numerically or alphabetically greater than or equal to the value on the right. |
| <= | Num <= lblAmt.Caption | The *less than or equal to* operator returns true if the value on the left side of <= is numerically or alphabetically less than or equal to the value on the right. |
| <> | txtAns.Text <> "Yes" | The *not equal to* operator returns true if the value on the left side of <> is numerically or alphabetically unequal to the value on the right. |

As you can see from Table 7.5, the comparison operators compare either variables, literals, control values, or combinations of those data sources. The comparison operators worked on both numeric and alphabetic values. You can compare any kind of number against another number or any kind of string against another string. To illustrate how these comparison operators produce true or false results, Table 7.6 shows the results of several comparisons.

**tip**

Learn these and the math operators! Almost all programming languages use similar operators. All programming languages perform some kind of data comparison, and what you learn here is applicable to any language you might learn in the future.

**TABLE 7.6** Examples of Comparisons

| Comparison | Result |
|------------|--------|
| 4 > 2 | True |
| 4 < 1 | False |
| 4 < 8 | True |
| "Apple" <= "Orange" | True |
| "Pearson" < "Person" | True |
| 0 >= 0 | True |
| 0 <= 0 | True |
| 1 <> 2 | True |
| 2 >= 3 | False |

Take extra care that the expressions on both sides of a comparison operator are the same data type or at least are compatible data types. In other words, you cannot compare a string to a numeric data type. If you try, you'll receive a type mismatch error because these data types do not match. You can compare any number against any other number most of the time regardless of the data type. In other words, you can test whether a single-precision value is less than or greater than an integer value.

In the next chapter, you will learn how to use the comparison operators to make decisions inside Visual Basic code.

# Summary

This chapter described Visual Basic data. Visual Basic supports several data types and you must know how to specify literals and declare variables that conform to those data types. Now that you understand data types and variables, you can perform calculations that assign the results of expressions to variables and controls.

- Each Form window has a corresponding code window that contains event procedure code for the controls on that window.

- All data in Visual Basic conforms to one of several data types that Visual Basic supports.

- Mathematical operators allow you to perform calculations. You don't need to understand math because Visual Basic does the math for you as long as you structure your expressions correctly.

- Comparison operators, combined with the decision statements you will learn in the next chapter, enable you to write programs that make decisions at runtime.

# IN THIS CHAPTER

- Making Decisions in Code
- Using `Else`
- Other Forms of Decision Making
- Nesting `If...Else` Statements
- Selecting with `Select Case`
- Looping in Visual Basic

# 8

# WORKING WITH DATA

Now that you know Visual Basic's mathematical and decision operators, you can put those operators to use in this chapter. The comparison operators enable you to set up complex decision-making and repetition statements in Visual Basic. One of the advantages that the computer offers to us is that the computer will repeat a task over and over without getting bored. In this chapter, you'll learn how to write programs that repeat sections of code.

The highlights of this chapter include the following:

- Use the `If` statement to make decisions.
- The `Else` branch enables you to write more powerful `If` statements.
- The `Select Case` statement is Visual Basic's compound `If` statement.
- Visual Basic supports several kinds of `Do` loops.
- The `For` loop enables you to repeat a section of code a specified number of times.

# Making Decisions in Code

One of the most important statements in a program is the If statement. With the logic that If provides, your application can begin to analyze data and make decisions based on the analysis. For example, your program can display a three-button message box and determine, with the If statement, which command button the user should click to close the message box.

If uses the comparison operators you learned in the previous chapters, such as < and >=. If performs one of two possible code actions, depending on the result of the comparison. In other words, If uses a comparison operator result to test data and might execute one or more lines of subsequent code, depending on the result.

Before If, code was executed sequentially, one statement after another. If enables your program to be more decisive and execute only those parts of the program the data warrants. For example, suppose you're writing an invoicing system. In such a system, no sales tax should be computed for tax-exempt organizations, so your program would skip over the tax computation code when processing such organizations.

If makes decisions. If a comparison test is true, the body of the If statement is executed. (In fact, the previous sentence is almost identical to Visual Basic's If statement.) The following is one format of If:

```
If comparisonTest Then
   One or more Visual Basic statements
End If
```

End If tells Visual Basic where the body of the If statement ends. Suppose that the user enters a sales figure into a text box named txtSales. The following computes a bonus amount based on sales:

```
If (txtSales.Text > 5000.00) Then
   sngBonus = txtSales.Text * .12
End If
```

This statement looks at a text box named txtSales on the Form window and analyzes the text box's contents, stored in the Text property. (All Text Box controls have a Text property that holds the current value of the text box.)

Visual Basic stores 0 (zero) in all numeric variables that you don't initialize first. Therefore, sngBonus equals 0 before the If executes. Then the code changes the sngBonus variable only if the value of the txtSales.Text property is more than 5000.00. In a way, the If reads like this:

*If the sales are more than $5,000.00, then compute bonus based on that sales value.*

Visual Basic stores a *null string* (also called an *empty string*) in string variables that you have not yet initialized. If you have an uninitialized Variant data type variable, the variable holds a null string that becomes zero if you assign the variable to a numeric variable.

The body of an If can have more than one statement. The body is often known as a *block*. The following If calculates a bonus, the cost of sales, and the reorder amount based on the value of the txtSales text box entry:

```
If (txtSales.Text > 5000.00) Then
    sngBonus = txtSales.Text * .12
    curCostOfSales = txtSales.Text * .41
    curReorderCost = txtSales.Text * .24
End If
```

The three statements that make up the body of the If execute only if the condition txtSales.Text > 5000.00 is true. Suppose that this code contains another assignment statement immediately after End If. That assignment statement is outside the body of the If, so the true or false result of the condition affects only the body of the If. Therefore, the tax computation in the following routine executes regardless of whether sales are more or less than $5,000.00:

```
If (txtSales.Text > 5000.00) Then
    sngBonus = txtSales.Text * .12
    curCostOfSales = txtSales.Text * .41
    curReorderCost = txtSales.Text * .24
End If
sngTax = .08 * txtSales.Text
```

> **tip**
>
> The parentheses are not required around the comparison test in an If, but they help separate the test from the rest of the code. In addition, the indentation helps illustrate the code that appears inside the If statement.

Can you see how the program makes decisions using If? The body of the If executes only if the comparison test is true. Otherwise the rest of the program continues as usual.

# Using Else

Whereas If executes code based on the comparison test's true condition, the Else statement executes code based on the comparison test's false condition. Else is an optional part of the If statement. Else specifies the code that executes if the comparison test is false. The complete format of the If statement with Else is as follows:

```
If comparisonTest Then
  One or more Visual Basic statements
Else
  One or more Visual Basic statements
End If
```

Typically, programmers called this full-blown `If` statement the `If...Else` statement. The `If...Else` statement is sometimes called a mutually exclusive statement. The term *mutually exclusive* simply means that one set of code or the other executes, but not both. The `If...Else` statement contains two sets of code—that is, two bodies of one or more Visual Basic statements—and only one set executes, depending on the result of the `If`. An `If` statement is either true or false because the `If`'s comparison produces either a true or false result. Therefore, either the first or the second body of code in an `If...Else` executes.

Suppose that a salesperson receives a bonus if sales are high (more than $5,000) or suffers a pay cut if sales are low (less than $5,000). The following `If...Else` contains the code necessary to reward or punish the salesperson. The `If` code body computes the bonus, as you saw in the previous section. The code body of the `Else` subtracts $25 from the salesperson's pay, which is stored in the `curPayAmt` variable, if the sales quota is not met. The following code computes such a payment amount based on the quota:

```
If (txtSales.Text > 5000.00) Then
  sngBonus = .05 * txtSales.Text
Else
  curPayAmt = curPayAmt - 25.00
End If
curTaxes = curPayAmt * .42
```

The fourth line of code might surprise you at first. The assignment appears to make the statement that the pay is equal to the pay minus 25. You know that nothing can be equal to itself less 25. In math, the = acts as a balance for the two sides of an equation. In Visual Basic and other programming languages, when the = is not used inside an `If`'s comparison test, it is an assignment that takes everything to the right of the = and stores that

**note**

When the variable appears on both sides of an equals assignment operator, in any programming language, the variable is being changed in some way.

value in the variable on the left of the =. Therefore, the fourth line subtracts 25 from the value stored in curPayAmt and assigns that result back to curPayAmt. In effect, it lowers the value of curPayAmt by 25.

To further your understanding of the If...Else statement and to demonstrate testing for an input box's return value, Listing 8.1 uses If...Else to respond to an input box. The code asks the user for a company name and then accepts the name or recognizes that the user clicked Cancel to close the input box without answering it. (When a user clicks Cancel in response to an input box, the input box returns a null string, "".)

**LISTING 8.1** Using an If...Else to Check an Input Box's Return Value

```
Dim strCompName As String
Dim intPress As Integer   ' MsgBox return value here
' Ask the user for a name
' Use XYZ, Inc. for the default value
➥strCompName = InputBox("What is the company name?",
  "Company Request", "XYZ, Inc.")
' Check the return value
If (strCompName = "") Then
  ' The user clicked Cancel
  intPress = MsgBox("Thanks anyway")
Else
  ' The user entered a company name
  intPress = MsgBox("You entered " & strCompName)
End If
```

# Other Forms of Decision Making

Most languages support additional kinds of decision-making statements. Virtually every language in existence uses the If statement as well as the Else option.

Table 8.1 lists three additional operators that work with the comparison operators you already know. These operators, called the *logical operators*, combine multiple decisions into one If statement.

**TABLE 8.1**   Logical Operators

| Operator | Use | Description |
|---|---|---|
| And | If (A > B) And (C < D) | Produces a true result if both sides of the And are true. Therefore, A must be greater than B, And C must be less than D. Otherwise, the expression produces a false result. |
| Or | If (A > B) Or (C < D) | Produces a true result if either side of the Or is true. Therefore, A must be greater than B, Or C must be less than D. If both sides of the Or are false, the entire expression produces a false result. |
| Not | If Not(strAns = "Yes") | Produces the opposite true or false result. Therefore, if strAns equals "Yes", Not turns the true value to false. |

An example will help clarify the reason for the logical operators. The logical operators help clarify an otherwise complicated If statement. Analyze the following If statement:

```
If (sngSales > 5000.00) And (intUnitsSold >
➥10000) Then
    sngBonus = 50.00
End If
```

This If statement rewards a salesperson if sales totals more than $5,000 and if the salesperson sells more than 10,000 units of a particular product. Without And you would have to embed an If statement in the body of another If statement like this:

```
If (sngSales > 5000.00) Then
    If (intUnitsSold > 10000) Then
        sngBonus = 50.00
    End If
End If
```

note

Unlike the other operators you have seen, the logical operators use words such as And instead of symbols such as *.

Your goal as a programmer is to make your code as clear as possible. The logical operator And is much more intuitive and easier to understand than the multiple-line If.

How could you rewrite this If to pay the bonus if the salesperson sells either more than $5,000 or more than 10,000 units? The logical Or operator does the trick like this:

```
If (sngSales > 5000.00) Or (intUnitsSold > 10000) Then
    sngBonus = 50.00
End If
```

# Nesting `If...Else` Statements

If you nest one `If...Else` statement inside another, you'll have to use `ElseIf` to start the nested statement. Consider the code in Listing 8.2.

**LISTING 8.2**  Combining Nested `If...Else` Statements with `ElseIf`

```
If (intHours <= 40) Then
   curOverTime = 0.0
' Now test for hours between 40 and 50
' and pay time and a half
ElseIf (intHours <= 50) Then
      curOverTime = (intHours - 40) * 1.5 * sngRate
   Else
      ' Must pay double time over 50 and
      ' time and a half for the hours between
      ' 40 and 50
      curOverTime = ((intHours - 50) * 2 + (10 * 1.5)) *
sngRate
End If
```

> ### caution
>
> The `Not` logical operator works on a single value, unlike the other two logical operators, which combine two or more decisions. The `Not` often negates a comparison test. Use `Not` cautiously. The `If` used for the `Not` operator example in Table 8.1 would be more readable if it were a simple `If` statement that eliminated the `Not`, such as `If (strAns <> "Yes")`.

The `ElseIf` statement in the fifth line starts a new `If...Else` block of code. If the value of `intHours` is not 40 or less in the first line, then it must be more than 40. Therefore, `ElseIf` tests to see if the hours are more than 40 but less than or equal to 50 (the fifth line would never execute unless the hours were more than 40). Time and a half is computed for those overtime hours. If the `ElseIf` produces a false condition, then the hours worked must be more than 50. The program then contains a complex expression that computes double time for all hours over 50 and time and a half for the 10 hours between 40 and 50.

Do nested `If...ElseIf...End If` statements like these get confusing and difficult to debug? Of course—and this simple example illustrates just how difficult they can be. In the next section, you'll see how the `Select Case` statement offers a better alternative than nested and confusing `If` statements.

# Selecting with `Select Case`

The `Select Case` statement is better suited to checking for multiple conditions than is `If`, even when utilizing the logical operators. The use of more than three or four embedded `If...Else` statements results in a complicated program. You get into messy logic such as "If this is true, then if this is true, then if one more thing is true, then do something, otherwise…" Here is the Select Case statement's format:

```
Select Case Expression
   Case expressionMatch
      Block of one or more Visual Basic statements
   [ Case expressionMatch1
      Block of one or more Visual Basic statements]
   [ Case expressionMatch2
      Block of one or more Visual Basic statements]
      :
   [ Case expressionMatchN
      Block of one or more Visual Basic statements]
   [Case Else
      Block of one or more Visual Basic statements]
End Select
```

Using Select Case is simple even though its format is long. Select Case selects from one of several conditions. The number of conditions, indicated by the [ Case expressionMatch# …] body, varies according to the number of conditions that you need to test. If none of the cases performs a match, the Case Else code body executes if you supply one.

Consider the example in Listing 8.3.

**LISTING 8.3** Using Select Case Statements to Compare Multiple Values

```
' Test for a child's letter grade
Select Case txtGrade.Text
   Case "A"
      lblAnnounce.Caption = "Perfect!"
   Case "B"
      lblAnnounce.Caption = "Great!"
   Case "C"
      lblAnnounce.Caption = "Study harder!"
   Case "D"
      lblAnnounce.Caption = "Get help!"
   Case "F"
      lblAnnounce.Caption = "Back to basics!"
   Case Else
      lblAnnounce.Caption = "Error in grade"
End Select
```

If the text box txtGrade.Text holds the letter *A*, the Case body on the third line executes and then Visual Basic skips all the remaining cases. Once that happens, the code that begins after End Select executes. If the txtGrade.Text text box holds the letter *B*, the Case body on the fifth line executes, and so on. The body of a Case can cover several lines, although only single lines of code are in this example. Visual Basic knows that once a Case *expressionMatch* is made, each line in that matching Case body executes until the next Case, at which point the entire Select Case has done its job and the program can continue.

If for some reason a grade other than A, B, C, D, or F appears in the text box, the Case Else takes over and warns of the error by setting the label's value.

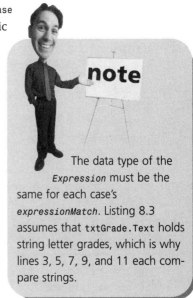

**note**

The data type of the *Expression* must be the same for each case's *expressionMatch*. Listing 8.3 assumes that txtGrade.Text holds string letter grades, which is why lines 3, 5, 7, 9, and 11 each compare strings.

Visual Basic supports another form of Select Case that lets you specify one conditional operator for each *expressionMatch*, using the Is keyword. Listing 8.4 rewrites the previous Select Case but uses numeric grades to take advantage of conditional Select Case choices.

**LISTING 8.4**  Using Conditional Select Case Comparisons

```
' Test for a child's numeric grade
Select Case txtGrade.Text
   Case Is >= 90
      lblAnnounce.Caption = "Perfect!"
   Case Is >= 80
      lblAnnounce.Caption = "Great!"
   Case Is >= 70
      lblAnnounce.Caption = "Study harder!"
   Case Is >= 60
      lblAnnounce.Caption = "Get help!"
   Case Else
      lblAnnounce.Caption = "Back to basics!"
End Select
```

Given this format and the numeric grades, each case is dependent on the numeric grade being 90 or above for the best message and below 60 for the worst message. Notice that no test had to be made for a numeric grade less than 60 because if the grade is not between 60 and 100, it has to be below 60. (This example assumes that the grade will fall between 0 and 100 and not be bad data to illustrate how the `Case Else` can work as one of the `Case` statement bodies.)

One final format of `Select Case` appears in the Visual Basic language that allows for a range of choices using the `To` keyword. The range determines which `Case` body executes. Use the range-based `Select Case` when you can order the possibilities sequentially, as shown in Listing 8.5.

**caution**

`Select Case` statements don't work for all nested comparisons. No `Select Case` format supports the inclusion of logical operators, so you cannot use `And`, `Or`, or `Not` in a `Select Case` test expression. You have to resort to a nested `If...ElseIf...End If` statement for complex nested conditions.

**LISTING 8.5** Using a Range for `Select Case` to Compare Grouped Values

```
' Test for a child's numeric grade
Select Case txtGrade.Text
   Case 0 To 59
      lblAnnounce.Caption = "Back to Basics"
   Case 60 To 69
      lblAnnounce.Caption = "Get help!"
   Case 70 To 79
      lblAnnounce.Caption = "Study harder!"
   Case 80 To 89
      lblAnnounce.Caption = "Great!"
   Case Else
      lblAnnounce.Caption = "Perfect!"
End Select
```

**tip**

You can combine the various forms of `Case` expressions into a single `Select Case` statement. Here's a `Case` that uses all the formats to check for a value:

```
Case 101, 102, 201 To
205, Is > 300
```

If the expression in the `Select Case` statement is `101`, `102`, `201`, `202`, `203`, `204`, `205`, or more than `300`, the body of this `Case` executes.

Notice that the order of cases in Listing 8.5 is different, because of the range format being used. The first `Case` test checks for the lowest possible range. If the numeric grade falls between 0 and 59, the worst message appears in the label (integers are assumed, to keep things simple; this could produce an error if `79.5` is entered for a grade). Each succeeding range moves up sequentially. You can also test for string ranges as long as the lowest strings, compared alphabetically, are tested earliest.

# Looping in Visual Basic

In addition to decision statements, all programming languages enable you to write statements that repeat themselves a certain number of times. These statement blocks are called *loops*. Loops play an important role in programs because you will need to repeat sections of a program to process multiple data values. For example, you might need to calculate a total of past due charges for all customers. A loop can read each customer's past due charges and add that amount to the running total.

## The `Do While` Loop

The `Do` statement is a fundamental looping statement in Visual Basic and in many other languages, and it comes in several formats. Visual Basic supports several versions of the `Do` statement. The `Do While` loop is perhaps the most common looping statement that you will use in your programs. `Do While` works with comparison expressions just as the `If` statement does.

The six comparison operators that you learned about earlier work inside loops. Rather than controlling the one-time execution of a single block of code, however, the comparison expression controls the looping statements.

As with the `If` statement that ends with `End If`, a loop will always be a multiline statement that includes an obvious beginning and end. Here is the format of the `Do While` loop:

```
Do While (comparison test)
  Block of one or more Visual Basic statements
Loop
```

The block of code continues looping as long as *comparison test* is true. Whether you insert one or several lines of code for the block does not matter. It is vital, however, for the block to somehow change a variable used in *comparison test*. The block keeps repeating as long as *comparison test* is true. Eventually, *comparison test* must become false or your program will enter an infinite loop and the user will have to break execution through an inelegant means, such as pressing the Ctrl+Break key combination.

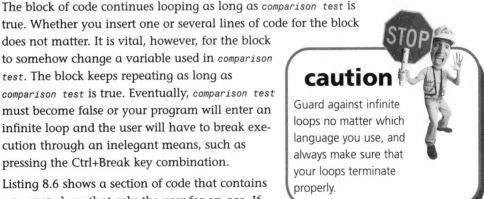

**caution**

Guard against infinite loops no matter which language you use, and always make sure that your loops terminate properly.

Listing 8.6 shows a section of code that contains a `Do While` loop that asks the user for an age. If the user enters an age less than 10 or greater than

99, the program beeps at the error and displays another input box asking for the age. The program continues looping, asking for the age, as long as the user enters an age that's out of range.

**LISTING 8.6**    A Do While Loop

```
Dim strAge As String
Dim intAge As Integer
Dim intPress As Integer

' Get the age in a string variable
strAge = InputBox("How old are you?", "Ask Age")
' Check for the Cancel command button press
If (strAge = "") Then
  End    ' terminates the application immediately
End If

' Cancel was not pressed, so convert Age to integer
' The Val() function converts strings to integers
intAge = Val(strAge)

' Loop if the age is not in the correct range
Do While ((intAge < 10) Or (intAge > 99))
  ' The user's age is out of range if true
  intPress = MsgBox("Your age must be between ",
     "10 and 99", vbExclamation, "Error!")
   strAge = InputBox("How old are you?", "Ask Age")
   ' Check for Cancel button again
  If (strAge = "") Then
    End    ' Terminate application now
  End If
  intAge = Val(strAge)
Loop
```

Figure 8.1 shows the message box error that Listing 8.6 displays if the user enters an age value that's less than 10 or greater than 99. Listing 8.6 does nothing with MsgBox()'s return value stored in intPress. The user simply presses Enter to close the message box, so checking for intPress's value would not help this particular section of code.

> **caution**
>
> You are beginning to see longer sections of code as you learn more commands. Soon you'll feel comfortable with code much longer than Listing 8.6. In the meantime, walk through the code one line at a time, making sure that you understand each statement before you move to the next. Keep in mind that the second half of Listing 8.6 is a loop that executes over and over if the user does not enter a valid age.

**FIGURE 8.1**

The user sees this message as long as the age is out of range.

The code in Listing 8.6 contains some redundancy. For example, two lines contain almost the same `InputBox()` function, and the same check for a Cancel button press appears twice in the program. There are other looping statements that the next section introduces and that you will master as you progress in your programming career. These other kinds of looping statements may be able to help simplify this code by removing some of the redundancy.

Perhaps the most important thing to note about the `Do While` loop in Listing 8.6 is that the body of the loop provides a way to terminate *comparison test*. The code contains an `intAge` variable that the body of the loop reassigns each time the loop's block of code executes. Therefore, assuming that the user enters a different value for the age, the loop will test against a different set of comparison values. The comparison test fails (which means that the age is inside the range), and the program will stop looping. If the loop's body does nothing with the comparison test variable, the loop will continue forever.

> **note**
>
> Listing 8.6 uses the built-in `Val()` function. `Val()` accepts a string argument and converts that string to a number (assuming that the string holds correct digits for a valid number). The `InputBox()` function returns a string, so the value the user enters into the input box must be converted to an integer before it is stored in the `intAge` variable.

## The `Do Until` Loop

Whereas the `Do While` loop continues executing the body of the loop as long as the comparison test is true, the `Do Until` loop executes the body of the loop as long as the comparison is false. A program's logic determines which kind of loop works best in a given situation.

`Do Until` works almost exactly like the `Do While` loop, except that the `Do Until` loop continues executing the body of the loop *until* the comparison test is true. Like `Do While`, `Do Until` is a multiline looping statement that can execute a block of code.

Here is the format of Do Until:

```
Do Until (comparison test)
    Block of one or more Visual Basic statements
Loop
```

Figure 8.2 shows how the Do Until loops.

```
' Shows Do...Until Loop

'

    strAns = InputBox("Again?")

Do Until (strAns = "N")

    strAns = InputBox("Again?")

Loop

" Program continues here
```

Two additional Do loops appear in Visual Basic. Here are their formats:

```
Do
    Block of one or more Visual Basic statements
Loop While conditional test
```

```
Do
    Block of one or more Visual Basic statements
Loop Until conditional test
```

Notice the placement of the While and Until sections. These sections appear at the end of the loop. By testing the condition at the end of the loop, the programmer ensures that the body of the loop always executes at least one time. With the conditional test at the top of the other Do loops, the body of those loops may not execute. Which loop you use depends on whether you want the loop to execute at least one time.

In summary, the following is a brief rundown of why Visual Basic supports four kinds of Do loops. You can see that the location and nature of the conditional test determine the proper loop to use. Almost all programming languages offer loops that work in a similar way.

- **The location of the conditional test**—If the conditional test appears at the top of the loop in the Do statement, the loop's body may never execute. If the conditional test appears at the bottom of the loop in the Loop statement, the body always executes at least once because Visual Basic does not perform the test until the bottom of the loop.

■ **The nature of the conditional test**—Do loops can continue either *while a* condition is true or *until* a condition is true. In the former case, the body of the loop keeps executing as long as the condition is true. In the latter case, the loop keeps executing until the condition is met.

Although there is not ample room here for examples of all the loops available within Visual Basic, you can see that programming languages include rich vocabularies. Many languages, including Visual Basic, contain several other kinds of loops. One nice surprise when learning programming languages is that your future knowledge builds on your current knowledge. Once you master a loop such as the Do While loop, the other kinds of loops are simply variations on the same theme.

## The For Loop

The For loop (sometimes referred to as the For...Next loop) also creates a loop. Unlike the Do loops, however, the For loop repeats a specified number of times. The format of the For loop is daunting at first, but after you master the format, you will have little trouble implementing a For loop when you need to repeat a section of code a specified number of times.

There is not one correct loop to use in all situations. The For statement provides the mechanism for yet another Visual Basic loop that you'll learn. A For loop always begins with the For statement and ends with the Next statement. Here's the format of a For loop:

```
For CounterVar = StartVal To EndVal
  block of one or more Visual Basic statements
Next CounterVar
```

CounterVar must be a variable and not a control or literal. StartVal and EndVal each can be a number, an expression, or a variable. A simple example helps to demonstrate how the For loop works. The loop inside Listing 8.7 computes the total of the numbers from 1 to 10.

**LISTING 8.7**   A For Loop to Total Numbers from 1 to 10

```
intSum = 0
For intNumber = 1 To 10
  intSum = intSum + intNumber
Next intNumber
```

Here, the CounterVar is intNumber, 1 is this loop's StartVal, and 10 is the EndVal.

Listing 8.7 assigns `intNumber` the value 1 at the top of the loop. The first time through the loop, the third line works as follows:

```
intSum = intSum + 1
```

The `Next intNumber` statement returns to the top of the loop (the `For` statement) and adds 1 to `intNumber`. The second time through the loop, the third line becomes this:

```
intSum = intSum + 2
```

The loop continues, adding 1 to `intNumber` each time the loop executes. When `intNumber` becomes 10 (the format's *EndVal*), the loop finishes and the statement following the `Next` statement continues.

As with most statements, you have alternatives to the `For` loop. For example, you can add the numbers 1 through 10 like this:

```
intSum = 1 + 2 + 3 + 4 + 5 + 6 + 7 + 8 + 9
➥+ 10
```

**tip**

Remember, the `For` loop terminates when the *CounterVar* becomes larger than the *EndVal*.

You could also code back-to-back assignment statements like this:

```
intSum = 0
intSum = intSum + 1
intSum = intSum + 2
intSum = intSum + 3
intSum = intSum + 4
intSum = intSum + 5
intSum = intSum + 6
intSum = intSum + 7
intSum = intSum + 8
intSum = intSum + 9
intSum = intSum + 10
```

Neither of these approaches is extremely difficult, but what if you needed to add the first 100 numbers? The previous assignments could become tedious indeed with 100 statements. With the `For` loop it's as easy to add 100 numbers as it is to add 10, as Listing 8.8 demonstrates.

**LISTING 8.8**   A For Loop to Add the Numbers from 1 to 100

```
intSum = 0
For intNumber = 1 To 100
  intSum = intSum + intNumber
Next intNumber
```

# Summary

Whew! You have moved from nonprogrammer to a Visual Basic decision-making and looping programmer in just a few short chapters! Your head may be spinning, and that's okay. The next chapter takes a quick break and has some fun with Visual Basic graphics. Then, Chapter 10, "Advanced Visual Basic Programming," continues your tutorial with a complete walkthrough of an application, from start to finish, using loops and decision statements. With this language background, by the time you finish the next two chapters, you will feel comfortable inside Visual Basic.

- Decision statements such as If and Select Case make your programs smarter. They can determine which code to execute based on data in variables or from controls on the form.

- The Select Case statement is a powerful but relatively simple statement to use when your program must select from multiple options.

- Loops enable your programs to repeat sections of code.

- Although four Do loops exist in Visual Basic, they work similarly and differ only in how they terminate.

- The For loop is useful when you need to execute a loop a fixed number of times.

## IN THIS CHAPTER

- Using Shapes
- An Aside About Controls
- The Line Control
- Mastering the Shape Control
- A Sample Shape Application
- The Picture Box Control

# 9

# HAVING FUN WITH VISUAL BASIC

Visual Basic is *visual*, and much of its visual effect is due to its graphics capabilities. You will learn in this chapter how to draw shapes on a form. In addition, you can place graphic images from files, such as the images you locate on the Internet, on forms that serve as your application's background images. Graphics generate user interest and help keep the user's attention focused on your program.

The highlights of this chapter include the following:

- Graphics spruce up your application and get the user's attention.

- The Shape control is one of the most versatile controls in Visual Basic.

- Use the Shape control to place various shapes on your form, with several fill patterns to choose from.

- The Picture Box control is more flexible than the Image control when you want to display graphics on your form.
- The LoadPicture() function stores the actual image in the Picture Box control.

# Using Shapes

You will need to draw circles, squares, and other shapes on your form because a picture is not always the most effective graphic. For example, you can place an oval around your company name to highlight the name at the top of your form.

The Shape control works to draw all kinds of shapes such as boxes and other figures on your form. By placing controls and setting appropriate properties, you'll be adding flair to your application. The properties of each control that you place on the form determine exactly what kind of image the control becomes.

Here are the primary graphics images that you can draw with the Shape control:

- Rectangles
- Squares
- Ovals
- Circles
- Rounded rectangles
- Rounded squares

Figure 9.1 shows a Visual Basic form with a sampling of these images. By combining these fundamental geometric images and setting appropriate color and size properties, you can draw virtually anything you need on the form.

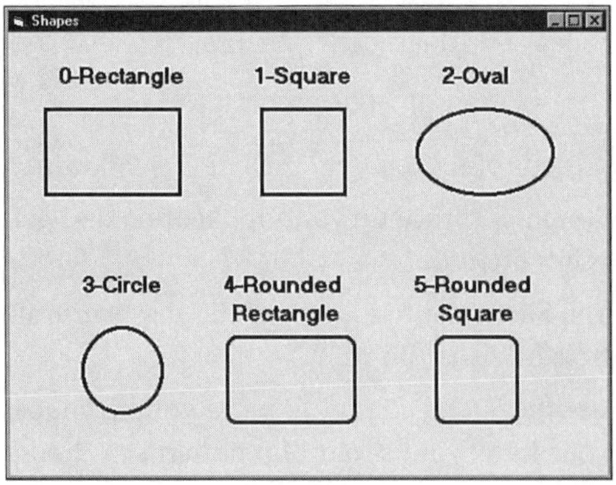

**FIGURE 9.1**

These are the images you can draw.

# An Aside About Controls

Now that you are somewhat familiar with Visual Basic, some of its controls, and property values for those controls, you should begin approaching Visual Basic differently. As you learn how to use a new control in your applications, study the properties that apply to that control. Visual Basic's online help lists all the details about any control you select. When you click on a control and press **F1**, the online help provides you with a list of properties, events, and methods related to that control.

By studying the various properties that a control supports, you learn about that control's characteristics. For example, in the next section, you learn about the Line control. The Line control's `BorderWidth` property determines the thickness of the line you draw. Therefore, you know a characteristic of the Line control just from the existence of the `BorderWidth` property—that you can control the thickness of any line you draw on your form.

# The Line Control

You use the Line control to draw lines of various widths, lengths, and patterns. The Shape control handles the drawing of all other fundamental shapes.

The Line control supports properties that specify the width and length of lines that you draw. In addition, you can change the pattern of each line that you draw. Table 9.1 lists several of the Line control's property values. Table 19.2 contains the values that you can specify for the `BorderStyle` property. The `BorderStyle` property determines the pattern that Visual Basic uses to draw the line. By specifying various `BorderStyle` values, you can vary the line pattern. If you assign a `BorderStyle` property at runtime, you can either specify a number that represents `BorderStyle` or use one of Visual Basic's named literals.

**TABLE 9.1**  The Line Control's Fundamental Properties

| Property | Description |
| --- | --- |
| BorderColor | Sets the line color. |
| BorderStyle | Contains one of seven values that specifies the pattern of your line. See Table 9.2 for available `BorderStyle` values. The default value is 1-Solid. `BorderStyle` has no effect on lines with `BorderWidth` greater than 1 twip. |
| BorderWidth | Specifies the size, in twips, that your line takes. |
| DrawMode | An advanced style that determines how the bit patterns of the line interact with the surrounding form's bit appearance. The default value, 13-Copy Pen, works well for virtually all Visual Basic applications. |

**TABLE 9.1**    (continued)

| Property | Description |
|----------|-------------|
| Visible | Holds True or False, indicating whether the user can see the Line control. You might want to set the Visible property in code so that the line appears as a highlighting tool. |
| X1 | Contains the number of twips from the left of the Form window to the start of the line. |
| X2 | Contains the number of twips from the left of the Form window to the end of the line. |
| Y1 | Contains the number of twips from the top of the Form window to the left starting point of the line. |
| X2 | Contains the number of twips from the top of the Form window to the lower ending point of the line. |

**TABLE 9.2**    The Line Control's BorderStyle Values

| Property | Named Literal | Description |
|----------|---------------|-------------|
| 0-Transparent | vbTransparent | Background comes through the line. |
| 1-Solid | vbBSSolid | The line is solid. |
| 2-Dash | vbBSDash | The line is dashed. |
| 3-Dot | vbBSDot | The line is dotted. |
| 4-Dash-Dot | vbBSDashDot | The line is composed of continuing dash-dot-dash-dot. |
| 5-Dash-Dot-Dot | vbBSDashDotDot | The line is composed of a series of one dash followed by two dots. |
| 6-Inside Solid | vbBSInsideSolid | Same as 1-Solid for lines. |

Figure 9.2 shows how various BorderStyle settings affect the lines you draw. BorderStyle determines how a series of dashes and dots composes the line's pattern. (Is this Morse Code we're speaking here?)

To draw a line, double-click the **Line** control on the toolbox. In the center of the form, a line appears with a handle on each end. To move the line to a different location, drag the center of the line with the mouse. To lengthen or shorten the line, drag either handle on the line. You can raise and lower either end of the line by dragging either end's handle with the mouse.

**FIGURE 9.2**

BorderStyle determines the line's pattern.

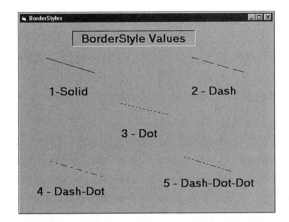

After you position the line with the mouse in the approximate location at which you need the line to appear, you can fine-tune the line's size and location by setting the various property values. If you're a patient programmer, you can even animate lines by changing the X1, X2, Y1, and Y2 property settings repeatedly through code.

Figure 9.3 shows why the drawing tools are useful. You never know what kind of form you must present to a user in the future. The lines and other shapes that you learn about in this chapter enable you to create more useful forms.

**FIGURE 9.3**

Accent your forms with simple graphics.

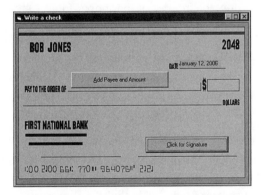

# Mastering the Shape Control

The Shape control gives you the capability to draw six different kinds of figures on the form. The various shading and color properties help you distinguish one shape from another. Table 9.3 lists the basic properties you'll use for the Shape control, the most important of which is the Shape property. The Shape property selects a particular shape from one of the six fundamental shapes.

**TABLE 9.3** The Shape Control's Fundamental Properties

| Property | Description |
|---|---|
| BackColor | Specifies a Windows color value that determines the background color of the shape. |
| BackStyle | Contains either 0-Transparent (the default) or 1-Opaque, which determines whether the background of the form appears through the shape or if the shape hides whatever it covers. |
| BorderColor | Specifies a color value that determines the color of the shape's bordering edges. |
| BorderStyle | Contains one of seven values that specifies the pattern of the shape's border. The Line control's BorderStyle values (refer to Table 9.2) provide the shape's BorderStyle possible values, also. The default value is 1-Solid. BorderStyle has no effect on shapes with a BorderWidth of more than 1 twip. |
| BorderWidth | Specifies the size, in twips, that the shape's outline takes. |
| DrawMode | An advanced style that determines how the bit patterns of the shape interact with the surrounding form's bit appearance. The default value, 13-Copy Pen, works well for virtually all Visual Basic applications. |
| FillColor | Specifies a color value that determines the color of the shape's interior lines. |
| FillStyle | Contains one of eight values that specifies the pattern of lines with which Visual Basic paints the interior of the shape. Table 9.4 contains the possible values for the shape's FillStyle. The default FillStyle value is 0-Solid. |
| Height | Specifies the number of twips high that the shape is (from the highest point to the lowest point in the shape). |
| Left | Specifies the number of twips from the form's left edge to the shape's far-left edge. |
| Shape | Contains one of six values that specifies the type of shape that the Shape control takes on. Table 9.5 lists the possible values for the shape's Shape property. The default Shape property is 0-Rectangle. |
| Top | Specifies the number of twips from the form's top edge to the shape's highest edge. |
| Width | Specifies the number of twips wide that the shape consumes (at the widest axis). |

Figure 9.4 shows a form with the various fill patterns that a shape can contain. Table 9.4 lists the possible values for the Shape control's FillStyle property.

**FIGURE 9.4**

The FillStyle property determines the shape's interior design.

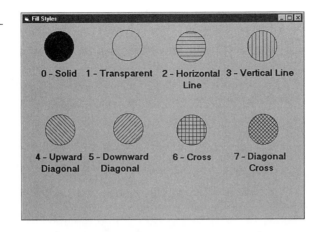

**TABLE 9.4**   The Shape Control's FillStyle Properties

| Property | Named Literal | Description |
|---|---|---|
| 0-Solid | vbFSSolid | Solid color fill with no pattern. |
| 1-Transparent | vbFSTransparent | The shape appears as an outline only. |
| 2-Horizontal Line | vbHorizontalLine | Horizontal lines fill the shape. |
| 3-Vertical Line | vbVerticalLine | Vertical lines fill the shape. |
| 4-Upward Diagonal | vbUpwardDiagonal | Upward diagonal lines fill the shape. |
| 5-Downward Diagonal | vbDownwardDiagonal | Downward diagonal lines fill the shape. |
| 6-Cross | vbCross | Crosshairs fill the shape. |
| 7-Diagonal Cross | vbDiagonalCross | Diagonal crosshairs fill the shape. |

Finally, Table 9.5 contains the possible values for the Shape control's Shape property. (Figure 9.1 showed the various shapes the Shape control can take.) Therefore, when you want to place a square on a form, you'll place the Shape control on the form and set the Shape property to 1-Square.

**TABLE 9.5**   The Shape Control's Shape Values

| Value | Description |
|---|---|
| 0-Rectangle | A rectangle |
| 1-Square | A square |
| 2-Oval | An oval |
| 3-Circle | A circle |
| 4-Rounded Rectangle | A rectangle with rounded corners |
| 5-Rounded Square | A square with rounded corners |

# A Sample Shape Application

By creating a simple application that changes a Shape control's properties, you'll master the Shape control quickly and you'll also learn something about the List control. To give you an idea where you're headed, Figure 9.5 shows the result of the application you'll create. By selecting from one of the two list boxes in the center of the form, you'll change the shape and pattern shown at the top of the form. The shape changes as soon as you select a new value from either list box.

**note**

The Visual Basic language contains commands with which you can draw graphics on the screen, but you don't have to dive into those programming specifics to place shapes, thanks to the powerful Shape controls you are learning here.

**FIGURE 9.5**

Select a shape and pattern from the list boxes.

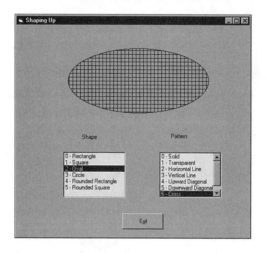

Follow these steps to create the application:

1. Open a new form.

2. Place controls from Table 9.6 on the form. You do not need to add the form; it appears automatically when you create a new application. Change the form properties listed at the beginning of Table 9.6. For the remaining properties, you'll need to add each control. Therefore, after you set the form properties, you'll add a shape to the form and set its properties. Then, add two labels, two list boxes, and a command button the same way.

3. The application requires code. You will need to initialize the list boxes so they have values to display as soon as the user runs the application and the form loads. An event procedure exists whose sole purpose is to do such housekeeping chores as soon as the program runs. The event is the form loading event. Select **View**, **Code** to display the code window and move any windows that may still overlap the code window out of the way.

4. At the top of the code window are two drop-down lists. The list on the left is a list of all objects in your application such as the form, the two list boxes, and so on. The right list box contains a list of all possible events for each of those objects. You need to add code only to the events you want your application to respond to. Select **Form** from the left drop-down list box at the top of the code window. Notice that Visual Basic automatically selected the Load event in the right drop-down list box and wrote the beginning and ending lines of code. Type the rest of the procedure with the code shown in Listing 9.1. The code is a list of special internal operations called *methods* (indicated by the period between the list box name and the method name, such as AddItem). Methods do little more than assign each item in each list box a value that will appear on the screen. An assignment operator, =, would not work because list boxes contain multiple areas of storage. In other words, you must create the list; the AddItem method does just that.

## LISTING 9.1   Initializing List Boxes

```
Private Sub Form_Load()
    ' Initialize the shape drop-down list box
    lstShape.AddItem "0 - Rectangle"
    lstShape.AddItem "1 - Square"
    lstShape.AddItem "2 - Oval"
    lstShape.AddItem "3 - Circle"
    lstShape.AddItem "4 - Rounded Rectangle"
    lstShape.AddItem "5 - Rounded Square"
    ' Initialize the FillStyle pattern drop-down list box
    lstPattern.AddItem "0 - Solid"
    lstPattern.AddItem "1 - Transparent"
    lstPattern.AddItem "2 - Horizontal Line"
    lstPattern.AddItem "3 - Vertical Line"
    lstPattern.AddItem "4 - Upward Diagonal"
    lstPattern.AddItem "5 - Downward Diagonal"
    lstPattern.AddItem "6 - Cross"
    lstPattern.AddItem "7 - Diagonal Cross"

    ' Set the first value of each list as default
    lstShape.ListIndex = 0
    lstPattern.ListIndex = 0
End Sub
```

5. Select the `lstPattern` list box object from the top-left drop-down code window list box. Visual Basic guesses correctly that you want to code the `Click` event procedure, as you can see from the right drop-down list box. Visual Basic always selects the most common event for each control that you select. Enter the code shown in Listing 9.2 for the first list box.

**LISTING 9.2   Changing the Pattern**

```
Private Sub lstPattern_Click()
 ' Change the pattern according to the selection
 shpSample.FillStyle = lstPattern.ListIndex
End Sub
```

6. Select the `lstShape` list box object from the top-left drop-down code window list box. Once again, Visual Basic guesses correctly that you want to code the `Click` event procedure, as you can see from the right drop-down list box on the code window. Enter the code shown in Listing 9.3 for the second list box.

**LISTING 9.3   Changing a Form's Shape**

```
Private Sub lstShape_Click()
 ' Change the shape according to the selection
  shpSample.Shape = lstShape.ListIndex
End Sub
```

7. Select the command button named `cmdExit` from the code window's left drop-down list box to begin coding the command button's `Click` event procedure contained in Listing 9.4. The `End` statement tells Visual Basic to end the program's execution as soon as the user clicks the command button.

**LISTING 9.4** Terminating a Program

```
Private Sub cmdExit_Click()
  End
End Sub
```

8. Press **F5** for the moment of truth! If you typed all the code correctly, and if you entered all the controls and their properties from Table 9.6, your application will run. Simply click on either list toward the bottom of the application to see a different shape and pattern in the center of the window. The true purpose of the program is to help you remember the information you learned earlier in this chapter about the Shape control. This program enables you to step through each shape and fill pattern possible. When you're ready to quit, click the **Exit** command button.

If your application doesn't seem to work properly, or if you get an error message, you probably typed something incorrectly in the code or failed to fill in a property for every control on the form (from Table 9.6). You will have to return to the code window, and if it checks out, you will have to click each property and check its property window values to make sure you've entered the values correctly.

9. You can save the project if you want to return to it later.

**TABLE 9.6** Properties and Values on the Shape Control Form

| Control | Description |
| --- | --- |
| Form Name | frmShape |
| Form Caption | Shaping Up |
| Form Height | 7005 |
| Form Left | 105 |
| Form Top | 105 |
| Form Width | 7965 |
| Shape Name | shpSample |
| Shape Height | 2025 |
| Shape Left | 1710 |
| Shape Top | 720 |
| Shape Width | 4560 |
| Label #1 Name | lblShape |
| Label #1 Caption | Shape |

**TABLE 9.6** (continued)

| Control | Description |
| --- | --- |
| Label #1 Height | 420 |
| Label #1 Left | 2160 |
| Label #1 Top | 3390 |
| Label #1 Width | 1215 |
| Label #2 Name | lblPattern |
| Label #2 Caption | Pattern |
| Label #2 Height | 420 |
| Label #2 Left | 5040 |
| Label #2 Top | 3360 |
| Label #2 Width | 1215 |
| List box #1 Name | lstShape |
| List box #1 Height | 1425 |
| List box #1 Left | 1560 |
| List box #1 Top | 3960 |
| List box #1 Width | 2010 |
| List box #2 Name | lstPattern |
| List box #2 Height | 1425 |
| List box #2 Left | 4680 |
| List box #2 Top | 3960 |
| List box #2 Width | 2010 |
| Command button Name | cmdExit |
| Command button Caption | E&xit |
| Command button Height | 495 |
| Command button Left | 3480 |
| Command button Top | 5880 |
| Command button Width | 1335 |

# The Picture Box Control

The Picture Box control and the Image control are similar: They both enable you to place graphic images such as scanned images on your form. The Image control is not quite as flexible as the Picture Box control because the Image control supports fewer file types and automatically resizes to fit around the size of your image file instead of letting you specify the size. In the past, the Image control was used a lot simply because it was more efficient than the Picture box control but with the speed of today's computers, the flexibility of the Picture box control outweighs its slightly less efficiency. The Picture Box control supports more properties and methods than the Image control does.

The key to understanding the Picture Box control is understanding the `LoadPicture()` function, which lets you set Picture Box control images at runtime.

## Picture Box Control Setup

When you need to display a graphic image, you'll select the Picture Box control or the Image control. Both support the same fundamental set of properties, methods, and events, but you'll find that the Picture Box control offers a better choice of property options. Table 9.7 lists the most important Picture Box control properties.

**TABLE 9.7**   Important Picture Box Properties

| Property | Description |
| --- | --- |
| Align | Determines the relative location of the picture on the form. |
| AutoSize | Specifies whether the control is to expand or contract in size to display an image or display only a portion of the image. |
| BorderStyle | Draws an optional border around the picture. |
| FontTransparent | Determines whether background text will show through the image. |
| Picture | Contains the pathname and filename of the graphic image. |

You can specify at design time the initial image to be displayed in the Picture Box control by entering the pathname and filename in the control's `Picture` property. Use the built-in `LoadPicture()` function when you want to display an image or change an image during runtime. Here is the syntax for using `LoadPicture()`:

`picPictureCtl.Picture = LoadPicture(strExpression)`

You can't directly assign the pathname and filename of the picture to the `Picture` property at runtime. You must enclose the pathname and filename inside the `LoadPicture()` function's argument. The following assignment statement replaces the Picture Box control's picture with a new image loaded from the root directory:

`Picture1.Picture = LoadPicture("c:\planes.bmp")`

## Picture Box File Types

Table 9.8 lists the graphic file types you can load with the Picture Box control.

**TABLE 9.8** File Types Displayed by the Picture Box Control

| Type | Extension |
| --- | --- |
| Bitmap | .BMP |
| Graphic Image File | .GIF |
| Icon | .ICO |
| JPEG | .JPG |
| Metafile | .WMF, .EMF |

> **note**
>
> The Picture Box control uses the AutoSize property to stretch the underlying control's size to the image being loaded. AutoSize allows this automatic resizing during runtime as you load different pictures into the same image location.

Suppose you had an image named Map.wmf on your disk that you wanted to display on the Form window when the user clicks a command button. You would create a Click event procedure for the command button that includes the LoadPicture() function. Such a command button event procedure might look something like the one in Listing 9.5; after running, it would display the Form window shown in Figure 9.6.

**LISTING 9.5** Using the LoadPicture() Function to Display Graphic Images

```
Private Sub Command1_Click()
  ' Loads the map into the Picture Box control
  '  when the user clicks the command button
  picPicture.Picture = LoadPicture("c:\Data\Map.wmf")
End Sub
```

**FIGURE 9.6**

The image of the map appears only after the user clicks the command button.

# Summary

A picture is worth a thousand words, and your Visual Basic application won't be complete with lines, shapes, and images. Don't overload the graphics and make your form look too busy. Instead, use graphics to accent your application's goals. This chapter showed you the fundamentals of placing graphics on your form. In the next chapter, you will walk through the creation of a complete Visual Basic application. The goal of the next chapter is to tie together some loose ends and help you gain a better overall picture of the way Visual Basic works and how you program in Visual Basic.

- Use the Shape control to draw various shapes on the form.
- Properties determine the kind of shape you place and its characteristics, such as the pattern used to fill in the center of the shape.
- Your application must initialize list boxes if the user is to see any data in them.
- The AddItem method initializes List Box controls on your form.
- Use the Picture Box control to display graphic images on your form.

## IN THIS CHAPTER

- Application: Interest Calculation
- Adding the Form's Labels and Text Boxes
- Adding Code

**10**

# ADVANCED VISUAL BASIC PROGRAMMING

The challenge with Visual Basic is not the language but the entire environment. To help complete your quick introduction in Visual Basic, this chapter walks you step by step through the creation of a complete working application. Finally, you will see the "big picture," and you will be able to put the pieces of the previous chapters together to begin creating your own Visual Basic programs as quickly as possible.

The highlights of this chapter include the following:

- You'll learn to arrange windows such as the Project window so that window placement optimizes your program-writing experience.
- Use the StartUp property to determine how the user's application window will appear when the application first begins.
- Hotkeys give your users more ways to access controls on the form.

- Focus indicates which control or window is active.
- Add error-checking to your code to guide users through proper data entry routines.
- Visual Basic applications can contain modules that are not tied to the Form window's controls.

# Application: Interest Calculation

This chapter creates an application that displays a simple form, shown in Figure 10.1. Behind the simple form is quite a lot of code that calculates an interest rate based on the user's entered values.

**FIGURE 10.1**

You will create an interest rate calculator that computes a future investment value.

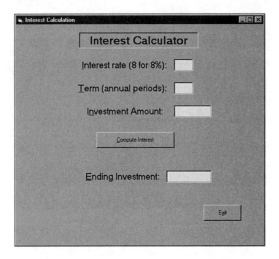

## Getting Ready to Write

The most important part of a program's design, the output definition, appears in Figure 10.1. Ordinarily, you won't have a figure to begin with when someone asks you to write a program for them. You will first have to interview that user and ask what kinds of information the program is to track and what are the goals of the program.

Suppose you didn't have Figure 10.1 and a user requested that you write a simple program to calculate interest on an investment. First, you would need to know exactly what the user meant by "calculate interest." Several methods exist to calculate interest, and many different kinds of investments are possible. For example, is the investment a lump-sum investment that grows over time or does the user plan to make fixed deposits over time (called a *cash flow interest calculation*)? Once you get an overview of the program's requirements, you then must gather all information the user is to enter and determine what the program is to output. With the help of Visual Basic's form-design tools, you might even sit in front of a computer with the user and lay out some text and text boxes to act as a prototype, a model of the finished application.

Once you define the way the output is to look, you are ready for the program internals. What exact calculations are required to produce the final result? Your user will need to supply you with this kind of information. Leave all the details of Visual Basic for later because your user doesn't care about event procedures or control properties. The user just wants a program that does what is expected. Once you have the screen and the necessary intermediate calculations defined, you then go back to your computer and develop the application.

## Creating the Application

Follow these steps to create the interest rate calculation application's form:

1. Start Visual Basic and select **New Project** from the **File** menu if the New Project window does not automatically appear.

2. Select **Standard EXE** from the New Project window. The form appears in the center of your window.

3. Change the form's Name property to frmInterest. Change the form's Caption property to Interest Calculation. Change the form's Width property to 3855 and the Height property to 7275.

4. Change the form's StartUpPosition property to 2-CenterScreen. You haven't seen the StartUpPosition property yet; it determines the location of the Form window when the user runs the program. Let Visual Basic center the form on your user's screen because you don't know the exact measurements of the screen a particular user will use. If you set StartUpPosition to 2-CenterScreen, Visual Basic always places the form in the middle of the screen no matter what the user's screen size and resolution are. (Use the WindowState property to open the Form window in its maximized state if you want a full-screen Form window when the application begins.)

**tip**

Click the **Window Maximize** button on the **Project** window. The **Project** window is the white window that appears behind the Form window when you create a new project. By maximizing the **Project** window, you will make your Visual Basic environment somewhat less busy, and you'll be able to focus more easily on the Form window that acts as your application's background.

5. You now need to add labels and text boxes. The form's title label is easy to generate. Place a label on the form and set the following properties:

Name: lblTitle

Alignment: 2-Center

BorderStyle: 1-Fixed Single

Caption: Interest Calculator

Font: Bold 18 (sets the Bold style and uses 18 for the default font's size)

Height: 495

Left: 2090

Top: 240

Width: 3855

6. You must now set up a series of three label/text box pairs. Notice that the labels in Figure 10.1 all have hotkeys (accessible by pressing the **Alt** key in conjunction with the hotkey [the underlined key] in each label). Figure 10.2 points out the hotkeys on the Form window.

> **note**
>
> Visual Basic automatically adds the first form to your project. Only in rare instances would you not want a form in a Windows application. The form comprises the program's primary window. Some Windows programs don't use a Form window because they work in the background and do not require user interaction through the use of controls. More often than not, a Windows application uses multiple windows. You can always add new forms to your applications by right-clicking inside the **Project** window, selecting **Add**, **Form**, and setting up the properties of your new form and its controls.

**FIGURE 10.2**

By adding hotkeys to your forms, you give users quick access to each label.

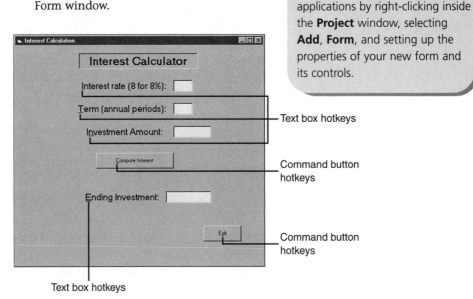

## Hotkeys and Target Controls

In Figure 10.2, you apply the hotkeys to the text labels such as the `Investment Amount` label. The label is text that appears on the form when the user runs the application. The Label control differs from a Text Box control in that the user does not interact specifically with a label on the form. Instead, the label simply identifies instructions, titles, and descriptions of other controls such as text boxes.

The interest rate calculation Form window's text boxes all have labels that describe what the user is to enter in each text box. In the interest rate calculation, a user might fill out the form and then, before clicking the Compute Interest button, realize that he entered an incorrect value in one of the text boxes. To edit the value, he can click that text box and edit the value. By adding a hotkey to that text box's description, however, you offer yet another way for the user to access the text box. From the keyboard, he can press Alt+T to edit the contents of the text box next to the `Term` label.

Visual Basic doesn't automatically connect a text box to a label's hotkey, though, even if that text box's purpose is to label the text box. Even if you place the label to the left of a text box, that does not mean that the label's hotkey will take the user's text cursor (often called the *caret*) to the text box. To ensure that a hotkey moves the user to another specific control such as a text box, you must master focus.

## A Detour: Understanding Focus at Runtime

Focus is a runtime concept in Windows. At runtime, only one window, form, or control can have the focus. The window or form currently in focus is the form whose title bar is highlighted (typically colored blue). The control with the focus has an outlined border or caption.

Focus is important because it determines what the next keystroke or Enter keypress will activate. With a windowed environment, the user interacts with objects such as command buttons and text boxes and not just with text from the keyboard. Focus enables the user to see which object on the screen will receive the next action.

Figure 10.3 shows a Visual Basic session with several windows, including two windows from the executing program. The center window has the focus; you know this because the title bar (at the top of the window) is highlighted. Therefore, the center window is receiving keystrokes if and when the user presses a key.

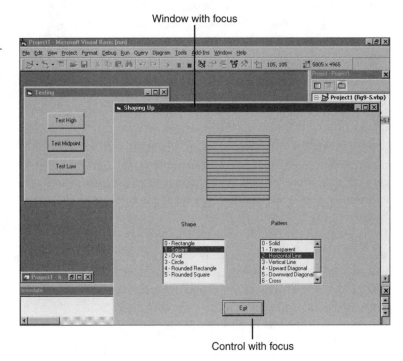

Window with focus

**FIGURE 10.3**

Learn to spot the window and control with the focus.

Control with focus

Only one control on the active window can have the focus. In Figure 10.3, the check box labeled AutoSize has it. Even though there are other windows on the screen, if the user presses Enter, the check box receives the Enter keystroke. A check box is either checked or unchecked, meaning that the control determines one of two states. If the user presses Enter, the AutoSize check box will turn to unchecked.

Different controls display the focus in different ways. Only one of the seven command buttons in Figure 10.4 can have the focus at any one time. Can you spot the command button that has the focus? The extra dotted outline lets you know that the Images command button has the focus and will receive an Enter keypress if the user presses Enter.

**FIGURE 10.4**

One of these
seven command
buttons has the
focus.

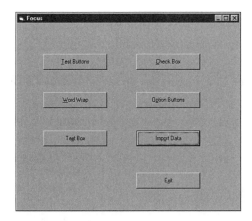

Of course, the user can
always click the **AutoSize**
check box with the mouse to
uncheck the control. In addition,
the user can click any control in
any window on the screen; that
window would get the focus, and
that control would receive the
click. Focus refers to the target
window and control that will
receive the next keystroke.

## Tab Order

The user can move the focus from control to control by pressing **Tab** (or **Shift+Tab** to move the
focus in a reverse direction). If you place eight controls on an application's form, what focus order
will result? In other words, as the user presses Tab,
will the controls get the focus from left to right or
from top to bottom?

Visual Basic sets the default focus order to be the order in which you place controls
on the form. Therefore, if you place the top control first and the bottom control second and then insert a third control in the middle of those two, the focus order will
not move down the form in the order the user expects.

You don't always place controls on a form in the same order in which you want to
set the focus. Therefore, controls that can receive the focus support the TabIndex property. The first control in the focus order has a TabIndex property of 0, the second control in the focus order has a TabIndex property of 1, and so on. If you place controls
on the form and later want to modify the focus order, you need to change the
TabIndex property values.

That brings you back around to the application you began developing earlier in this
chapter. You now have the background to understand that the labels have hotkeys
so that the user can quickly jump to any text box next to those labels.

# Adding the Form's Labels and Text Boxes

You now can add the labels and the text boxes to the interest rate calculation application. In this section, you will learn a shortcut method for adding multiple occurrences of the same control to the same form.

## Putting on the First Label and Text Box Set

Follow these steps to add the first set of label and text box controls:

1. Add the Interest Rate label as follows:

   Name: lblRate

   Alignment: 1-RightJustify

   Caption: &Interest rate (8 for 8%):

   Font: Regular 14

   Height: 375

   Left: 2040

   Top: 1080

   Width: 2895

2. Set up the Interest Rate text box as follows:

   Name: txtRate

   Alignment: 0-LeftJustify

   Font: 10

   Height: 375

   Left: 5160

   ToolTipText: Actual rate investment grows

   Top: 1080

   Width: 615

3. Blank out the text box's Text property so that nothing appears in the text box at startup (do this by deleting the default value that appears in the Text property).

> **caution**
>
> Not all controls can accept the focus. For example, a label cannot receive keystrokes, so a label never gets the focus. The Label control does include the TabIndex property, however. By setting the label's TabIndex value to one less than a text box to the right of the label, you can add a hotkey to the label's Caption property, and the user then has a hotkey to the text box. Text boxes don't support hotkey keystrokes by themselves, so by assigning the text box's label a hotkey and setting the next Tab in the order to be the text box, the focus jumps to the text box when the user presses the text box label's hotkey.

## Completing the Controls and Learning About Control Arrays

Notice that the Interest Calculator screen's Term and Investment Amount labels and text boxes look similar to the Interest Rate label and text box you just placed on the form; the font information and Height properties are all the same. Therefore, although you could enter the remaining labels and text boxes individually, you can utilize the Windows Clipboard to make the job go faster.

Highlight both the existing Interest Rate label and text box. Select the two by pressing the **Ctrl** key while you click each control. When you select both controls, sizing handles appear around them, as Figure 10.5 shows.

**FIGURE 10.5**

Sizing handles show that two controls are now selected.

Selected controls —

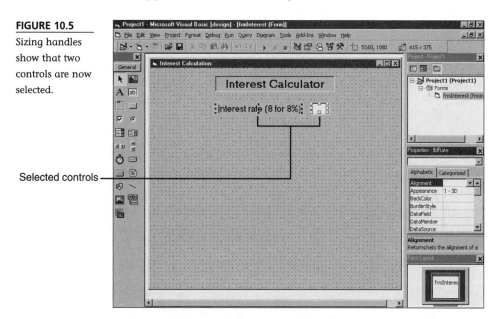

To add the rest of the controls, follow these steps:

1. Now that you've selected the two controls, select **Edit**, **Copy** to copy the selected controls to the Windows Clipboard. (The Windows Clipboard holds much more than just text, as you can see.)

2. Select **Edit**, **Paste** to paste those two items right back onto the form. Visual Basic displays a warning box that says You already have a control named 'lblRate'. Do you want to create a control array?

3. Answer **No** to the dialog box and answer **No** again when Visual Basic asks you about creating a control array for the text box.

A *control array* is a group of more than one control of the same type. The group has one name, and you distinguish between the controls by an index number. For this particular example, you should not create a control array because the form does not have enough controls to justify the extra code explanations needed to work with control arrays.

### ARRAYS: BOTH DATA AND CONTROLS

An *array* is a common element found in virtually all programming languages. Arrays help you step through large groups of data efficiently. In Visual Basic, control arrays are easy to master because of the visual nature of Visual Basic. The concept of control arrays extends to arrays of any kind of data.

Suppose you need to add a list of 100 sales totals for your region in a program. Your program could declare 100 different variables, perhaps named `sngSales1`, `sngSales2`, `sngSales3`, and so on. To add them would take a rather large assignment statement such as this:

```
SngTotal = sngSales1 + sngSales2 + sngSales3 + ...
```

Instead of 100, suppose your region had 1,000 or 10,000 sales values you needed to add. The number of different variables and the typing needed to add them would be tedious indeed.

Instead of naming each variable separately, you could create an array of single-precision variables. Each would have the same name, but you'd refer to each of them by an index such as `sngSales(1)` and `sngSales(89)`. With the index, a simple `For` loop would add them like this:

```
sngTotal = 0    ' Initialize the total
For i = 1 to 100
   sngTotal = sngTotal + sngSales(i)
Next i
```

If you then had 10,000 values to add, you would need only to change the 100 to 10,000 and the same code works!

Although control arrays are generally much simpler to work with than individually named controls, you need to master more of the Visual Basic language to see the full advantages of control arrays. Nevertheless, you now have a basic understanding of what control arrays are. If you pursue Visual Basic or any other language, you will be better prepared to tackle arrays of all kinds.

Continue adding controls as follows:

1. Move the pasted label and text box to their correct positions under the first pair. Click anywhere on the form's background to deselect the two controls. Click on the Label control and set these properties for the label:

   ```
   Name: lblTerm
   ```

   ```
   Caption: &Term (annual periods):
   ```

   ```
   Left: 2040
   ```

   ```
   Top: 1800
   ```

   ```
   Width: 2895
   ```

The Height and Font properties are already correct because you borrowed these properties from the control you copied from. Make sure the alignment is set to Right Alignment.

2. Set these properties for the text box:

   Name: txtTerm

   Left: 5160

   ToolTipText: Number of periods

   Top: 1800

   Width: 615

   As you can see, you don't have to set as many properties when you paste from existing controls.

3. Select the first label and text box and copy them to the Clipboard once again so you can paste them under the existing controls on the form. Refuse the control array prompts once again and set the following properties for the new label:

   Name: lblInvest

   Caption: I&nvestment Amount:

   Left: 1920

   Top: 2520

   Width: 2895

4. Set the text box's properties to the following:

   Name: txtInvest

   Left: 5160

   ToolTipText: Money you invested

   Top: 2520

   Width: 1215

   Your screen should look similar to Figure 10.6.

5. You now can quickly finish the form's controls. Select a label and text box once again and paste them below the existing controls. Set the label's properties to these values:

   Name: lblEnding

   Caption: &Ending Investment:

   Left: 1800

   Top: 4560

   Width: 2895

**FIGURE 10.6**

The form shapes up nicely.

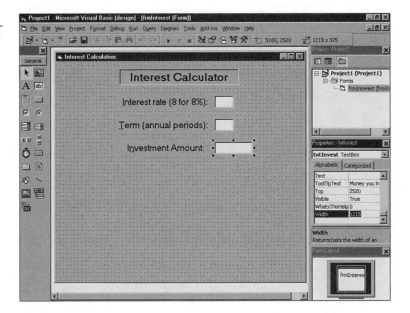

6. Set the text box's properties to these values:

   Name: `txtEnding`

   Left: `4920`

   Locked: `True`

   TabStop: `False` (so the user cannot send the focus to this text box; it's an output-only text box)

   ToolTipText: `Compounded Investment`

   Top: `4560`

   Width: `1455`

   The new property you just set is the `Locked` property. When you lock a control, Visual Basic allows no user editing of the control. Therefore, the code you'll add to the form can modify the text box's `Text` property, but the user cannot. The final text box will be a holding place for the calculated compound investment amount, so the user should not be allowed to edit the control even though it's a Text Box control.

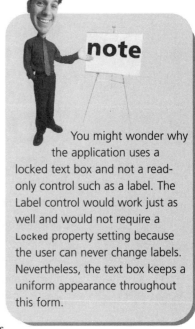

You might wonder why the application uses a locked text box and not a read-only control such as a label. The Label control would work just as well and would not require a `Locked` property setting because the user can never change labels. Nevertheless, the text box keeps a uniform appearance throughout this form.

7. Add a command button with these property values:

```
Name: cmdCompute

Caption: &Compute Interest

Height: 495

Left: 2640

ToolTipText: Click to compute final investment

Top: 3360

Width: 2535
```

8. Add a final command button named cmdExit to the lower-right corner of the form with E&xit for the Caption property.

# Adding Code

Often, programmers run their applications as they build them despite the fact that no code yet exists to make the application do real work. You should be able to run your application now (by pressing **F5**, the Visual Basic shortcut key for compiling and running the application) to make sure that the labels and text boxes all look correct. Check out the ToolTip text to ensure you've entered the text properly. Click the application window's **Close** button to stop the program so that you can add the final code.

The code is going to use loops to calculate interest. When the user clicks the middle command button, the calculation should take place, assuming the user has filled in all the necessary text boxes for the calculation. Therefore, you'll need an event procedure that executes when the user clicks the cmdCompute command button. The Click event procedure is named cmdCompute_Click().

## The Calculation Code

To open the code window for the command button and begin coding the Click event code (the code that executes if the user clicks the command button), double-click the Form window's command button labeled Compute Interest to open the cmdCompute_Click() event procedure. (Fortunately in this case, Visual Basic defaults to the Click event procedure when you double-click a command button on the Form window. Otherwise, you would have to select the Click event from the code window's drop-down list box.)

Add the code in Listing 10.1 to the event procedure. Visual Basic already wrote the first and final lines for you.

**LISTING 10.1** The Command Button Procedure

```
Private Sub cmdCompute_Click()
' Use a For loop to calculate a final total
' investment using compound interest.
'
' intNum is a loop control variable
' sngIRate is the annual interest rate
' intTerm is the Number of years in the investment
' curInitInv is the investor's initial investment
' sngInterest is the total interest paid
  Dim sngIRate As Single, sngInterest As Single
  Dim intTerm As Integer, intNum As Integer
  Dim curInitInv As Currency

  ' Error-checking
  If ErrorCheck() = 1 Then
    Exit Sub
  End If

  sngIRate = txtRate.Text / 100
  intTerm = txtTerm.Text

  curInitInv = txtInvest.Text
  sngInterest = 1    ' Begin at one for first compound

  ' Use loop to calculate total compound amount
  For intNum = 1 To intTerm
     sngInterest = sngInterest * (1 + sngIRate)
  Next intNum

  ' Now we have total interest,
  ' calculate the total investment
  ' at the end of N years
  txtEnding.Text = Format(curInitInv * sngInterest, "$###,##0.00")

End Sub
```

The code is rather complex for your first complete application, but you should have little trouble following most of it. At first, the code contains comments that explain the purpose of the procedure and describe the purpose of each variable. The code then declares each of those variables using Dim statements.

The code contains error checking. Immediately after the `Dim`, you see this:

```
If ErrorCheck() = 1 Then
   Exit Sub
End If
```

Visual Basic does not contain any statements or built-in functions called `ErrorCheck()`. That is the name of a procedure you will need to write in a moment. When a procedure is not associated with a control, that procedure is not an event procedure but one that is called from another place in the code. Technically, this kind of a procedure is called a *function*, indicated by its parentheses. (Sometimes the parentheses inside a function call contain values, as you saw with the two built-in functions named `MsgBox()` and `InputBox()`.) The `ErrorCheck()` function you write will execute and send back a return value to this procedure.

In this case, the `ErrorCheck()` function will return a number 1 if an error appears on the form. The error will be that the user did not fill in one of the required text boxes on the form, so the calculation cannot take place. You will write the error-checking code in the section "Error Checking," later in this chapter.

Assuming the user entered all the required text box values properly, four assignment statements take place that set up the interest rate calculation loop. The `For` loop actually calculates the investment's final value given the values the user entered in the text boxes above. The `For` loop steps through every period (usually a year), or *term*, of the investment. If it's a 10-year investment (a 10-term investment), the `For` loop will loop 10 times, calculating each year's final investment value and adding that to the total investment.

At the end of the event procedure, the code assigns the text box named `txtEnding` the ending value of the investment. A special built-in Visual Basic function named `Format()` converts the answer into a dollars and cents format that rounds the calculation to dollars and cents and displays the answer in the text box with a dollar sign and proper separating commas. If you reside in a country other than the United States, you will want to modify the string contents inside the `Format()` function to match your country's currency format.

You must also add the terminating code for the Exit command button so that the user can quit the application. Here's how you can add the code from within the code window:

1. Click the top of the code window's left drop-down list box and select `cmdExit`. A list of events that exist only for command buttons immediately fills the right list box.

2. Select the `Click` event from the right list box if it's not already selected.

3. Add the following code for the command button's `Click` event procedure:

```
Private Sub cmdExit_Click()
    ' Unload the form and terminate application
    Unload frmInterest
    End
End Sub
```

## The `Unload` Statement

The Exit command button's `Click` event procedure contains a Visual Basic statement you have not seen until now. `Unload` unloads a form from memory. If the form to unload is currently displayed, Visual Basic removes the form and resets all the form's control values to their original state before you added code.

In most cases the `Unload` statement is unnecessary, especially when your application contains only a single form. If you add multiple forms to the application, however, the user could have closed one of the Form windows (by clicking the window's close button), and the `End` statement could fail to release that form's resources properly.

One of the primary rules of programming is that if your program begins a process or creates a resource, such as a form, it should eventually quit that process and release that resource. Therefore, a graceful exit for a Visual Basic application is to unload all forms that were used. In most cases, Visual Basic will do that for you, but as a programmer concerned about your user environment (after all, you want your user to like your code's efficiency), you should unload all forms that you use before your program terminates.

Here is the format of the `Unload` statement:

```
Unload formName
```

You should include an `Unload` statement for all forms in all applications that you write. The investment application contains only a single form, so you need only the single `Unload` statement in the `cmdExit_Click()` event procedure. That is the last of your procedures to execute, so the `Unload` statement works well there.

## Error Checking

A potential problem exists every time your application interacts with a user. Just because your user should enter data a certain way doesn't mean that he will do it. Error-checking code often accounts for as much as 40% of an application.

This chapter's investment application uses only some rudimentary error checking that ensures the user entered proper values in the text boxes. Although the application is not *bulletproof* (meaning that it can handle anything the user enters, which would require extensive code), the error-checking routine that you will enter contains a fair amount of checking for such an introductory application.

If the user does not enter one or more values in the text boxes, the calculation will not work properly. Even worse, an error such as a divide-by-zero error could occur and stop the running program with a nasty error message.

The error-checking code should ensure that your users enter positive values greater than zero in each of the text boxes before clicking the computation command button. The check is simple: Convert each text box value to a number and, if any text box contains zero or less, do the following:

1. Tell the user about the problem in a message box.

2. When the user closes the message box, set the focus on the control with the bad value so the user can more easily enter a corrected value.

3. Test the control again before any calculation begins to ensure that the problem is fixed.

Several approaches exist for handling this error. The approach used here is slightly advanced, but it gives you a chance to see how an external module—the function—ties into an application's event procedure code. Remember that a control's event procedure code always applies to the Form window that holds that control. The code resides in a code module, a section of the project that holds the event procedure code. Code not tied to a particular control or form resides in its own code module. You can place such a standalone module in one or more projects simply by saving the code on the disk and inserting it into any modules that can use that same code.

**note**

Division by zero is said to be *undefined* in our mathematical system. Therefore, 4 / 0 is undefined. Some might say that 0 goes into 4 an infinite number of times, but the answer is not infinity but strictly undefined by definition. Other areas of our mathematical system would fall apart if we allowed division by zero to be defined in any way. Although it seems like a cop-out to say "Just don't do it," by accepting the undefined nature of such a division, the rest of the mathematical world works more smoothly than a well-oiled machine. You now have some interesting tidbits to discuss at your next cocktail party. Aren't you glad you don't have to know a lot about math to program computers?

To add the `ErrorCheck()` procedure, perform these steps:

1. Select **Project**, **Add Module** to add a new module (that you can view in a code window) to the project. You could also right-click over your Project window and add the module from the pop-up menu that appears.

2. Double-click the **Module** icon in the Add Module dialog box. Visual Basic adds a new module with the default name Module1 (and the filename will be `Mdule1.bas`). The Project window in Figure 10.7 shows the new module in your project. Your code window will now display a blank module where you can type the code.

**FIGURE 10.7**

You've now added another code module to the project.

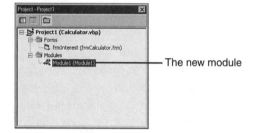

The new module

3. You can always maneuver between modules and the form by double-clicking the Project window object you want to work with. For now, however, stay inside the new module and type the function code you see in Listing 10.2.

**LISTING 10.2** Error-Checking Code

```
Public Function ErrorCheck() As Integer
   ' Error-checking for the form
   If Val(frmInterest.txtRate.Text) <= 0 Then
      intPress = MsgBox("Enter a value for the rate", vbCritical)
      frmInterest.txtRate.SetFocus
      ErrorCheck = 1
      Exit Function
   End If
   If Val(frmInterest.txtTerm.Text) <= 0 Then
      intPress = MsgBox("Enter a value for the term", vbCritical)
      frmInterest.txtTerm.SetFocus
      ErrorCheck = 1
      Exit Function
   End If
   If Val(frmInterest.txtInvest.Text) <= 0 Then
      intPress = MsgBox("Enter a value for the investment", vbCritical)
      frmInterest.txtInvest.SetFocus
      ErrorCheck = 1
```

**LISTING 10.2**   (continued)

```
     Exit Function
   End If
   ' No error occurred if execution gets here
   ErrorCheck = 0
End Function
```

The first differences you'll notice between the event procedure and this procedure are the opening and closing statements. The keyword Function distinguishes a function procedure, which always must return some value, from a subroutine procedure, which simply performs some kind of task. The procedures you've seen so far have been subroutines that used the Sub keyword to define them. In addition, the error-checking function procedure's opening line ends with As Integer. This qualifier tells Visual Basic that the function procedure will return an integer value. Functions can return any data type as long as you define the function to return the proper data type with the As keyword.

The function then checks each text box on the form. All form references include the form name. Therefore, instead of referring to the Interest Rate text box as txtRate, the code qualifies the text box with a form name as follows:

frmInterest.txtRate

Remember that an external module such as this one is not part of a specific form's code. Such a function may need to access or check on several controls in several different forms. The qualifying form name before the control tells Visual Basic exactly which form's control that function refers to.

If a text box is found to contain a bad value typed in by the user, a message box pops up to describe the problem. The code then sets the focus to that control with the SetFocus method. The user can edit the control and correct the problem as soon as the error box goes away.

> **tip**
>
> SetFocus is not a property or an event; it is a method. Controls usually support all three: events, controls, and methods. A *method* is a built-in operation that appends to the end of a control name, separated by a period. Read methods from right-to-left to understand them fully. For example, frmInterest.txtTerm.SetFocus tells Visual Basic to set the focus on the control named txtTerm located on the frmInterest form.

At the end of the code, the error-checking routine sets the function's return value to 1 if an error was found and exits the function and returns to the calling code, which was the form's event procedure code. To return a value from a function, simply assign the value that you want to return to the function name.

Figure 10.8 shows the message box that appears if the user enters a term value that's zero or less.

You've now completed the entire application! Save the project (InvestCalc.vbp would be a good name). When you save the project, Visual Basic asks for a form and a module name as well (use InvestCalc.frm and InvestCalc.bas, to follow the naming convention you started with the project name). Visual Basic understands the purpose of a file by its extension.

Run your application and enter values until you determine how much money you'll want to make from programming to retire in 10 years.

# Summary

This chapter developed a complete application. Through the development process, you saw how even a simple project can require detailed components such as error-checking and proper form management. This chapter gave your early programming experience a needed boost by strengthening what you already knew and by helping you focus more on the mechanics of building a complete working application.

- Use hotkeys to give users quick access to all needed controls on the form.
- Although labels never accept the focus, you can add a hotkey combination to a label, and the focus jumps to the text box next to that label.
- Unload all forms that your application uses in an application.
- Error-checking accounts for a large part of any application. Error-checking helps prevent your users from receiving system error messages.
- A code module can access any form's controls by prefacing the form's name to the control name with a period.

## IN THIS CHAPTER

- Introducing Visual Basic Wizards
- Using the Wizard for the Internet
- Sampling the Internet Controls
- A Preview of Advanced Issues

**11**

# ONLINE VISUAL BASIC PROGRAMMING

Visual Basic is one of the easiest programming tools available today to use for Internet access. Bear in mind, however, that even with Visual Basic, Internet access via programming is challenging. This short chapter only scratches the surface and offers a glimpse of how Visual Basic views and works with the Internet.

The highlights of this chapter include the following:

- How Visual Basic's Internet connection works.
- Visual Basic includes additional controls not shown on the toolbar.
- You can add a Web browser to any Visual Basic application.
- Encapsulation saves time and helps automate programming tasks.

■ ActiveX documents bring Internet pages to life.

■ You can turn virtually any Visual Basic application into an Internet application.

# Introducing Visual Basic Wizards

Before learning how to implement Internet access from within your applications, you should take a moment to learn one of Visual Basic's most interesting features, especially for newcomers. The Visual Basic Application Wizard helps you build applications without requiring that you write any code and without requiring that you place one control on a form!

Visual Basic is not magic and cannot read your mind. The Visual Basic Application Wizard actually creates a *shell* (also called an outline) of an application with some general features that you request. The reason the Application Wizard is useful for Internet-based Visual Basic applications is that it can create an initial application with Internet access that you then can complete with your own specifics to behave exactly the way you need.

Before getting into the Internet portion of the Application Wizard, this section walks you through an application's generation and creates a generic Visual Basic application that includes a blank window. Once you see the wizard's basics, you then can modify the wizard to generate an Internet-based application.

**note**

The wizard is a sequence of dialog boxes that present standard Windows application options that you can add to applications, such as the number of form windows, menus, and other common interface elements. The wizard then creates a skeleton application that you then must fill in with the specific controls and code you require.

Perform these steps to generate your first Visual Basic application with the Application Wizard:

1. Select **File**, **New Project**.

2. Instead of selecting Standard EXE as you've been doing, double-click the icon labeled **VB Application Wizard** to select it. The dialog box in Figure 11.1 appears.

**FIGURE 11.1**

The opening Application Wizard dialog box starts the application's generation.

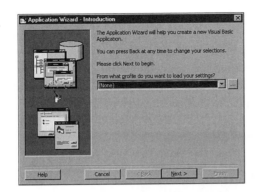

**caution**

The Application Wizard generally benefits advanced Visual Basic programmers more than beginning ones. To add code and controls to the shell of a Windows application requires some deciphering of the shell's contents. If you feel comfortable with the previous chapter's application, you are well on your way to using the wizard to create the shell of your next application. However, many newcomers are better off creating all their applications from scratch until they learn the language and how all the standard controls work.

3. Read through the wizard's first dialog box. A *profile* is a saved list of settings you can specify and save that will determine the nature of the application you create. For now, just bypass the opening dialog box by clicking **Next** without changing the option.

4. The second wizard dialog box wants to know if your application is to be a multiple-document interface (MDI) application, a single-document interface (SDI) application, or a Windows Explorer–like application. An MDI document is a Windows application from which you can open multiple data windows, such as a Windows word processor in which you can have more than one document open for editing at the same time. The SDI style is the same as the applications you've been creating, with a single Form window. An Explorer-style application includes a tree of high-level options on the left of the screen, with more detailed information on the right. The tree enables the user to select detailed information such as you might find in the Windows Explorer window, with a list of drives and directories on the left of the screen and the selected drive and directory's contents on the right.

If you click the option buttons in the center of the screen, the wizard's graphic changes to show the kind of application you select. If you click the SDI option, you'll see an application with a single window in the dialog box's graphic.

For now, click the **Single Document Interface** option. Enter a project name of First and click **Next** to move to the next wizard dialog box.

5. The Menus dialog box, shown in Figure 11.2, gives you the ability to create a Windows-like pull-down menu and add it to your application. Although you can add a menu through the toolbox and programming, the wizard is probably the easiest way to do so. Many advanced programmers use the wizard only to create the menu structure of their applications quickly, and then they finish the rest of the application's details by hand.

**FIGURE 11.2**

You can select menu items that you want placed in your application.

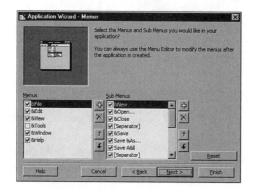

For this example, accept all the menu defaults. You'll see that the wizard adds these menu options to your application: **File**, **Edit**, **View**, **Window**, and **Help**, along with the standard submenu options. Click **Next** to continue.

6. The next dialog box enables you to select a Windows toolbar that will appear toward the top of your application beneath the menu. Accept the defaults and click **Next**.

7. *Resource files* contain bitmap graphic images, text, and other elements of a typical Windows application. Although you can embed resource items directly inside your application through various methods, by placing them outside an application in a resource file, you can more easily change them without having to change your application.

Don't select a resource file. Click **Next** to move to the next dialog box.

> **tip**
>
> Use a resource file for your application's text. Every text value that appears on your application's form can reside inside a resource file. If you then want to sell your application in a foreign country, all you need to do is translate and provide a new resource file and you never have to change one line of code. If you embed text inside code, you have to locate, change, and recompile every file that includes any text at all.

8. The dialog box you see next is the subject of the next several sections of this chapter. As you can see, the wizard can add Internet connectivity to your application. For now, do not change anything; accept the defaults, and click **Next** to move to the next dialog box.

9. Click the appropriate wizard options to add these elements to your generated application: a *splash screen* (a window that appears when your application first starts, to introduce your program to the user) and an *About box* (a dialog box that lists details and contact information for your program, accessible from the Help menu). Click **Next** to continue the wizard.

10. The wizard gives you a chance to access a database program, such as Microsoft Access. You would use a database in applications such as online inventory or ordering systems. For now, click **Next** to move to the final wizard dialog box.

11. Click **Finish** to watch Visual Basic's wizard put the application together, add the forms, and build the menus. If this is the first time you have used the wizard to generate an online-related application, Visual Basic will display a message box window telling you that the application may take a few minutes longer than normal. The first time Visual Basic creates such an application, it must unpack several Internet controls from its installation folder.

12. Click the closing dialog box and close the final instructions. The wizard leaves your development environment fairly clear of items, but you can double-click any object in the Project window to see forms and code modules that are there. For now, press **F5** to compile and execute the program; you will the screen shown in Figure 11.3.

**FIGURE 11.3**

The Application Wizard generated a working, albeit plain, application.

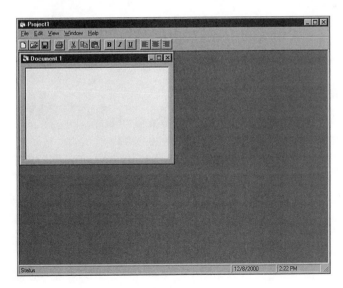

The program generated looks somewhat like a word processor because of the large editing area in the center of the screen. Try the menus and click the toolbar buttons. Things look good. Select **Help**, **About** to see the standard About box that Visual Basic created for you. As you can see, the wizard created a structure that saved you a lot of work.

You will find that the application doesn't respond to your keystrokes as you might expect, however. If you attempt to perform certain tasks, a small dialog box will appear, telling you that what you requested has not been implemented by the programmer (you).

Remember that the wizard's job is to generate a fully working application, albeit a generic one, that performs basic start-up tasks such as displaying a program window, setting up a menu structure, and adding some special elements such as toolbars and the Help About box. After the wizard does its job, you then add the specifics.

In the next section, you will use the wizard to add full, working Internet access to your skeleton application.

# Using the Wizard for the Internet

Visual Basic's Application Wizard does lots of work for you when you want your application to access the Internet. If you make the correct choice within the wizard, Visual Basic automatically adds the access and gives your application worldwide communication capabilities.

Visual Basic's Application Wizard provides Internet access. It specifically gives your application the capability to browse World Wide Web pages.

## Working the Wizard

When you create an application shell with Visual Basic's Application Wizard, the fifth dialog box (see Figure 11.4) is the Internet Connectivity dialog box, which sets up Web access for the application you're building.

> **note**
>
> The Internet tools described in this chapter work equally well for Internet and intranet applications. The Internet is the worldwide networked system of computers, whereas an *intranet* is a local networked system (perhaps a network inside a single building or even a small area on the same floor) that provides the same connectivity and Web page display as the Internet itself.

**FIGURE 11.4**

You can select
Web access from
the wizard's
Internet
Connectivity
dialog box.

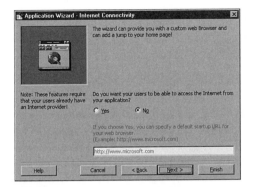

When you select the **Yes** option button, the wizard
actually inserts the engine for a Web browser in the
application.

## Default URL

A *uniform resource locator (URL)* is a Web site
address. Every Web site has a unique URL. If you
opt to add the Internet access capability to the wizard's application, you can supply a default URL Web
page site for the application's browser. When a user
triggers the browser inside the application, the
browser logs on (through the user's own Internet
provider) and connects to the URL you specify in
the wizard.

Always begin the URL with `http://`. *HTTP* stands for
*Hypertext Transfer Protocol* and designates the standard communication procedure used to access Web
pages.

## Creating an Internet-Aware Application

Follow these steps to add an Internet-browsing feature to your wizard's generated application:

1. Create a new project and double-click the
   icon labeled **VB Application Wizard**.

2. Click **Next** to bypass the Introduction dialog box if you see it. You can keep
   the dialog box from appearing in subsequent sessions by clicking the check
   box labeled **Skip This Screen in the Future**.

note

Your users must already
have an Internet service
provider (ISP, an organization that
connects to the Internet), or they
can't access the Web with your
application. Also, you must have
Internet Explorer 3.0 or later
installed on your own development system. Internet Explorer
contains shared code that the wizard uses to add appropriate code.

note

The wizard supplies a
default URL—Microsoft's
home page—so you need to
change this default if you want
your users to see something else.

3. Select **Single Document Interface (SDI)** to keep the application simple.

4. Click **Next** to move through the next three dialog boxes and to accept the default menu options.

5. At the Internet Connectivity dialog box, click **Yes**. For this example, leave Microsoft's Web site URL in the text box.

6. Click **Finish** and **OK** to finalize and generate the application.

When you return to Visual Basic's development environment, notice the toolbox. Figure 11.5 shows the tools the wizard added to the usual collection of standard Visual Basic controls, such as text boxes and labels. You've used these controls before in this tutorial: Common Dialog Box, Toolbar, Image List, and Slider.

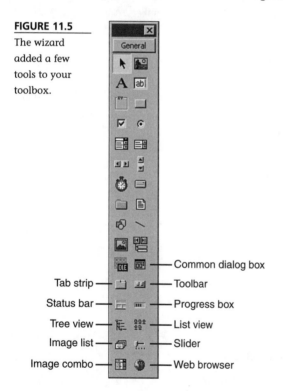

**FIGURE 11.5**
The wizard added a few tools to your toolbox.

Common dialog box
Tab strip —— Toolbar
Status bar —— Progress box
Tree view —— List view
Image list —— Slider
Image combo —— Web browser

The extra tools give the application's Web-browsing function the control it needs. Obviously, the WebBrowser control is the tool this chapter is primarily concerned with.

note

The section "Sampling the Internet Controls," later in this chapter, explains more about the Internet controls that come with Visual Basic's Professional and Enterprise editions.

The Web browser includes the standard browsing tools that you are used to if you've ever used a browser. You can do the following from your application's browser:

■ Click a Web page's hotspots to jump to related Web pages.

■ Enter a new URL in the Address text box to see a different site.

■ Browse backward through the pages you've seen by clicking the toolbar's Back button.

■ After you back up, return to a Web page by clicking the toolbar's Forward button.

■ Click the toolbar's **Stop** button to freeze a page at its current loaded state if it takes a long time to load its graphics. (Usually, text will load long before graphics, and you might not need to view the rest of a page's graphics.)

■ Finish a Web page that you've stopped from loading or update a page to see new information by clicking the toolbar's **Refresh** button.

■ Access the home page you set up for your ISP, if you have one, with the toolbar's Home button. You can select **View**, **Options**, **Navigation** to set a different home page.

■ Locate other sites on the Internet with the toolbar's **Search** button.

All this is possible, and you never coded one programming statement to gain the Internet functionality.

## Trying the Application

Get a feel for the application's shell by pressing **F5** to run the application. The screen you see looks no different from other wizard-generated applications you've seen. The Internet feature appears, however, when you choose WebBrowser from the **View** menu. In the middle of the application's screen, a Web-browsing dialog box appears and requests that you log on with your typical provider's logon dialog box (assuming you are not already logged

**note**

Internet Explorer is actually a small application wrapped around a huge ActiveX control. An *ActiveX control* is a control that you can insert into any Visual Basic application, as well as in virtually any other application you write using a Microsoft-based development environment. The Web browser that Visual Basic's wizard inserted is a sample of such an ActiveX control. Although the application's Web browser is simpler than the full-blown version of Internet Explorer (fewer toolbar buttons appear and no menu exists), the embedded browser supplies all the common browser features needed, such as a previous page button, next page button, home page button, and so on. If you click the **Search** toolbar button, Internet Explorer uses Microsoft's search site to launch the search request.

on when you start the application). After you enter your logon username and password, an Internet Explorer–like window appears in the center of your application screen and displays Microsoft's Web site (see Figure 11.6).

**FIGURE 11.6**

Your application is hooked into Microsoft's Web site.

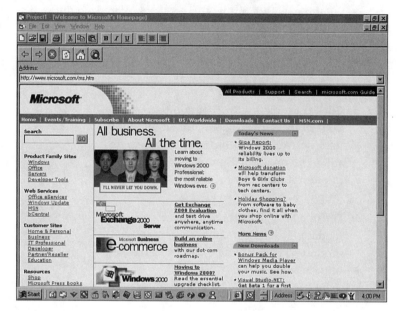

If you want to log off the Internet, you must close the Web browser, double-click your service provider's Taskbar icon, and select the logoff option. Although the Web browser doesn't include a logoff feature, you can add one through programming.

# Sampling the Internet Controls

If you use Visual Basic's Professional or Enterprise edition, you can use several advanced Internet-based (and ActiveX) controls to add and control Internet access from within your applications. The previous section's example demonstrated the power of one single control, the WebBrowser control. This section explains more about these controls.

Several Internet controls appear when you choose Components from the Project menu. Here, you'll review those controls and understand how and when you can use them in projects that access the Internet.

As you learn more about programming, especially object-oriented programming as you'll do beginning in Chapter 14, "Programming with C++," you will run across the term *encapsulation*. Encapsulation refers to different things, depending on whether you're encapsulating data, code, or both. Nevertheless, in a broad sense, encapsulation always refers to packaging. Visual Basic includes some Internet controls that encapsulate, or package, your existing applications and code so that they work across Internet technology.

Among the more common encapsulation controls that Visual Basic contains are these:

**note**

*Internet access* can mean many different things in today's world, including complete applications that users access and run from the Web. The Internet provides more services than Web page viewing and file downloading these days, especially with the new ActiveX controls that work across the Internet as easily as they work inside single-computer applications. When you activate Web pages with programs, Visual Basic can be the engine that you use.

- **Internet Transfer control**—Encapsulates the three most popular Internet protocols: HTTP, FTP (File Transfer Protocol), and Gopher (a searching protocol to help you locate information on the Internet). You can download files directly from within your Visual Basic applications by using FTP.

- **WebBrowser control**—Encapsulates a Web browser directly inside your application.

- **WinSock control**—Gives you a Windows common connection and data-exchange control that provides two protocols: User Datagram Protocol (UDP) and Transmission Control Protocol (TCP), the more common).

You saw one of these encapsulation controls—the WebBrowser control—in the previous section. The Application Wizard uses the WebBrowser control to insert the browser in the generated application. As you saw, the WebBrowser control isn't as full functioned as Internet Explorer, but it does provide simple and direct access for any user who subscribes to an Internet service.

Visual Basic comes with several controls you can add to a project so that the project can interact with the Web. These controls begin with the abbreviation IE in the Components dialog box.

Table 11.1 helps you locate the controls described in this section. Often, the control names don't describe their capabilities. Table 11.1 describes the control you select from the Components dialog box to get the functionality you need. (To access the Components dialog box, choose **Components** from the **Project** menu.)

**TABLE 11.1**   The Component Names You Select for Internet Controls

| Component Name | Description |
| --- | --- |
| IE Animated Button | Animated display showing IE's connection |
| IE Popup Menu | A menu control that appears on the Web page |
| IE Popup Window | A tabbed window control that opens a new connection window |
| IE Preloader | Preloads a site before the visible Internet access begins |
| IE Super Label | A Web page label |
| IE Timer | Provides timing operations for Internet services |
| Microsoft Internet Controls | Web browser control |
| Microsoft Internet Transfer Control | The transfer protocol control |
| Microsoft WinSock Control | The Windows connection to common Internet protocols |

# A Preview of Advanced Issues

Assuming that you want to interact with the Internet and Visual Basic, you've already seen a start of what's in store. The simplest way to add Internet capabilities is to use the VB Application Wizard to add the wizard, as was done in this chapter's first section. If you go further than that, you have a steep learning curve ahead of you.

Here, you will see some of the terms and concepts you'll face as you dive into the VB-to-Internet foray. By learning what's in store now, you won't be faced with a completely new environment if and when you learn to provide comprehensive Internet interaction from your applications.

If you use the Microsoft Network online service, a set of controls comes with Visual Basic that offers Microsoft Network–related services from the applications you write, such as the MSN mail control. These controls begin with the MSN abbreviation in the Components dialog box.

## ActiveX Documents

If you want to develop a pure Internet application, you can use ActiveX documents to get started. An *ActiveX document* acts and looks just like a regular Visual Basic application on a Form window, except that an ActiveX document sends ActiveX controls to the user's computer if the computer doesn't contain the ActiveX controls used by the document. (The document comes to the user looking like a regular HTML page.) The ActiveX document can contain hypertext links (ActiveX controls that are either downloaded or already there, depending on the user's machine contents). The ActiveX document's menus replace its parent application's menus.

The ActiveX document links to an HTML page that you create or use. When the user clicks the link to your ActiveX document, your document activates, the controls get to the user's computer, and the Web page's ActiveX document code executes as the user views the page.

Perhaps the most important reason for creating ActiveX documents is that Internet Explorer can run them as though the Internet Explorer were a control program or operating system program launcher. The ActiveX document's menus merge with Internet Explorer's (and override functionality when needed), and you don't have to learn a new language such as Java to activate Web pages.

> **note**
>
> The ActiveX document isn't static. The document in the ActiveX document is a running application in every respect. A document concept helps programmers see how Web pages use the embedded ActiveX document.
>
> The New Project dialog box contains two icons—ActiveX Document EXE and ActiveX Document DLL—that create ActiveX document shells. After you start creating an ActiveX document, you can add whatever features you like to the Form window, just as for regular applications.

## HTML and VBScript

Although you need to know the Visual Basic programming language only to access all the Internet connectivity features found in Visual Basic, you need to master two auxiliary languages to tie things together well. HTML is the formatting language behind Web pages. The HTML language is designed to achieve the following goals:

- Format Web pages in columns, with graphics, and appropriate titles.
- Allow the integration of additional Internet service programs, such as VB ActiveX documents and Java (the C++-like programming language that activates Web pages; you'll learn about Java in Chapter 20, "Java Programming").

HTML is an interpreted language, so HTML code doesn't compile and become executable as Visual Basic programs do. Instead, HTML formats Web pages, specifies where graphics and dividing frames go, and allows for embedded activated applications such as ActiveX documents and Java programs.

*VBScript*, as the name implies, is another scripting language, but Microsoft designed VBScript based on the Visual Basic programming language. Visual Basic programmers often feel right at home with VBScript. VBScript is useful when you want to add key Visual Basic features to a Web page, such as pop-up messages, input boxes, loop-through calculations, and so on. Despite its foundation in Visual Basic, VBScript doesn't replace Visual Basic's ActiveX documents but instead loads them into an HTML page for execution. Therefore, VBScript is the medium through which HTML documents locate and execute Visual Basic ActiveX document applications. You'll learn more about VBScript in Chapter 15, "Macro, Batch, and Scripting Languages."

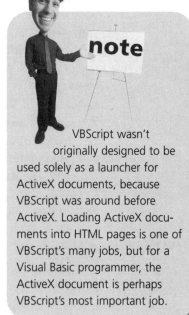

**tip**

You can add the ActiveX Document Migration Wizard to the Add-In Manager menu option. This wizard converts existing applications to ActiveX documents so that you can place whatever applications you've already created onto the Web.

**note**

VBScript wasn't originally designed to be used solely as a launcher for ActiveX documents, because VBScript was around before ActiveX. Loading ActiveX documents into HTML pages is one of VBScript's many jobs, but for a Visual Basic programmer, the ActiveX document is perhaps VBScript's most important job.

# Summary

This chapter previewed Visual Basic's role as an Internet player. Obviously, one chapter cannot cover even a small fraction of the details needed to turn Visual Basic into an Internet programming tool. A huge background is needed just about Internet technology before you tackle Visual Basic's interface. As you've seen, Visual Basic provides full online support and supplies an Internet browser wizard that adds online capabilities to virtually any program.

- Both intranet and Internet program support can be vital to a company.
- Visual Basic supports online programming in many ways.
- With the Visual Basic Application Wizard, you can install an Internet Web browser in your application.
- Advanced Internet tools are available for the programmer who must use Visual Basic to exploit Internet programming fully.

# PART IV

# PROGRAMMING IN VARIOUS ENVIRONMENTS

12    Program Algorithms . . . . . . . . . . . . . .197

13    Programming with C . . . . . . . . . . . . .211

14    Programming with C++ . . . . . . . . . . .227

15    Macro, Batch, and Scripting Languages  .243

16    Internet Programming Concepts . . . . . .259

17    HTML Programming . . . . . . . . . . . . .273

18    Dynamic HTML . . . . . . . . . . . . . . . .285

19    Introduction to XML . . . . . . . . . . . . .295

20    Java Programming . . . . . . . . . . . . . .305

21    JavaScript . . . . . . . . . . . . . . . . . . .323

## IN THIS CHAPTER

- Counters and Accumulators
- Swapping Values
- Sorting
- Nested Loops
- Searching Arrays
- A Brief Introduction to Data Structures

12

# PROGRAM ALGORITHMS

This chapter is more theory oriented than the previous ones. You'll learn about programming algorithms that are common across all programming languages. An *algorithm* is a common procedure or methodology for performing a certain task. To keep things familiar, you'll see the algorithms in Visual Basic, but the concepts you learn here are important no matter which programming language you use.

The highlights of this chapter include the following:

- Counters and accumulators enable you to keep running counts and totals.
- The use of temporary variables is vital for data swapping.
- The bubble sort is a fundamental data-sorting technique.

- The binary search is a far more efficient search technique than the simple sequential search.

- Data structures enable programmers to write code that manipulates complex data.

# Counters and Accumulators

When you see a statement such as the following, what do you think?

```
number = number + 1
```

Your first impression might be that the statement is not possible because nothing can be equal to itself plus one. This works in programming, because a programming equals symbol acts like a left-pointing arrow. The assignment statement says "take whatever is on the right side of the equals symbol, evaluate it, and put it in the variable to the left."

When your program reaches the statement just shown, it adds 1 to the variable named number. If number is 7 to begin with, it now is 8. After it adds 1 and gets 8, it then stores 8 in number, replacing the 7 that was originally there. The final result is one more than the initial value.

Such an assignment increments a variable and can be extremely useful. Many programmers put such an assignment statement inside a loop to count items when the loop repeats. When the loop finishes, the counter variable has the total.

The routine in Listing 12.1 uses such a counter. It is a number-guessing game. This program gives the user a hint as to whether a guess is too low or too high and counts the number of guesses. The intTries variable holds the count.

**LISTING 12.1** A Number-Guessing Game That Uses a Counter Variable

```
' Number-guessing routine
intTries = 0     ' The counter variable
intNum = 47      ' The computer's guess

Do
  intGuess = InputBox("I'm thinking of a number...What is your guess
➥ (between 1 and 100)")

  If (intGuess < intNum) Then
    MsgBox ("Your guess was too low. Try again.")
  ElseIf (intGuess > intNum) Then
```

## LISTING 12.1   (continued)

```
    MsgBox ("Your guess was too high. Try again.")
  End If
  intTries = intTries + 1    ' Add to counter
Loop Until (intGuess = intNum) ' Loop stops when user guesses correctly

MsgBox ("You guessed it in only " & intTries & "!")
```

Without the counter, the program would not be able to tell the user how many guesses he made.

An *accumulator* is similar to a counter in that the same variable name appears on both sides of the equals symbol. Unlike counter variables, accumulators usually add something other than 1 to the variable. Use accumulators for totaling dollar amounts, sales figures, and so forth. To add a series of sales values entered by the user, for example, a statement such as this would be in order:

```
sngTotalSales = sngTotalSales +
➥sngSingleSales
```

Chapter 10, "Advanced Visual Basic Programming," briefly introduced you to arrays. You may remember that an array is a list of variable values with one name that you distinguish in your code with an index (called a *subscript*). With an array of variables instead of a bunch of variables named separately, your program can step through each value in the array using a loop that increments the array subscript.

Listing 12.2 uses a For loop to accumulate a total. Assuming the array has 100 values, the loop adds all 100 array variables and displays the total.

By the way, you can display strings only from within a message box. Both previous listings displayed strings and numeric values in the MsgBox() function. Visual Basic converts any nonstring value to a string when you concatenate that value to a string.

## LISTING 12.2   Using an Accumulator to Total an Array

```
curTotal = 0.00        ' Initialize the accumulator

For i = 1 To 100
  curTotal = curTotal + curCosts(i)
Next i
MsgBox ("The total costs are $" & curTotal)
```

# Swapping Values

The cornerstone of any sorting algorithm is data swapping. As you sort data, you have to rearrange it, swapping higher values for lower values. As Figure 12.1 shows, swapping values simply means replacing one variable's contents with another's and vice versa.

**FIGURE 12.1**

Learn to swap two variable values with code.

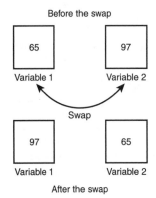

Before the swap

65
Variable 1

97
Variable 2

Swap

97
Variable 1

65
Variable 2

After the swap

Suppose you assign two variables named `var1` and `var2` with the following statements:

```
var1 = 65
var2 = 97
```

The concept of swapping them is simple. How would you do it? If you said the following, you would not be quite correct:

```
var1 = var2    ' Not quite accurate
var2 = var1
```

Can you see why these two assignment statements do not swap the values in the two variables? The first statement assigns `var2` to `var1`, which wipes out `var1`'s original value. The second statement is then redundant, because both variables already hold the same value after the first statement.

**caution**

Visual Basic has a `Swap` command that performs a swap of two variables, but most programming languages do not. If you want to write programs that are easily ported to other languages, you should use the procedure shown here.

An accurate approach to swapping variables is to use a third variable, often called a *temporary variable* because you do not use its value once you swap the original variables. Here is the code to perform the swapping accurately:

```
temp = var1
var1 = var2
var2 = temp
```

# Sorting

Your programs can sort lists of values in different ways. Perhaps the list was sorted previously, and now you want to reverse the sort. A reversed sort may be appropriate, for example, to print customer balances from the highest balance to the lowest.

Consider the following list of numbers that is not sorted:

**10  54  34  46  23**

Here is the list sorted in *ascending order* (from lowest to highest):

**10  23  34  46  54**

Here is the list sorted in *descending order* (from highest to lowest):

**54  46  34  23  10**

Of course, your program can also sort character string data, such as a list of names. When sorting strings, the computer uses the ASCII table to sort the values in alphabetical order.

There are several ways to sort data. The most popular one for beginning programmers is called a *bubble sort*. A bubble sort is not extremely efficient but, unlike other sorting algorithms, it is easy to understand and program. As Figure 12.2 illustrates, the lower values in the unsorted list seem to float up to the top, one for each pass made through the data.

The sort's name is actually misleading. In reality, the typical bubble sort algorithm moves the larger values in the list down. Ultimately, the list gets sorted from low to high (assuming you are performing an ascending sort), but the high values are the ones that the algorithm targets, as you'll see in the code that follows.

The data that you want to sort is typically stored in an array. Using the array subscripts, you can rearrange the array elements, swapping values, until the array is sorted in the order you want.

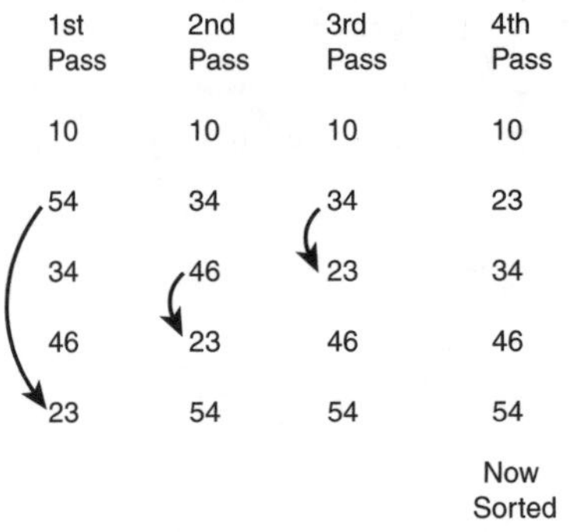

**FIGURE 12.2**

At each pass, the list gets closer to being sorted.

| | 1st Pass | 2nd Pass | 3rd Pass | 4th Pass |
|---|---|---|---|---|
| | 10 | 10 | 10 | 10 |
| | 54 | 34 | 34 | 23 |
| | 34 | 46 | 23 | 34 |
| | 46 | 23 | 46 | 46 |
| | 23 | 54 | 54 | 54 |
| | | | | Now Sorted |

In a bubble sort, the elements of an array are compared and swapped two at a time. Your program must perform several passes through the array before the list is sorted. During each pass, a bubble sort compares each pair of values in the list and, if the first value in the pair is higher than the second, swaps the two to force the higher value down one entry.

As Figure 12.2 shows, after the first pass of a bubble sort, the routine places the highest value (54) at the bottom of the array. In the second pass, 46 is placed right before 54, and so on until no more swaps take place. Listing 12.3 shows a bubble sort being used on the five values shown earlier.

## LISTING 12.3   Sorting a List of Values with a Bubble Sort

```
' Bubble sorting algorithm
Dim intValues(5) As Integer    ' Reserve the array

' Fill the array with an unsorted list of numbers
intValues(1) = 10
intValues(2) = 54
intValues(3) = 34
intValues(4) = 46
intValues(5) = 23

' Sort the array
For outer = 1 To 5       ' Outer loop
   For inner = 1 To 4     ' Inner loop to form the comparisons each pass
      If (intValues(inner) > intValues(inner + 1)) Then
         temp = intValues(inner) ' Swap the pair currently looked at
         intValues(inner) = intValues(inner + 1)
         intValues(inner + 1) = temp
      End If
```

**LISTING 12.3**   (continued)

```
    Next inner
Next outer
' The array is now sorted
```

At the heart of any sorting algorithm is a swapping routine, and you can see one in the body of the bubble sort's For loops.

If Listing 12.3 worked with a string array that contained string values instead of integer values, the code would alphabetize the strings.

# Nested Loops

A bubble sort requires a nested For loop. As with the If statement, you can nest one loop inside another. Anytime your program needs to repeat a loop more than once, use a nested loop. Figure 12.3 shows an outline of a nested For loop. Think of the inside loop as looping faster than the outside loop. The inside loop iterates faster because the Inner variable goes from 1 to 10 in the inside loop before the outside loop's first iteration is completed. Because the outside loop does not repeat until the Next Outer statement, the inside For loop has a chance to finish. When the outside loop finally does iterate a second time, the inside loop starts all over again.

The inner loop in Figure 12.3 executes a total of 40 times. The outer loop iterates four times, and the inner loop executes 10 times for each of the outer loop's iterations.

Figure 12.4 shows two loops nested within an outer loop. Both loops execute completely before the outside loop finishes its first iteration. When the outside loop starts its second iteration, the two inside loops repeat all over again.

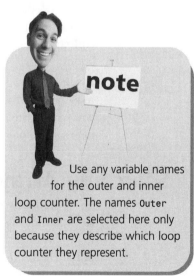

**tip**

If you want a descending sort, you have to change only one statement in Listing 12.3. Instead of swapping the values if the second item of the pair is lower, swap them if the second item of the pair is higher, like this:

```
If (intValues(inner) <
➥intValues(inner + 1))
➥Then
```

**note**

Use any variable names for the outer and inner loop counter. The names Outer and Inner are selected here only because they describe which loop counter they represent.

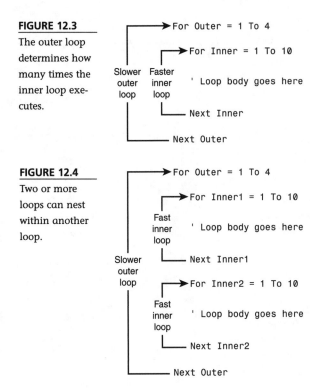

**FIGURE 12.3**

The outer loop determines how many times the inner loop executes.

```
       ┌──────►For Outer = 1 To 4
       │
       │       ┌──►For Inner = 1 To 10
Slower Faster  │
outer  inner   │   ' Loop body goes here
loop   loop    │
               └── Next Inner
       │
       └────── Next Outer
```

**FIGURE 12.4**

Two or more loops can nest within another loop.

```
         ┌──────►For Outer = 1 To 4
         │
         │       ┌──►For Inner1 = 1 To 10
         │       │
  Fast   │       │   ' Loop body goes here
  inner  │       │
  loop   │       └── Next Inner1
         │
Slower   │       ┌──►For Inner2 = 1 To 10
outer    │       │
loop     │       │   ' Loop body goes here
  Fast   │       │
  inner  │       └── Next Inner2
  loop   │
         └────── Next Outer
```

The blocks of code inside Figure 12.3's innermost loops execute a total of 40 times each. The outside loop iterates four times, and each inner loop executes in its entirety, first the top and then the bottom, each time the outer loop iterates once again.

Be sure that you match Next with For statements when you nest loops. Each Next must go with the most recent For before it in the code. Visual Basic issues an error if you write a program whose inside loop's Next statement appears after the outside loop's Next statement.

# Searching Arrays

There are many methods for searching arrays for a specific value. Suppose you have several arrays with inventory data. The first array, PartNo(), holds all your inventory item part numbers. The second array, Desc(), holds the description of each of those parts. The third array, Price(), contains the price of each corresponding part. You might keep all the inventory data on the disk and then read that data into the arrays when it is time to work with the data.

An inventory program often needs a lookup routine. A user could type a part number, and the computer program would search the `PartNo()` array for a match. When it finds one, for example at subscript 246, you could then print the 246th element in the `Desc()` and `Price()` arrays, to display the description and price of the part number just entered.

Several ways exist to search arrays for values. The various searching methods have their own advantages. One of the easiest to program and understand, the *sequential search*, is also one of the least efficient. The search method that you select depends on how much data you expect to search and how skilled you are at understanding and writing advanced searching programs.

## The Sequential Search

The sequential search technique is easy but inefficient. With it, you start at the beginning of the array and look at each value in sequence until you find a value in the array that matches the value for which you are searching. (You then can use the subscript of the matching element to look in corresponding arrays for related data.)

Listing 12.4 shows you a sequential search algorithm. The code asks the user for a part number, and then the sequential search routine finds the matching description and price in the other two arrays. After you study the code, you should find that the sequential search is very easy to understand.

> **tip**
>
> You often have more disk space than internal memory. Computers have more than 25 times the disk space than internal memory. Because your disk drives hold data more often than memory does, you often cannot fit a disk file into memory arrays all at once. When you begin writing programs with data that needs more memory than your computer has, you will begin using an advanced programming technique called *random-access file control*. Random-access files enable you to treat your disk file as if it were a huge array. Thus, you could rearrange values on the disk as you would in an array. Most programming languages support random-access disk files.

**LISTING 12.4**   Using a Sequential Search in an Inventory Application

```
' Sequential search for an item's description and price.
'
' This code would be part of a larger inventory program.
' ** This program assumes that the variable named intTotal
'    contains the total number of items in the inventory
'
```

**LISTING 12.4** (continued)

```
' First, get the part number the user wants to look up
  strPart = InputBox("What is the number of the part you want to see?")

For i = 1 To intTotal     ' Look through all inventory items
   If (strPartNo(i) = strPart) Then
      MsgBox("Part Number " & strPart & "'s description is" &
➥      strDesc(i) & "With a price of $" & curPrice(i))
      End    ' Quit the program early once it is found
   End If
Next i       ' Get the next item since it did not match

' If the program flow gets here (and did not end in the loop),
' the searched part number must not be in the inventory arrays.
MsgBox("Sorry, but that part number is not in the inventory.")
```

## The Binary Search

If your array is already sorted, a *binary search* offers tremendous searching speed advantages over a sequential search. A binary search is more complex than a sequential search but, as with most things in the programming world, it is worth the effort in many cases.

The binary search technique uses a *divide and conquer* approach to searching. One of the primary advantages of a binary search is that with every comparison you make, you can rule out one-half of the remaining array if a match is not found. If you are searching for a value in a 1000-element array, and the first comparison you make fails to match, you have only 500 elements at most left to search (with the sequential search, you would still have a possible 999 elements left to search). On the second search, assuming there is no match, you rule out one-half of the remaining list, meaning that there are only 250 more items to search through.

> **tip**
>
> The array being searched does not have to be sorted for the sequential search to work. The fact that sequential searches work on unsorted arrays makes them more useful than if the technique required sorted arrays, because you do not have to take the time to sort the array before each search.

The multiplicative advantages of a binary search will surprise you. If you have a friend write down a number from 1 to 1,000 and then use the binary search technique to guess (your friend will only have to tell you if you are too low or too high with each guess), you can often zero in on the number in 8 to 10 guesses. This is an amazing feat when there is a pool of 1,000 numbers to choose from!

The binary search technique is simple. The first guess should be exactly in the middle of the sorted list. If you guess incorrectly, you need to know only if you were too high or low. If you were too high, your next guess should split the lower half of the list. If you were too low, you should split the higher half of the list. Keep splitting the list with each guess.

Suppose your friend thinks of the number 390. Your first guess would be 500 (half of 1,000). When your friend says "too high," you would immediately know that your next guess should be between 1 and 499. Splitting that range takes you to your second guess of 250. "Too low," replies your friend, so you know the number is between 250 and 499. Splitting that gives you 375. "Too low" means the number is between 375 and 499. Your next guess might be 430, then 400, then 390 and you've guessed it. One out of 1,000 numbers, and it took only six guesses.

Listing 12.5 uses the binary search technique to find an inventory part. As you can see from the code, a binary search technique does not require very much code.

## LISTING 12.5 A Binary Search

```
' Binary search for an item's description and price.
'
' ** intTotal contains the total number of inventory items
'
' Get the part number the user wants
  strSearch = InputBox(""What is the number of the part you want to see?")

first = 1    ' Must begin the lower-bound of the search at 1
last = intTotal    ' The upper-bound of the search

Do
' Compute mid subscript value. Integer variable discards fraction
  intMid = (intFirst + intLast) / 2
  If (strSearch = strPart(mid)) Then
    MsgBox("Part number " & strSearch & "'s description is" &
      strDesc(mid) & "With a price of $" & Price(mid))
    End    ' Found! Stop the program
  ElseIf (strSearch < strPart(mid)) Then    ' Must divide array
    last = mid - 1    ' New subscript for next loop iteration
  Else
    first = mid + 1
```

**LISTING 12.5** (continued)

```
    End If
Loop While (first <= last)

' The searched part was not found if the code gets here (the END
' statement above would have been triggered otherwise).
MsgBox("** Sorry, but that part number is not in the inventory.")
```

# A Brief Introduction to Data Structures

A *data structure* is a collection of one or more variables taken as a group. Consider the storage of an inventory item. The computer needs to track the following values for each item:

**caution**

A binary search always requires that you sort the array before you begin the search.

- Part Number
- Quantity
- Description
- Cost
- Retail Price

Of course, the company will have many items, so these values will be stored on the disk, probably read into five arrays, and managed from there.

## Data Structures Help Group Data

The problem with using separate arrays is that your code must keep track of multiple arrays for the same inventory file. It's as though you must break the single inventory file into five pieces (the arrays) while your program works with the inventory, then combine the five arrays into a single disk file at day's end.

Most programming languages support the concept of a data structure, sometimes called a *structure*, *record*, or *object*. The advantage of a structure is that it's a single unit, treated as a single variable, but with different data types within the same structure. Figure 12.5 shows a diagram of how an inventory record might look. Although this structure has five parts (called *members*), and the parts are not all the same data type, the program treats the structure as a single variable. The structure might be named stInventory. The inventory will have many items, so the programmer creates an array of these structure variables, referring to them as `stInventory(1)`, `stInventory(2)`, and so on.

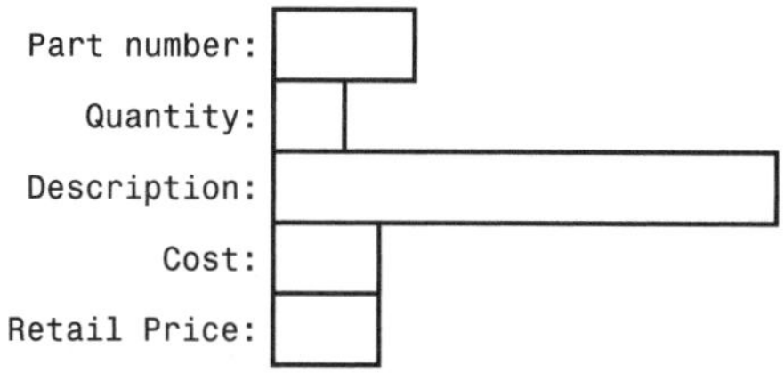

**FIGURE 12.5**
The inventory structure value is composed of different data types.

```
Part number: [      ]
   Quantity: [   ]
Description: [          ]
       Cost: [    ]
Retail Price: [  ]
```

## Referencing Data Structure Items

Often, a period (.) enables the program to access individual items within a structure variable. Therefore, the program might refer to the fifth inventory part's cost like this:

`strInventory(5).curPrice`

In Visual Basic, you could print the description inside a message box like this:

```
MsgBox("The item costs $ " &
➥strInventory(5).curPrice )
```

Unlike arrays where every element must be the same data type, structures allow you to group data more as it appears in the real world. As you learn more about programming, you'll find many uses for data structures such as these.

A data structure does not always refer to a group of data where multiple data types come together as just described, however. Data structure theory runs long and deep and is part of a foundational education for a programming career. As you program, you'll run across fancy data structure names such as queues, linked lists, and double-linked lists. These refer to the way programmers can connect data structures to one another for fast sorting and searching.

**caution**

Just because a data structure is sometimes called an object doesn't necessarily mean the language being used is object oriented. As you'll learn in Chapter 14, "Programming with C++," an object is not just a data structure with data only but one with actual code inside the object itself.

**tip**

Read a structure item from right to left. The previous statement, in effect, says "Print the cost from the fifth inventory item." Some languages begin array subscripts at zero, so using subscript number 4 would actually reference the fifth item in a zero-based array.

**MOVE OVER, GRACE HOPPER!**

A man famous for his study and an early promoter of data structure technology is Dr. Donald Knuth. Dr.

Knuth was one of the first to tell the world about the bubble sort, and then he proceeded to tell the world (the programming world) how poor the bubble sort performs with large amounts of data and how other kinds of more esoteric and complex sorting techniques are faster. (Dr. Knuth was one of the first to analyze the value of a binary search, for example.)

Although programming languages rarely include built-in sorting and searching routines, most of today's programming environments do, especially object-oriented programming environments.

As you learn Visual C++, for example, you will not only learn the C++ language but you'll also learn about the code libraries available inside the Visual C++ environment that will perform advanced sorting and searching techniques, such as the binary search. Although you'll rarely if ever have to write a binary search routine on your own, you should understand how such a search works.

In addition, as you learn about advanced data structures such as linked lists, consider how such routines are programmed. Even though you may not have to write code that mimics these built-in efficient routines, you should understand the coding theory beneath so that you'll have a better understanding of when to use them and why. For example, if your code works with unsorted data, you know that you cannot apply a binary search because a binary search requires a sorted list. You might pick a different search routine, one that does not require sorted data.

# Summary

The techniques you learned in this chapter will be useful throughout your entire programming career. Sorting and searching techniques are central routines in the data processing world. The computer, thanks to your programs, can do mundane tasks such as sorting a huge list of inventory values while you concentrate on less mundane jobs such as customer service.

- A typical counter and accumulator assignment updates the value of a total variable.

- A bubble sort makes several passes through the data, sending the small value of each pass to the top of the list.

- Nested loops control sorting routines by stepping through a list's values multiple times.

- A sequential search provides a simple searching algorithm, but a binary search is far more efficient.

- Although data structures appear in many varieties, a structure or record often appears as a data type in modern programming languages and enables you to work with a group of data values of different data types.

## IN THIS CHAPTER

- Introducing C
- Analyzing a C Program
- Using the main() Function's Format
- Using the #include Statement
- C Data
- C Comments
- Declaring Variables
- C Functions
- C Operators
- C Control Statements

13

# PROGRAMMING WITH C

C is one of those programming languages that most programmers never predicted would take off. Designed as a highly efficient, somewhat cryptic language used to write in the Unix operating system, C is a language designed by system programmers. The application programming community never intended to use C seriously.

Today, virtually every program you see on the store shelves is written in either C or, more likely, a language based on C. A C-based compiler is on a high percentage of programmers' computers. C's importance to modern computer languages cannot be stressed enough.

The highlights of this chapter include the following:

- C is an efficient language.
- C is a small language with very few commands.
- C's operators are more numerous than in most previous languages.
- Many of C's looping and decision statements work like Visual Basic's.

# Introducing C

Compared to an assembly language, C is a highly efficient language in which to write operating systems. C is more maintainable, and programmers are able to update the operating system and produce accurate code.

To achieve its efficiency, C has one drawback that other high-level languages don't: C is more cryptic than most other programming languages. Its cryptic nature comes in the form of a huge collection of operators and a small number of keywords. Table 13.1 lists C's keywords. The standard C language has only 32 keywords, an extremely small number compared to other languages such as Visual Basic. C relies on its assortment of operators to perform tasks more than other languages do; whereas Visual Basic may require three statements to loop or add to a variable, C sometimes requires only one statement or even one operator to perform the same task.

**caution**

Notice that C's keywords all appear in lowercase, quite a change from Visual Basic. C is case sensitive, so if you use an uppercase letter anywhere inside a command, your program will not compile properly.

**tip**

Notice that many of C's keywords match Visual Basic's. The `case`, `do`, `else`, `for`, and `if` keywords work much like their Visual Basic counterparts. Therefore, you already know how five commands work—you know one-sixth of the C language already!

**TABLE 13.1** C Keywords

| auto | double | int | struct |
|---|---|---|---|
| break | else | long | switch |
| case | enum | register | typedef |
| char | extern | return | union |
| const | float | short | unsigned |
| continue | for | signed | void |
| default | goto | sizeof | volatile |
| do | if | static | while |

C has more operators than any other programming language, with the exception of APL. As you know from Visual Basic, an operator is usually a special character that performs some operation on data. Not all operators are mathematical, but the primary math operators are the most obvious way to learn about operators because you are already used to them. In the expression 5 + 6, the plus sign (+) is an operator. As with Visual Basic and others, most programming languages use the same four operators that C uses (see Table 13.2).

## Table 13.2 Standard Math Operators in C

| Operator | Example | Description |
|---|---|---|
| + | 5 + 6 | Performs addition |
| - | 10 - 4 | Performs subtraction |
| * | 4 * 7 | Performs multiplication |
| / | 27 / 9 | Performs division |

Learning how C's operators work is of utmost importance. Most of your time learning C will be spent working with C's operators. The large number of operators make people think C is a cryptic or mathematical language. Actually, C's operators (Table 13.3 shows a complete list) are not all mathematical. Many of them take the place of commands used by other languages. It is the abundant use of operators in C that makes it very efficient and succinct.

## TABLE 13.3 C Operators

| Operator | Description | Operator | Description |
|---|---|---|---|
| ++ | Increment | -- | Decrement |
| * | Multiply (and dereference) | / | Divide |
| + | Add | - | Subtract |
| % | Calculate remainder | = | Assign |
| < | Less than | > | Greater than |
| <= | Less than or equal to | >= | Greater than or equal to |
| == | Equal to | != | Not equal to |
| \| | Bitwise or | & | Bitwise and |
| ^ | Bitwise 1's complement | ~ | Bitwise 2's complement |
| >> | Bitwise shift right | << | Bitwise shift left |
| \|\| | Logical or | && | Logical and |
| ! | Logical not | ?: | Condition comparisons |
| () | Grouping and argument lists | [] | Subscript |
| . | Member of structure | -> | Pointer |
| += | Increment by a value | -= | Decrement by a value |
| *= | Multiply by a value | /= | Divide by a value |
| %= | Update with a remainder | >>= | Bitwise shift right update |
| <<= | Bitwise shift left update | ^= | 1's complement update |
| &= | Bitwise and update | \|= | Bitwise or update |
| , | Sequence operator | (type) | Convert to a data type |
| (sizeof) | Return the size of type | | |

# Analyzing a C Program

Listing 13.1 contains a short but complete C program.

**LISTING 13.1**   A Small Sample Program in C

```
/* Prints a message on the screen */
#include <stdio.h>
    main()
    {
        pnintf('C is efficient.\n');
        return 0;
    }
```

Listing 13.1 produces this message on the screen:

```
C is efficient.
```

The program required seven lines to output one simple sentence. With C's compiled efficiency and power comes the responsibility to master the language and all its nuances.

Listing 13.1 contains three sets of grouping symbols: angled brackets <>, braces {}, and parentheses (). Be extremely careful when typing a C program because the correct and exact symbol is important. C doesn't handle ambiguity very well, so if you type the wrong symbol, C won't work properly.

# Using the `main()` Function's Format

The cornerstone of every C program is the `main()` function. Because `main()` is a function and not a command, the trailing parentheses are required. A C function, just like a Visual Basic procedure, is a section of code that does something. `main()` is required because execution of a C program always begins in its `main()` function. Programmers use `main()` to control the rest of the program. `main()` often includes a series of procedure calls. (All procedures in C are known as *function procedures*; you'll learn more about C functions in the section "C Functions," later in this chapter.)

The actual code for `main()`, as with all C functions you write, begins after the opening brace, {, and `main()` continues until the closing brace, }, where `main()` terminates and other functions often begin. Other sets of braces, always in pairs, may appear within a function such as `main()` as well.

Notice in Listing 13.1 that many of the statements end with a semicolon (;). Full statements require the semicolon. For example, assignment statements and lines that perform I/O require the semicolon, but formatting and grouping statements don't. In Listing 13.1, the line with `main()` doesn't require a semicolon because `main()` doesn't terminate until the final closing brace in the last line. The brace requires no semicolon because it is a grouping character and does nothing on its own.

## Using the `#include` Statement

Surprisingly, you'll never see `#include` in a list of C commands because `#include` is not a C command. Statements in a C program that begin with the pound sign are called *preprocessor directives*. The compiler analyzes the directive and, instead of compiling the statement, acts upon the statement immediately during compilation.

The `#include` preprocessor directive tells the compiler to insert another file that resides in source code form at the location in the program where the directive resides. Therefore, before the program is actually compiled, more code is inserted at the programmer's request at the place where `#include` occurs. That code is compiled along with the programmer's code.

The `stdio.h` file is a source code auxiliary file that helps a C program perform input/output (I/O) properly. C files that end with the `.h` extension are called *header files*, as opposed to C program source code files that end with the `.c` filename extension. All C programs perform some kind of I/O, and the most common header file used to help C with its I/O is `stdio.h`. As you learn more about C, you'll learn additional header files that can be helpful, such as the `time.h` header file that includes definitions that help with time and date conversions.

note

The fact that C doesn't include support for a built-in string data type isn't a huge problem because built-in functions are available in the language to work with string data. Also, C does allow for string literals, such as strings that you type directly in the code, just not string variables. Unlike Visual Basic, however, string data is not inherently supported in the fundamental language, which sometimes makes for some interesting programming.

## C Data

C supports data formats that work much like Visual Basic's data formats. For example, C supports the following kinds of data:

- A single text character
- Integers
- Floating-points (decimal numbers)

C supports several types of integers and floating-point data such as long and short integers as well as single-precision and double-precision floating-point decimal data. Unlike Visual Basic, C does not support a string data type. Although C has some built-in functionality to handle strings in some situations, generally the C language leaves it to the programmer and functions to handle strings. C doesn't support an intrinsic string data type. Therefore, the only text-based data type that C supports is a single character.

All of C's character literals must be enclosed in apostrophes, often called single quotation marks. The single quote differentiates character data from other kinds of data such as numbers and symbols. All of the following are character literals:

```
'Q'      '8'      '*'      ' '      'a'
```

None of the following are character literals because none of them appear inside single quotes:

```
Q      8      *      a
```

Listing 13.1 contains a special character, \n. At first, \n doesn't look like a character, but it is one of the few two-character combinations that C treats as a single character. \n tells C to drop the cursor down to the next line. Listing 13.1 didn't use \n as a single character, but \n is always considered a single character as well as most occurrences of a letter that follows a backslash.

Listing 13.1 included a string literal as well. String literals (remember that C does not support string variables) are always enclosed in quotation marks. Therefore, the following are string literals:

```
"C is efficient.\n"
```

```
"3"
```

```
"443-55-9999"
```

# C Comments

A C comment is the same as a Visual Basic remark. Comments document the code. A comment begins with /* and ends with a closing */, even if the comment spans several lines of code. C comments can go anywhere in a program, including the end of a line.

What does the following C statement do?

```
return ((si < s2) ? si : s2));
```

How could anyone expect to know what that statement does? Even an advanced C programmer will have to analyze the statement for a while to understand it. A simple comment makes everything much easier, as the following statement shows:

```
return ((s1 < s2) ? s1 : s2); /* Finds the smaller of 2 values */
```

From the comment, you know that the statement locates the smaller of the two values stored in s1 and s2 (s1 and s2 are variables).

# Declaring Variables

Keeping in mind that no string variables exist in C, declaring variables in C is about as simple as declaring them in Visual Basic. Consider the following section of a main() function:

```
main()
{
  char initial;
  int age;
  float amount;
```

This code declares three variables: initial, age, and amount. They hold three different types of data: a character, an integer, and a floating-point value. These variables are local to the function and cannot be used outside main(). (You can declare variables before main(), and those variables are known as *global*, but global variables are generally not recommended.)

C does not initialize variables to zero as Visual Basic does. The assignment statement works just as it does in Visual Basic. You can initialize variables like this:

```
initial = 'G';
age = 21;
amount = 6.75;
```

# C Functions

C is built on a foundation of functions—both those functions that you write and the functions supplied by C. The next two sections should help you understand the nature of C functions.

## Using Built-In Functions

Unlike just about every other programming language in the world, C has no input or output statements. Look through Table 13.1 once more. You don't see a Print statement or anything else that might be considered an I/O statement.

C performs all its I/O through functions that your C compiler provides. By letting the compiler makers implement I/O in functions, the C language is highly *portable*, meaning that a C program that runs on one kind of computer should run on any other computer than is capable of running C programs. A C program written for a Macintosh will work on a PC without change, assuming that you compile the program using each computer's own C compiler.

## The `printf()` Output Function

The most common I/O function is the `printf()` function. `printf()` outputs data to the screen in most cases (although the programmer can route the output to other devices if needed through operating system options). Here is the format for `printf()`:

```
printf(controlString [, data]);
```

`controlString` determines how the output will look. `controlString` will format any data values that you specify (separated by commas if more than one value is output) in the data area. Consider the following `printf()`:

```
printf("Read a lot");
```

This `printf()` doesn't include a data list of any kind. `controlString` is the only argument to this `printf()`. When you use a string of text for the `controlString` value, C outputs the text directly to the screen. Therefore, `printf()` produces this onscreen when the user runs the program:

```
Read a lot
```

When you print numbers and characters, you must tell C exactly how to print them. You indicate the format of numbers with conversion characters that format data. The conversion characters format data in functions such as `printf()` (see Table 13.4).

### **caution**

Remember to use the `\n` character if you want output to force the cursor to the next line. If the previous `printf()` was followed by this `printf()`:

```
printf('Keep learning);
```

the output would look like this:

```
Read a lotKeep learning
```

Obviously, the first `printf()` should have used the `\n` character like this:

```
printf(Keep learning\n");
```

With `\n`, subsequent `printf()` output would appear on the next line.

**TABLE 13.4**    C Conversion Characters

| Character | Description |
|-----------|-------------|
| %d | Integer |
| %f | Floating-point |
| %c | Character |
| %s | String |

When you want to print a value inside a string, insert the appropriate conversion characters in the `controlString`. Then, to the right of the `controlString`, list the value you want printed. Figure 13.1 shows how a `printf()` can print three numbers—an integer, a floating-point value, and another integer.

**FIGURE 13.1**

The conversion characters determine how and where the output appears.

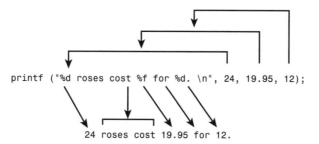

```
printf ("%d roses cost %f for %d. \n", 24, 19.95, 12);
```

24 roses cost 19.95 for 12.

Strings and characters have their own conversion characters as well. You don't need `%s` to print strings by themselves because strings included inside the `controlString` that don't have the formatting percent sign before them print exactly as you type them. Nevertheless, you might need to use `%s` when combining strings with other data.

The next `printf()` prints a different type of data value using each of the conversion characters from Table 13.4:

```
printf("%s %d %f %c\n", "Sam", 14, -8.76, 'X');
```

This `printf()` produces this:

```
Sam 14 -8.760000 X
```

The string `Sam` needs quotation marks, as do all string literals, and the character `x` needs single quote marks, as do all characters. C formats floating-point numbers with full precision, hence the four zeros at the end of the value. You can limit the number of places printed by using format specifiers. If the `printf()`'s conversion characters for the floating-point number had been `%5.2`, the `-8.76` would have been output in five spaces, with two of those five spaces used for the decimal portion.

## WORKING WITH STRINGS

Although C doesn't support string variables, a way exists to store strings. C represents all strings with a *null zero* character at the end of the string. This character has an ASCII value of zero. When C encounters it, C knows that it has reached the end of the string. You never see this null zero, and you never do anything to add it, because C adds it.

If a string includes `0` as part of its text, such as the following address: `"190 S. Oak Road"`, the embedded zero is not the null zero; it is a regular ASCII character (ASCII number 48).

Figure 13.2 shows how the string `"Sams"` is stored in memory as a string. The `\0` character is C's representation for the null string. The length of a string includes the characters within the string but never includes the null zero.

C uses a character array to hold strings, including the string's null zero. All of C's data types can appear in their own arrays, but when a character array appears and a null zero is included at the end of the data, C treats that character array just like a string. C uses brackets instead of parentheses for array subscripts. To define a character array that holds a 10-character string, you could declare the following:

```
char month[10] = "September";  /* Declare and initialize the string */
```

You should always leave room for the null zero in the array. C uses zero-based arrays, so month can hold a 10-character string in elements 0 through 8 and the null zero in element 9. You can also assign the array at runtime using a special strcpy() function like this:

```
strcpy(month, "September");  /* Assigns September to the month array */
```

To use strcpy(), you must include the header file named string.h in the same area of the program where you include stdio.h.

**FIGURE 13.2**

Strings always terminate with a null zero character.

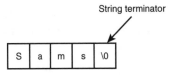

String terminator

## The scanf() Input Function

Getting keyboard input is much more difficult than producing output on the screen. Use scanf() to accept keyboard input; scanf() is fairly simple now that you understand printf(), but it does act funny at times. Here is the format for scanf():

```
scanf(controlString [, data]);
```

If you remember the following rule, scanf() should work for you every time:

> Prefix each variable inside scanf() with an ampersand unless that variable is an array.

Therefore, the following scanf() function gets an age value entered by the user:

```
scanf(" %d", &Age);
```

The following scanf() function gets the user's first name into a character array as a result of the user following the prompting printf():

```
printf("What is your first name? ");
scanf(" %s", name); /* Get the name */
```

note

Do you see the blank before the %d in scanf()'s controlString? Always include the blank because sometimes input of values works better with the blank. (A reason does exist for this, but it's technical and not important here.)

scanf() is a mirror-image function to printf(). Often, you will write programs that ask the user for values with a printf() and get those values with scanf(). When your program gets to scanf(), C stops and waits for the user to type values. The variables listed inside scanf() (following the *controlString* argument) will accept whatever the user types, and scanf() quits receiving input when the user presses Enter.

Despite its problems, scanf() is useful to learn early in your C tutorial so that you can practice getting user input. There are many other ways to get user input in C, and often they work better than scanf(), but scanf()'s similarity to the simpler printf() makes scanf() an acceptable keyboard-input function for beginners.

Listing 13.2 shows a complete program that prompts for user input and gets output. You can study the program to gain a better understanding of the material you've covered so far in this chapter.

## LISTING 13.2    Using scanf() and printf() for Input and Output

```c
#include <stdio.h>
main()
{
  int age;
  float weight;
  char first[15], last[15];   /* 2 char arrays */

  printf("\nWhat is your first name? ");
  scanf(" %s", first);   /* No ampersand on char arrays */
  printf("What is your last name? ");
  scanf(" %s", last);

  printf("How old are you? ");
  scanf(" %d", &age);       /* Ampersand required */
  printf("How much do you weigh? ");
  scanf(" %f", &weight);   /* Ampersand required */

  printf("\nHere is the information you entered;\n");
  /* Notice the space between the following printf()'s
     two %s occurrences to ensure that the first
     and last names are separated. */
  printf("Name: %s %s\n", first, last);
  printf("Weight: %d", age);
  return 0;   /* Always best to do this */
}
```

Here is a sample execution of Listing 13.2:

```
What is your first name? Joe
What is your last name? Harrison
How old are you? 41
How much do you weigh? 205

Here is the information you entered:
name: Joe Harrison
Weight: 205
Age: 41
```

## Writing General Program Functions

As with a Visual Basic program's collection of event procedures, C programs are modular and comprise many functions. Although you can put all of a C program's code in the `main()` function, `main()` is intended to be used as a controlling function for the rest of the program. Listing 13.3 illustrates the outline of a C program that has proper form.

**LISTING 13.3** Using `main()` to Control the Rest of the Program

```
#include <stdio.h>
main()
{
  getNums();    /* Get a list of numbers */
  sortNums();   /* Sort the numbers */
  printNums()   /* Print the list */
  return 0;     /* End the program */
}

getNums()

{

  /* Body of function goes here
     that gets a list of values
     from the user */
}

sortNums()
```

**LISTING 13.3** (continued)

```
{
   /* Body of function goes here
      that sorts the values */
}
printNums()
{
   /* Body of function goes here
      that prints the values */
}
```

C calls a function procedure when it encounters the function's name. Therefore, `main()` is composed of a series of function calls to three separate procedures. (The code bodies appear in comments in this example.)

`main()`, and hence the entire running program, terminates when the `return 0` statement is reached. `return` often appears at the end of a function that is returning a value to the calling function. `main()` is returning `0` to the operating system. Zero is a standard return value that the operating system can check. (If you perform error checking, you could return a different value to the operating system if an error occurs and program the operating system to do something in response to a non-zero value.)

> **note**
>
> C distinguishes between a function's declaration and its call by the trailing semicolon. A semicolon always follows a function call (such as the lines in `main()`), but a semicolon never follows the first line of a function (called the function declaration).

As with all languages, one problem with C is that its local data is known only to function procedures that declare that data. In other words, if no global variables exist in Listing 13.3, the local array holding the user's values will be known only to the `Get Nums()` function. To pass this data to the other functions for sorting and printing, you would write the program in such a way as to pass the list from function to function, or perhaps declare the list locally in `main()`, which can pass the list between the called functions. Passing takes place within the parentheses after a function name.

A discussion of the ways C programmers pass data would take several chapters. For now, it is enough that you understand much of the structure of a C program.

# C Operators

Many of C's operators, such as the plus sign, work exactly like those in other languages. Nevertheless, C's rich collection of operators requires some review so that you can grasp what C is all about. This section provides a quick overview of some of C's more interesting operators.

C supports increment and decrement operators. In Chapter 12, "Program Algorithms," you learned about the concept of adding or subtracting 1 (one) to or from a variable to keep track of a count. C's ++ and -- operators add and subtract 1, respectively, from whatever variable you apply them to. The following statements add 1 to the variables a, b, and c:

```
a++;
b++;
c++;
```

The following statements decrease a, b, and c by one:

```
a--;
b--;
c--;
```

C also supports *compound assignments*, operators that update the value of a variable: +=, -=, *=, and /=. The following statement

```
a += 25;   /* Add 25 to a */
```

is identical to this statement:

```
a = a + 25; /* Add 25 to a */
```

These operators help the programmer do his job more quickly and make the compilation of the program more efficient. However, at times they do make for cryptic code.

# C Control Statements

C supports an if...else statement that works a lot like the Visual Basic If...Else statement. Table 13.5 lists the relational operators with which you can compare data.

**TABLE 13.5**   C Relational Operators

| Relational Operator | Description |
| --- | --- |
| == | Equal to |
| > | Greater than |
| < | Less than |
| >= | Greater than or equal to |
| <= | Less than or equal to |
| != | Not equal to |

Use braces to group the body of an `if` statement as shown in the following statement:

```
if (age < 18)
 { printf("You cannot vote yet\n");
   yrs = 18 - age;
   printf('You can vote in %d years.\n", yrs);
 }
else
{
  printf("You can vote.\n");
}
```

The individual statements in the `if` statement end with semicolons, but not the `if`. The `if...else` spans several lines, so you don't put semicolons after the first line of an `if` statement.

C also supports several kinds of looping statements that use the relational operators. For example, the following code shows a `while` loop that continues as long as the relational expression evaluates to true:

```
while (amount < 25)
  {
    printf('Amount is too small.\n");
    wrongVal++;   /* Keep track of number of problems */
    printf("Try again... What is the new amount? ");
    scanf(" %d", &amount);
}
```

C's `For` looping statement is more succinct than Visual Basic's because C does not require a `Next` statement. In addition, the C compiler can determine the entire loop structure from the For statement's parenthetical values. In Visual Basic, the following set of statements prints the numbers from 1 to 10:

```
For ctr = 1 To 10
   Print ctr
Next ctr
```

In C, the same code is shown here:

```
for (ctr=1; ctr<=10; ctr++)
{   printf(" %d\n", ctr); }
```

Although the C code appears more cryptic to people, the compiler gains efficiency because a Next statement does not have to be processed each time through the loop. The C compiler knows the end of the loop occurs at the closing brace.

Several other control statements also work like those in Visual Basic, such as C's switch statement, which produces virtually the same relational testing control that Visual Basic's Select Case statement provides.

# Summary

Are you a C expert after one chapter? No way. Do you understand the fundamentals of C? You might be surprised at how well you already understand the language. With your Visual Basic background, you understand the nature of many of C's controlling statements. C's syntax and operators certainly take some time to master, but you will have little trouble progressing from here.

The next chapter describes C's successor, C++. Many times, C++ code is identical to that of C. Instead of focusing on specific language statements, our introduction to C++ focuses more on the object-oriented programming aspects of C++.

- C's operators enable the language to be efficient.
- All C programs require at least one function named main().
- Use #include to supply header information required by your C program.
- Make sure that a semicolon terminates every C statement.
- C's looping statements can be written succinctly to keep the code small and efficient.

# IN THIS CHAPTER

- Learning C++
- Object Terminology
- Fundamental Differences Between C and C++
- Introducing Objects
- Benefits of OOP

**14**

# PROGRAMMING WITH C

The language competing with Visual Basic for the top programming language in use today is C++. Whereas C was the original Windows programming language, C++ is the Windows programming language of choice today for those not wanting to use Visual Basic, or for those who want another language to use in addition to Visual Basic.

C++ is considered to be a better language than C. It offers full support for *object-oriented programming* (*OOP*). In Visual Basic you work with objects, because Visual Basic is not a true OOP language. In this chapter you'll learn how and why C++ provides strong OOP support and how the mechanics of C++ provide for more flexible, maintainable, and efficient programming than C.

The highlights of this chapter include the following:

- C++ is a better C than C.
- OOP increases your productivity.

- Classes are the holders of object families.
- C++ object libraries extend your programming skills.
- C++'s inheritance feature can decrease programming time.

# Learning C++

In the previous chapter, you learned about C's increment operator, ++, which increases a variable's value by 1 (one). C++ is an incremental improvement over C, hence its name. Much of a C++ program looks like pure C code, and it is just that. The C++ language does introduce some new language elements, but the keywords and structure are similar to C.

Most of C++'s changes from C are a result of injecting OOP technology. The primary differences between C and C++ aren't commands and keyword differences but rather how the language supports the use of objects.

There is disagreement as to whether it is best to learn C before C++. One side argues that learning C without dealing with the OOP issues makes it easier to learn C's mechanics; then you can learn the OOP additions to the language. Others argue that object-oriented programming is simpler than programming without objects so the programmer learns bad habits when the OOP structure is not present. They say that C++ should be learned first without taking the time to deal with C. The majority of C++ programmers first began with C, and learning C doesn't seem to slow them down too much.

Virtually every C program in use today is compiled by a C++ compiler. C++ compilers support C as well as the OOP additions that C++ provides. The compiler distinguishes between C and C++ programs by the source code's extension; C programs use .c, and C++ uses .cpp. Not all C++ compilers support programming in the Windows environment, but most PC-based C++ compilers sold today do, including support for a visual interface such as a toolbox with controls, as Visual Basic provides.

# Object Terminology

OOP is laden with terminology that seems daunting at first. The actual implementation of OOP is fairly easy to understand, but to prepare you for the terms ahead, take a moment to study the following OOP-related characteristics:

- **abstraction**—The internals of an object do not always have to be known by the programmer to use an object.
- **class**—The definition of a related group of objects.

- **inheritance**—The capability to create a new class of objects from an existing class. Inheritance enables you to create new objects with behaviors and characteristics based on existing objects and classes.

- **message**—A command that acts on specific objects, as opposed to language commands that are not tied to specific objects.

- **object**—A collection of characteristics and behaviors, perhaps even two or more variables treated as a single unit, that appear in OOP programs.

Most OOP languages, not just C++, support these same characteristics.

- **polymorphism**—A name given to the capability of different objects to respond differently to the same command (called a *message*).

- **reuse**—The capability of a language to utilize objects defined in other programs.

These complex terms are not that difficult to understand. Unfortunately, one chapter is not enough to teach C++'s details, but by the time you finish this chapter, you will know the foundation of C++, you will be more familiar with the terms associated with OOP, and you will understand exactly what's in store for you if you become a C++ programmer.

# Fundamental Differences Between C and C++

Some of the new language features that C++ provides over C have nothing directly to do with OOP. The following sections preview some of the non-OOP language differences that you'll find between C and C++.

## Comments

One of the differences is the way that C++ allows you to place comments in your C++ programs. (A comment in C or C++ is the same as a remark in Visual Basic.) Any text that follows a double slash, //, is considered by C++ to be a comment. Therefore, you don't need a closing comment symbol, such as */, as you need in C. The following shows the same comment in C++ and then in C:

```
intCust++;  // Add to customer count

intCust++;  /* Add to customer count */
```

The C++ format is often simpler to code because the programmer does not have to terminate the comment. In addition, fewer bugs appear because, if a programmer fails to terminate a C comment, code that should not be included in the comment is included until the next closing comment symbol.

## Name Differences

Some differences between C and C++ are simple changes. For example, instead of C's #include <stdio.h> directive, C++ programs almost always include the #include <iostream.h> directive.

**note**

C++ recognizes C's /* and */ comments. Many of today's C compilers also recognize the C++ // comment.

As with the C header files, C++ programmers will include many other header files in addition to iostream.h, but iostream.h is the most commonly included file. iostream.h is the header file that defines basic input and output.

## I/O Differences

C++ includes several new operators. The two most common C++ are the *insertion* operator (<<) and the *extraction* operator (>>). These operators are usually combined with the two stream objects cout and cin. A *stream object* is nothing more than a series of data that is being input or output.

A few examples will quickly show you how to combine the insertion and extraction operators with stream objects. The following statement sends a string and a number to the screen (typically the output stream goes to the screen, although you can change that to a different destination device):

```
cout << "Here is the total: " << 1000.00;
```

In C, you would use printf() like this:

```
printf("Here is the total: %f7.2", 1000.00);
```

If you want to write several lines of output, you can do so by embedding the newline character in the output stream. The following line

```
cout << "Line 1" << '\n' << "Line 2" << '\n' << "Line 3" << '\n';
```

produces this output:

```
Line 1
Line 2
Line 3
```

C++ combines the `cin` input stream with the `>>` extraction operator to support keyboard input. As with `scanf()`, keyboard-based input with C++ is fairly simple to understand and implement, but as with `scanf()`, in all but the most fundamental cases, C++'s input capabilities are limited when you use `cin`. Most introductory courses and texts teach `cin` and `>>` just to get the student started with a way to get keyboard input quickly, but keep in mind that more advanced and better input methods exist that you would go on to master if you were to pursue the C++ language.

To get a keyboard value into an integer variable named `intAge`, you could do this:

```
cin >> intAge;
```

Of course, you would probably prompt the user first with a `cout`, so the I/O would more likely look like this:

```
cout << "How old are you? ";
cin >> intAge;      // Get the age
```

> **tip**
>
> Generally, C++ programmers do not use the newline character, `'\n'`, at the end of a statement with `cout`; they use a special object called `endl`. `endl` is an object that not only produces a newline character but also empties the *output buffer* (a temporary holding place in memory for output as you build it) if you send data to a device that buffers output, such as a printer. Therefore, the following statement would be more likely than the one shown before this tip:
>
> ```
> cout << "Line 1" << '\n'
> ⮡<< "Line 2" << '\n' <<
> ⮡"Line 3" << endl;
> ```

# Introducing Objects

You've already seen examples of objects. All data values are potential objects in the C++ language. Variables are objects. Although objects can get much more complex than simple variables, a variable is a valid object. In addition, you've now been introduced to the objects `cin` and `cout`. Although `cin` and `cout` are predefined language objects and are not like many other objects in programs, they do work in the same way that all other objects work. You'll learn about this in the rest of this chapter.

An object is like a package that exists inside a C++ program. All objects have behaviors and properties. Consider the following object definition:

```
int intObj = 17;   // Defines an integer object
```

The integer variable `intObj` has properties; the object can hold nondecimal, whole number values that can be negative, zero, or positive. In addition, the object has behavior; when you output the object, an integer appears. When you assign a decimal value such as `12.34` to `intObj`, the object throws out the fractional portion and receives only `12`.

Obviously, the idea of OOP-based objects goes far beyond simple variables. Objects can be as simple as variables, but often an object represents a non-language item such as a database table, a printer, or a keyboard. After developing a collection of several object classes, you will be able to manage an object such as a color printer as easily as you manage a variable, through code. Of course, that's the goal of OOP; in reality, abstracting real-world objects to programming-language equivalents is not so easy, but the goal of OOP is to make programming as simple as using objects that you define.

The cornerstone of objects in C++ (as well as any other OOP-based language, such as Smalltalk) is object reuse. Once you develop an object, you can easily port that object to other programs. Even objects written by others are available to your program. Therefore, if someone in your company develops a collection of objects that represent company data, such as a company personnel record, your program can also use the object. The details of how the object is formed are unimportant; your program can access the object without knowing everything about the object. In other words, you can reuse an object declared elsewhere without knowing all the details of the object, knowing only enough to use it in your code.

### OBJECTS BUILD UP THE LANGUAGE

Input and output streams provide the fundamental I/O capabilities of C++ but, through classes, you can increase the capability of these streams to input and output more than single characters. Through OOP-related techniques such as inheritance and abstraction, you can route any kind of data to any kind of object.

For example, a C++ program might send the contents of a database record to a series of text boxes with the following simple statement:

```
txtSet << dtaRecord;  // Write record to text boxes
```

**tip**

Everything electronic today is composed of modules. Your television set is a collection of electronic modules; if something goes wrong with your TV, the repair center will probably replace a whole circuit board, even if a small part on the board is the only fault. Your stereo might be made up of a collection of components that you can add, remove, and interchange with others. This kind of object reuse is the lofty goal of OOP. When someone develops an object, others can use that object in their own programs without having to design and declare the object all over again and without having to know all about the object's internals. Of course, before a programmer reuses an object, that programmer must study the object's definition to learn what kind of data the object contains. With object reuse, the backlog of programming projects, in theory, should be reduced. The problem is that the backlog is not reduced, due to the demand for programs in today's computing world. Without OOP, however, that backlog might be even greater than it already is.

Figure 14.1 shows what might take place with such a statement. You can output a huge record with a simple statement when using objects. Getting to the point where you can output consolidated records to a set of text boxes requires quite a bit of programming. Nevertheless, C++ makes that intermediate programming simpler than would otherwise be the case, due to the OOP foundation of C++. Once you build these special and powerful I/O streams, your programs become much easier to manage and maintain. In another language, writing a database record to a set of text boxes on the screen would take many statements.

**FIGURE 14.1**

A simple-looking output statement can produce quite a bit of output when you print objects.

This simple statement:
```
txtSet << dtaRecord; // Write record to text boxes
```

could produce this if the dtaRecord object contains this data:

The customer's record is up to date and contains the following:

Customer name:  George Primrose
Address:        14 West Elm Street
City:           Carmel
State:          Indiana
Zipcode:        49982
Balance:        $562.09
Payment code:   4-G78

# Defining Classes

In general, to declare a C++ object, you must declare a class. A class is not an object but is a description of an object. The C++ language includes a new keyword called `class` that you use to define a class.

Consider the following class declaration:
```
class Person {
  char strLastName[25];
  int  intAge;
  float flSalary;
};
```

The class name is `Person`. The class is said to have three *members*. The member names are `strLastName`, `intAge`, and `flSalary`. This class, therefore, describes objects that contain three members. Individually, each member could be

**caution**

Remember, a class is a description of an object but not the object itself. In a way, `int` is a keyword that defines a class. `int` is a data type that describes a type of numeric value or variable. Only after you define integer variables do you have an integer object. In the same way, only after declaring variables from a class does an instance of that class—or more accurately, an object of that class—exist in code.

considered a separate variable, but taken together (and C++ will always consider the members to be part of the class) the members form the class. The members are not objects but parts of objects that you can define with this class.

# Declaring Object Variables

Consider the following statement that declares a simple C++ integer variable:

```
int intCount;
```

You do not have to tell C++ what an integer is because C++ already understands the integer class. The integer class is internal to the language. Therefore, intCount will be an integer variable that takes on all the characteristics of all integer variables.

C++, without your help, would have no idea what the Person class would be, however, because Person is not an internal class native to C++. Therefore, the multiline class statement shown earlier tells C++ exactly what the class's characteristics are. After you define the class, you then can declare variables or, more accurately, objects of the class. The following statement declares a Person object called Mike:

```
Person Mike;    // Declares an instance of the Person class
```

Figure 14.2 shows what the object (or variable or instance of the class) looks like. The object named Mike is a three-part object. The characteristics are as follows: Mike is an object that begins with a 25-character array, followed by an integer, followed by a floating-point value.

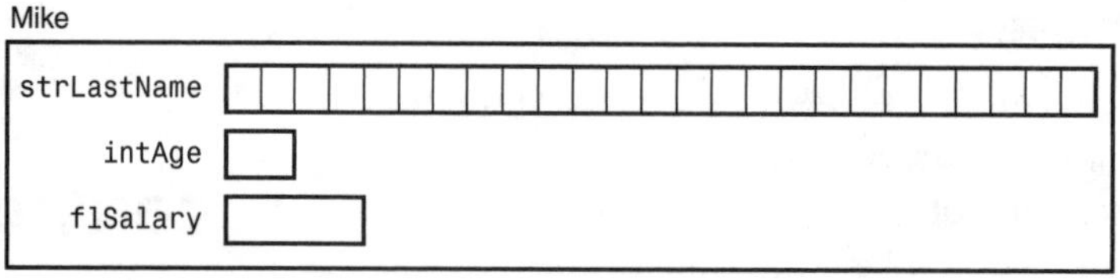

**FIGURE 14.2**

The object named Mike internally contains three members.

All Person objects that you declare from the Person class will look like Mike, but they will have different names just as integer variables in a program have different names. In addition, the objects will have local or global scope, depending on where you declare them.

The following statement would declare three additional objects that take on the characteristics of the Person class:

```
Person Judy, Paul, Terry;
```

## Accessing Members

You'll use the dot operator . (period) to access members in an object. For example, the following assignment stores a value in the Mike object's intAge member:

```
Mike.intAge = 32;   // Initialize the member
➥named age
```

As long as you qualify the member name with the object name, C++ knows which object to assign to. Therefore, if several Person objects are declared in the program, the object name before the member informs the program exactly which object member you want to initialize. Anywhere you can use a variable, you can use a member name as long as you qualify the name with the object. For example, you cannot directly assign a string literal to a character array in C++ (or in C), but you can use the strcpy() function like this:

```
strcpy(Mike.strLastName, "Johnson");   //
➥Assign the name
```

You could print one of the members like this:

```
cout << Mike.intAge;   // Display the age
```

If you wanted to print the three members, you might do so like this:

```
cout << Mike.strLastName << ", " <<
➥Mike.intAge << ", " <<
        Mike.flSalary << endl;
```

**tip**

Generally, programmers place the class definition globally, or even stored in a header file that they include in subsequent programs.

Once the class definition appears globally (such as before the main() procedure), the rest of the program can use that class to declare object variables. The variables might be global, but they will probably be local if the programmer follows the suggested standards and maintains only local variables to a procedure. As with any variables, you can pass object variables between procedures as needed.

## Adding Behavior to Objects

Until now, you've only seen how to add characteristics to a class by defining the class members. You can also define the class behaviors. The behaviors describe what objects in the class can do. Adding behaviors to a class requires much more coverage than the rest of this chapter will allow. Nevertheless, an example or two of a class with

**note**

If you've ever seen C's struct statement, you will recognize that class is identical in every respect, until you begin to add characteristics to the class, as you'll learn in the next section.

defined behavior will show you how objects begin to take on a life of their own in a way that simple variables cannot do.

The following `Person` class definition is more complete than the previous one because it defines not only the characteristics (the members and their data types) but also the behaviors (called *member functions*):

```
class Person {
  char strLastName[25];
  int  intAge;
  float flSalary;
  // Member functions appear next
  void dispName( void )
    { cout << "The last name is ";
      cout << strLastName << endl;
    }
  void compTaxes(float taxRate)
    {  float taxes;
       taxes = taxRate * flSalary;
       cout << "The taxes are ";
       cout << taxes << endl;
    }
  char [] getName( void )
    { return strLastName; }
  int getAge ( void )
    { return intAge; }
  float getSalary ( void )
    { return flSalary; }
};
```

Just as a member can be an instance of a variable, a member can also be a function. The embedded function, the member function, applies only to objects declared from this class. In other words, only `Person` objects behave exactly this way, but those `Person` objects can perform the operations defined by the member functions. In a way, the objects are smart; they know how to behave, and the more member functions you supply, the more the objects know how to do.

Many programmers elect to use function declarations (the declaration, or first line of a function, is called the function's *prototype*) in the `class` statement but then define the actual function code later. By placing function prototypes after the `class` itself, you keep the class cleaner:

```
class Person {
  char strLastName[25];
```

```
  int  intAge;
  float flSalary;
  // Member functions appear next
  void dispName( void );
  void compTaxes(float taxRate);
  char [] getName( void );
  int getAge ( void );
  float getSalary ( void );
};

void Person::dispName( void )
  { cout << "The last name is ";
    cout << strLastName << endl;
  }
void Person::compTaxes(float taxRate)
  {  float taxes;
     taxes = taxRate * flSalary;
     cout << "The taxes are ";
     cout << taxes << endl;
  }
char [] Person::getName( void )
  { return strLastName; }
int Person::getAge ( void )
  { return intAge; }
float Person::getSalary ( void )
  { return flSalary; }
```

The `class` statement is more compact because only
prototypes appear in the definition and not member function code. The member function code could
appear elsewhere in the program or, more likely,
would be included from a library file of member
functions. Notice that if you place the function's
definition later in the program, you must preface
the definition with the class name followed by the
`::` operator. The class name qualifies the function
because different classes may have member functions with the same name as other classes in the
program.

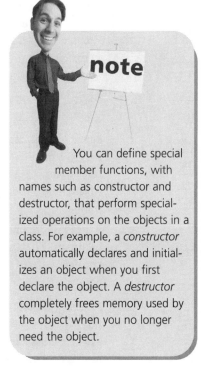

You can define special
member functions, with
names such as constructor and
destructor, that perform specialized operations on the objects in a
class. For example, a *constructor*
automatically declares and initializes an object when you first
declare the object. A *destructor*
completely frees memory used by
the object when you no longer
need the object.

Before we discuss how to apply the member functions to objects, you need to understand how scope affects objects and their member functions.

## Working with Class Scope

The class statement defines a class and its members and member functions, as you know. However, special consideration must be given to the scope of individual data and function members. In the previous class definition, all members were known to be private, which makes the class virtually unusable. By adding special public and private qualifiers, you make the class available to code.

Consider this modified Person class definition (the member function code is omitted for brevity):

```
class Person {
  char strLastName[25];
  int   intAge;
  float flSalary;
  // Member functions appear next
public:
  void dispName( void );
  void compTaxes(float taxRate);
  char [] getName( void );
  int getAge ( void );
  float getSalary ( void );
};
```

All members are considered to be private unless you precede them with the public keyword as is done here. All members before public are private, but you can place private: before the first member to make sure that other programmers know your intention is that the class members up to the next public keyword remain private. All members (both data members and function members) that follow public: are public.

Being private means that any program that uses the class can never access private members. This is critical for data protection that the class provides. Earlier in this chapter, you saw the following statement:

```
cout << Mike.intAge;   // Display the age
```

Actually, this statement will not work in the program because the program does not have access to the intAge data member. intAge is a private member, so no code outside the class can access intAge. By protecting the data members, you keep the object intact, and you ensure that only predefined functions available in the class can access the age. That's why you often see member functions that begin with get, as in the getAge() function shown previously. The fact that getAge() is in the public section of the class means that any program that defines Person objects can use the getAge() function. Therefore, you cannot display intAge directly, but you can call the getAge() function like this:

```
cout << Mike.getAge();  // Display the age
```

Notice that when you apply the member function to the object, you use the dot operator just as you do for data members. Other class objects may be defined and also have functions named getAge(), so you must qualify the member function by letting the program know you want the getAge() function applied to one specific object variable in the program named Mike.

Keep in mind that complete college courses and huge texts exist that teach object-oriented programming in C++. You're getting only an overview here, although the overview is actually rather complete. After mastering this introductory chapter, you should be able to understand the early portions of a course or text on C++ much more easily.

> **tip**
>
> Actually, when you see a member function combined with an object, you are sending a message to the object. The object, by containing the getAge() member function, knows how to return its age value when properly requested with the getAge() member function. Therefore, the code Mike.getAge() is known to be sending a message to the object named Mike telling Mike to return its intAge value. When a getAge() message is applied to Mike, Mike returns the age because of the member function.

# Benefits of OOP

With this introduction to C++, you can better understand the advantages that C++ provides over more traditional, non-OOP languages. One of the benefits of OOP is that you can create your own operators. More accurately, you can change the way an operator works when the program uses that operator with one of your objects.

By writing special operator overloading member functions, you can make any C++ operator work on your own objects. For example, a plus sign is the addition operator that automatically works on all numeric values. The plus sign, however, cannot work on a Person object such as Mike. Therefore, if you wanted to add two Person objects together to get a total of the salaries, you could write a function that adds the salaries of two or more flSalary data members. When you apply the totaling function members to objects, you can produce the total of the salaries, but you can also overload the plus sign operator so that plus works not only for two numbers but also for two Person objects.

Once you overload the operator, therefore, the code `Mike + Terry` works just fine, whereas you could never ordinarily use a plus sign between two `Person` objects that contain three data members of different data types. Such operator overloading means that you can simplify a program's code. Instead of using a function to simulate a common operation, you can apply the operator itself to your own objects. The member function that describes the operator overloading determines exactly which data members are affected and used by the operation.

The concept of polymorphism makes the overloading of operators possible. For example, the same operator applied to an integer variable behaves much differently if you apply it to a class object that you define.

In addition to overloading operators, you can create your own data types. Keep in mind that a class simply defines a collection of data that is composed of data members that conform to an ordinary data type. Therefore, for example, you could create a `String` class whose only data member is a character array. By overloading the appropriate operators, you can make C++ behave like Visual Basic and support string-like variables.

The `String` class is just one example of the many classes you and others can write to support object reuse. Over time, you will build a large library of classes that you can use for your future programs. As you build classes, the amount of code that you have to write should lessen, and you should complete applications more quickly. In addition, as you build and debug object class libraries, your programs should become more maintainable. Using operator overloading and other OOP advantages means that your code will be less bulky. When you need an object, you will simply take one from a class library, just as you add new stereo components when you want to expand your music system.

One of C++'s most productive features is inheritance. When you or someone else writes a class that you use, you are not limited to objects of that class. The C++ language supports inheritance so that you can derive new classes and create new objects that have all the benefits and features of their parent classes but with additional features as well.

# Summary

You cannot master OOP with C++ in one chapter, but you've already learned the fundamentals of how C++ works. At its most basic level, the C++ language offers improvements over C even if you don't use object-oriented programming. Nevertheless, when you begin to use OOP, you will learn to create classes that define objects that seem to take on lives of their own. The objects understand how to perform some duties based on their member functions, and you can extend the objects through inheritance to derive new classes that you can use later.

- OOP increases your flexibility because objects take on a life of their own and decrease programming time.

- The object's class determines which properties the object contains.

- By reusing objects, you reduce the amount of coding effort you must do.

- By using inheritance, you do not have to specify all the details for an object when you create that object.

## IN THIS CHAPTER

- Batch: The One That Started Everything
- Macro Languages
- Visual Basic for Applications (VBA)
- Scripting in Windows

15

# MACRO, BATCH, AND SCRIPTING LANGUAGES

Some programming languages exist not to write applications in, but to control the operating system and other applications. You can automate common operating system tasks so that with a single keystroke you can trigger a series of operating system commands that execute as though they resided in a program. In addition, Windows programs such as Excel and Word offer macro languages that enable you to collect a series of program commands in a single module, not unlike a program, and when you issue the command to start that module, the commands automatically execute as if you were at the keyboard typing them yourself.

Some Web page languages also provide a scripting language that helps to automate tasks done on the Web. This chapter introduces you to these concepts.

The highlights of this chapter include the following:

- Batch files control computer processes such as installation routines and file copies.
- Scripts work like batch files but for Web-based tasks.
- Batch and script files are interpreted and never compiled programs.
- A macro can be a set of recorded keystrokes or a scripted control language for an application.

# Batch: The One That Started Everything

From the very first PC (the original IBM PC), DOS supported a batch language that automated certain DOS tasks. Today, DOS windows inside Microsoft Windows still support batch files. Batch files contain commands from the batch language. A surprisingly large number of computer users still rely on this text-based DOS-controlling language for certain tasks such as disk copies and directory traversal.

A batch program differs quite a bit from a program you would write in C. A batch file is never compiled because the PC executes the batch file one line at a time as it reads each line. Although interpreting batch commands takes longer than executing compiled code, batch files are never large enough to take very long to execute.

Even if you could compile a batch file, the batch file's execution speed is limited to the speed of the operating system in handling the batch commands. In other words, if the operating system takes a moment to delete a file, compiling the file deletion command will not speed up the process. It will only speed up the capability of the operating system to read the command.

## Batch File Usage

Although batch files are used less and less, they were the forerunner of many scripting languages today and are still in use at times. Mainframe users often automate tasks with batch-like files (see the sidebar "JCL: The Original Batch File Language," later in this chapter).

Batch files always end in the .bat filename extension. You can execute batch files directly from the DOS prompt or from the Windows Start, Run command, and you can even assign an icon to a batch

**note**

One of the most common batch file uses today is in the installation of individual software installations, network setup routines, and *deployment* (installing the same program across an entire network of computers).

file and execute the batch file from the Windows Start menu or from the desktop. The icon-starting batch file is probably the most common use of batch files in Windows. When you select the icon, Windows automatically opens a DOS window and begins executing the batch file.

The most typical command that is found in a batch file is the name of a program. Whenever DOS encounters a program name in a batch file, it executes the program. For example, a DOS-based text editor program stored in the file `edit.com` comes with Windows. Any program that ends in the `.com` or `.exe` filename extension begins executing if you type its filename (with or without the extension) at the DOS prompt or in a batch file. If the word `edit` or `edit.com` appears on a line in a batch file, DOS will start the DOS editor at that point in the batch file's execution. When you exit the editor, the batch file resumes its execution and continues if other batch commands are in the file or Windows regains control.

As with all programs that end with the `.com` or `.exe` filename extension, a batch file, all of which end in the `.bat` extension, executes when you type its name with or without the `.bat` extension.

> **tip**
>
> In Windows, if a batch file contains the name of a Windows program, the Windows program executes. Therefore, you not only execute DOS programs from within a batch file but you can also run Windows applications. I use such a batch file for a shared PC as follows: When I click on my icon, a batch file quickly copies my data files into a work area and starts an application. When a co-worker clicks the same icon that has her name listed, the batch file copies her data files to that work area. The same application works with both our data files without our having to locate our files each time we begin the program.

Therefore, you can start executing a batch file named DOIT.BAT from the DOS prompt by typing DOIT or DOIT.BAT (you can also mix uppercase and lowercase letters).

## JCL: THE ORIGINAL BATCH FILE LANGUAGE

Mainframe environments support *Job Control Language (JCL)*. JCL to a mainframe is like the DOS batch language to a PC. JCL controls the automatic execution of mainframe programs and commands.

JCL has been around since the 1960s. If you go to work for a large organization that uses a mainframe, you'll certainly need to know some JCL. Still, as with PCs, the graphical interface of mainframes has reduced the dependency on JCL. Some college programming degrees still require a class in JCL for mainframe-based degrees. Although you may never have to master all the ins and outs of JCL, you'll almost certainly encounter it at some point and will probably have to change it in programs that you use. By mastering JCL, you learn a lot about the file structure of the machine.

## Reviewing the Batch Language

Although you'll never have to become a batch command wizard, as a review, Table 15.1 lists a few of the more common batch commands that DOS supports.

**TABLE 15.1** Some Common Batch File Commands

| Command | Description |
|---|---|
| Any DOS command | Any valid DOS command, such as COPY or FORMAT, works in a batch file. |
| Any program name | Any executable program or batch file name (with or without the file's extension) works in a batch file. |
| call *batch file* | Pauses the current batch file and begins another, just as Visual Basic uses Call to execute a procedure. When the called batch file completes its task, control returns to the current batch file. If you do not use call but place a batch filename as a command in another batch file, the first batch file's execution stops as soon as the named batch file begins. The call batch command makes the second batch file operate as a subroutine. |
| cls | Erases the DOS window screen. |
| echo | Specified as either echo on (the default) or echo off and determines whether or not DOS displays each batch command on the screen as the batch file executes. Turning off the echoing of commands keeps the screen clear of clutter but also makes debugging batch files more difficult. |
| pause *message* | DOS displays the message following the pause and displays Press any key to continue on the next line. The batch file pauses and waits for the user to press a key before continuing with the next command. pause is useful when the user has to indicate that an action has occurred, such as a disk being put in a disk drive. |
| rem | Remarks that document the batch file. The remarks will appear during execution unless you've turned off the echoing of commands. |

Suppose you want to send a directory listing to your printer. You might create a batch file named PRDIR.BAT that contains the commands shown in Listing 15.1.

**LISTING 15.1** Printing a Directory Listing

```
rem Directory Print
echo off
pause Turn on your printer
dir c:\>prn:
```

When you run PRDIR.BAT from a DOS window or
when you assign a Windows icon to the batch
file and execute the batch file, the following output occurs on the screen:

```
c:\>rem Directory Print

c:\>pause Turn on your printer
Press any key to continue . . .
```

After you turn on your printer and press a key, a
wide directory listing of your root directory will
print. Actually, many Windows users utilize this
very batch file for simple and quick directory listings because Windows Explorer, while a super
directory-traversal program, does not print simple
directory listings easily.

Given that batch files are in use much less today
than before because the DOS environment is
much less important today, mastering the batch
language is less critical than before when DOS
was the most common environment in which you
executed programs. But even though they are still
used, they will probably be used less and less as
time goes by. So why even bother discussing
them? Primarily because the nature of batch files
is easy to grasp and other kinds of scripting languages work in a similar, interpreted manner. The
rest of this chapter (as well as Chapter 21,
"JavaScript,") discusses a style of programming that
builds on the batch file concept.

**tip**

One would think that a
simple task such as deleting
files that match a particular
naming format would be
simple in Windows Explorer.
For example, suppose you
wanted to delete all your
accounts payable files for years
1990 through 1999. The names
are ActPay90, ActPay91, and so on.
The following DOS command is
much simpler to use than trying to
do the same thing in Windows
Explorer:

```
Del ActPay9?
```

The question mark is a *wildcard*
character that stands for any other
single character in the file. In this
command, you are telling DOS to
delete all files that begin with
ActPay9 and end with any single
character.

Not only games but some utilities such as disk-repair and imaging programs are
sold today for the DOS mode only. The multitasking of Windows sometimes causes
these programs to report incorrect results, so their authors return to the DOS mode
for the program's execution. These utilities often use batch commands to automate
their tasks. If you knew a few batch commands, you could wrap some commands
around the program and create backup files, clear the screen, or possibly process
two or more disk drives using the utility without intervening as you'd otherwise have
to do.

# Macro Languages

At its most basic level, a *macro language* does nothing more than imitate keystrokes the user of the application might type. There is not one, single macro language. Many software applications support their own unique, nonstandard macro languages. The simplest form of a macro is the keystroke-recording feature, although other forms exist. Once you record a series of common keystrokes in a macro file, you then can trigger those keystrokes by executing the macro within the application. Many of today's Windows applications enable you to assign a new toolbar button or create and assign an Alt+keystroke to a macro so that you can start a macro's execution with a single click or keystroke.

## The Need for Macros

Suppose you found yourself saving a backup of a Word document to drive D every few minutes. The original document appears on C, and the built-in Ctrl+S keystroke saves the document to C, but just for safety you want to save the file to drive D once in a while so that a second backup is available.

The following lists the steps you must perform, including the necessary menu commands and values you might type, to perform such a backup save to drive D:

1. Select **File**, **Save As**. The Save As dialog box appears.

2. Press the **Home** key to move the text cursor to the beginning of the default filename. The file normally saves the file in the current folder and disk, although you are going to override that location.

3. Type `d:\` so that Word will save the file on the D drive.

4. Click **Yes** to override your previous backup file on D. (This assumes that you've saved the file at least once before in D's `root` folder.)

5. Click the **OK** button to save the file. The default disk drive and folder will now be on D, so you must restore the default to its original location.

6. Select **File**, **Close** to close the file from Word's work area.

7. Select **File**, **2**. The 2 on the **File** menu will be the second-to-last file you edited, which was the file in its original location before you saved it to D. You are now working, once again, with the original file from drive C, and you've placed a copy on drive D.

The last two commands had to close the document and reload it from drive C. Otherwise, your edits would all go to D after you'd saved the file to D, and you would not have two copies being saved.

Although macros are not as complex as other kinds of programs, you still must test them to ensure that they perform as you expect them to. Try the macro on different data scenarios; for example, if the macro is to save a portion of a spreadsheet, erase all the values in the spreadsheet and see whether the macro behaves as expected or issues an error message. If the macro prints a report, see what happens when the printer is not turned on. Although macros don't have to handle these extreme unexpected conditions as gracefully as an application written in Visual Basic, you should make sure that they operate reasonably when the environment changes from an expected one.

## Using a Keyboard Macro

If you use Microsoft Word, you can follow along with this series of steps to see the screens that appear. However, performing these seven steps every few minutes to save the backup file while still keeping the original file in its original location is tedious. Instead of typing these keystrokes over and over, let Word record them as a keyboard macro that you can trigger easily. A macro is an interpreted set of commands that an application supports for tasks that you automate. Word, as well as most Windows applications that support macros, will enable you to record your keystrokes in a macro file and later play those keystrokes by executing the macro's commands.

Here are the steps you would use in Microsoft Word to record the macro:

1. Select **Tools**, **Macro**, **Record New Macro**. Word displays the Record Macro dialog box, shown in Figure 15.1.

**FIGURE 15.1**

Word can record your keystrokes and store them in a macro file.

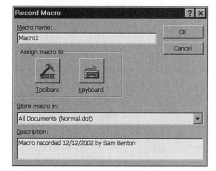

2. Click the **Keyboard** button to assign the macro you're about to record to a keystroke combination.

3. Press **Ctrl+D** or another keystroke that you want to use to trigger the macro. If the keystroke is already assigned (such as **Ctrl+S**, which is already assigned

to **File**, **Save**), Word tells you about the previous assignment and gives you a chance to replace the previous assignment or type a new keystroke.

4. Press **Enter** to begin recording the macro. Word places a small floating Stop Recording dialog box on your screen.

5. Perform your macro's step-by-step commands. If you are following along with this example and are creating a macro to save the current Word documents back on drive D, perform the keystrokes listed in the previous steps.

6. After you've finished typing all the macro's commands, click the **Stop Recording** button on the floating dialog box to let Word know that the macro is completed. (Word will not save the click of the **Stop Recording** button in the macro.)

When you press the macro's keystroke, Word runs them as if you were at the keyboard typing them yourself.

A keyboard macro is probably the easiest to create because you only need to type the keystrokes that you'd normally type and select the commands you'd normally select to place that command in the macro. The macro can contain any keystroke you'd normally use in Word, even those that enter text in a dialog box or move the focus from one control to another.

Obviously, creating generic keyboard macros is not always trivial. For a keyboard macro to work, you must ensure that the application is ready to receive those exact keystrokes. Using the previous example, if you had never saved the document to drive D, Word would not prompt you to replace the original backup with the new version (in step 4 of the file backup steps). The macro assumes that the prompt to replace the backup file will always appear, and if that prompt does not appear, the macro will still assume the prompt is on the screen and will try to select the Yes button when none appears. Such bugs are not always easy to find, and sometimes the easiest thing to do is start over and create a new macro.

In addition, keyboard-recording macros are just that; they record keyboard actions but not mouse actions. No mouse clicks or moves are recorded with the keyboard macros, so you must use only keyboard commands when recording macros. The graphic elements and windows that you might normally use the mouse

**note**

Most properly written Windows applications provide keyboard-equivalent ways of performing mouse actions. Therefore, you can use the keyboard in a recorded macro to do almost anything you might otherwise do with a mouse.

to control might differ each time you run the application, so you should not and cannot perform a mouse action while recording a macro.

Every keyboard-based macro language is different for every application because every application has somewhat different keystroke requirements for issuing commands. For example, Microsoft Excel uses a different set of menu commands from Excel to print a worksheet. Therefore, keyboard macros differ from program to program.

# Visual Basic for Applications (VBA)

Not all macros are keyboard based. In addition to keyboard-recording macros, many macros provide additional commands that go beyond the simple selection of menu options. Again, each application may support its own set of macro commands, but Microsoft standardized Visual Basic among all applications a few years ago. The result was Visual Basic for Applications (VBA).

Even non-Microsoft products have begun to provide support for VBA as the internal macro language for the application. If the VBA trend continues, eventually all applications could support the same macro language. (The keyboard-recording macro capabilities will probably differ among applications, however, because applications have different menus.)

Microsoft has offered Visual Basic for Applications for several years in its major software packages, such as the Office products. The problem in the beginning was that no VBA standard existed. Therefore, even a Visual Basic programmer did not automatically know the VBA language because VBA differed not only from Visual Basic, but also from the software programs that used VBA.

Beginning with Visual Basic 5, Microsoft began to combine both Visual Basic and VBA, as well as all the products that support VBA, so that a Visual Basic programmer now knows not only Visual Basic but also VBA. VBA now follows the same standards and conforms to the same rules, syntax, commands, functions, procedures, and control capabilities as Visual Basic. As a matter of fact, when you want to write a VBA program to control Word in some way, the screen that appears in Word looks much like a Visual Basic screen, as Figure 15.2 shows.

## caution

The VBA environment does not supply all the bells and whistles, such as supplementary extra controls, that the stand-alone Visual Basic development package supplies, but the fundamental language tools are all there for VBA that you find in Visual Basic.

FIGURE 15.2

When you write a macro in VBA to control an application, you use Visual Basic's own environment.

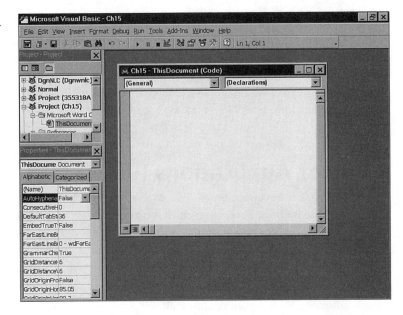

You might wonder how VBA can supplement and add functionality to a Windows application. For example, Excel supports VBA, but with all the worksheet power and commands that Excel already provides, how could a VBA program controlling an Excel environment and worksheet add any benefit to the Excel user?

Suppose at the end of the month, an Excel user consolidates 25 divisions' sales report worksheets into a company-wide summary worksheet. Such a consolidation of cells could be tedious, but it requires only fundamental Excel skills. To automate the task, the employee could easily record a keyboard macro to load each of the 25 division worksheets and update the summary worksheet.

In the previous section on macros, you learned some of the problems with keyboard macros. The most critical part of using a keyboard macro is making sure that the macro runs in exactly the same environment and with the same set of worksheets and columns each time. The keyboard

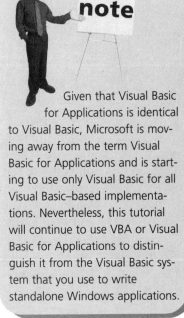

note

Given that Visual Basic for Applications is identical to Visual Basic, Microsoft is moving away from the term Visual Basic for Applications and is starting to use only Visual Basic for all Visual Basic–based implementations. Nevertheless, this tutorial will continue to use VBA or Visual Basic for Applications to distinguish it from the Visual Basic system that you use to write standalone Windows applications.

macro has no room for ambiguity. For example, what if one division were to shut down for remodeling one month? The keyboard macro that always expects and consolidates all 25 divisions would either consolidate a blank worksheet or one that doesn't even exist, producing an error.

Because Visual Basic for Applications is a complete programming language, the employee who needs such a report might want to create a series of commands that handles these unexpected conditions more gracefully than keyboard macros could. Perhaps the VBA code could read each worksheet and, if data other than zeros appears for the totals, add that worksheet to the summary but ignore any other worksheet where the division had no activity for that period. Such a macro—a Visual Basic program with code that is capable of analyzing worksheets—would come in handy.

The VBA language is identical to Visual Basic, but some extensions to the language must be made available by the application's authors as well. For example, the fundamental Visual Basic language supports variables, controls, and data files but contains no direct support for worksheet files or cell processing. Therefore, the Excel implementation of VBA will provide some support for reading and writing worksheet cells and data files.

For example, in Excel, a collection of worksheets can appear in the same workbook. Figure 15.3 shows such a workbook with tabs that indicate individual worksheets for each division. VBA distinguishes the worksheets from one another using a subscript. `Worksheets(1)` would be the first worksheet in the workbook, `Worksheets(2)` would be the second worksheet, and so on. You can access a worksheet by name instead of by the subscript by placing the name in parentheses, such as `Worksheets("Division1")`. A single cell or range of cells is referenced by the `Range` keyword, so the first cell in a worksheet named `Division14` would be `Worksheets("Division14").Range("A1")`. The cell value works just like a variable or control property because you can assign to or from the cell. To place the value 25 in the cell, you could write this assignment statement:

```
Worksheets("Division14").Range("A1") = 25
```

All the Visual Basic–based event procedures work, and you can even design a visual interface to a worksheet by adding controls that respond when the user clicks a command button or selects from a list box. The event procedure code that you write might process worksheet cells instead of variables as a standard Visual Basic application might process, but the idea is the same. Therefore, you have all the power of a full-fledged Windows programming language with a visual interface that is capable of manipulating Excel worksheet data.

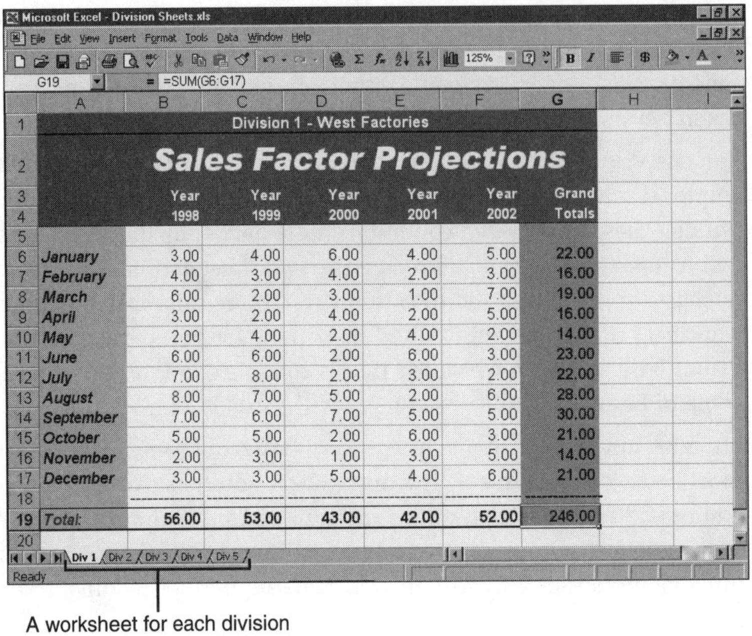

**FIGURE 15.3**

A single Excel
workbook can
hold multiple
worksheets.

A worksheet for each division

# Scripting in Windows

Although Windows does not support the same kind of batch language DOS does, the
Windows 98 operating system provided a start with a controlling language called
*Script* or *Windows Scripting Host (WSH)*. WSH is a set of commands that controls
Windows applications and provides some control over activities that take place in
Windows.

One of the places where the Windows scripting language helps the most does not
fall into the typical automated command and program-launching category.
Windows scripting has played a major role for several years in controlling dial-up
access to online providers. Online services, such as Microsoft Network or America
Online, each require different protocol commands. *Protocol* refers to the way that
one computer communicates with another. American Online requires a certain
stream of characters to be sent to its computers when someone dials up AOL from
home with a PC. Microsoft Network requires a series of different characters. Not only
must your PC be able to communicate the proper protocol to the service you are
dialing, but also other dial-up factors may be required. Perhaps you must dial a certain combination of digits to access a long-distance carrier before you dial up an
online service if that service is in another calling area.

Creating a communications script file can be tricky; by its very nature, online communication is fairly technical. The Windows scripting language comes with its own help file, located in your Windows `Script.doc` folder. You can open this file using WordPad. In `Script.doc`, you will see that the script language looks a lot like C in the way that it supports multiple procedures. Fortunately, the script language is even easier than C because it supports high-level communication commands, such as the `waitfor` command that watches your communications port and waits for a signal to come through from the remote computer.

Listing 15.2 shows the script file necessary to communicate with the CompuServe online service. Fortunately, you don't have to write this file yourself if you use CompuServe. Instead, the file comes with the CompuServe service when you install the CompuServe access software.

**note**

Each Windows application that supports Visual Basic for Applications provides its own object model. The *object model* is the collection of objects that are specific to that application. For example, Word would have document objects that can contain special attributes such as bold text, and Excel would have worksheet objects as described previously. VBA uses the application's object model to store, retrieve, and analyze data in the application's format.

## Listing 15.2   A Script File

```
;
; This is a script file that demonstrates how
; to establish a PPP connection with Compuserve,
; which requires changing the port settings to
; log in.
;

; Main entry point to script
;
proc main

    ; Set the port settings so we can wait for
    ; non-gibberish text.

    set port databits 7
    set port parity even

    transmit "^M"
```

**LISTING 15.2**   (continued)

```
waitfor "Host Name:"
transmit "CIS^M"

waitfor "User ID:"
transmit $USERID, raw
transmit "/go:pppconnect^M"

waitfor "Password: "
transmit $PASSWORD, raw
transmit "^M"

waitfor "One moment please..."

; Set the port settings back to allow successful
; negotiation.

set port databits 8
set port parity none
```

```
endproc
```

Even though you may not understand script commands, you can glance through Listing 15.2 and fairly easily follow the script. The script first sets some communications port parameters, then transmits a ^M character (^M mimics the Ctrl+M keystroke first required by CompuServe when you make a connection). When CompuServe sends the user ID request to the user's PC, the user's ID and password (stored in system variables named $USERID and $PASSWORD, respectively, set up when the user first installed CompuServe) go to the CompuServe computers. Once logged in, final communications port settings are specified. When the script file terminates, the user is logged into CompuServe and controls the session from that point on.

Most online communication services supply their own script, so you'll rarely have to write a script file for communications. Nevertheless, if you want to access a company mainframe or a friend's PC, you may want to create a script file, possibly by making a copy of one that already exists and modifying it, so that you can automate the protocol needed to access the remote PC.

All script files require the `.scp` filename extension.

When you want to automate an online session, study `Script.doc` to learn the scripting language that controls protocol and study any examples that exist on your PC. (Use the Windows Start menu's Find command to look for any files that end with the `.scp` extension.) You are probably better off modifying an existing script file than starting a new one on your own until you become better acquainted with the script language.

Beginning with Windows 98, the Windows Scripting Host gained new commands so that users and programmers could take Windows automation beyond online communications. The WSH now has the capability to work with Windows objects such as the file system, icons, and windows. One of the most powerful new features of WSH is its capability to support ActiveX objects so that the language can manipulate and work with virtually any Windows application's objects. (Chapter 16, "Internet Programming Concepts," explains more about ActiveX controls.)

The capability to work with ActiveX objects enables the WSH language to manipulate worksheets, word processor documents, and even database files.

Unlike the scripting language you saw earlier that controls online communication connections, the WSH supports several different scripting languages. In the next chapter, you will see examples of VBScript, a scripting language based on Visual Basic. In addition, WSH will execute script files written in JavaScript (sometimes called JScript), as well as others. The future of Windows scripting is uncertain due to the new nature of the language, but programmers will often be able to supplement their applications with installation scripts and system-management scripts that prepare the user's computer for the application.

# Summary

Several interactive languages exist to control system functions. These languages—such as DOS's batch language, JCL, and the Windows scripting languages—enable you to automate a series of commands to simplify your use of the system and common tasks such as logging into online services. If you find yourself typing the same operating system commands, consider automating the task with a scripting language.

Not only can you automate operating system tasks, but also, many applications include an automation macro language. For example, you can automate the Microsoft Office products by recording the keystrokes of commands that you type. You can also write background applications in Visual Basic for Applications, a language that is finding its way into many Windows applications.

## IN THIS CHAPTER

- Internet Programming Considerations
- The Need for Simple Navigation
- HTML Programming
- ActiveX Controls
- Scripting in Internet Applications
- ASP and .NET Technologies

# 16

# INTERNET PROGRAMMING CONCEPTS

All Internet activities require underlying programs written by programmers. Several ways exist to write applications for the Internet. However, the Internet technology that you learn today will probably change tomorrow. One of the ways to stay abreast of Internet programming is to master the terminology first. This chapter focuses primarily on the terms and languages that you'll need to know to master Internet programming. Subsequent chapters focus more specifically on the topics introduced here.

- How information is sent throughout Internet connections.
- HTML is the primary language behind Web pages.
- ActiveX controls are small routines that can appear inside Web pages to activate those pages.

- ASP technology might change the way people use the Web.

- Software may be rented and run from Web servers in the future, using ASP instead of buying the software.

# Internet Programming Considerations

Once you understand Internet-related terminology, you'll have little trouble understanding the technology required to program Internet applications. It's impossible to understand Internet-based programming if you do not have a grasp of the hardware and software technology related to Internet communications.

Because communication between computers is the ultimate goal of the Internet, the data is always sent along a serial wire from one computer to the next until the final machine receives the signal. The connection between computers—a phone cable in most cases—transmits only a single bit of information at a time. Binary 1s (ones) and 0s (zeros) are all that travel the lines between Internet computers. Fortunately, the programming languages behind many Internet applications hide the low-level binary data foundation of Internet communications.

## Internet Connections

Several ways exist to connect to the Internet. A modem is still the primary method for most users. Many businesses install high-speed connections to the Internet, and some users even receive Internet signals from high-speed satellite dishes. The serial method of data communication means that the faster the connection, the faster a user will receive and transmit Internet data.

**tip**

Keep in mind that the Internet is a network of networks. Think of it as an *interconnected network*. The first requirement of any Internet communication is to locate the computer for which a message is intended.

**note**

Although communication technology ultimately sends only one bit at a time back and forth between two computers, almost all Internet connections are *full duplexed*, meaning that you can issue commands and send them while the remote computer responds to a previous request. The speed of today's computers makes this possible. Although the wire allows only one bit at a time to be sent from either computer, the Internet connection can combine these single bits at high speeds to make it appear to the user that data is traveling back and forth at the same time.

Your Internet applications will not need to distinguish the way that a computer interacts with the Internet. The type of connection is unimportant, but you must keep in mind that not all users will have fast Internet access. Therefore, as you develop Internet applications, remember to keep your applications as efficient as possible. Graphics and video can take a while to load on the user's machine if the connection is slow. The Internet applications that you write should not make users less likely to view the Web page due to sluggish load time.

---

**THE ULTIMATE DEMOCRACY: THE INTERNET?**

All Web pages—good or bad, fast or slow—are equal in one respect: They are available to users on an equal-access basis. If a user doesn't like your Web site, he can go to another.

As a developer of Web pages, your goal should be to design pages that are effective at capturing and keeping the user's attention, even while competing with millions of other Web pages. Part of this goal is to create fast-loading Web sites. If your user has to wait too long for your page to load, he will quickly lose interest and move to another page.

---

A computer receives the signal that another computer sends to it via *point-to-point (PPP)* connections. Switches exist all along the communication route between Internet connections. The correct combination of switches must be made for a signal to travel from one Internet machine to another. Figure 16.1 shows an overview of the point-to-point process.

**FIGURE 16.1**

Several computers route the signals between your two PCs conversing over the Internet.

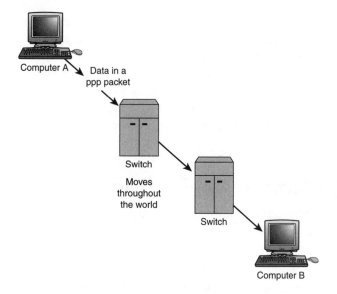

Computer A

Data in a ppp packet

Switch

Moves throughout the world

Switch

Computer B

## Internet Communications

When one Internet-based computer communicates with another, the data is rarely if ever sent all at once. Instead, the server breaks up the message into packets of data. The receiving machine informs the sending machine that a packet has been properly received before the next packet is sent. Error correction is made simpler, and a bad packet can be sent again before too much time passes.

Billions of packets travel from one computer to another every few minutes. The biggest challenge is not transmission or receipt but getting the right packet to the proper recipient. Often, a computer does not receive a packet but sends it down the line to the next computer on the Internet. A packet gets to its proper location through a value known as a *packet address*. An address appears as a 12-digit value such as 255.111.001.233. Each computer connected to the Internet has its own unique Internet address, just as each postal address is unique. If a computer receives a packet with an address that does not match that of the computer, it sends the message on down the line until the packet address matches the computer's Internet address. Fortunately, data transmits at the speed of light (even though modems do their best to slow things down at times), so the transmission of data packets occurs quickly enough to make the Internet a viable communications tool.

**note**

This PPP connection is used not only for sending and receiving e-mail but for communicating all Internet information back and forth between computers. Web pages and Internet programs themselves must travel an appropriate set of switches before they appear on the computer that is to receive the signal.

This text does not require that you be an Internet guru to understand Internet programming concepts. Nevertheless, it's assumed that you've used the Internet enough to understand home pages and maneuver around the *World Wide Web* (*WWW* or just *the Web*).

# The Need for Simple Navigation

An Internet site might contain several Web pages; the first screen that you visit for any site generally is its home page. The home page often contains links to other pages on the site and to other home pages on the Internet.

For example, if you visit Que Publishing's Web site at http://www.quepublishing.com, you'll see a home page like the one in Figure 16.2. The mouse cursor changes shape when you move it over a hypertext link to another page or to a definition box, which pops up when you click the mouse.

Each page that you see on the Web is located somewhere on someone's computer. How in the world does your Web browser find the correct page? Each Web site contains a unique address called the *uniform resource locator (URL)*. Instead of requiring that you type each page's URL (which can become quite lengthy), the current page's hypertext links direct your Web browsing software to the next URL that you want to display.

The first Web browsers on the market were known as Mosaic browsers, named after *Mosaic*, the first true Internet graphical browsing program. Students at the University of Illinois at Urbana-Champaign created Mosaic for the National Center for Supercomputing Applications (NCSA). Mosaic took the Web one giant leap forward, making Web-crawling accessible to anyone with an Internet connection and the Mosaic software. The Mosaic-based browsers are still in use, notably with Microsoft's Internet Explorer and Netscape's Navigator, although today's browsers have greatly extended the Web page programming language that you'll learn about in the next section.

## tip

The routing of data to and from Internet computers works a lot like the air travel of people between cities. For example, many people might travel from Chicago to New York, but not all at the same time or by the same route. Instead, small groups (packets of people) travel throughout the day on different flights.

Just as passengers often travel through different airports to get to the same final destination, data is routed through several servers from the origination point to the final user.

**FIGURE 16.2**

Web pages are graphical and often connected to other sites.

# HTML Programming

One of the goals of Web page designers is to make pages uniform no matter what kind of computer (or, more accurately, which *platform*) is used. The *Hypertext Markup Language (HTML)* is a machine-independent language that Web developers use to design Web pages. A page's HTML listing is actually a set of text commands that, when viewed with a Web browser, produces a Web page that conforms to the look the author intended.

Listing 16.1 contains some of the HTML commands that produced the Web page in Figure 16.2.

> **note**
>
> Unless you write extremely low-level Internet applications, you will rarely need to concern yourself with packets and packet addressing. This discussion simply informs you how Internet computers communicate between each other. If you ever need to write system-level programs that perform connections to various addressed Internet computers, you will have an understanding of the connection and packet processes.

**LISTING 16.1** HTML Commands to Produce the Web Page in Figure 16.2

```
<html>
<title>Que Publishing</title>
<script language="JavaScript"
src="/includes/javascript/global.js">
</script>
<script language="JavaScript">
bgcolor="#FFFFFF" marginheight="0" marginwidth="0"
topmargin="0"
leftmargin="0">
<table border="0" cellspacing="0" cellpadding="0">
   <tr>
     <img src="/images/network/que_tab.gif" width="91" height="20" border="0"
     alt="Que Publishing"></a></td>
       <td><a href="http://www.informit.com/">
       <img src="/images/network/informit_tab.gif" width="91" height="20" border="0"
     alt="InformIT"></a></td>
       <td><a href="http://safari.informit.com/">
       <img src="/images/network/safari_tab.gif" width="94" height="20" border="0"
     alt="Safari"></a></td>
       maxlength="255"><input type="image"
       src="/images/leftnav/search_button.gif" border="0" name="Click Here2"
       value="Submit" width="53" height="15" align="middle"></center>
   <tr>
       <td valign="top" align="left" colspan="3"><img
       src="/images/basics/spacer_ffffcc.gif" width="164" height="1"
border="0"></td>
```

**LISTING 16.1** (continued)

```
    </tr>
<tr>
    <td valign="top" align="left"><img
    src="/images/leftnav/arrow_left_1hi.gif" width="27" height="21"
    border="0"></td>
    <td valign="middle">
<p>
<a href="/member/login.asp?session_id={55F4C9C4-D05F-4873-B60F-B04E0622D763
}" class="navleftmajor">Register with Que</a>
</p>
    </td>
</tr>
```

Take a moment to look at how Listing 16.1 produced the Web page in Figure 16.2. The HTML listing looks a little forbidding. Nevertheless, as you compare the code to the home page, you'll see how the HTML language produced parts of the Web page. If you want to look at HTML code for any Web page that you display, select View, Source from your Web browser to see the code.

The terms within the angled brackets (< and >) are called *tag references* (or *tag commands* or just *tags*). Tags are central to the HTML program. Many commands contain a beginning tag and an ending tag; a forward slash, /, precedes an ending tag. For example, <TITLE> marks the beginning of a title and </TITLE> marks the end.

Tags do not contain formatted text; they offer formatting instructions that your Web browser is to follow. Therefore, when your Web browser sees the <CENTER> tag, your Web browser knows to center the text that runs up to the subsequent </CENTER> ending tag.

Tags primarily determine the placement of figures, the format of text, links to other Web sites, and table information. Many of the tags in Listing 16.1 are formatting tag codes that specify font style and size instructions for the Web browser.

A nonbracketed text item is a literal constant, such as a title, that is to appear on the Web page. For example, in the third code line of Listing 16.1, the words Que Publishing are not within brackets. These words are the title that appears on the page.

When you navigate to a Web page, the remote server sends only the HTML text to your browser. It responds to the commands by formatting text appropriately and placing links and graphic images where the HTML dictates they should appear. Your browser first receives the full HTML page and then receives whatever graphic images and multimedia content are needed to complete the page.

Browsers provide a Stop button that you can click to keep from receiving graphics and multimedia images for those times when you don't want to wait on them but want to read the text that has already been sent to your browser. In place of the images and multimedia content, your browser places an icon that lets you know where the image would appear if you had let the image load to your computer.

Chapter 17, "HTML Programming," teaches you HTML coding fundamentals.

# ActiveX Controls

Even as recently as two or three years ago, Web page designers often had to write active Web page content in C or C++ to embed Web browsing technology in applications. No longer is that the case. Many Web-based ActiveX controls now appear in Web applications, and the trend is increasing. An *ActiveX control* is a small program, compiled into an ActiveX object that conforms to specific browser requirements, that you can embed inside any ActiveX control reader container. Many Windows applications support ActiveX technology so that you can extend the application by inserting the ActiveX control into the application.

Developing ActiveX controls is easier to do with today's programming environments than when they were first introduced. Nevertheless, the development can still be complicated. Visual Basic includes some tools to help streamline the process, and if you want to develop ActiveX controls, Visual Basic might be the best platform from which to start.

For the Internet developer, ActiveX controls are important because Web browsers such as Internet Explorer support them, and the user can interact with them. You can place common Web page functions inside an ActiveX control that you write and then include that ActiveX control in all Web pages that are to use that function. Therefore, if you develop a routine in Visual Basic that performs a service, such as calculating interest, if you use an ActiveX development platform, such as the Visual Basic ActiveX development tool, your routine works both as a standalone application and as an embedded ActiveX control inside a financial Web page.

> **tip**
>
> An ActiveX control works like a C++ object in that it supports characteristics and behaviors you control in your program.

You've already seen an interesting use of ActiveX controls: Visual Basic's Internet control. You used Visual Basic's ActiveX Internet control in Chapter 11, "Online Visual Basic Programming," when you created an application with an embedded Web browser. To add Internet access to any Visual Basic application, you need only to drop the Internet ActiveX browser control into your Visual Basic application's Form window.

The big advantage of ActiveX controls is that they are *scalable* and work on multiple platforms. A scalable object is limited only by the properties and method routines defined for it. You can incorporate scalable objects inside other objects, and their power grows as the container object gathers more ActiveX controls. In addition, you can place ActiveX controls in many languages, including Visual Basic, Visual C++, and Java.

Given the cross-platform support of ActiveX objects, you as a programmer have many thousands of ActiveX controls to choose from. You need only to drop these controls into your project, whether you write Visual Basic or Visual C++. The controls then attach to your development toolbox, where you manipulate the control just like the default Visual Basic controls. The power of ActiveX really takes off when you consider that most of today's Web browsers in use support ActiveX. You can build an active Web page by dropping ActiveX controls inside your HTML-based Java applet. The Web browser automatically senses the ActiveX control and executes the control's functionality.

# Scripting in Internet Applications

Web browsers such as Internet Explorer support not only HTML pages but also other languages and applications. The Internet Explorer browser is actually little more than an ActiveX container. Therefore, any application that can present itself to the Web browser as an ActiveX control appears inside the Web browser.

In addition to HTML, ActiveX controls, and Java programs that you'll learn about in Chapter 20, "Java Programming," Web browsers can also support special scripting languages called *JavaScript* and *VBScript*. These special scripting languages enable you to embed controlling code inside HTML code that interacts with and reacts to other objects on the Web page. Whereas JavaScript is similar to the Java language, VBScript is similar to Visual Basic. Listing 16.2 shows a partial listing of a VBScript program. The code is virtually identical to Visual Basic's programming language. The HTML tags show that programmers embed VBScript right inside HTML code. The scripting languages give more analysis power to the code behind Web pages.

**LISTING 16.2**   A VBScript Example

```
<SCRIPT Language="VBScript">
    Call PrintWelcome
    Call ModMessage
```

**LISTING 16.2**    (continued)

```
Sub PrintWelcome
    If Date() = "2/2/2002" Then
        document.write ". . . .Kathy's Birthday!"
    End If
    If Date() = "2/5/2002" Then
        document.write ". . . .Eric's Birthday!"
    End If
    If Date() = "5/17/2002" Then
        document.write ". . . .Michael's Birthday!"
    End If
    If Date() = "7/25/2002" Then
        document.write ". . . .My Birthday!"
    End If
End Sub
Sub ModMessage
    Document.Write "<BR>This page was last modified: "+Document.lastModified
➥+"</FONT><BR>"
End Sub
</SCRIPT>
```

With a background in Visual Basic, you'll feel right at home with VBScript. One problem with VBScript, however, is that it never gained a foothold, so it is shown here only briefly. JavaScript has caught on to a greater extent, and you'll find an entire chapter on JavaScript in Chapter 21, "JavaScript."

VBScript is useful when you want to add key Visual Basic features to a Web page, such as pop-up messages, input boxes, loop-through calculations, and so on. Despite its foundation in Visual Basic, VBScript doesn't replace Visual Basic's ActiveX controls and documents but instead loads them into an HTML page for execution. VBScript is the medium through which HTML documents locate and execute Visual Basic ActiveX document applications. If you created the ActiveX interest rate calculation control described in the previous section, you would use VBScript inside a Web page's HTML code to inform the Web browser displaying the program about the interest rate ActiveX control. The VBScript would inform the Web browser when to display the control (such as when the user clicks a button to request it).

# ASP and .NET Technologies

Instead of going to a computer store to purchase software, many individuals and companies will soon be renting software over the Internet.

*Active Server Pages (ASP)* provides the technology to deliver programs from the authoring company to a specific Web site's computer. As an example, instead of buying a copy of the Microsoft FrontPage Web design program, you would go to Microsoft's Web site and simply rent the program, which would be delivered to your computer and run for a specified period of time.

Active Server Pages (ASP) are just text file scripts that end in the filename extension .asp. Actually, ASP is not a new language in itself; it is a definition of how a Web page developer can combine tools already on the market to produce interactive Web pages. The code inside the file is HTML code with some extensions and languages that often make the ASP code look a lot like Visual Basic code. The beauty of ASP is that you can apply your knowledge of Visual Basic to ASP without learning another language such as C++.

According to an October 16, 2000, article in *InfoWorld*, analysts are projecting that revenues in the ASP sector will reach $23 billion by the end of 2003, a major sum given its 1999 inception.

Although an ASP tutorial would take far too long to cover here, a simple example might be helpful to show how ASP code combines with HTML and mimics Visual Basic's language elements. Listing 16.3 shows an extremely simple ASP example. Listing 16.3 prints the words Learning ASP 10 times in a Web browser.

## LISTING 16.3  ASP Code Appears Inside HTML

```
<%@ Language=VBScript %>
<html>
  <head>
    <title>ASP Code inside HTML</title>
  </head>

  <body>
    <% titleVar = "Learning ASP" %>
    <%For i=1 To 10%>
      <%=titleVar%>
    <%Next%>
  </body>
</html>
```

Listing 16.3 uses a Visual Basic For...Next loop to do its job. Here is a step-by-step breakdown of the code:

1. The line `<%@ Language=VBScript %>` informs the Web browser that VBScript will be used inside the code. Actually, VBScript is the default language, so you could omit this line. You can use other scripting languages such as JavaScript.

2. The `<title>` HTML command tag defines the text that appears at the top of the Web page's window. Therefore, the words Learning ASP will appear in the title bar area of the Web browser that displays this code.

3. A variable named varMessage is defined with learning ASP as its content. All ASP variables are of the Variant data type, so no distinction is made between numeric and string variables.

4. A For...Next loop executes 10 times. The body of the loop simply displays the variable's contents in the browser window.

One technology that is sure to affect Web programmers and users is Microsoft's .NET technology. Although .NET is still being defined at the time of this writing, it is touted as a system development platform for all kinds of applications, both Web and standalone. The goal is to write to a preset list of standards so that code will port easily to online and offline environments.

A program written for a computer will also work across the Internet for anyone to execute from his browser window. In a way, .NET technology is a wide-scale ActiveX control standard; when you develop an ActiveX routine, you can run that code on a standalone computer or on a Web page in which you embed the control. When you write a program that conforms to the .NET standard, that program works on a standalone computer as well as a Web site. That's the standard, for instance, to which Microsoft might conform future versions of its Office applications. A user will be able to buy a copy of Office, but he also can log on to the Office Web site and use the system online without it being installed on his computer.

If a computer is connected to the Internet and contains code that conforms to the .NET standard, any other computer connected to the Internet will be able to execute that code, no matter what processor or operating system the other computer contains. By requiring that standalone applications also conform to the .NET standard, Microsoft hopes to help ensure that code eventually ported to an online environment from a standalone one still works as expected without modification.

---

**C# SO YOU WON'T BE FLAT**
**(THAT'S AN ATTEMPT AT A LITTLE MUSICAL HUMOR...)**

Microsoft's backbone language for the .NET development environment is C#, a language strongly based on C++ and Java. The C# development environment uses the same Development Studio environment that Visual Basic uses. As a matter of fact, Microsoft's goal is for you to use that same development environment no matter in what language you are writing.

The strength of C# has yet to be proven. .NET is still too new to know if programmers will adopt C# or stick with Java or whether some completely new language will crop up. As a programmer who wants to keep current, you should watch C# and follow its adoption by the programming community. If it begins to take over Java installations, that might be a sign that Microsoft's .NET will take hold. Other companies will be competing for a Web development standard similar to C#'s, however. Sun Microsystems, the creators of Java, will certainly have a competing system of development tools that will bridge the online and offline programming divide that now exists.

---

# Summary

One of the first steps in learning to program Internet applications is to learn how the underlying communication technology works. HTML is the code that formats Web pages to display text and graphics properly. HTML is the container and format-ter of all that appears on a Web page, including scripts and Java code. Adding Internet browser technology is one of the foundations of today's applications, because of the importance of the Internet.

A move is underway to standardize software for both standalone use and online exe-cution. Given that ActiveX controls are browser compatible, most of today's Internet applications contain some form of ActiveX control. In the future, other technologies such as .NET and ASP will compete for the programmer's time.

Now that you have an introduction to Internet programming concepts, the next few chapters describe the details of the more common languages and tools that you will surely be exposed to as a developer. With the Visual Basic background that you now have, you will have little trouble gaining insight into the languages discussed.

- The Internet defines point-to-point contacts to pass along data throughout the Internet.

- HTML code describes the way a Web page looks and defines hyperlinks to other Web pages.

- An ActiveX control is a routine that you write that runs both as a standalone routine and inside Web pages that contain the control.

■ ASP combines a predetermined standard, implemented by HTML, VBScript, and other existing Web languages, to provide large-scale program execution from Web browsers without those programs' code actually appearing on the user's computer.

■ Microsoft's .NET technology extends ActiveX and defines ASP-like programming standards so that software written to the .NET standard works both in a standalone environment and over the Internet.

## IN THIS CHAPTER

- Understanding HTML
- Simple HTML
- Simple HTML Text Formatting
- Simple HTML Graphics
- Using Hyperlinks
- E-mail HyperLinks

**17**

# HTML PROGRAMMING

As you learned in the previous chapter, Hypertext Markup Language (HTML) is the code behind Web pages. Using HTML, you place text, graphics, Java and other active content, and hyperlinks throughout Web pages to give those pages the look you desire. Unlike traditional programming languages, HTML is interpreted as your Web page loads. Your Web page, formatted with HTML code, goes across the Internet to whatever user requests it. That user's browser then interprets your HTML commands to format the page properly. This chapter is an introduction to HTML coding.

- HTML is a formatting language that you type using a text editor.
- HTML commands are stored in tags.
- HTML controls the online browser experience including the title at the top of the browser's window.

- You can embed hyperlinks that send your Web page visitors to other linked pages.

- Graphics are simple to place in Web pages, and you can even turn a graphic image into a hyperlink to another page.

# Understanding HTML

Even simple HTML commands can produce quite attractive and complete Web pages. For example, consider how simple the HTML code is in Listing 17.1. You should have little trouble following the commands even if HTML is new to you.

**tip**

Thanks to WYSIWYG (What You See Is What You Get) HTML editors, most HTML commands can be produced automatically. For example, Microsoft FrontPage enables you to drag items onto a screen from a toolbox and type text in text boxes to create your Web pages visually. FrontPage then translates the page into HTML commands for you. Microsoft Word and other word processors can often save documents (with formatted text as well as embedded tables, graphics, and multimedia) as HTML pages that Word translates to HTML code.

**LISTING 17.1**   Simple HTML Commands

```
<HTML>
 <HEAD>
  <TITLE>Beany Hat</TITLE>
 </HEAD>
<BODY>
 <CENTER>
   <H1>Fancy, yet simple!</H1><P>
 </CENTER>
<HR NOSHADE>
<CENTER>
   HTML is the key to attractive Web pages. Your Web pages will
   carry with them text, images, and multimedia content that the
   HTML code formats into the resulting Web pages.
  </Center>
  <Center>
   <IMG SRC="Beany.gif" ALT=" ">
  <H1><I><A HREF=www.microsoft.com>Click here to see Microsoft's Web site
  </A></I></H1>
  </Center>
  <MARQUEE >This text scrolls across the screen</MARQUEE><P>
 </BODY>
</HTML>
```

Figure 17.1 shows the Web page that results from Listing 17.1. As you can see, the Web page is attractive and fairly complex despite the simple HTML code that created it.

**FIGURE 17.1**

A nice Web page that requires only simple HTML code.

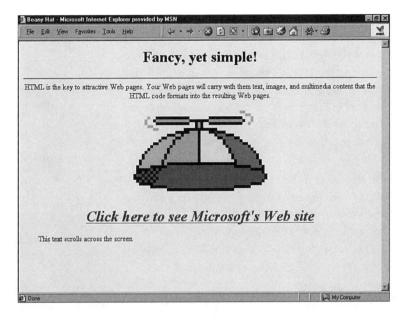

Developers add to the HTML language constantly. As the Web becomes more complex, the needs of the HTML language expand. For example, HTML did not originally support frames that allow for two separate scrolling windows on a single Web page, but frames are now standard. One of the most important additions to the HTML language was the capability of a Web page to become active using an embedded program. You'll learn how to use Java to embed a program directly inside HTML code in Chapter 20, "Java Programming."

Transferring a packet of HTML code such as that in Listing 17.1 is much less time consuming than transferring a graphic image of the entire Web page. In other words, if you were to scan a Web page, then send the scanned image as a graphic file to a browser, the transfer and subsequent wait for the Web page would be long because graphics files are quite large. Your Web browser reads the HTML commands and then formats the included text and small graphic images according to the HTML instructions.

**tip**

The next time you log onto the Internet, locate your browser's menu option that lets you view the HTML source code. If you use Internet Explorer, the source display command is **View**, **Source**. In Netscape Navigator, the command is **View**, **Document Source**.

Several tools exist to create Web pages using modern graphical cut-and-paste methods. You can create a fancy Web page simply by using a text editor and knowing the HTML language. For example, the Macintosh SimpleText and BBEdit text editors work well for HTML pages, as does Windows Notepad. The large development environment of Visual Basic is not required for Web page development because of the dependence on HTML's text nature.

On the other hand, development environments for Web pages are becoming quite advanced with tools such as FrontPage or Dreamweaver, so that you can create advanced Web pages without working inside HTML code as much as you would if you used a straight text editor. Often, programmers use graphic development tools to lay out the overall Web page and then use a text editor to hone the HTML source code to finalize the page.

## Simple HTML

All Web pages require a fundamental set of HTML codes. Listing 17.2 shows the minimal HTML code needed to display a Web page.

**note**

To prove that you need only a simple text editor to create fancy Web pages, start your computer's text editor (such as Notepad or BBEdit) and type the code in Listing 17.1. Save the file but don't use the text editor's default .TXT extension; instead, use the required Web page extension of .HTM (Web pages also support the .HTML extension). Open your Web browser and select File, Open, locate your HTML file, and click OK to see the Web page appear inside your browser. A problem will appear because you won't have the graphic file named BEANY.GIF on your computer. Substitute the filename and path for a graphic image you have on your computer to display the image in the center of the Web page.

**LISTING 17.2**   A General HTML Format

```
<html>
  <!-- This is a comment -->
  <head>
    <title>The window's title bar text goes here</title>
  </head>
  <body>
    <!-- The bulk of the Web page text, graphics, and HTML
         code goes here -->
  </body>
</html>
```

The commands between the angled brackets are the HTML command tags that format the page's data and instruct the browser on how to display the page. Most

HTML tags appear in pairs, such as <body> and </body>. The closing tag, indicated with a slash (/), tells the browser where the tag command ends.

You have the freedom to use as much whitespace as needed to make your HTML code clear. The following title tag set

```
<title>Jerry's home page</title>
```

is identical to this one even though the following code uses three lines of HTML to achieve the same result:

```
<title>
Jerry's home page
</title>
```

This code places the title, Jerry's home page, at the top of the user's browser window title bar when the user views the Web page.

You can document your HTML code, just as you can add remarks to Visual Basic code, with the comment tag. Comments always begin with <!-- and end with the comment's closing angled bracket, >. Unlike many command tags, a comment does not require a closing tag.

Notice that the first tag in all Web pages should be <html>, indicating the beginning of the HTML code. The end tag is </html>, indicating that the Web page is through.

The heading section, enclosed with <head> and </head>, contains title bar information using the <title> and </title> tags and other preliminary Web page data such as *metatags*, advanced HTML code that programmers can place inside Web pages to get noticed by search engines. Often, the title bar is the only text that appears in the heading section.

The body section, enclosed with <body> and </body>, includes the bulk of the Web page content. The user is most interested in the data between these two tags.

## Simple HTML Text Formatting

When you want text to appear on the browser's screen, you enter the text inside the HTML code. Your Web page body could simply include lines of text like this:

```
<body>
This text will appear
on whatever Web browser screen
opens this HTML code.
</body>
```

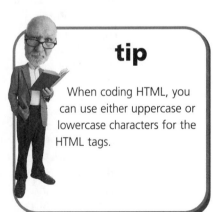

**tip**

When coding HTML, you can use either uppercase or lowercase characters for the HTML tags.

Web browsers do not automatically format text. These three lines of text all appear on one line inside the browser, like this:

```
This text will appear on whatever Web browser screen opens this HTML code.
```

If you want to add line breaks, you must include the `<br>` tag (no ending `<br>` tag exists). `<br>` tells the Web browser to break the line at that point and move to the next line. The following `<body>` section displays three lines of text:

```
<body>
This text will appear<br>
on whatever Web browser screen<br>
opens this HTML code.
</body>
```

Again, the text breaks onto three lines only because of the `<br>` tags and not because the lines happen to end there.

Text automatically appears right-justified on the browser's window. You can change the alignment to centered, right-aligned, or left-aligned with these tags:

`<p align=center>` and `</p>`

`<p align=right>` and `</p>`

`<p align=left>` and `</p>`

You can add italic, boldfacing, and underlining to your text. The following HTML code contains such formatting:

```
This line contains <u>two underlined</u>
➥words.
This line contains <i>two italicized</i>
➥words.
This line contains <b>two boldfaced</b>
➥words.
```

The `<h>` tag controls the size of headlines that you use as titles on your page. Use `<h1>` (the largest) through `<h6>` (the smallest) to display headlines. Figure 17.2 shows the Web page created by the HTML code in Listing 17.3.

## tip

As you will notice in Listing 17.2, `<center>` does the same as `<p align=center>`, with the added benefit of centering pictures as well as text.

## caution

Generally, Web page designers refrain from using underlining on Web pages because most hyperlinks appear as underlined text. Therefore, if you include underlined text that does not serve as a link to another Web page, your users may waste time trying to click on those underlined words to see what happens.

**LISTING 17.3**    Examples of the `<h>` Tag

```html
<html>
  <head>
    <title>Headline sizes</title>
  </head>
  <body>
    <!-- An automatic line break
         occurs after each headline -->
    <h1>Number 1 headline size</h1>
    <h2>Number 2 headline size</h2>
    <h3>Number 3 headline size</h3>
    <h4>Number 4 headline size</h4>
    <h5>Number 5 headline size</h5>
    <h6>Number 6 headline size</h6>
  </body>
</html>
```

**FIGURE 17.2**

You can specify up to seven headline sizes.

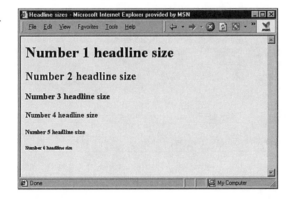

Using a method similar to the headline tag, you can control the size of your text using the `<font size>` tag. You can specify a font size from 1 (the smallest, which is exactly the opposite of the `<h>` tag's numbering system) to 7, as Listing 17.4 demonstrates.

**LISTING 17.4**    Examples of the `<font size>` Tag

```html
<html>
  <head>
    <title>Headline sizes</title>
  </head>
```

**LISTING 17.4**   (continued)

```
<body>
  <font size=1>Smallest text size</font> <br>
  <font size=2>Growing...</font> <br>
  <font size=3>Growing...</font> <br>
  <font size=4>Growing...</font> <br>
  <font size=5>Growing...</font> <br>
  <font size=6>Growing...</font> <br>
  <font size=7>Largest text size</font>
</body>
</html>
```

**FIGURE 17.3**

Text size grows
as you increase
the font size.

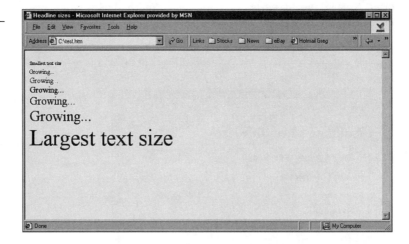

# Simple HTML Graphics

The `<img src>` tag places images on your Web pages. After you designate an image's location and filename, the image appears. Graphics are simple to display and, unless you want to apply advanced formatting techniques to your Web page images, the `<img src>` tag is all you'll need for many of your Web page graphics.

Here is a simple Web page command that displays an image on the screen:

```
<img src="images/myphoto.jpg"
```

The image appears wherever this `img src` tag appears inside the HTML code. It's up to you to ensure that the image is formatted in a type of file that browsers can display. The common image formats are JPEG and GIF, and most graphics programs produce images in these two formats.

You can easily place a border around a graphic, in effect adding a framed image to your Web page. The `border` tag is an extension of the `img src` tag. In addition, you can align your graphic image to the left, center, or right edge of the screen by placing the `align=` option inside the `img src` tag. Consider the following complex image tag:

```
<img src="/images/Dogs.gif" align=left
➥border=10>
```

The image comes from a Web folder named `images` where all the site's images are located. The `align` option instructs the browser to left-align the image to the left browser window. The `border=10` option instructs the browser to place a border around the picture and to make the border 10 points wide. Given that a point is approximately 1/72 of an inch, the border will be about 1/7 of an inch thick.

> **tip**
>
> Web page developers often store all of a site's images in a single directory named `images`. Therefore, if one page accesses the same image as another page, the image consumes disk space only one time. If the designer stored images in several locations, duplicates would surely appear over time and consume disk space.

When used in the HTML code in Listing 17.5, the Web page begins to take on a more complete feel, as Figure 17.4 illustrates.

**LISTING 17.5** Using the `img src` Tag

```
<html>
  <head>
    <title>Our Pups</title>
  </head>
  <body>
    <h1>These are our mutts.</h1>

    <font size 4>Although they don't know it, they are animals.<br>
    <br>
    Their names are Zucchi (girl) and Casper (boy).<br><br><br>

    <img src="\images\dogs.jpg" align=left border=10>

    <br><br><br>They are of the Bischon Frise breed.<br>
    (They won't like it if you call them poodles!)
  </body>
</html>
```

**FIGURE 17.4**
Place a border
around your
image to help
focus the pic-
ture.

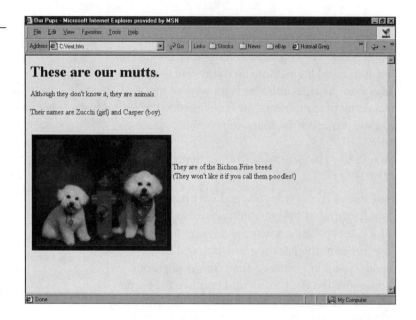

In Figure 17.4, you can begin to see the advantage of aligning your graphic images
to the left or right of the screen. Subsequent text prints to the side of the image.

# Using Hyperlinks

An anchor *tag*, indicated by <a> and </a>, creates a hyperlink to another page location. The browser that displays your Web page creates the underlined link at the
point of your HTML's <a> tag.

The following lines send the user to the Que Publishing Web site when the user clicks
the hyperlink:

```
<a href="http://www.mcp.com">
Get some great books
</a>
```

Everything between the <a href> tag and the closing </a> tag comprises the hyperlink. The four words, Get some great books, will be underlined on the Web screen, and
the user can click anywhere in that text to move to the corresponding Web site.

You can even specify graphics and multiline text as hyperlinks. When the user clicks
the hyperlink, the page changes to the linked Web page. The user can click the
browser's Back button to return to the current page.

The HTML statement that follows shows you how to use an image as a hyperlink. Remember that everything you place between the initial `<a href>` tag and the `</a>` ending tag is a hyperlink, whether you place graphics, text, or both there.

```
<a href="http://www.MinskeyFamilyPics.htm">
  <img src="images/Flag.gif">
</a>
```

When the Web page that includes this statement appears, the user's mouse pointer will change to a hand when the user points to the image on the screen that is named `Flag.gif`. If the user then clicks the image, the browser opens the page located at `http://www.MinskeyFamilyPics.htm`.

# E-mail HyperLinks

You can use the hyperlink tag to place an e-mail–requesting link inside your Web page. When your user clicks the text or graphic image you use as an e-mail hyperlink, an e-mail message window such as the one in Figure 17.5 opens, preaddressed to the address your hyperlink specifies.

**FIGURE 17.5**

Make it easy for your users to send you e-mail.

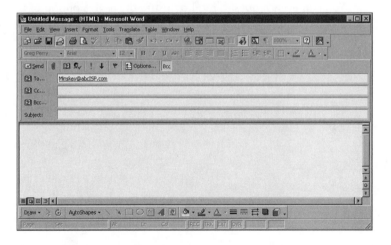

To specify an e-mail–based hyperlink, use the `mailto` tag option like this:

```
<a href="mailto:Minskey@abcISP.com">
  Write to us!
</a>
```

When the user clicks the words `Write to us!`, the e-mail message shown in Figure 17.5 opens, already addressed.

# Summary

You now have a basic understanding of Web page coding. Once you understand the general nature of HTML code, creating and formatting Web pages becomes a simple matter. When you are ready to add tables, frames, and other advanced elements to your page, you'll need to master more advanced command tags, but you should have little trouble doing so as long as you build gradually on the knowledge you have already. Using only the tags discussed in this chapter, you can create nice-looking, although simple, Web pages that contain text, graphics, and links to other sites.

- HTML text files end in the .htm or .html extension.
- Use command tags to format your HTML commands.
- The <title> tag determines the words that appear at the top of your browser window.
- Control the size of HTML headlines and text with the proper font size and H*n* tags.
- The <img src> tag places graphics in your HTML code.
- You can even request e-mail by using the mailto option of the <a href> tag.

## IN THIS CHAPTER

- Introducing DHTML
- A Sample DHTML Page
- The Technology Behind DHTML
- The Microsoft and Netscape Battle
- The Rollover Effect

**18**

# DHTML PROGRAMMING

Dynamic HTML (DHTML) has been around long enough that most browsers support and properly display Web pages based on it. Many browser companies raced to support DHTML because of the active Web pages that it provides. DHTML does its job after the Web page loads onto a user's computer. Before DHTML, the user would have to reload the Web page to see a change such as text color, but DHTML provides such changes inside the user's browser without requiring a page reload. Several of today's common Web page elements, such as buttons that change when the user moves the mouse cursor over them, are possible due to DHTML.

- DHTML extends HTML.
- You can activate your Web pages with DHTML code.
- Elements such as menus and rollover effects appear when you code them in DHTML.
- JavaScript serves as one of the most popular languages for implementing DHTML.

# Introducing DHTML

DHTML is not actually a different language from HTML but instead is a set of add-on technologies. To create more self-activating Web sites, you piece together the tools you want to use. Therefore, to master DHTML you don't learn new HTML commands; instead, you learn new items you can place on the Web pages that you develop.

If you use a Web development package such as Dreamweaver, you'll be able to add many DHTML options easily by dragging and dropping them into your Web page and setting certain options. As with HTML, however, you will want to modify the DHTML elements at times, and to do so you'll need an advanced knowledge of HTML. Therefore, make it a point to become an expert in HTML before DHTML.

This chapter will not actually teach you DHTML, because of its advanced nature and the complex tools required at times. However, you will gain insight into what you'll be required to master if you want to create DHTML-based pages.

The following list provides an overview of some DHTML elements you'll find on many of today's Web pages:

- **Menus**—Your Web page can support a system of pull-down menus that cascade out, much like the Windows Start menu. Figure 18.1 shows Microsoft's Web site that includes such menus.

Menu

**FIGURE 18.1**

DHTML enables active menus on Web sites.

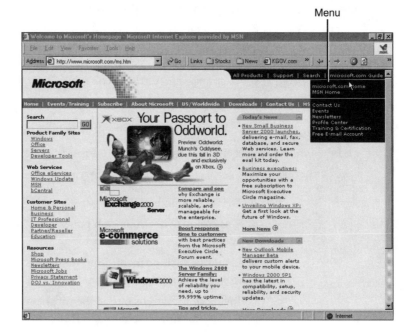

- **Help systems**—Developers can use DHTML to provide a help system for Web pages. This same technology can be applied to company intranets and individual software packages that provide HTML-based hyperlinked help.

- **Automatic adjustment of fonts and colors**—Your Web page text and graphic sizes and colors can change, depending on your Web page user's actions. For example, you could display a catalog of items that you sell and their descriptions. When the user clicks on a description, the description would increase in size and become boldfaced so that the user can read it more easily.

- **Common database manipulations**—Web pages that display data from a database provide the user with tools to perform common sorting, filtering, and searching within the Web browser without requiring a secondary download and delay from the serving computer.

In addition, a single DHTML-based Web page is routed to all users of your Web site. Depending on any user's individual actions, that user's Web site behaves differently from another user who views the same site but performs different actions on that page.

Keep in mind that programming Web pages, either in DHTML or the simpler HTML, is quite different from writing programs in Visual Basic. When creating Web pages, you are providing formatting commands primarily that the user's Web browser is to adhere to. You are not writing a program that processes data and includes graphic controls such as text labels and command buttons in the way you do with Visual Basic. As you progress through the rest of this lesson, you will see an example of DHTML's code.

# A Sample DHTML Page

Before discussing additional DHTML aspects, it would be useful if you visit a Web page that contains DHTML-based Web page code. When you access the following Web address,

`http://msdn.microsoft.com/workshop/default.asp`,

you'll see the Microsoft Web page shown in Figure 18.2.

The text at the left of the Web page is activated by DHTML code. As you point to each item on the left, the description in the center of the page changes to describe the item pointed to.

## caution

Remember, no page reloading occurs when the page changes, because of DHTML elements. The user does not have to click on an item on the left of the page to see that item's description. The user only has to move the mouse cursor over an item; that item's description instantly appears in the center of the page.

**FIGURE 18.2**

A DHTML-based
Web page looks
like other Web
pages at first.

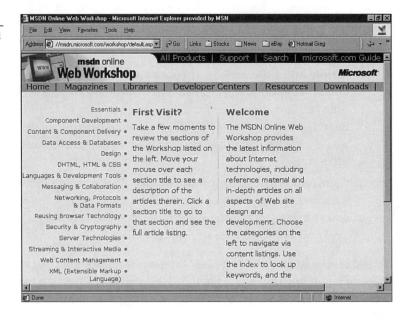

Figure 18.3 shows what happens when the user points to the description labeled
DHTML, HTML, & DSS. The best thing about this Web site is that the same link points to
a site that describes DHTML. You can go to that site (when you've finished with this
chapter, of course!) and learn more about DHTML.

New description

**FIGURE 18.3**

The center item
changes as a
result of the
mouse cursor
resting on any
item to the left.

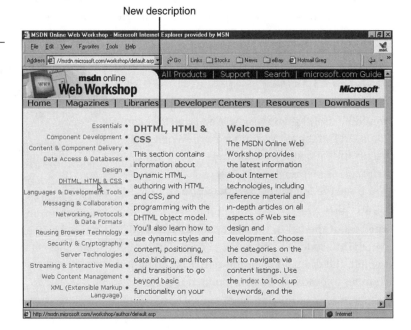

# The Technology Behind DHTML

One of the most important components of DHTML technology is the Document Object Model (DOM), designed for Web pages. The DOM is really a description that explains how to access any element on a Web page as an object. These objects, similar to Visual Basic's controls and C++ objects, have properties that you can change on-the-fly simply by changing its properties. All of the following can be objects subject to the Document Object Model:

- Text
- Graphics
- Individual HTML tags
- Hyperlinks
- Menus
- Multimedia controls such as video clips
- Command buttons and other controls that can appear on Web pages

With DHTML comes a new name for scripts—*scriptlets*. A scriptlet is the same as the scripts you learned about in Chapter 15, "Macro, Batch, and Scripting Languages," and may be authored in JavaScript, VBScript, or another scripting language. In other words, JavaScript code that performs on a DHTML object, such as a command button that changes colors, would be called a scriptlet. A scriptlet is a routine written in a scripting language just as an applet is a routine written in Java. (You'll learn about Java applets in Chapter 20, "Java Programming," but for now a Java applet is little more than a program written in Java.)

Scriptlets appear inside HTML code using the `<a href>` hyperlink tag you learned about in the previous chapter's lesson. The tag informs the browser to expect a DHTML scriptlet and the scriptlet's language. The following informs HTML about a Javascript routine that appears in the Web page:

```
<a href="javascript:">
```

Here is what you know so far about DHTML: A Web page based on DHTML changes in response to the user's actions. That change occurs because the objects on the Web page, defined by the DOM standard, are manipulated by scriptlets. These scriptlets are routines written in scripting languages such as VBScript and JavaScript.

> **note**
>
> Microsoft's VBScript has not gained the DHTML acceptance of JavaScript. Because of JavaScript's acceptance, an entire lesson is devoted to JavaScript in Chapter 21, "JavaScript." There, you will learn some of the details of coding in JavaScript.

# The Microsoft and Netscape Battle

Microsoft and Netscape implement DHTML differently, much to the dismay of many Web developers. (Netscape is the company that provides the Netscape Navigator Web browser.) The two companies provide browsers that approach DOM differently. The original Navigator browser that provided DHTML support recognized only a fraction of the object-based elements that Internet Explorer recognized. If you write a DHTML Web page for the Internet Explorer browser, you can make almost all Web-page elements objects that your scripting code can manipulate. In Navigator, only a subset of those objects can be manipulated.

Therefore, DHTML-based Web pages are more active when viewed inside Internet Explorer than the same pages viewed in Navigator. Fortunately, Internet Explorer has a broader user base than Navigator. Also, the newer versions of Navigator promise to implement the full DOM specification that the Microsoft browsers support, so as users adopt the new versions of Navigator, more DHTML Web-page documents will be available to both browsers.

# The Rollover Effect

One of the most common DHTML elements in Web pages is the *rollover effect*. When the user points to a button on a Web page, that button changes color or format. By highlighting a button this way, you help show the user that the button is being pointed to and that a mouse click will activate that button.

In the days before DHTML, when a user clicked a button, the click sent a message back to the Web page's server to fetch another page or part of a page. The user had to wait for this to occur.

Buttons that appear on Web pages often have graphic images on them. The graphic image may have the button's text and color and a design of some kind. DHTML scriptlets handle the rollover effect by changing the picture on the button to another picture. In other words, when the DHTML scriptlet senses that the mouse pointer is over the button, the scriptlet switches the graphic image to a different image. The second image might be a brighter or otherwise highlighted image of a button.

As you learned in the previous chapter, the `<src img>` command tag defines a graphic image that appears on a Web page. The scriptlet replaces the default `<src img>` with a different graphic image.

Listing 18.1 shows a JavaScript scriptlet that produces the rollover effect. For now, don't worry about the details, which you'll learn about JavaScript in Chapter 21. Just look through the code; you should be able to understand the basic nature of the scriptlet from what you already know about programming.

**LISTING 18.1** A Scriptlet to Replace the Graphic on a Button

```html
<html>
<body>
 <a href="javascript:"
  onmouseover="changeOver('Img1');"
  onmouseout="changeOut('Img1');">
  <img name=Img1 src="Img1.gif">
 </a><br>
 <a href="javascript:"
  onmouseover="changeOver('Img2');"
  onmouseout="changeOut('Img2');">
  <img name=Img2 src="Img2.gif">
 </a><br>

<script>
function changeOver(anImage) {
   if (anImage == "Img1") {
     document.images[anImage].src = "Img1over.gif";
   }
   else if (anImage == "Img2") {
     document.images[anImage].src = "Img2over.gif";
   }
}

function changeOut(anImage) {
   if (anImage == "Img1") {
     document.images[anImage].src = "Img1.gif";
   }
   else if (anImage == "Img2") {
     document.images[anImage].src = "Img2.gif";
   }
}
</script>
</body>
</html>
```

One of the first signs of a DHTML Web page is the `javascript` keyword. Listing 18.1 implements the `javascript` command as follows:

```html
<a href="javascript:"
  onmouseover="changeOver('Img1');"
  onmouseout="changeOut('Img1');">
  <img name=Img1 src="Img1.gif">
 </a>
```

By the way, if you save this and the surrounding HTML code in a text file, with the .htm filename extension, the code will not seem to work because you will probably not have the code's required image files on your computer named Img1.gif, Img2.gif, Img1over.gif, and Img2over.gif. You need to have two graphic button images and two similar button images that appear when the user rolls the mouse pointer over one of the two buttons. If you want to take the time to locate four graphic images with the .gif filename extensions, you can copy those images to the disk folder where you store Listing 18.1 and change the gif filenames in the code to your files' names. Then, when you load the text file into your Web browser (use the **File**, **Open** menu option), two images will appear and they will change to the other two as you run your mouse over them.

If you pursue further education in DHTML, you'll learn better ways of coding rollovers than shown in Listing 18.1. A common improvement to the code makes the scriptlet much more general-purpose to handle several sets of buttons instead of writing the scriptlet just for two specific buttons and graphic images.

onmouseover is a JavaScript command that checks to see whether the mouse pointer is over one of the buttons. If the mouse pointer rests over the image (named Img1 here), the changeOver procedure executes. changeover replaces the currently displayed image with another in this code that appears later:

```
function changeOver(anImage) {
   if (anImage == "Img1") {
     document.images[anImage].src = "Img1over.gif";
   }
   else if (anImage == "Img2") {
     document.images[anImage].src = "Img2over.gif";
   }
}
```

When the user's mouse pointer leaves the image, the onmouseout event defined as changeOut executes to restore the original image, using this code:

```
function changeOut(anImage) {
   if (anImage == "Img1") {
     document.images[anImage].src = "Img1.gif";
   }
   else if (anImage == "Img2") {
```

```
        document.images[anImage].src = "Img2.gif";
    }
}
```

The HTML specification and browsers had to be changed to support DHTML elements such as scriptlets. The tag command `<script>` was not included in HTML until version 4, and no browser that supported earlier versions of HTML could support any DHTML options such as a rollover effect. Today, however, most browsers in use support either the full DHTML implementation (as most Internet Explorer browsers do) or the Navigator subset (that supports rollover effects) of many common DHTML effects.

For an example of button rollover effects, visit the Brady Games site at `http://www.bradygames.com/` to see what happens when you point to a button on the left of the page. Figure 18.4 shows the rollover effect, which not only changes the appearance of the button but also displays a description of what clicking that button produces. (The black-and-white figure cannot show the button's color change.)

**FIGURE 18.4**

The button and its description change when the user points to the button.

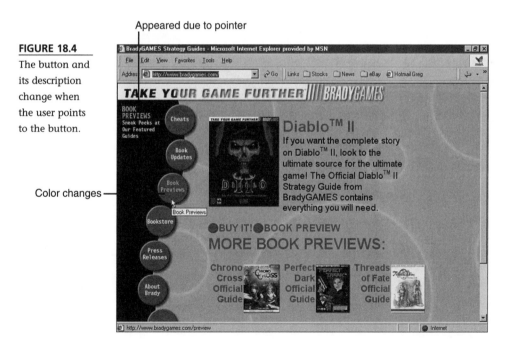

## Summary

DHTML activates Web pages by enabling the use of objects that can be manipulated by scripting code such as JavaScript or VBScript. DHTML is not fully supported by every browser in use today, but it will be in the future. (By then, another technology will probably replace DHTML; such is the way with these things.) Most Web sites can safely use it now because most current browsers support it, at least partially. DHTML enables you to create Web pages that are more active, adding to the user's browsing experience.

- DHTML allows you to add menus, help systems, and active button effects to the Web pages you develop.

- The active DHTML code appears in a scriptlet that you write and place inside your HTML code.

- The `<a href>` command tag informs the Web browser of an upcoming scriptlet.

- JavaScripts are interpreted line by line as the Web browser reads them.

## IN THIS CHAPTER

- XML and Its Impact
- Multiple Platforms
- A Complete XML Example

19

# INTRODUCTION TO XML

Pundits believe that the next decade of Web activity will be better than the previous one because of eXtensible Markup Language (XML). Only time will tell whether or not XML will meet these expectations, but most agree that XML provides the means for more advanced Web page technology and, more importantly, provides a way for companies with large Web sites to maintain those sites, create additional sites more easily, and share data with other sites. In this chapter, you will get a glimpse into the technology of XML.

- XML describes both the format and the content of a Web page.
- XML extends routine HTML command tags.
- XML code must be both valid and well formed to work properly.
- The DTD, Document Type Definition, defines the XML command tags in your Web pages.

# XML and Its Impact

How important is XML? The Gartner Group, an Internet research company, says that 80% of business-to-business (also known as *B2B*) traffic uses XML. XML is much like HTML, and in many ways is identical. An XML listing includes standard HTML command tags, but XML command tags are far more numerous.

An XML coder can define and use, on-the-fly, brand-new command tags that are also available to other Web pages. In defining your own XML command tags, you are using the extensible portion of XML. Code examples throughout the rest of this chapter will help show how the XML coder does this.

Whereas HTML describes the format of a Web page, XML describes the content of a Web page. XML does more than just tell the Web browser where and how to place Web page elements.

Consider the following possible XML section from a Web page:

```
<CARMAKE>Swifty</CARMAKE>
<CARMODEL>Dove</CARMODEL>
<ENGINEPARTNO>546-32Xs</ENGINEPARTNO>
<WHOLESALE>$21,039</WHOLESALE>
<SUGGESTEDRETAIL>$32,483</SUGGESTEDRETAIL>
```

Over time, industries will begin to standardize their XML tags. Therefore, <ENGINEPARTNO> might be standardized by automobile Web site designers to designate any automobile manufacturer's engine part number. As other automobile Web developers standardize and use <ENGINEPARTNO> (and its corresponding ending tag of </ENGINEPARTNO>), Web pages can be combined and borrowed and used as the basis of other Web pages that also contain such parts.

When learning XML, you would not learn a <CARMAKE> tag because no such tag exists. As soon as a Web site uses <CARMAKE>, however, the tag is defined and should be used in that context. As a Web designer, you will learn the standard XML tags being used for the type of Web site you are developing. Your XML tags then define data categories, not actual data specifics.

One problem at this time is that XML is too new for globally agreed-upon definitions. Even within industries, one company might create XML tags that differ greatly from another's. The move toward organization will come only as companies that both support XML begin to agree on a standard and that standard grows. For example, if your company's Web site is to interact with a vendor's XML-based Web site, one of you will have to adopt the other's XML tags or a combined system must be put into place. This agreement process will continue and grow as more companies begin to move to XML.

HTML has a defined set of formatting and hyper-link tags, and you could very easily learn all of them. XML is defined as Web designers use it. You'll never learn all the XML tags, because new tags will continue to be developed as long as the language is in use.

# Multiple Platforms

The mainframe and PC are not the only comput-ing devices used today. On handheld palm devices that display Web content on small monochrome screens; content-limited WebTV screens; control devices wired to the Web in the home such as security cameras and control pan-els; and cell phones that display 8-line Web pages, Web content is being routed to many devices other than the typical color PC screen.

What is a company to do when it wants to enable its Web pages for PC users and for every other pos-sible device that can display Web content? If the company produces an HTML-based Web page that is formatted for PCs, the company will have to implement different HTML code to format the page for a cell phone. The company then will have to change the code again so that the page works on WebTV. With HTML, the conversion is tedious. With XML tags, the Web designers need only to transfer the XML tags and the content to each new format, a much simpler process. A special set of XML definitions called the DTD, or *Document Type Definition*, contains the XML definitions and as long as all Web pages adopt the same DTD, they can each interact.

HTML is still, and will always be, required. Without HTML, a Web page cannot appear no matter how many DHTML scriptlets and no mat-ter how many XML tags you place in a file. HTML is the Web browser's only known language. Special extensions to HTML, supported by today's

**tip**

For the first time, Web search engines can begin to search across industries for categories of items instead of performing time-consuming, tedious, and resource-grabbing searches for spe-cific text embedded in Web pages. A search engine could scour Web page tags for the exact tag `<ENGINEPARTNO>` to locate specific engine parts for automobile manufacturers quickly instead of wasting search time and resources scanning non–automobile Web site inventories.

**caution**

Don't discount XML's importance. Although the definition of XML may seem fuzzy (it still is), many companies are moving to convert all their Web pages from straight HTML code to XML code. Cisco, Incorporated, claims to process 95% of its busi-ness over the Internet. When Cisco converted to XML in mid-2000, it began saving $175 million annually over traditional HTML-based tech-nology.

browsers, help to extend the routine HTML job such as describing the format of text and graphics. HTML still defines most of a Web page's appearance and hyperlinks. XML is an internal layer that defines the Web page's data. As you see an example built in the next few sections, you will better learn how XML works internally on a Web page while HTML performs the external formatting.

# A Complete XML Example

In spite of the freedom that a Web programmer has with XML, certain rules do apply. All XML code must conform to two requirements:

1. XML code must be well formed and must begin with the `<?xml version=1.0?>` tag, which is never used in another context. In addition, all tags must appear between the `<list>` and `</list>` tags. Browsers do not handle poorly defined XML code as well as they do HTML. If you write badly formed HTML code, such as forgetting a terminating tag before another beginning tag, a browser would not display an error message; instead, the browser would show an incomplete sentence or a badly placed graphic image. When some of the HTML is incorrect, later HTML code is affected. Bad XML code produces actual error messages.

2. The XML code must be valid. Simple XML code cannot be validated, but by using the XML technology called Document Type Definition (DTD), you ensure that your XML code follows your own validation rules.

The next two sections explore the concepts of well-formed XML code and XML-based validity. You will see how to determine whether XML code is well formed and you will see how to define the DTD. By the time you finish these sections, you will be well on your way to comprehending the goals of XML.

## Using Well-Formed XML Code

Listing 19.1 contains an XML file. The file is a description of a company's personnel records. Listing 19.1 shows only one employee in the file.

note

In addition to being well formed and valid, all XML code should reside in a file with the XML filename extension.

## LISTING 19.1    A Well-Formed XML File

```xml
<?xml version="1.0"?>
<list>
   <employee>
      <firstname>James</firstname>
      <lastname>Wilson</lastname>
      <emp_codes>
         <startcode>C8</startcode>
         <currentcode>B7</currentcode>
      </emp_codes>

      <employees_managed>
         <emp_mngd>Julie Brown</emp_mngd>
         <emp_mngd>Anthony Harris</emp_mngd>
         <emp_mngd>Kay Bell</emp_mngd>
         <emp_mngd>Mavis Gray</emp_mngd>
      </employees_managed>

      <review_text>
Mr. Wilson has maintained consistency as an above-average
employee of the company. He works well with his peers as
well as his subordinates.
      </review_text>
   </employee>
</list>
```

The location of the starting and ending command tags determines groups within the file. For example, this employee, James Wilson, manages four other employees. The tags `<employees_managed>` and `</employees_managed>` enclose the names of four employees whom Mr. Wilson manages. If Mr. Wilson managed 20 employees, 20 names would appear between `<employees_managed>` and `</employees_managed>`. The name of each employee Mr. Wilson manages is enclosed between `<emp_mngd>` and `</emp_mngd>` tags.

Listing 19.1 is well-formed. No XML-compatible browser will have a problem with the file. However, if this code's author had not grouped the tags properly, the browser would issue an error message.

Here is a badly formed section of code that would not work:

```
<employees_managed>
    <emp_mngd></employees_managed>Julie Brown</emp_mngd>
    <emp_mngd>Anthony Harris</emp_mngd>
    <emp_mngd>Kay Bell</emp_mngd>
    <emp_mngd>Mavis Gray</emp_mngd>
```

The closing </employees_managed> tag is out of place. The employee names would not appear within the managed employees group, the goal of the grouping would be lost, and the mismatched start and end tags would cause the browser problems. The <employees_managed> and </employees_managed> tags should enclose the names of the employees Mr. Wilson manages.

## Validating XML Code

In many ways, badly formed XML code acts like a syntax error in a regular, compiled, programming language. As with a syntax error, badly formed XML code produces an error message. Invalid XML code acts just as a logic error in a regular, compiled program acts. That is, the browser issues no error message but the displayed Web page will not conform to the developer's goals. Bad data is likely to appear because of the invalid XML.

Suppose you omitted a required piece of data within an XML file, such as an employee's last name. The first few lines of such a file might look like this:

```
<?xml version="1.0"?>
<list>
   <employee>
      <firstname>James</firstname>
      <lastname></lastname>
      <emp_codes>
         <startcode>C8</startcode>
         <currentcode>B7</currentcode>
      </emp_codes>

      <employees_managed>
```

Such an entry in the XML code is incorrect, assuming that all employees have last names. Such an omission could be overlooked, and a search of employee records wouldn't turn up this employee because you failed to include the name.

Of course, some tags might not contain data, and such an omission could still be correct. For example, an employee who is not in a supervisory position would not have any employees beneath them. The content of `<employees_managed>` and `</employees_managed>` could be left blank until the employee in question was promoted to a position in which he had subordinates.

Given the fact that XML codes are defined as you go along (until de facto standards are determined by a company or industry sector), you will want to eliminate all possible mistakes such as the omission of required data.

Therefore, the second half of learning XML requires that you master Document Type Definition. DTD is simply a set of rules you make up for every XML tag you define.

Suppose you make a DTD entry for `<employees_managed>` that says the group may be left blank. A DTD entry for `<lastname>`, however, states that `<lastname>` can never be omitted. If you fail to list a last name, the browser will read your DTD, see the problem, and alert you to the data error.

If you write XML-based Web pages that are to be used in conjunction with another company's XML, you will want to use a uniform set of XML tags. Therefore, you will need access to the other company's DTD. The DTD appears right inside the Web page's source code and is open to all. Therefore, locating a Web page's DTD is as easy as looking at the Web page's HTML source code. In most browsers, you'll simply select View, Source to do just that.

Keep in mind that this XML file might contain hundreds of employees. Creating a complete set of DTD rules for one employee's entry would be overkill, but creating one set of DTD rules that covers one, ten, or hundreds of similar entries in the XML file makes a lot of sense. DTD entries ensure that you follow your own requirements.

## Defining the DTD

One requirement of a DTD is defining whether an entry requires data or can be left blank. As indicated in the previous section, the `<employees_managed>` tag can be left blank if the employee doesn't supervise others, but the employee's last name is required.

The first line in your DTD must be this:

```
<!DOCTYPE list [
```

The opening bracket begins the DTD. Most of the subsequent lines in the DTD will follow this format:

```
<!ELEMENT XMLtag (requiredTag1, requiredTag2, requiredTag3, ...)>
```

*XMLtag* is the tag you are defining, and the tags between the parentheses are those that must appear between the opening and closing *XMLtag* tags and the order in which they must appear. Consider the following line:

```
<!ELEMENT employee (firstname, lastname, emp_codes, employees_managed,
➥review_text)>
```

This DTD entry states that the tags following it must appear between the `<employee>` and `</employee>` tag pair. If the XML code does not conform to the DTD's requirement, the code will be invalid and the browser can issue an error.

If the DTD contained only the single line defined so far here, it would be rather limiting. With the `!ELEMENT` definition just shown, the DTD provides for no optional tags or data values between the tags.

DTD uses the `#PCDATA` keyword to designate text. `#PCDATA` is a parameter that your XML code will replace with a specific value. Consider this DTD entry:

```
<!ELEMENT firstname (#PCDATA)>
```

**tip**

Without a DTD, your browser has no way to determine the validity of your XML code. Therefore, you should always define a DTD for all XML code you write.

This entry tells the browser that the `<firstname>` tag must have a data value. The `#PCDATA` tells the browser that something must appear between the `<firstname>` and `</lastname>` tags.

So far, you have seen the following lines of the DTD built:

```
<!DOCTYPE list [
  <!ELEMENT employee (firstname, lastname, emp_codes, employees_managed,
➥review_text)>
  <!ELEMENT firstname (#PCDATA)>
```

To summarize, you (and your browser) now know the following about the XML requirements:

- A DTD is being defined that will state the format of the XML entries.
- The `<employee>` and `</employee>` tags must include (at a minimum) the following tags (their end tags are assumed): `<firstname>`, `<lastname>`, `<emp_codes>`, `<employees_managed>`, and `<review_text>`.
- A value is required for the `<firstname>` tag.

The next line indicates that a last name also is required for all employees:

```
<!ELEMENT lastname (#PCDATA)>
```

Assume that the `<emp_codes>` tag must contain a `<startcode>` (because all employees started working at some point) and a `<currentcode>`. This must be some kind of pay code or years-of-service code. Therefore, depending on how long the employee has worked, the current code may be different from the start code, but both are required. The following DTD entry ensures that both tags are included:

```
<!ELEMENT emp_codes (startcode, currentcode)>
```

Both tags require values even though the values may be identical if the employee has not worked long. The following ensures this:

```
<!ELEMENT startcode (#PCDATA)>
<!ELEMENT currentcode (#PCDATA)>
```

The DTD is coming right along. No way yet exists for optional data, however. You can designate optional tags using the character *. The * works like the DOS wildcard character: It represents zero or more items. An example will clarify this character.

<employees_managed> is the first tag that may or may not include other tags, the <emp_mngd> tags. You would use * to designate the optional tags:

```
<!ELEMENT employees_managed (emp_mngd)*>
```

The asterisk informs the browser that <emp_mngd> might appear between <employees_managed> one or more times or not at all.

Listing 19.2 shows the complete DTD with the XML code that it defines. As you can see, the DTD appears before the XML code that it defines.

## LISTING 19.2    DTD and corresponding XML.

```
<?xml version="1.0"?>

<!DOCTYPE list [
  <!ELEMENT employee (firstname, lastname, emp_codes, employees_managed,
➥review_text)>
    <!ELEMENT firstname (#PCDATA)>
    <!ELEMENT lastname (#PCDATA)>
    <!ELEMENT emp_codes (startcode, currentcode)>
      <!ELEMENT startcode (#PCDATA)>
      <!ELEMENT currentcode (#PCDATA)>
    <!ELEMENT employees_managed (emp_mngd)*>
    <!ELEMENT review_text (#PCDATA)*>
]>

<list>
  <employee>
    <firstname>James</firstname>
    <lastname>Wilson</lastname>
    <emp_codes>
      <startcode>C8</startcode>
      <currentcode>B7</currentcode>
    </emp_codes>
```

**LISTING 19.2**   (continued)

```
    <employees_managed>
        <emp_mngd>Julie Brown</emp_mngd>
        <emp_mngd>Anthony Harris</emp_mngd>
        <emp_mngd>Kay Bell</emp_mngd>
        <emp_mngd>Mavis Gray</emp_mngd>
    </employees_managed>

    <review_text>
Mr. Wilson has maintained consistency as an above-average
employee of the company. He works well with his peers as
well as his subordinates.
    </review_text>
  </employee>
</list>
```

# Summary

You now have an understanding of basic XML language. Perhaps more important than the language specifics is understanding why XML is so vital to the Web's future. The XML tags define data and don't just work to format a Web page as HTML does. Your Web page will still need HTML to format the look and behavior of the page, but the underlying XML code will make your page more easily accessed by sites that recognize the XML tags you use. In the future, search engines and other processes will be able to perform more accurate searching, sorting, and manipulation of Web data.

**caution**

You are well on your way to mastering XML, but please be warned: Much more XML knowledge is needed to make XML work well for your Web pages. You've only scratched the surface here, but you do have a good understanding of XML fundamentals. In Chapter 25, "Your Programming Future," you will find other XML resources that will help you increase your XML knowledge.

- The use of XML will grow as standards are agreed upon.
- Unlike HTML which comes with predefined command tags, the XML programmer creates new command tags that describe content within Web pages.
- XML code must be well formed or errors will result when a user displays the XML-based Web page.
- Document Type Definition (DTD) entries describe and define XML tags used in a Web page.

## IN THIS CHAPTER

- Introducing Java
- Java Provides Executable Content
- Multiplatform Executable Content
- The Java Usage Summary
- The Security Issue
- Give Java a Spin
- Visual J++: A Sample Java System
- The Java Language Specifics
- Exception Handling

20

# JAVA PROGRAMMING

The world of Web pages gained an unexpected boost in capabilities when the Java language was introduced. Originally designed for embedded programming applications such as the programs inside automobile computer modules, Java quickly became the standard language used to activate Web pages. Java almost single-handedly rescued static HTML-based Web pages and turned the Web into an interactive medium.

If you plan to work as a programmer on Web-based applications, you will have to learn Java. Java is simple to learn, however. The inventors of Java used C and C++ as their models, and Java is a small language. Its strength is in its size because small programs can load quickly along with HTML pages to present interactive Web pages to users on the Internet.

The highlights of this chapter include the following:

- A description of how Java works in Web pages.
- How Java programs travel with their associated Web pages.
- Java programs are small for efficiency.
- Java is OOP but is not C++.
- Visual programming environments, such as Visual J++, improve the Java programmer's efficiency.
- Java programs compile differently from programs in other languages.
- How to extend the built-in Java classes for your Java programs.
- Java handles exceptions for you to improve error-checking.

# Introducing Java

The colorful, Internet browser screens now require advanced programming concepts and languages. With their simple navigational tools and appealing graphical nature, the new Web browsers made the Internet accessible to anybody and everybody with their simple to-and-fro navigational tools and appealing graphical nature. Soon, millions of users all over the world were moving back and forth between Web sites as easily as they moved from page to page in their word processors.

Internet browsers have been around for several years. From the beginning, they have brought text, graphics, and hyperlinks to Internet users. Yet, within two or three years, the original Internet browsers were considered obsolete due to the static nature of their screens. In other words, despite the colorful and cross-linked pages that Internet browsers make available for the world, the pages did not have enough action in them to keep users occupied. More importantly, the browser technology was too static to make Web sites truly come alive.

Users seem to want more from the Internet than just a distributed set of interconnected graphical screens. Despite the Web's hypertext nature, those hypertext links simply take you from one page to another without doing any work for you except eliminating the need to type long Web page addresses. Users want real computing power coming at them from the Web sites they visit. For example, instead of reading about the rules of baseball, you might want to see a baseball game in action or get an introductory graphical tutorial on the basics of the game. In addition, the ability to access online database technology over an Internet connection, for e-commerce and remote inventory control, requires more than regular, HTML-only Web pages can handle.

Java, developed by Sun Microsystems in the mid-1990s, changes the way that Web sites operate. Instead of using Web browsers to view data, the browsers seamlessly download programs written in Java and those programs execute on the user's computer, as opposed to the remote server serving up the Web page. You can actually interact with the Java program as you would with any software program that runs on your computer. All traces of the Java program then go away when the applet ends, or when the user leaves the Web page.

You can write two kinds of Java programs:

- **Java applets**—Java applets are small programs that travel with HTML code and execute on the Web user's computer.

- **Java applications**—Java applications are complete standalone programs that do not require a Web browser or HTML to execute.

## caution

Don't make the mistake of thinking that all the sounds and animation you've seen on the Web represent Java technology. For example, when you listen to a Web page's sound file, your own computer's sound-producing software is probably playing the sound data that comes from the Web site to your browser. Java takes computer interaction a step further.

Most Java programs so far appear as Java applets. After all, the primary goal of Java is to place executable code on Web pages so that users gain more interactivity with Web sites. In addition to writing applets that appear in Web pages, you can also create standalone programs that execute without the need for a Web browser. For example, if you wanted to write a rental property management application that runs independently of an Internet connection, you could select Java as the programming language you use to develop the application.

# Java Provides Executable Content

When working with Java, you'll often hear and read about executable content. Executable content is what Java is really all about. A Web page contains executable content via HTML commands in the form of a Java applet. Any Web page's Java-based content exists on the target user's computer. Figure 20.1 shows an overview of an HTML document with two embedded Java applets.

**FIGURE 20.1**

HTML serves up Java's executable content.

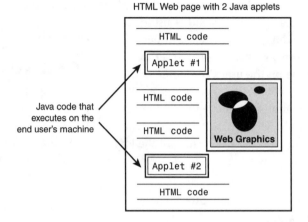

HTML Web page with 2 Java applets

Java code that executes on the end user's machine

When the user enters or clicks the URL that displays the page seen in Figure 20.1, the user's Web-browsing software loads the HTML code, formats the page's text according to the HTML tags, displays any graphical images that appear on the page, and loads the executable content (as applets) so the content can execute. The executable content executes either immediately or upon a predetermined event, such as a mouse click over a hot spot on the Web page.

The best method of running Java applets is not always obvious to the user. The user might think he is viewing a busy Web page, when in reality an applet is providing animation. The look of that animation is smooth because the animation software runs on the user's computer. Because of the applet, the speed of the animation is not dependent on the download time or Internet traffic.

note

As you'll see in this chapter's code, the <APPLET> tag indicates that a Java-enabled applet appears inside HTML. The Java code follows the <APPLET> tag until the closing </APPLET> tag appears.

Before Java-enabled Web pages, the user did have some interaction with the remote site. Nevertheless, that interaction was severely limited. Web page animation was controlled by the user's animation software. If a computer system had no software that could display animation, that feature of the Web page was lost for that system's users.

# Multiplatform Executable Content

Now that you've seen how Java-enabled Web sites appear to the user, think about the requirements of such executable content. When you write a Java-based Web page, you want the code to work on the user's remote computer no matter what kind of computer the remote user uses.

*Common gateway interface (CGI)* programming provides the primitive interaction you often see on non-Java Web sites.

Whereas most language compilers such as Visual C++ turn programs into a machine-dependent executable program, Java development tools do not go quite that far. All Java compilers compile your Java code into a special machine-independent module called *bytecode*. Your Java-enabled Web browsing software translates this compiled bytecode into instructions that your computer can execute.

No computer can really read bytecode, but each computer's Java-enabled browser can. In other words, given a Java applet's bytecode, a PC can run the applet using a Web browser, and a Unix-based minicomputer can run the same bytecode using its own Java-enabled browser such as HotJava. Each Web browser interprets the machine-dependent bytecode and then translates that bytecode into machine-specific instructions that particular computer can understand.

Figure 20.2 shows the Java compilation/translation scenario. You'll use the Java language to produce bytecode for a virtual machine and not a specific machine, because the bytecode is machine independent. The bytecode is sent to the Web page that is to contain the applet, and when the user requests that Web page, the user's Web browser reads the bytecode and automatically interprets the bytecode into code readable by the user's computer. The user is unaware that all this took place; he simply displays the Web page and sees the executing applet along with the rest of the Web page's content.

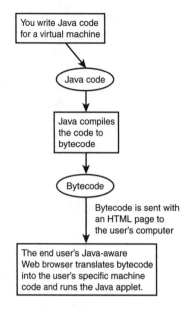

**FIGURE 20.2**

Your Java session produces compiled bytecode that subsequent computers translate to run the program.

# The Java Usage Summary

As a newcomer to Java technology, you might benefit from a summary of how to view a Java-enabled Web page with a Java-aware Web browser such as Internet Explorer. Here are the steps that occur:

1. You log on to the Internet, using your Web-browsing software.

2. You see your Web browser's default home page.

3. You enter a Java-enabled Web site's URL.

4. The serving computer sends the HTML document to your Web browser.

5. The HTML-based document's <APPLET> tag informs your browser of the page's Java-based executable content.

6. If any graphics appear on the Web page, your browser downloads them.

7. Depending on how the Java applet is to be triggered (either automatically or by a user's event), the server will also send the bytecode to your computer when the time is right.

8. Your computer's Web browser interprets the bytecode and executes the Java executable content.

9. When you leave the Web page, the executable content goes away. (Some Web browsers will keep the Java code in memory for a while in case you return to the page.)

Whereas the previous steps were based on the user's perspective, this would also be a good time to explain what you, the Java programmer, will go through to create Web pages with Java applets. Here are the general steps you'll follow:

1. Start your Java compiler.

2. Write the Java applet.

3. Create the HTML Web page that will contain the Java applet. Use appropriate tags to indicate the applet and its parameters.

4. Compile the Java applet. Your Java development system will place the applet in its appropriate location needed for the HTML Web page that will contain the applet.

5. If the compiler finds errors, fix them and recompile the file.

6. Test and debug the applet.

7. Store the applet and HTML on your Web server, where they will await an Internet user's request.

# The Security Issue

Security should always be your concern when writing online applications. In practice, Java-enabled applets could be prone to security problems without the proper precautions being in place. After all, when you visit a Java-enabled Web page, you are not always sure whether an applet is running or what that applet is trying to do to your computer's disk or memory.

Fortunately, Sun Microsystems developed Java to be a network-based programming language. Therefore, security is inherent in the language, both for the developer and for the Internet user. What follows are some of the security-related protections built into the Java language:

- A Java applet is not allowed to venture into the user's memory areas where it does not belong.

- A Java applet cannot create, read, rename, copy, or write files on the user's file system.

- A Java applet cannot connect to additional machines on the user's network.

- Applets cannot call system routines on the user's system.

**caution**

You can load and run a Java applet locally from your own browser by loading an applet from your own disk drive or network. A locally loaded applet generally has permission to read and write to the local file system. In addition, some applet viewers let the user specify a list of files that a Web applet can access.

As you can see, Java developers understand the need for security, and the most obvious security footholds are barred from an applet's access. As more people write Java applets, additional security concerns are sure to enter into the picture.

# Give Java a Spin

Now that you know more about Java, you can take a look at a Java-enabled Web page. Use Internet Explorer 3.0 (or later) or Netscape's Navigator to locate the following Web site:

`http://java.sun.com/`

The Sun Web site presents some of the most up-to-date information on Java technology. When you display the Web page, a Java applet loads and you can read changing industry news as it rotates in the upper-right corner of the screen. Figure 20.3 shows the page and the location of the Java-based news ticker.

The Java-based news ticker

**FIGURE 20.3**

Java applets can enliven a Web page.

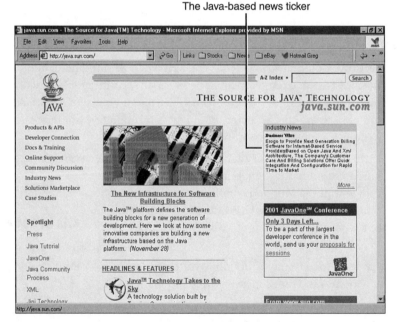

# Visual J++: A Sample Java System

Several implementations of Java exist. One of the most popular due to its similarity with the Visual Basic development environment is Visual J++, one of Microsoft's newest languages. The Visual J++ technology supports the entire Sun

Microsystems–developed Java language. Visual J++ is a programming platform used to develop Java-enabled applets and standalone applications. It includes not only a Java compiler (the tool that translates your Java programs to bytecode) but also an editor, debugger, and online documentation provider.

Therefore, if you already know Visual Basic, you'll feel at home with Visual J++ after you learn it. The numerous windows and screen elements are the same as Visual Basic's because both use a standard interface called the Microsoft Visual Studio.

Several Java-based programming systems exist on the market, and Visual J++'s big advantage is its visual interface that is so similar to the other Microsoft languages that you might use. The early Java compilers were command-line based. Surprisingly, the graphical nature of computers and the Web did not make it to the Java language development tools until programmers used Java for about a year. In late 1995 and early 1996, graphical Java development tools, such as Visual J++, began to appear on the market.

**note**

Actually, all of Microsoft's current languages use the Visual Studio platform. Therefore, the programming tools remain the same although you can write programs in different languages.

Keep in mind that Visual J++ is not a Java replacement, nor is it a competing product to the Java language. In fact, Microsoft makes it clear that Visual J++ implements the same Java technology developed by Sun Microsystems. Therefore, when you work with Visual J++, you are working with the Java language, just as Visual C++ programmers write code in C++. Visual J++ is a complete development platform, or program development tool, with which you can create Java-enabled applets.

Just to give you a better idea of what a full-fledged Java programming system can offer, here are just a few Visual J++ features you'll run across if you use the Visual J++ platform (competitors might offer some, all, or more of these kinds of features):

- The Visual J++ editor contains a powerful set of word-processing text features, including the usual search, cut, paste, multipane viewing, moving and copying between windows, bookmarks, a full-screen viewer, and advanced windowing features.

- Visual J++ contains a complete online help system that includes all available documentation, including a version of Microsoft's Books Online technology.

- You'll want to take advantage of Visual J++'s interactive debugger. Online debugging enables you to specify breakpoints and examine data contents at any point in your program. You'll learn about online debuggers, such as the one in Visual J++ and Visual Basic, in Chapter 22, "The Importance of Maintenance."

■ Microsoft's famous wizard technology enables you to build your initial Java applet or application quickly. After the wizard creates the application shell, you then can fill in the missing pieces to customize your own Java program requirements.

■ You can use the Visual J++ applet viewer, JView, to test the applets and applications that you write before sending them out onto the Web with your Web server.

■ You can create dialog boxes and menus with the Resource Wizard.

■ The included Java wizards can also create your initial HTML Web page containing your Java-based executable content.

■ Visual J++ integrates the Component Object Model (COM) so that you can integrate external applications, such as a working Excel spreadsheet, into your own Java applet.

■ ActiveX technology is an integrated part of Visual J++, and you can create applications that combine Java applets and ActiveX controls.

# The Java Language Specifics

Java is not a difficult language to learn. Java includes several prebuilt procedures that you often use to perform standard operations such as I/O (*input and output*). Java programs are typically small; the smaller the applets you write, the faster those applets will load and run on the user's machine. Java is an OOP language and is identical to C++ in many ways. Both languages have common keywords, comments, and built-in functions. Java's OOP nature means that you can extend language objects that others write to complete applications faster.

## The Language Format

Listing 20.1 shows a very simple Java program so that you can familiarize yourself with the format of

**tip**

The developers of Java borrowed many elements from the C++ language but improved upon many of C++'s features. For example, unlike C++ (or C), Java supports the string data type. Java also supports true arrays; C++'s arrays are actually pointers to memory, which can complicate the programming process.

the language. Right away you should recognize the C++ elements that you read about in Chapter 14, "Programming with C++."

**LISTING 20.1** A Simple Java Program

```
//*********************
// A simple Java applet
//*********************

import java.applet.*;    // Required support files
import java.awt.*;


//-------------------------------------------------
// Main class
//-------------------------------------------------
public class Simple extends Applet
{
  public void init()
  {
    resize(320, 240);     // Applet's window size
  }
  //-------------------------------------------------
  public void paint(Graphics g)
  {
    // Change subsequent text color to red
    g.setColor(Color.red);
    // Write a simple message in the window
    g.drawString("Very simple!", 75, 100);
  }
}
```

Listing 20.1 is simple and displays the message Very simple! in red on the screen 75 *pixels* (*picture elements*, the dots on the screen) from the right edge and 100 pixels from the top of the screen. The screen in this case would be whatever Java-enabled Web browser the user views the page with.

## Java Details

Before going into the specifics of Listing 20.1, take a moment to consider these points:

- All Java programs are case sensitive. Therefore, if you initially name a variable intSum, don't refer to it later as INTSUM; Java will not recognize that both are the same.

- Java is a free-form language. You can indent and include lots of whitespace to make your programs easier to read and maintain.

- A semicolon generally follows each complete executable line. No semicolons follow comments or braces, however. Also, a class or procedure's definition line (the first line in a class or procedure) does not end with a semicolon, because those statements define classes and procedures but do not execute or produce output.

- A pair of braces encloses a group of lines that Java treats as a single block of code. Generally, a block can appear anywhere that a single statement can appear. The braces also designate start and stop points for procedures.

These Java coding principles apply to small as well as to large Java programs. When you first begin writing Java programs, you may forget some of these coding conventions. A full-featured Java compiler, such as Visual J++, will catch simple syntax errors during and after you write your applet.

## Understanding the Code

The details of Listing 20.1 are simple to understand. All text that follows a double slash, //, is comment text. In Listing 20.1, comments help divide the sections of the applet from one another as well as document some lines in the code.

The `import` commands in Listing 20.1 appear in almost every Java program that you'll write. The `import` command is analogous to the C and C++ `#include` preprocessor directive, except that `import` is a Java command and not a language directive. `import` inserts classes from special class packages provided by your Java compiler. Remember that in OOP, a class defines an object. A class package is a collection of classes that are logically grouped together. For example, graphics routines often appear in a class package. You can use the graphics objects from the class as long as you import that class package.

The `import` command follows these two formats:

```
import specificPackage.specificClass;

import specificPackage.*;
```

When you know the name of a class that you want to use, you can specify that name inside the `import` command. `specificPackage` is the name of the class package from which you want to import the class named `specificClass`.

The second format of `import` uses the * wildcard character to specify that you want to import all classes from a class package. Listing 20.1 uses this `import` format for its imported classes. The `java.applet` class package is necessary when the applet is to be embedded in a Web page. Therefore, you'll always import `java.applet` and all its classes at the top of every applet that you write. The `java.awt` class package contains graphics routines that enable you to send output to a Web page's applet window. Instead of printing text on the screen, your applet must draw the text pixel by pixel. Listing 20.1 contains a `drawString()` function that is a class procedure defined in the `java.awt` class package.

The following line from Listing 20.1 defines a class named `Simple`:

```
public class Simple extends Applet
```

The opening brace that follows this `public` statement makes up the body of the applet's class named `Simple`, and the class does not terminate until the closing brace. A statement such as this must appear in your applet because your applet is actually an entirely new class from the predefined `Applet` class, which you are extending. In this example, the applet is taking the generic class called `Applet` (defined in the `java.applet` class package) and extending into the copy `Simple`; the code in the body of `Simple` is the added functionality for this newly extended class. Without the added code, `Simple` would be no different from the built-in `Applet` class, and the applet would appear in the Web page but could do nothing. The new code is what makes the applet perform.

The next few lines in Listing 20.1 define a new method called `init()`. Methods act much like functions except that you apply the methods to objects such as the screen window object. In reality, the listing is redefining a method that already exists. When the subclassed `Applet` became `Simple`, a method named `init()` came with the `Applet` class but does nothing except prepare the applet to run. `init()` is applied to the `Simple` class. Every Java programmer must redefine `init()`, and almost every Java applet includes the `resize()` function in the body of `init()`:

```
public void init()
   {
     resize(320, 240);    // Applet's window size
   }
```

The `resize()` method informs your class of your applet's window size in the target Web page. You can also insert any other code inside `init()` that you want executed right after the initial loading of the applet. `resize()` requires two arguments: an x coordinate and a y coordinate. Enter the coordinates in pixels. In Listing 20.1, the `resize()` function is defining the Java applet's window size (the window will appear inside the Web page on the user's machine) as 320 pixels wide by 240 pixels high.

The `paint()` method should appear in every applet that you create and should follow `init()`. Your applet executes `paint()` every time your applet window needs redrawing. If the user hides the applet's window with another window and then unhides it, the hidden portion must reappear; `paint()` determines what happens when the window is redrawn. As long as you've supplied a `paint()` method as you must, your applet window will reappear properly with the text, colors, and whatever else `paint()` puts on the window.

In Listing 20.1, the `paint()` method looks like this:

```
public void paint(Graphics g)
  {
    // Change subsequent text color to red
    g.setColor(Color.red);
    // Write a simple message in the window
    g.drawString("Very simple!", 75, 100);
  }
```

The `setColor()` method, therefore, sets the color for all text that will subsequently appear on the output window, g, until another `setColor()` appears. Although the window's background remains gray

**note**

Unlike `init()`, `paint()` requires an argument inside its parentheses. The argument is a value that the `paint()` method operates on. `Graphics g` represents your Web page's graphical applet window. Whatever `paint()` does to the value named g happens to your applet's window.

(you can change the background color if you want), text that appears will be red. After the applet sets the text color to red, two red words appear in the applet's window because of this line:

```
g.drawString("Very simple!", 75, 100);
```

`drawString()` is a commonly used Java method that sends text strings to the applet's window. `drawString()` respects the color set by `setColor()`, so the text Very simple! will appear in red. Notice the g before the method name. If you opened several different windows with an applet, you could send text to different windows by prefacing `drawString()` with each window's designated context name, such as g for this application's single window. The two arguments that end the `drawString()` method indicate how wide and high the text is to appear, in pixels.

You now know all there is to know about the applet in Listing 20.1. As you can see, Java programming is not difficult to understand, but some of the statements can get tricky because of the inheritance brought on by OOP.

# Exception Handling

One programming element that has come into existence recently is *exception handling*. Exception handling did not exist before C++ came on the scene, and Java is one of the best languages at handling exceptions that exists today.

Have you heard of the phrase *management by exception*? This *MBE* management style is designed for employees who need little supervision to complete their jobs. Generally, the employees who work best under MBE are those who fall into one of the following categories: self-starters, owners, star performers, and quick learners. Instead of wasting time managing these kinds of employees, a manager can spend time managing other parts of the business that need more than routine attention.

Good exceptions should flag management's attention as well as bad exceptions. If an employee's typical sales figures grow from 20,000 widgets to over one million units in a month, management must look into the good exception as well. That employee may have wrongly cut prices below wholesale, the accounting department may have made a bookkeeping error in their records of sales, or the employee may have landed an international contract to supply all of Italy—that employee indeed needs to be praised.

As you can see, MBE operates when things don't go as expected. A Java program can also handle exceptions in a similar manner. A Java program's exception occurs when something happens that Java was not expecting; most often, a runtime bug occurs. C++ is currently one of the other major languages to handle exceptions.

## Setting Up Exceptions

*Exception handling* refers to a Java program that manages certain exceptions. Just as you cannot always predict every bug that can occur, you cannot always predict the exceptions that you need to handle. Generally, if you find yourself adding extensive error-detecting code to certain actions, such as files that your program expects but cannot find, and your error-detection code handles the situation (such as informing the user about the problem), that situation deserves an exception-handling process.

When you set up a Java program with exception handling, you tell the program to *throw* an exception if the exception situation occurs. Other code must *catch* the exception, meaning that the catching code will take over if and only if the exception (such as an error) takes place. The idea is that the

> **note**
>
> Your programs already contain exception handling. If your program attempts to open a file that does not exist, your program will throw that exception to the runtime system and you (or worse, your end user) will get a frustrating error message. For example, a file might not be on the user's disk that the program expects to see. When you write your own exception-handling routine, you attempt to catch the error yourself instead of the error being thrown to the user, resulting in unhandled error messages that frustrate users.

catching code will handle the problems seamlessly without runtime errors entering into the foray and onto the user's screen.

Whenever you want Java to throw an exception that your code can handle, use the throws keyword. The following statement defines a method without exception-handling code:

```
public String getAppletInfo()
    {      // Body of method goes here
```

Here is the same method definition with the exception-handling code:

```
public String getAppletInfo() throws exceptionName
{        // Body of the method goes here
```

Not only does this method's definition include the throws keyword, but the method tells the name of the exception that might be thrown: exceptionName. When you call this getAppletInfo() method from any other location in the Java program, the throws keyword tells the system that you will handle the exception, not the operating system. If an error occurs, the system will not issue an error but will execute your routine named exceptionName.

## Using try and catch

At first, this discussion of exceptions might seem daunting. Exceptions, however, make a lot of sense. The biggest reason to use exceptions is to let your programs handle problems gracefully and not halt productivity with a messy runtime error message appearing in your user's face. Of course, some exceptions will be so severe that you will have to halt the program, but you can do so with a more friendly error message such as, "You are missing a file named Actdata.dat. Be sure to create this file before you run this application again." Such an error message is better for users than a cryptic "File not found" message. Sometimes, you will be able to handle the error fully; special code called catch code can create the missing file in this case so that the rest of the program can continue.

**note**

Perhaps the designers of Java added exception handling to the language because Web users who are the most common Java program users often are far from you, the designer of the Java program. Unlike a corporate environment where the data processing department can send a technician to a user's desk to help with an error message, your Web page user might reside on the other side of the world. You need to ensure that any errors that occur are handled as gracefully as possible on the end user's computer.

When an exception is thrown (when it occurs due to an error or any other exception trigger you've defined in the program), your program will not handle the exception unless you placed the exception-causing code inside a *try block*. A try block is a block of code that begins with the `try` keyword, such as the following:

```
try
  {
     avg = CalculateAvg();     // Computes a divided average
     g.drawString("The average is " + avg);   // May not execute!!
```

In other words, if the average calculation triggers a mathematical error and you have defined the error as an exception using `throws`, or the error is predefined as is the case for many mathematical problems such as attempted division by zero, the exception will be handled by your exception handling code.

Place the exception-handling code inside a *catch block*. A catch block handles a particular exception. In other words, you must code a catch block for each exception your program might try to throw. Here is a possible catch block you could write for the ArithmeticException for the code you just saw:

```
catch(ArithmeticException excep)
    { g.drawString("An error occurred when you calculated the average.");
      g.drawString("Run payroll's pre-process before this application.");
    }    // The exception will not produce a runtime error now
```

Obviously, this discussion only scratches the surface of exception handling and Java. But you now can add exception handling to your tool belt of programming topics that you now know more about. Many of today's programmers do not take the time to familiarize themselves with exceptions and in doing so, they forgo writing simple error-handling routines and allow their users to see nasty system messages if a problem occurs in the running program.

# Summary

The goal of this chapter was to introduce you to the Java language. Java activates Web pages by sending small active applications called applets along with Web pages. Part of that introduction has to be a language overview. Unlike more traditional programming languages such as FORTRAN and Visual Basic, a Java program is almost always part of something else, most notably a Web page. The program travels with the Web page to the user's machine and executes using the user's own computing power.

You may not understand much of the Java language yet, but you can understand a simple Java program better now that you've finished this chapter. An applet is actually a subclass, or an inherited version of a predefined class that comes with the Java compiler. You add functionality to the Java `Applet` class to make the program your own.

■ Java applets travel with Web pages.

■ A Java applet runs on the user's computer, not on the computer that sends the Web page to the computer.

■ It's possible to write stand alone Java applications that are not tied to Web pages.

■ Visual development environments such as Visual J++ enable you to work with Java applications as easily as you work with Visual Basic.

■ Java is similar to C++, but incorporates more security than C++ because of its online nature.

■ An exception arises when something fails to go according to plan.

■ By expecting and handling as many exceptions as you can predict, you'll help reduce or eliminate runtime error messages that would otherwise appear on your user's screen. Your own messages will appear in their place and you can better explain the problem and correction than the user's system.

## IN THIS CHAPTER

- What JavaScript Can Do for You
- Reviewing JavaScript's Objects
- JavaScript's Events and Handlers
- JavaScript's Language Is Complete

**21**

# JAVASCRIPT

JavaScript enables you to add multimedia capabilities to your Web site. JavaScript is linked to DHTML, as you learned in Chapter 18, "Dynamic HTML," but it is a separate entity from DHTML. Although DHTML relies on JavaScript, DHTML is a collection of technologies that surpasses HTML alone. By itself, JavaScript is a script-based programming environment that you use to spruce up Web sites and make those sites more interactive.

- JavaScript is loosely based on the Java programming language.
- A Web page can contain a JavaScript scriptlet that executes in response to the user's actions.
- A scriptlet executes on the end user's computer, not on the Web server.
- For a scripting language, JavaScript is quite extensive.

# What JavaScript Can Do for You

JavaScript provides the activation of Web page elements, such as command button rollover effects. In addition, JavaScript code can verify user entries on a Web page. In addition, it works with other Web technologies to build effective and intelligent Web pages.

Netscape, the company that authored Netscape Navigator, created JavaScript several years ago. All major browsers version 3.0 and later support the use of JavaScript so Internet Explorer 5, for example, has no trouble with JavaScript code that appears on a Web page.

JavaScript is not the same language as Java. Java is a programming language based on C++, and it includes industrial-strength language elements; JavaScript is somewhat simpler than Java. JavaScript is a scripting language that requires less learning than a full-fledged, compiled programming language. In addition, unlike most programming languages, JavaScript is interpreted, meaning that you won't have to recompile your JavaScript code every time you make a change.

JavaScript is tied closely to rollover effects, but it also ties in well with Web page forms such as the one in Figure 21.1. JavaScript controls the text boxes, list, and list boxes on forms. One of the great things about a JavaScript scriptlet is its speed; all the script code loads and then executes on the user's computer (the *client*, as opposed to the *server* computer that hosts the Web site). JavaScript can interact with the mouse and keyboard to respond immediately when the user makes a movement.

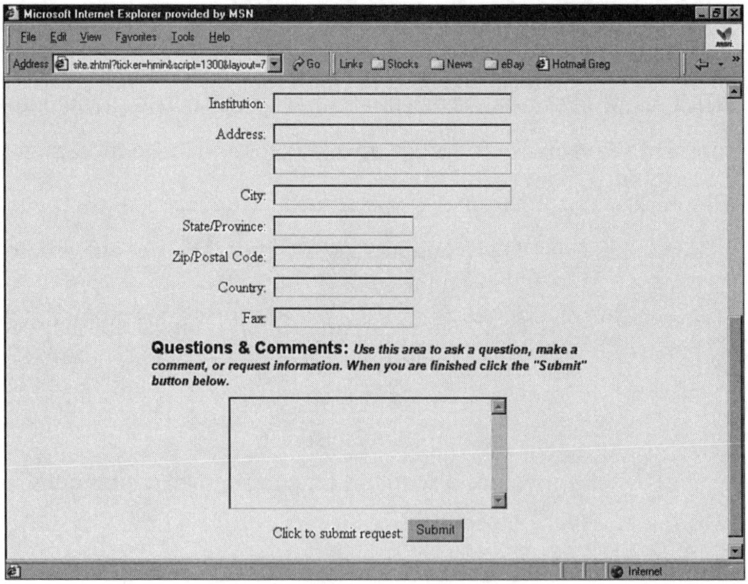

**FIGURE 21.1**

JavaScript works behind the scenes with Web forms.

The designers of HTML didn't intend to make HTML a complete language that would perform all Web page activity, formatting, and control. The designers of HTML added the `<script>` tag (and a corresponding `</script>` tag) to enclose extensions to HTML, such as JavaScript code.

The Web browser does not interpret code between `<script>` and `</script>`. This allows the Web page designer to put whatever he wants inside the extensible script area. It's up to the browser to support whatever the Web designer puts between the scripting tags. As a further precaution to protect JavaScript code from HTML formatting attempts, you'll add all your JavaScript code inside HTML not only between `<script>` and `</script>` tags but also between comments.

The following section of HTML code demonstrates how a one-line JavaScript statement, hidden by a comment with the `<script>` tags, appears inside the HTML code:

```
<html>
  <script language="JavaScript">
  <!--
     document.form1.CoTitle.Text="King
Chemicals, Inc."
  // -->
```

You can always view the source code of any JavaScript scriptlet. JavaScript source code travels with HTML, embedded within the HTML code. If you view a Web page with JavaScript code, you can select View, Source from the browser's menu to see both the HTML and JavaScript code. If you want to pursue a career in JavaScript programming, you'll want to look at a lot of code. The noncompiled JavaScript language allows you to see how other programmers perform their JavaScript scriptlet magic.

**note**

You can store JavaScript scriptlet code outside an HTML file. The `<script>` tag supports the loading of a scriptlet from an external file. All JavaScript code that you place in a single scriptlet file must end in the `.JavaScript` filename extension.

If JavaScript scriptlets did not travel with the HTML, the server computer's power would have to be utilized to interact with the user. An older Web technology named *CGI* (for *Common Gateway Interface*) utilized server-side computing power primarily for forms. Therefore, if you filled out a form on a Web page that used CGI, you would fill in the form's blank areas and click a button such as a Submit button that sent that information to the server's CGI code to check. The transfer would take a few moments and if you made a mistake in the form such as enter an invalid state abbreviation, the CGI code would have to resend the HTML page and an error message back to you. This slow back-and-forth process continued until you gave up on the form or got it correct.

With JavaScript, the JavaScript code comes with the HTML code with the embedded form itself. The code runs on the user's computer, on the client's computer, and not on the Web server. Therefore, if you made a mistake on the form's state abbreviation blank, the JavaScript code could immediately warn you of the problem so you could easily back up to the previous blank and correct the problem.

# Reviewing JavaScript's Objects

Every element on your Web page is an object to JavaScript. By naming each element, you can manipulate those elements through JavaScript code. You might be surprised at the plethora of objects JavaScript recognizes. JavaScript even recognizes your browser's history list as an object. Table 21.1 lists a few of the Web page–based objects that JavaScript can view.

**Table 21.1** JavaScript recognizes many kinds of objects.

| | | |
|---|---|---|
| window | document | form |
| applet | anchor | area |
| button | checkbox | fileUpload |
| image | password | radio |
| reset | select | submit |
| text | textarea | ids |
| link | plugin | tags |
| frame | history | location |
| menubar | scrollbar | statusbar |

As with the Visual Basic controls, the JavaScript objects all support characteristics that your JavaScript code can modify to change the behavior of those objects. For example, the checkbox object supports the Checked property. When Checked is True, the check box is selected on the screen; False means that the user has not selected the check box.

In addition to properties you can set and test for, JavaScript objects support methods. A JavaScript method is a built-in routine designed to do something with that object. For example, a document object is the Web page itself. When you want your JavaScript scriptlet to write text to the screen, you'll apply the write method to the document object like this:

```
document.write("This appears on the screen.")
```

This is only an overview. If you later study JavaScript in more depth, you will learn the common methods that most Web page objects support.

### PUTTING TOGETHER THE PUZZLE

In many ways, working with JavaScript requires little more than knowing Web page object names and knowing which methods you can apply to those objects to do the things you want to do. The pieces are all there: objects and methods that work with specific objects. Your job as a programmer is to collect the object you want to manipulate and locate the methods that perform that manipulation.

Object-oriented programming (OOP) shines brightly in a graphical interface such as a Web browser. The packaged objects such as the Web page elements all come with a predefined set of characteristics (properties) that you can set to make the objects appear a certain way. They also come with a predefined set of methods that you can use to make the objects behave a certain way.

Variables provide a means for you to store data temporarily for calculations, data-swapping, sorting, and other routines that do not lend themselves to onscreen controls. As with most languages, JavaScript supports a wide range of variables and operations on variables. You don't even have to define your variable types explicitly; JavaScript will attempt to guess the variable's type from the context of its usage.

The following section of JavaScript code defines three variables and then calculates with them. No screen object is being used to perform this calculation:

```
var hoursWorked, rate, totalPay
hoursWorked = 40
rate = 9.85
totalPay = eval(hoursWorked * rate)
```

The code is similar to but not quite in the same form as it would be in Visual Basic. JavaScript does not support arithmetic calculations directly. You call a built-in function named `eval()`, and JavaScript passes the formula to its internal calculator to return the result.

**tip**

In today's complicated graphical world, JavaScript is a good first programming language to learn. Not only are JavaScript programmers in demand now, but JavaScript is a simpler language than most others. Although its roots are in C and C++, JavaScript borrows from the old, interpreted versions of BASIC in its variable data types. You don't have to tell JavaScript what a variable's type is. You can store a string in a variable at one place in a program and store a number and perform math with the same variable. JavaScript adjusts the variable so that it holds whatever kind of data is needed at the time.

At this point in the book, it would be understandable if you were beginning to confuse methods and functions. A survey of languages can clear up a lot of questions but create even more. If all languages were identical, there would be little need for more than one. You have to keep straight not only all the languages discussed, but also how the elements work within each language.

In JavaScript code, a method is always separated from its object with a period. A function call always has parentheses in which you pass a parameter that the function is to work with, such as the previous calculation being passed along to eval() to evaluate.

# JavaScript's Events and Handlers

Like Visual Basic event procedures, JavaScript supports events and event handlers. When an event occurs, such as the user clicking the mouse, that event's handler executes if you've supplied the handler code. For example, if the user clicks the mouse over a button on a Web page form, the button's onClick event is triggered only if you have written code for it.

In Chapter 18, you saw a JavaScript rollover routine that uses the onMouseOver and onMouseOut event handlers. The code for the onMouseOver event executes automatically when the user viewing the Web page moves the mouse pointer over the button assigned to the onMouseOver event. The code for the onMouseOut event executes automatically when the user viewing the Web page moves the mouse pointer off the button to elsewhere on the page.

Figure 21.2 shows a Web page with JavaScript-enabled buttons before the user moves the mouse pointer over one of the buttons. Figure 21.3 shows how the top button, GoHome, changes when the user moves the mouse pointer over the button. This rollover effect is possible only because the scriptlet that contains code to handle the rollover comes to the user's computer inside the HTML Web page. The code must run on the user's computer to respond immediately to the mouse movement.

Listing 21.1 repeats the code you saw in Chapter 18. Now that you've learned a little more about JavaScript, the code should make more sense to you, although not all the code will be clear even after you complete this chapter; JavaScript can't be taught or learned in one short chapter.

**FIGURE 21.2**

A Web page with JavaScript looks like any other until the user activates a JavaScript scriptlet.

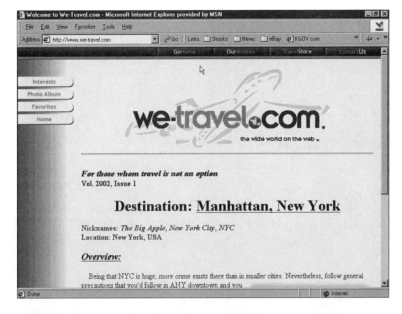

**FIGURE 21.3**

When the mouse pointer moves over an onscreen button, GoHome, the JavaScript code changes the button's appearance.

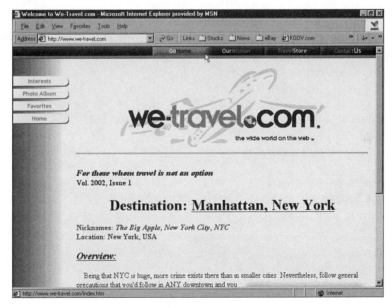

**LISTING 21.1**  A JavaScript Script That Performs a Button Change When the User Points to the Button

```
<html>
<body>
 <a href="javascript:"
  onmouseover="changeOver('Img1');"
  onmouseout="changeOut('Img1');">
  <img name=Img1 src="Img1.gif">
 </a><br>
 <a href="javascript:"
  onmouseover="changeOver('Img2');"
  onmouseout="changeOut('Img2');">
  <img name=Img2 src="Img2.gif">
 </a><br>

<script>
function changeOver(anImage) {
    if (anImage == "Img1") {
      document.images[anImage].src = "Img1over.gif";
    }
    else if (anImage == "Img2") {
      document.images[anImage].src = "Img2over.gif";
    }
}

function changeOut(anImage) {
    if (anImage == "Img1") {
      document.images[anImage].src = "Img1.gif";
    }
    else if (anImage == "Img2") {
      document.images[anImage].src = "Img2.gif";
    }
}
</script>
</body>
</html>
```

You'll notice in the following section of Listing 21.1 that two events, onmouseover and onmouseout, trigger the execution of a function: changeOver() and changeOut() respectively. (Uppercase and lowercase do not matter when you write JavaScript methods, functions, and event handlers.) Therefore, the programmer has supplied the handler code for those two events.

```
onmouseover="changeOver('Img1');"
onmouseout="changeOut('Img1');"
```

When the `onmouseover` event occurs, the `changeOver()` function, defined later in the script, swaps the image on the button after checking to see which picture is showing currently. The button is stored in an image array, indicated by the subscript named `anImage` inside these brackets: `document.images[anImage]`. So, if the first picture (called `Img1`) is under the mouse, the function displays the replacement image, `Img2over.gif`.

# JavaScript's Language Is Complete

JavaScript supports almost as many language elements as a fully compiled language such as Visual Basic or C++. This massive vocabulary is rare for a scripting language. As you look through JavaScript code, you'll find many statements that appear in C and C++ that quickly show the roots of the JavaScript language. (Chapter 13, "Programming with C," and Chapter 14, "Programming with C++," contain the review for C and C++.)

The size of the JavaScript language is crucial to give programmers the ability to respond to the user's actions. Pictures on the Web page swap due to mouse clicks and movements, calculations are performed for financial services, and menus can appear when the user needs to select an option.

Here are some of the statements you'll find in JavaScript:

- `for` loops
- `do` loops
- `while` loops
- `if...else` statements
- Comments (comments can begin with `//`, or you can enclose multiple-line comments between `/*` and `*/`)
- C-like increment and decrement operators (`--` and `++`)
- `switch` for multiple selections

# Summary

JavaScript is an interpreted language that works within HTML code to activate Web pages. Not only can JavaScript manipulate objects on the screen by changing the objects' properties, it can also interact with the user through forms by controlling and inspecting controls such as text boxes, lists, and command buttons. The object-oriented nature of JavaScript objects makes working with most onscreen objects relatively simple because of the predefined set of methods from which you can choose.

- The JavaScript code comes from the Web server with the Web page that is stored in HTML.

- JavaScript code executes on the user's computer and responds to the user's actions.

- As with Visual Basic, a JavaScript scriptlet executes code stored in event procedures.

# THE BUSINESS OF PROGRAMMING

22    The Importance of Maintenance . . . . . . .335

23    Distributing Your Applications . . . . . . .357

24    The Programming Business . . . . . . . .373

25    Your Programming Future . . . . . . . . .389

## IN THIS CHAPTER

- Flowcharts
- Pseudocode
- Introduction to Structured Programming
- Structured Programming Techniques
- Proper Testing Is Vital
- Debugging

# 22

# THE IMPORTANCE OF MAINTENANCE

Chapter 2, "Anatomy of a Program," asked the question *Is programming an art or a science?* Perhaps you've realized now that programming is a combination of both. Certainly the more you write programs, the better you will become and the more you'll develop a style that suits the best coding method for you. In addition, you'll learn objective, productive techniques that can help you and any other programmer become better. As you develop applications, use the techniques that you learn in this chapter to improve your code and make your programs more maintainable later.

The highlights of this chapter include the following:

- Flowcharts enable you to lay out your program's logic.
- Pseudocode assembles your program logic into readable prose so you can check for completeness.

■ Structured programming keeps your code readable and maintainable.

■ Only after extensive testing should your program be released as a final product.

# Flowcharts

*Flowcharts* and related logic-development tools are the staple item of computer professionals. The complexity of programs requires that you somehow find a way to depict the logic of a program before writing it. It is said that a picture is worth a thousand words, and the flowchart provides a pictorial representation of program logic. The flowchart provides the logic for the final program. If your flowchart is correctly drawn, writing the actual program becomes a matter of rote. After the final program is completed, the flowchart can act as documentation to the program itself.

## Flowchart Symbols

Flowcharts are made up of industry-standard symbols. You can buy plastic flowchart symbol outlines, called *flowchart templates*, at an office supply store to help you draw better-looking flowcharts instead of relying on freehand drawing. In addition, several flowcharting software tools are currently available over the Internet and in common drawing programs.

Several flowcharting symbols are possible. Nevertheless, only a handful are used a lot. This chapter teaches you about the most common flowcharting symbols. With the ones you learn about here, you can write any flowchart that you'll ever need. The remaining symbols are simply refinements of those you learn here.

Figure 22.1 describes the flowcharting symbols used in this chapter. You should take the time to learn these symbols because they are extremely common in the programming literature that you will come across. As with top-down design (see Chapter 2), you can use flowcharts to help map out any event, not just computer programs. There are many noncomputer "how-to" books on the market that use these very same flowcharting symbols.

Table 22.1 describes each of these symbols and how to use them.

The common
flowcharting
symbols and
their meanings.

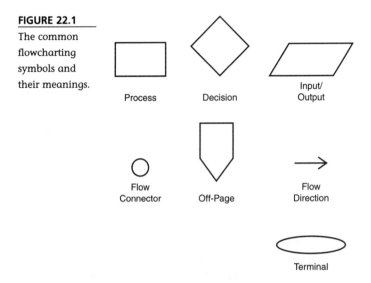

## TABLE 22.1 The flowcharting symbols and their usage.

| Symbol | Description |
| --- | --- |
| Process | Contains a description of what is being done. Use a process symbol when straight processing of data is taking place, such as a calculation or program initialization. |
| Decision | Use when the program must make a decision based on two outcomes, such as printing either to the screen or to the printer, depending on where the user requested the printing. |
| Input/Output | Use for any input or output the program does, such as asking the user a question, or printing a report. (The slanted shape of the I/O symbol gives you a clue as to what it means; the slash in *I/O* slants the same way.) |
| Terminal | A terminal symbol with the word *Begin* or *Start* written in it always begins every flowchart. A terminal symbol with the word *End* or *Finish* written in it always ends every flowchart. When you refer to the flowchart later, there will be no question where it begins or ends. |
| Off-page | Put an off-page connector at the bottom of any flowchart that is continued to another page. Put the next page's page number inside the off-page connector. Put an off-page connector at the beginning of each page that concludes a previous page's flowchart. Put the previous page's number inside the off-page connector that begins the new page of the flowchart. |

**TABLE 22.1** (continued)

| Symbol | Description |
| --- | --- |
| Flow connector | Use when one logic flow of the flowchart is to merge with existing logic. You typically see an alphabetic letter inside the flow connectors. A matching flow connector (one with the same letter) indicates the re-entry point to the existing logic. |
| Flow direction | These arrows connect every symbol in the flowchart and indicate the direction of the program flow. |

# The Rules of Flowcharting

Although every programmer draws flowcharts differently, there are some distinct rules that you should acquaint yourself with before going further. Because these rules are almost universally followed, you should understand them so the flowcharts you write will be readable by others. With each rule, you will see an example that both follows and breaks the rule so you can get an idea of how to use the rule.

*Rule #1—Use standard flowcharting symbols.* If you stick to the conventional symbols, others can understand your flowchart's meaning, and you can understand theirs.

*Rule #2—The flowchart's logic should generally flow from the top of the page to the bottom of the page, and from left to right. If your flowcharts do not follow this standard, they could become disorganized and hard to follow.*

Some flowcharts have no need to move to the right because they describe sequential program logic, but most have some kind of flow going in either of the two recommended directions. There might be times when a proper flowchart seemingly breaks this rule; you will see one shortly. Because of repetition in logic, the flowchart might have areas that go back up and to the left to repeat sections of the logic, but eventually the logic must continue in the preferred directions. The *overall* logic must flow from top to bottom and from left to right.

*Rule #3—The decision symbol is the only symbol that can have more than one exit point, and it always has two.* Most flowcharting symbols have one entry point and one exit point. The direction flow arrows indicate the entry and exit points. The decision symbol always has two exit points because, at that place in the logic, one of two things takes place, and the next flow of logic is determined by the result of that decision.

*Rule #4—A decision symbol should always ask a yes or no question.* A flowchart's decision should always have two and only two outcomes (hence, Rule #3's two-exit reasoning). You will see the decision in the symbol itself. Most flowcharting symbols have words in them that describe what is taking place at that point in the flowchart.

You should clearly label the exits of each decision symbol as well. Because the exits are the result of a yes or no question, label the exit *Yes* or *Y* and *No* or *N* so you know what the exits indicate.

You might wonder whether it is reasonable to expect all decisions to have only two possible results. There are times when your program must choose between one of many values, based on the data it receives. However, multiple decision symbols will take care of any number of possibilities. When you were a child, you may have played Twenty Questions, a game in which someone thinks of an object or person, and you can ask only yes or no questions to determine what the object is. Ask enough yes or no questions, and you can determine anything. The same concept applies to decisions in a program. In the chapters on Visual Basic programming, you will see how to direct programs to handle more than two possibilities.

*Rule #5—Instructions inside the symbols should be clear English descriptions, not* computerese *or programming language statements.* You should develop a flowchart before you write a program. You should not include programming statements inside flowcharting symbols. If you were ready for the programming language at this point, you wouldn't need to take the time flowcharting.

The flowchart is your own development of the logic. You will eventually convert the flowchart into programming language statements, but only after you are clear that the flowchart performs the logic you need, and not before.

## A Real-World Flowchart

As with the wedding plans that helped show how to approach top-down design in Chapter 2, it might be helpful to see a common everyday problem described with a flowchart before seeing a more traditional flowchart for a computer program. Always keep in mind that the logic dictates what the machine does, so you cannot leave out any details.

Figure 22.2 shows the flowchart for calling a friend on the telephone. To keep the example reasonable, the flowchart includes the important aspects of the problem, but there are many other ways to write the same flowchart. See whether you can follow the flowchart. The direction arrows show you how to do it. Follow the flowchart several times, from start to finish, given each of these conditions:

1. Assume your phone is dead when you begin the call.
2. Assume your friend is home and answers the phone.
3. Assume your friend's phone is busy.
4. Assume nobody is home at your friend's house.
5. Assume your friend is not home, but her roommate answers.

Notice that the flowchart does not leave out the details of an actual phone call. It tries not to assume too much either. Calling a friend, to you, might just mean picking up the phone and calling, but when you flowchart the details, you begin to see how much you take for granted.

Notice also how the connector symbols work to keep the flowchart clean and tidy. There are several places where parts of the flowchart repeat. For example, if the friend's phone is busy, the connector circle with the *A* directs the flow back up to the top of the flowchart. Repetitive logic such as this might appear to go up the flowchart, breaking the second flowcharting rule, but it does not because the repeating logic eventually continues down and to the right when the friend's phone is finally answered.

Moving to a problem that uses a computerized solution, suppose you have to flowchart the logic of many payroll systems with overtime. You have to detail the procedure necessary to compute net pay given the possibility of time-and-a-half and double overtime. Before getting the flowchart, try to decipher these details:

1. If an employee works 40 hours or less, the employee gets paid an hourly rate times the number of hours worked.

2. If an employee works between 40 and 50 hours, the employee gets paid the regular pay rate times 40 hours, plus time-and-a-half (1.5 times the hourly rate) for those hours between 40 and 50.

3. If an employee works more than 50 hours, the employee gets double time (2 times the hourly rate), plus 10 hours of time and a half (for those hours between 40 and 50), and 40 times the regular hourly rate for the first 40 hours.

Even though you can follow these details if you had to, the flowchart provides a much easier way of depicting the logic. Follow the flowchart in Figure 22.3. Take any number of hours worked and follow those hours through the flowchart. The flowchart keeps you on the right path of logic flow without the details that don't apply getting in the way. Trying to write a program from the previous three-point list is much more difficult than writing a program from the flowchart.

**FIGURE 22.2**

One possible
flowchart for
calling a friend
on the tele-
phone.

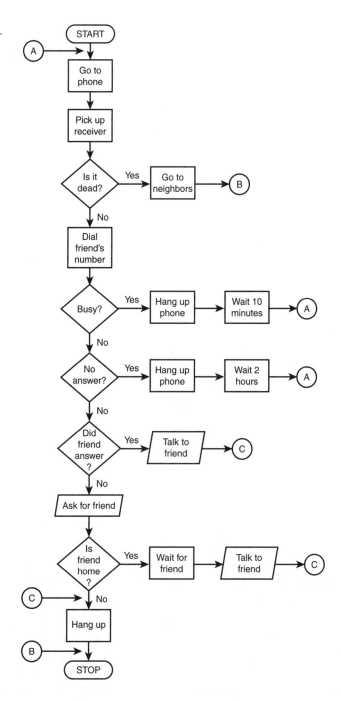

**FIGURE 22.3**

The flowcharting of a payroll example shows the breakdown of overtime.

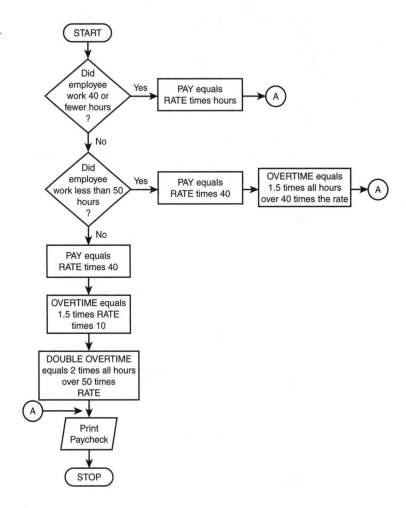

## Pseudocode

Despite the power and ease of flowcharting, some companies prefer another method for logic description called *pseudocode*. Pseudocode, sometimes called *structured English*, is a method of writing logic using sentences of text instead of the diagrams necessary for flowcharting.

Flowcharts take a long time to draw and a lot of paper doing so. Even though you can buy flowcharting programs, they are often limited and do not offer the flexibility that a lot of programming logic needs. Therefore, you must often resort to drawing flowcharts by hand. When you finish a flowchart and realize that you left out two critical symbols, you have to redraw much of the flowchart. Because of their nature, flowcharts take lots of time to draw, and some companies do not want their programmers taking the time to flowchart when pseudocode can take its place and is more time efficient.

The only tool you need for pseudocode is a word processor. Word processors offer the power to insert, move, and delete text. Because pseudocode requires no drawing, it is faster than flowcharting and easier to maintain.

As with flowcharts, there is no way to teach some pseudocode techniques unless you have been programming for a while. The term *pseudo* means false; therefore, pseudocode literally means *false code*. The more you know about programming languages, the more you will adapt to pseudocode, so just read the next example and try to get a feel for pseudocode.

Pseudocode does not have any programming language statements in it, but it also is not free-flowing English. It is a set of rigid English words that allow for the depiction of logic you see so often in flowcharts and programming languages. As with flowcharts, you can write pseudocode for anything, not just computer programs. A lot of instruction manuals use a form of pseudocode to illustrate the steps needed to assemble parts. Pseudocode offers a rigid description of logic that tries to leave little room for ambiguity.

Here is the flowchart for the payroll problem, presented earlier in the chapter, in pseudocode form. Notice that you can read the text, yet it is not a programming language. The indention helps keep track of which sentences go together. The pseudocode is readable by anyone, even by people unfamiliar with flowcharting symbols.

*For each employee:*
    *If the employee worked 0 to 40 hours then*
        *net pay equals hours worked times rate.*
    *Otherwise,*
        *if the employee worked between 40 and 50 hours then*
            *net pay equals 40 times the rate;*
            *add to that (hours worked −40) times the rate times 1.5.*
        *Otherwise,*
            *net pay equals 40 times the rate;*
            *add to that 10 times the rate times 1.5;*
            *add to that (hours worked −50) times twice the rate.*
    *Deduct taxes from the net pay.*
    *Print the paycheck.*
*End the problem.*

# Introduction to Structured Programming

Perhaps no other aspect of programming will better provide you with the ability to write clean, maintainable code than structured programming techniques. Structured programming techniques are available no matter what programming language or platform you use.

In the late 1960s, programming departments began to wallow in programming backlogs that grew at tremendous rates. More people were writing more programs than ever, but many programmers had to be hired to maintain the previously written programs.

When you finish a program, you are finished only temporarily. That program's assumptions about the job it performs will change over time. Businesses never remain constant in this global economy. Data processing managers began recognizing that the programming maintenance backlog was beginning to take its toll on development. Programmers were pulled away from new projects to update older projects. Maintenance was taking too long.

It was during the maintenance crisis of the 1960s that data processing people began looking for new ways to program. They weren't interested in

> ## tip
>
> It has been said that a program is written only once, but it is read and changed numerous times. Learn to write readable and maintainable programs. By using a conscientious approach (instead of the old "throw a program together" approach that some programmers use), you help ensure your future as a programmer for many years. Companies save money when a programmer writes code that is maintained easily.

new languages necessarily but in new ways to write programs that would make them work better, faster, and most importantly, that would make them readable so that others could maintain the program without too much trouble. Structured programming techniques were developed during this time.

## Structured Programming Techniques

The idea of structured programming is that programs should be written in an orderly fashion without a lot of jumping to and fro. A program that is made easier to read while it is being written can be changed more easily. People have known for years that clear writing is important, but it became obvious to computer people only after about 20 years of using nonstructured techniques.

There is some debate as to exactly when beginning programmers should be introduced to structured programming. Some feel that programmers should be trained in structured programming from the beginning so that they know no differently. Others feel beginners should learn to program using any way that gets the job done, and then they should adapt to structured programming only when they are comfortable in a programming language.

The latter group argues that a beginning programmer doesn't know any programming languages to which to relate structured programming techniques. They say a beginning programmer doesn't know enough to understand structured programming. However, because you now understand flowcharts and pseudocode, you can see what structured programming is all about with those tools. Then, when you learn a programming language in the second half of this book, you will be thinking in structured programming mode and will naturally fall into a structured programming pattern from the beginning.

> **tip**
>
> You don't write well-written code just for others to read. As you begin to write more and more programs, you tend to forget exactly what you did in earlier programs. Often, programmers go back to code they wrote months earlier, and the code is as foreign as if someone else had written it. Therefore, you help yourself as much as anybody when you write easy-to-read, well-written programs.

## Structuring Problems

To give you a feel for the need for structured programs, consider the following list of directions given to you when you ask how to get to the local grocery store:

1. First, go to steps 8 and 9.
2. Drive one mile straight.
3. Drive one mile straight again.
4. Drive one mile straight again. You will see the store on your right.
5. If the store is closed, go to step 11.
6. Stop and get out of your car.
7. Go to step 13.
8. Drive straight to Harvard Avenue.
9. Turn right at 51st Street.
10. Go to step 2.
11. Turn left on Yale Street.
12. Go four miles straight and you will see another grocery on your left.
13. Go in and shop.

There is nothing wrong with this list of directions, but shouldn't they be a little more organized? A total stranger to your town probably wouldn't think they were good directions. The problem is that they seem to have been thrown together, and even though you could follow them, you couldn't do so without frustration and slow-down.

The following list contains the same directions. You can see that it makes more sense:

1. Drive straight to Harvard Avenue.

2. Turn right at 51st Street.

3. For the next three miles, keep driving straight. You will see the grocery on your right.

4. If the grocery is open, go inside.

5. If the grocery is closed, turn left on Yale Street. Go four miles straight and you will see another grocery on your left.

6. Go inside whichever grocery is open and buy groceries.

The second list gives the same directions, but it uses less than half as many statements as the first list. The smaller size isn't the primary advantage of the second list; its advantage is that it is thought out much better. Anyone would find the second list easier to follow than the first.

A well-written and easily read program doesn't necessarily mean it's structured. Structured programming is a specific approach to programming that generally produces well-written and easily read programs. Nothing can make up for a programmer rushing to get a program finished by what he thinks is the fastest way. The following is heard a lot: "I'll make it structured later, but for now I'll leave it as it is." "Later" never comes, and people begin to use the program until one day when changes have to be made, and the changes take longer than if the entire program were rewritten from scratch.

**note**

Keep the importance of program size in perspective as you learn to program. Better-written, well-documented, well-structured programs often take longer to type and consume more disk space. Remember, though, that a program is written once but read and changed many times. Put some effort into writing readable code. Disk space is cheaper these days than ever, and file size shouldn't be a prime consideration when writing programs.

## The Constructs of Structured Programming

Structured programming includes the following three constructs:

- Sequence
- Decision (also called *selection*)
- Looping (also called *repetition* or *iteration*)

A *construct* (from the word *construction*) is a building block of a language and one of the language's fundamental operations. As long as a programming language supports these three constructs (most do), you can write structured programs. An unstructured program contains lots of *branching*. A branch occurs when a program goes this way and that with no order. The first list of directions to the grocery branched on its very first statement.

---

**JUMPING AROUND**

Most programming languages enable you to branch with a GOTO statement. The GOTO works as it sounds; it tells the computer to go to another place in the program and continue execution there. Having to search down in a program for the next instruction to execute makes you break your train of thought.

Some programmers and programming textbooks warn you to stay away from the GOTO statement completely. The GOTO statement by itself isn't a bad statement when used conservatively, but it can wreak havoc on a program's readability if you overuse it.

---

The three structured programming constructs aren't just for programs. You will find that you can use them for flowcharts, pseudocode, and any other set of instructions you write. The constructs ensure that a program doesn't branch all over the place and that execution is controlled and easily followed.

# Structured Programming Techniques

The following sections explain each of the three structured programming constructs. Read them carefully and you'll see that the concept of a structured program is easy to understand. Learning about structure before learning a language should help you think of structure as you develop your programming skills.

## Sequence

*Sequence* is nothing more than two or more instructions one after the other. Sequential instructions are the easiest of the three structured programming constructs because you can follow the program from the first statement to the last within the sequence. Figure 22.4 uses flowcharting to demonstrate sequence logic.

**FIGURE 22.4**

The sequence structured programming construct executes the program in order.

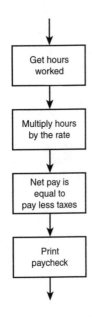

Here is a pseudocode description of the flowchart as you follow the flowchart from top to bottom:

*Get the hours worked.*
*Multiply the hours by the rate.*
*Subtract taxes to compute net pay.*
*Print paycheck.*

Because computers must be able to make decisions and perform repetitive tasks, not all of your programs can consist of straight sequential logic. When sequence is available, however, it makes for straightforward program logic.

## Decision (Selection)

You have seen the decision construct before. The decision symbol in a flowchart is the point at which a decision is made. Anytime a program makes a decision, it must take off in one of two directions. If a program can break off in more than two directions, you will break up the decisions into multiple two-pronged selection statements to maintain structured code. Obviously, a decision is a break from the sequential program flow, but it is a controlled break.

By its nature, a branch must be performed based on the result of a decision (in effect, the code that is not to be executed must be skipped). A decision, however, as opposed to a straight branch, ensures that you don't have to worry about the code not being performed. You won't have to go back and read the part of the program skipped by the decision. Based on new data, the program might repeat a decision and take a different route the second time, but again, you can always assume that the decision code not being executed at the time is meaningless to the current loop.

Figure 22.5 shows a flowchart that contains part of a sales strategy program's logic. The flowchart's diamond shape indicates a decision pattern. Only one of two outcomes is possible depending on the result of the decision.

Here is a description for the decision shown in the flowchart:

*If the employee sells more than $10,000,*

  *give the employee a raise.*

*Otherwise:*

  *have the employee sign a sales pledge commitment card;*

  *Downgrade the employee's status.*

Notice that the decision construct works just like Visual Basic's If statement.

## Looping

Perhaps the most important task done by computers is *looping*: repeating or iterating lines of program code. A computer can repeat sections of a program millions of times and never get bored. A computer makes the perfect companion for workers who have lots of data to process, because the computer can process the data, repeating the calculations needed throughout the data, and the person can analyze the results.

Looping is prevalent in almost every program. Rarely do you write a program that is a straight sequence of instructions. The time it takes to design and write a program isn't always worth the effort for a straight series of tasks. A program is most powerful when it can repeat a series of sequential statements or decisions.

Figure 22.6 shows a flowchart that repeats a section in a loop. Loops temporarily break the rule that flowcharts should flow down and to the right. Loops within a flowchart are fine because eventually the logic will stop looping.

Here is a description of the flowchart in Figure 22.6:

*If there are more customers,*

  *do the following:*

    *calculate the next customer's balance;*

    *print an invoice.*

*Otherwise,*

  *print the total balance report.*

**FIGURE 22.5**

The decision structured programming construct offers one of two choices.

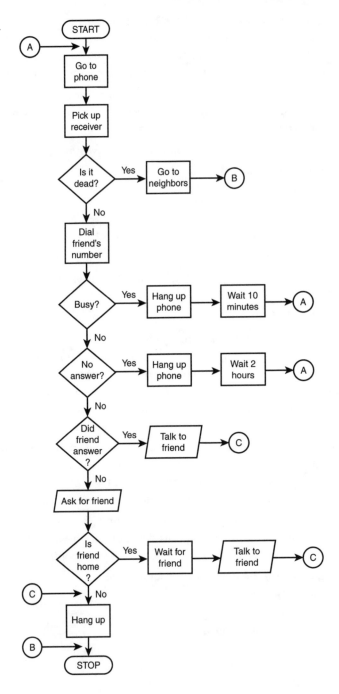

**FIGURE 22.6**

**FIGURE 22.6**

The looping structured programming construct repeats parts of the program.

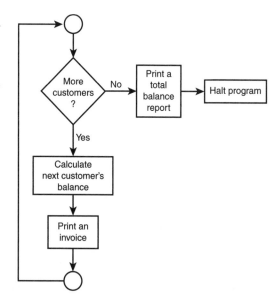

As you can see, eventually there won't be any customers and the loop (beginning with *do*) will stop looping so that the rest of the logic can take over. This conforms to Visual Basic's Do loops.

As long as you keep these three constructs in mind as you write your program and resist the temptation to start branching all over the program, you will write well-structured, easy-to-maintain programs and ensure your position as a programmer for many years.

### THE DANGER OF SPAGHETTI CODE

Spaghetti code often results when a programmer doesn't design the program properly. If you go straight to the keyboard and begin typing code before thinking through the program and developing its logic, you are almost sure to leave elements out of the program. When you add them, it is too easy to stick them wherever they work and branch back and forth to the new code instead of integrating it into the existing logic.

## caution

Be aware of the dreaded infinite loop. An *infinite loop* is one that never ends. If your computer gets into an infinite loop, it continues looping, never finishing, and it is sometimes difficult to regain control of the program without rebooting the computer. A loop should always be prefaced with a decision statement that eventually triggers the end of the loop, enabling the rest of the program to finish.

Proper planning helps ensure that when you get to the programming step, the program will be well thought out, and your structured programming techniques will be included in the final code.

# Proper Testing Is Vital

When you finish writing your application, you aren't completely done with the program. You must now turn to the task of debugging the program. You want to get as many bugs out of the program as possible. For obvious reasons, you don't want the user of your program finding all kinds of mistakes that you made. Therefore, you must thoroughly test the program. Here are the typical testing steps that programmers should follow before distributing a final version of the program to users:

1. Perform desk checking.

2. Perform a beta test.

3. Compare results of the beta test against the old system's parallel test results.

## Desk Checking

Most programmers go through a series of desk checks on their programs. *Desk checking* is the process of checking the program using as many different scenarios of data as possible, trying to find weak spots and errors in the code. During desk checking, the programmer should try extreme values, type bad input, and generally try his best to make the program fail. He should also try every option available in the program, using different combinations to see what happens.

## Beta Testing

When desk checking is completed and the programmer is as confident as he can be about the program's correctness, he should set up a series of users to try the program. This is known in the industry as the *beta testing* stage. The more beta testers (test users) you find to test the program, the better the chance that errors will be found. Users often try things the programmer never thought of while writing the program.

---

**BETA TESTING NOW EXISTS ON A GRAND SCALE**

More and more companies are openly inviting the public to help beta test products. Microsoft, for example, is extremely open about distributing beta test copies of its applications and operating systems long before the final release is available for sale. Most of these beta versions are available for download over the Internet. Beta tests give reviewers and testers an early peek at the software, and it also helps Microsoft because these testers can inform Microsoft of bugs they find.

As the beta audience grows, so does the time a company takes for the test. If a company thoroughly tests a product internally and then releases the product after extensive and controlled beta testing, the company will produce a better product. Today's software is highly complex, taking as many as 100 programmers to produce a new version of Windows, for example. Therefore, structured testing is not always possible in-house. A large-scale beta test is about the only way that these companies will discover some of the bugs that are fixed before the product is released.

## Parallel Testing

A user should never abandon an old system and switch to the new program right away. A period of *parallel testing* should be performed. For instance, if you write a payroll program that's going to replace the manual payroll system for a dry cleaner, the dry cleaner shouldn't get a copy of your program and use only that. Instead, it should continue using its manual payroll system and your program at the same time. Although this means payroll takes a little longer each pay period, the results of the program can be compared against those of the manual system to see that they match.

Only after several pay periods of well-matched parallel testing should the user feel confident enough to use the program without the manual backup.

During this testing period, the programmer may have to make several changes to the program. Expect that changes will be necessary, and you won't feel disappointed or lose your programming confidence. A programmer rarely writes a program correctly the first time. It usually takes many attempts to get a program correct. The thorough testing described in this section doesn't ensure a perfect program; some errors might appear only after the program is used for a while. The more testing you do, the less likely it is that errors will creep up later.

## Debugging

Programs are easy to write, but correct programs are a different story. Locating program bugs can be difficult. Fortunately, most language distributors supply debugging tools to make your life as a programmer easier. Although the compiler locates syntax errors for you, logic errors often take extra time to locate, and you must find them before your users do. When a payroll amount comes out incorrectly because of a bug, you will need to locate the problem as soon as possible.

The debugging tools of programming languages have become very sophisticated. In a programming environment such as Visual C++ or Visual Basic, most debugging aids are similar enough that you can learn one and understand the rest. The Windows environment enables debuggers to take on extremely powerful features with which you can locate problems in your code. For example, you can view an application's output in one window and see the content of individual variables in another window (often called the Immediate window).

The following is a sample of the features you'll find in debugging systems that come with Windows programming languages. The list should help you realize the importance of a powerful debugger in writing bug-free systems.

- You can analyze variables at runtime (in an Immediate window). For Windows programming, you can also analyze the contents of controls, such as the current value of a text box even if the text box doesn't yet appear in the output window. Therefore, you can easily check to see which value has been stored in a control property.

- You can change the contents of variables during the execution of the program so that the rest of the program acts as though the code had assigned those values.

- You can set breakpoints throughout the program. A *breakpoint* halts execution of a program at the code line where you set the breakpoint but maintains all variable and control values so that you can inspect the data at that point in your program's execution. This often helps you pinpoint trouble spots in code that does not produce the results you expect.

- You can set *watch variables* that halt the program's execution when they receive a specific value or range or values.

- You can skip statements that you don't want to execute during a debugging session so that you can test only key areas of your program.

Figure 22.7 shows the best feature of Windows-based debuggers. When you halt a program during a single-step session or with a breakpoint, you can view the contents of a variable just by pointing to the variable. The value in the variable appears in a pop-up window at the mouse pointer's location.

In addition to the usual debugging features, you can also retrace your steps through a program. When you need to see exactly which parts of a program have executed up to a breakpoint, you can look at the call stack. The *call stack* appears in a dialog box and shows all procedures that have executed. If you double-click a procedure name, the code window opens to that procedure, and all variable values are still intact so that you can see what values have been computed.

**FIGURE 22.7**

The debugger can pop up a variable's value.

curGrossPay contains 312.

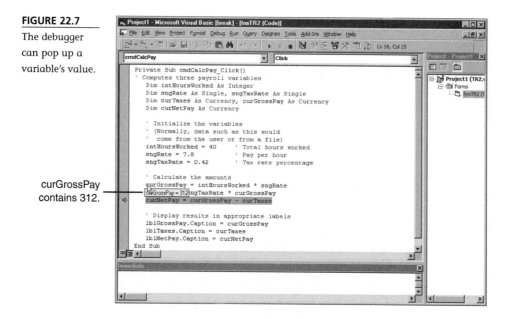

Figure 22.8 shows a Call Stack dialog box displayed over a Visual Basic code window. In addition, a Debug toolbar appears, so you have one-button access to common debugging operations such as viewing watch window variables and stepping through code.

**FIGURE 22.8**

The Call Stack dialog box retraces your program's procedures that have executed.

The Debug toolbar

The Call Stack dialog box

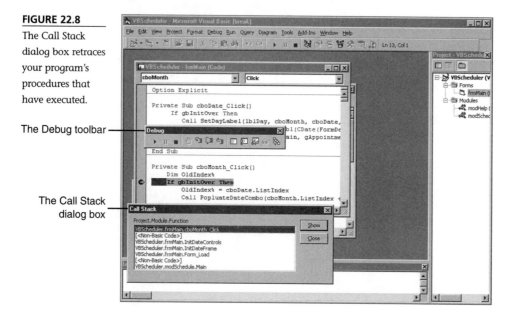

# Summary

This chapter returned you to programming theory by showing you how to write programs that you can more easily maintain. Before coding, sketch out your logic with flowchart diagrams, especially tricky, and convert your flowcharts into pseudocode to ensure that your logic is correct and complete. With structured programming techniques, you help clarify the code that you write. If you or another programmer must later make changes, those changes are far more easily implemented when you've written structured code. One of the ways that you determine whether a program has bugs or not is by following the testing techniques described in this chapter. Then, if your code needs debugging, you will appreciate the power of today's language debugging tools that enable you to halt a program in the middle of its execution and inspect data values.

- Flowcharts use symbols to represent logic.
- End users can read your pseudocode to help ensure that you are thoroughly integrating all the necessary components into your program design.
- Structured programming techniques improve your programming productivity.
- The three structured programming constructs are sequence, decision, and looping.
- Today's development environments often supply built-in debuggers to help you locate problems in your code.

## IN THIS CHAPTER

- Issues Surrounding Software Distribution
- Distribution Used to Be Easy
- Windows Application Distribution
- Deploying Your Application
- After Generating the Setup
- More Helpful Tools

**23**

# DISTRIBUTING YOUR APPLICATIONS

After you write, test, and debug a program, you must get it into the hands of users. One of the problems with the software industry is a lack of installation standards for new software. Although Windows provides some uniformity for installing software, not all software producers conform to that standard.

This chapter introduces you to the problems associated with software distribution. You want to be sure that your users find it easy to install the programs you write. Today's distribution tools help a lot when it comes to creating distributable software. You will see how Visual Basic creates a customized installation for you.

The highlights of this chapter include the following:

- ■ Software distribution comes in many forms.
- ■ Windowed environments present challenges for software distribution because of the large number of files required for windowed applications.

- Major software development environments, such as Visual Basic, provide installation creation routines to help you properly distribute your software for users.

- Always supply unistallation routines with your software.

# Issues Surrounding Software Distribution

The hardest part of software distribution is not in the selling of the product. More mail-order outlets and computer-related stores are open than ever before. Even discount stores and warehouse chains carry software as if software were a staple item for our daily lives. Through ASP technology, you'll soon be renting software over the Internet. Software companies are looking for new titles to distribute and new programmers to write the code. Software mail-order catalogs are numerous. The business of computers today gives you many avenues in which to market your product.

Just because you wrote a program that works on your computer with your software settings certainly does not mean that the program will work on others' computers. For happy users, you must make sure that the program installs on the user's computer and that the program will run once installed.

# Distribution Used to Be Easy

Before Windows, the text mode environments of microcomputers made program distribution and installation painless. Many programs were compiled into a single file. At most, the installation routine would create a subdirectory on the user's hard disk and store the program there.

Today's graphical environments make the process much more difficult. A Windows program, for example, is not one file but a series of files that are to be installed in several places. System files (many with the extension .DLL) are often stored in the Windows directory, the program-related files go in their own directory, and several Windows bookkeeping entries must be made, such as modification of the Windows *Registry* (a repository of installed program information). An installation routine becomes a necessary part of your application's distribution because users do not have the ability, nor should they be expected to have, to install all files and Registry entries exactly as expected by your program.

The next section explains how you can use a distribution system to install your Windows applications. Although this discussion focuses on the Windows environment, the concepts apply to other graphical environments, such as Macintosh computers.

# Windows Application Distribution

Throughout the rest of this section, you will see the steps required by a common distribution method. Microsoft Visual Studio, the same development environment that supports Visual Basic and Visual C++, supports a standard distribution system that collects all files related to a Windows project and packages those files into a distributable set of disks, CD-ROM, or networked distribution. Visual Studio even creates an installation script that controls installation of the entire program.

**caution**

Almost all Microsoft languages use the Visual Studio interface and distribution system. If you use a non-Microsoft language or a different installation distribution system, the steps you follow will not match exactly those in this chapter, but the general nature of the system will mimic that of the Visual Studio system.

## Your First Step: Compilation

As mentioned earlier, you will need to compile whatever Windows application you distribute. The compiled file is a final executable with the .EXE filename extension. All related Windows application modules and forms work together to form the executable file. Although auxiliary files might still be necessary, such as a Microsoft Access database file used for initial data, most of your project's files combine into the executable to make distribution easier.

Your compiled application runs much faster than the application running within Visual Basic's development environment. You want your application to run as quickly and smoothly as possible without your users doing more than necessary. The compiled executable file makes the application's execution simple.

When you're satisfied that you have your program running as accurately as possible, the Visual Studio File, Make option actually performs the compilation. Other programming platforms use a similar, if not identical, menu option to compile. Visual Studio then displays a Make Project dialog box that is little more than an open file dialog box. You

**note**

The compiled application is more secure than a distributed source project. If you distribute the source code (the project and its related files), anyone with a Visual Studio language such as Visual Basic can modify your work. However, most people couldn't even run the source code for your program because they do not have Visual Basic to load and run the program. Therefore, a compiled file is necessary so that all can use your application.

need to select the folder where you want to store the compiled application and the name for the executable file. (The project will have the executable filename extension .EXE.) If you do not have Visual Studio, you won't be following along with this exercise step-by-step, but the actual specifics are less important than the general installation process.

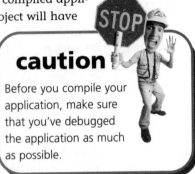

**caution**

Before you compile your application, make sure that you've debugged the application as much as possible.

Before clicking **OK** to start the compilation, you can set compilation options by clicking the **Options** button to display the Project Properties dialog box, seen in Figure 23.1. The dialog box lets the programmer specify version information for the compiled application, common information needed by developers. If you plan to release several versions of the software, the version numbers let you determine the order of versions. You can specify the version information from the development environment's Project Properties dialog box so that you don't have to specify versions only at compile time. The version numbers and description information stay with the project's source code.

**FIGURE 23.1**

Set the compiled project's options in the Project Properties dialog box.

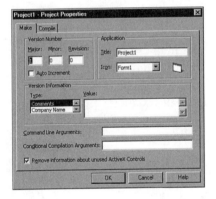

The Icon field entry designates the icon that indicates the application on the Windows **Start** menu and on a taskbar button. Generally, you leave the primary form name in the Icon field. The form's Properties window contains an Icon entry from which you can select an icon for the form and, therefore, for the compiled application.

The **Compile** tab (also common in compilers) displays the Compile options page shown in Figure 23.2. To optimize the compiled project to make it run as quickly as possible, you could set options such as **Compile to Native Code.** (If you compile to *p-code*, a special intermediate language used by some compilers such as Visual

Basic, the application requires that your user keep a runtime Visual Basic–based DLL file in his Systems folder. Native code runs faster and requires fewer files.)

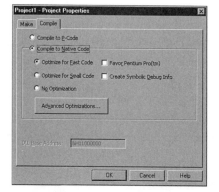

When you close the Project Properties dialog box by clicking **OK**, Visual Studio compiles your code. Assuming that no compile errors exist, Visual Studio creates the .EXE file (you'll see the compilation status in the upper-right corner). You can exit Visual Studio and run the application by selecting the **Start** menu's **Run** option after locating the .EXE file. The form's icon that you selected appears in the taskbar when you run the program.

Of course, at first your users will not be able to run your application as easily as you can, because the application is already loaded on your system. The next section shows a tool that automatically creates an installation script for your users so that they can install your application with minimal trouble.

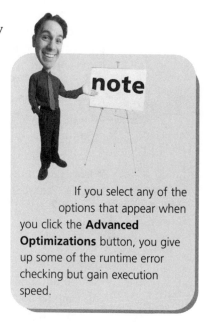

**note**

If you select any of the options that appear when you click the **Advanced Optimizations** button, you give up some of the runtime error checking but gain execution speed.

# Deploying Your Application

In Visual Studio, beginning with release 6, a special wizard walks you through the creation of a Windows-based installation for your application. Although you may not have a Visual Studio–based product now, and although you may use a different vendor's product in the future, you can learn a lot about such products by following the process described here.

Visual Studio's Package and Deployment Wizard does the following:

- Compiles the application and compresses the files.

- Creates a setup program that your users can use to install the application.

- Determines the best fit for installation floppy disks, creates the numerous setup disks, and splits files across multiple floppy disks for extra large files. The Package and Deployment Wizard tells you in advance how many floppy disks the setup requires.

- Copies your compiled application to a hard disk so that you can install it over a network or onto a CD-ROM creator.

- Sets up your application for distribution across the Internet for Internet Explorer users.

The Package and Deployment Wizard generates a list of files needed for setup. A single Setup.exe doesn't come out of the setup routine. Often, a Windows application requires system-related files (such as those with the .DLL and .OCX extensions that represent *Dynamic Link Libraries* and ActiveX controls, respectively). Those files reside in the targeted setup area (floppy disks or a hard disk) with the compiled program and the Setup.exe file.

note

Most installation files that contain the installation script for an application are named Setup.exe.

Before you can run the Package and Deployment Wizard, you must load your application's project into the Visual Studio environment. Therefore, if you use Visual Basic, you would load your Visual Basic project files as if you were going to work on the application.

Only after you have debugged and compiled your project are you ready to create the installation module. The installation routine, the Package and Deployment Wizard, will compile your code one final time if you've made an edit since your most recent compilation. Figure 23.3 shows the opening screen of the Package and Deployment Wizard.

**FIGURE 23.3**

Use the Package
and Deployment
Wizard to create
a Setup.exe file.

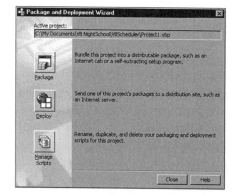

**FIGURE 23.3**

Use the Package
and Deployment
Wizard to create
a Setup.exe file.

The first Package and Deployment Wizard option, which is the option you'll probably select most of the time, creates a standard Setup.exe routine that your users can install. The Package and Deployment Wizard can prepare this installation routine on a disk, floppy disks, or a CD-ROM writer or in special .CAB files that you can send out over the Internet for online distribution. The second option sends the install routine to an Internet server that can install the application remotely. During the installation/creation routine, the Package and Deployment Wizard creates a script file that describes the setup routine. In subsequent sessions, you can either modify the setup script that you've already created or create the setup from the original project. The third option on the Package and Deployment Wizard's opening window lets you manage your installation scripts.

The first option generates the most common forms of an installation routine for most applications. It is this option that most other software installation routines follow. After you click the first option, you'll see the window shown in Figure 23.4. Unless your application requires external ActiveX controls or database files, you can keep the first option selected.

**caution**

Because of the size of most Windows applications today and the abundance of CD-ROM recorders, few applications come on disks.

**tip**

If you want to set up an ActiveX control, you need to select the Dependency File option so that the wizard can collect the proper files in the order the application needs them. If you don't tell the wizard that other dependent files must appear in the project, it will be unable to collect all the necessary files.

**FIGURE 23.4**

Determine the kind of setup package to create.

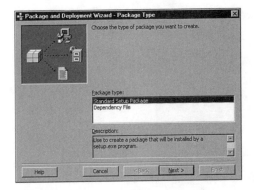

You'll need to specify a folder on your computer where you want the distribution files saved. The Package and Deployment Wizard needs to know where your final setup application should go. The directory you select should be empty so that other installation routines don't get in the way. Therefore, as a developer, you will have many folders on your disk drives, with each folder holding one complete set of installation files for each application that you write. You should document these folders so that you can later go back and collect the proper files you need for applications that you distribute to others.

**tip**

By saving the installation to a new and empty folder, you'll know when the wizard finishes that all the files in that directory are there as the result of the wizard.

One of the most powerful features of an installation/creation system such as the Package and Deployment Wizard is that the wizard can scan your project file to determine which program files your application needs. (The wizard can't determine which database drivers are needed if your application contains any data-related controls, so you'll have to select them from a dependency-file screen as described earlier in this section.)

A dialog box such as the one shown in Figure 23.5 appears after the wizard finishes collecting all the application's files that you've specified. Make sure that every file your application needs is listed. You might need to add more files (by clicking **Add**), such as Readme.txt or a database file. Additional database support files may be needed, and you will need to add those to the file list so that the installation routine stores them with the installation files in the setup package.

**FIGURE 23.5**

Look through the files to make sure the Package and Deployment Wizard collected the files your project needs.

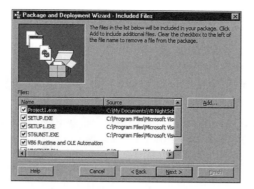

The Package and Deployment Wizard's next dialog box requests distribution information. You can create a single distribution file or request that the setup routine be placed across multiple floppy disks or other kind of media. After you determine how you want the Package and Deployment Wizard to divide your installation routine, you can display the Installation Title screen to type the title that appears in the installation dialog box that the user sees. When you click **Next**, you are given the choice of **Start** menu locations where your program will be installed, as shown in Figure 23.6.

**FIGURE 23.6**

You can determine the way the application will appear on the user's Windows Start menu.

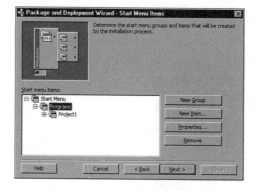

From the dialog box, create the submenu that will appear on the installed PC's Start menu. Click the **New** button and display the New Group dialog box. Doing so enables you to add new folders to the user's **Start** menu. You can specify the application's submenu items, which might include a Readme.txt file you want to add to the project or an auxiliary program, such as a system utility.

Several additional screens might appear, depending on your installation options. The Install Locations screen determines the location of each of the installed files. You'll want the majority of the files installed in the folder that the user selects during the installation procedure, as specified by the AppPath system variable. You can select individual files in the Package and Deployment Wizard's list and send those files to an alternate folder, such as the user's Program Files folder (specified by a system variable called ProgramFiles).

Click **Next** to select any files that you want to designate as shared files. A file may be shared not only by other users (such as a database file the application might access) but also by other programs on the computer, such as an ActiveX control that your project contains. Designate which files are shared by placing a check mark in the box next to that file.

One of the finishing touches of the Visual Studio Package and Deployment Wizard is a screen that asks what you want to call your installation's script file (see Figure 23.7). By creating a script file, you will not have to answer the long list of wizard queries that you've had to answer to this point the next time you create the installation routine. In addition, you can modify the script without having to redo the installation screens if something changes in the installation process, such as the removal of a shared file.

> **note**
>
> As you can see, installation systems such as the Visual Studio Package and Deployment Wizard require numerous decisions. With those decisions, however, comes complete control over how and where your application arrives on the user's system.

**FIGURE 23.7**

Save your installation script so you do not have to re-create it later.

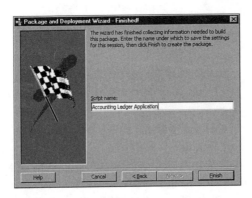

When you are finished, the Package and Deployment Wizard builds the installation script, creates the installation routine, and places that routine in one of several files, depending on the options you selected. When finished, a setup file will reside on your PC in one or several files that you can distribute. These setup files will install and re-create your application on other computers.

# After Generating the Setup

After your installation wizard generates a setup routine, test it. To test the routine, run the setup program to make sure that no bugs appear and the final application runs smoothly on the computer.

The simplest way to test the generated setup routine is to choose **Run** from the Windows **Start** menu and find the Setup.exe file. Click the **Run** button to start the application's setup. A typical setup installation will occur. The setup program will analyze the target computer to ensure that no programs are running that may conflict with a file that is about to be installed.

**tip**

Test the setup routine on a computer that has never contained your application and has never run Visual Studio. This helps ensure that your application installs properly on users' computers. Some business copier centers allow you to rent a PC; if you are allowed to install new software on such a computer, this is a good candidate.

## Remember the Networks

One of the most ignored areas of software installation is the availability of enterprise installation routines that install software uniformly across a network of computers. Consider a large company that has 150 computers networked to servers around the company. Suppose the company decides to purchase an accounting application you sell. The company will not want to send technical support personnel around to all 150 computers to perform a manual installation. Rather, the company wants a single network-aware installation that installs the software from the server to all the computers on the network.

The cost of individuals installing individual software on individual computers is quite expensive considering the number of computers that exist in many of today's organizations. Therefore, depending on the scope of your software, you may need to obtain the assistance of a network engineer who can help you create a correct installation script that works in a networked environment.

**note**

If you cancel the setup program at any time before it finishes, it closes after removing any files copied to that point. Therefore, if you cancel the process at any time, all traces of the application's setup are removed.

## Uninstalling the Application

Installation wizards such as the Package and Deployment Wizard generate not only the installable setup routine but also an application uninstaller that lets users uninstall all the application's files at any time. The Package and Deployment Wizard hooks to the system Control Panel's Add/Remove Programs icon. Therefore, if a user wants to remove the application from his system, he needs only to follow these steps:

**caution**

After you develop the installation for the network, be sure to test the install thoroughly. If the installation has a problem, that problem is multiplied by a hundred or more times as it goes to all the machines on the network.

1. From the **Start** menu, choose **Settings** and then **Control Panel**.

2. Double-click the **Add/Remove Programs** icon.

3. Select the application from the list of installed applications. After receiving verification that the user wants to remove the application, the uninstall routine takes over and removes the program and all its related files from the user's computer.

The Package and Deployment Wizard stores the uninstall information in the same directory as the application. The file that contains the removal instructions is named ST6UNSTLOG and holds the necessary details for the Add/Remove Programs system utility to do its job. Not all files should be removed, especially system files that might be shared by other programs. Before removing these files (such as ActiveX controls), the removal utility displays a warning dialog box that lets the user decide how to remove them.

# More Helpful Tools

As you develop more programming skills and work with more programming language environments, you will run across tools that you will want to add to your bag of coding tricks. The following sections briefly describe tools that you may run across as a programmer that you'll want to look into.

## Profilers

One programming tool, called a *profiler*, analyzes parts of your program and determines exactly which parts are sluggish. It is thought that 90% of a program's execution time is spent in less than 10% of the code. Of course, this rule of thumb is probably not scientifically provable but its concept is understandable.

Perhaps a sorting algorithm is inefficient and needs looking into to speed it up. Perhaps you are performing a sequential search when a binary search might be faster. Perhaps a calculation is inefficient and you can combine operations to make the program compute results more quickly. A profiler can analyze the execution of your program and tell you where the time is being spent during the execution.

Many of the major programming languages on the market either have a profiler or their authors are producing one. A balance can be met between efficient code and clear, maintainable code. Sadly, programmers don't use profilers enough. Often, a program contains a sluggish section that could use some honing that would not risk the code's maintainability. The backlog of programming jobs right now and in the foreseeable future also keeps programmers from taking the time needed to check the execution profile of their applications.

## Version Controllers

Version control used to be important only in the mainframe world where programming teams wrote computer information systems for large groups of people within the company. Perhaps one department might use a version of the software that contains extra features than the other departments. The programming staff developed a way to keep the versions straight. They assigned unique version numbers to each program they sent into production that was used by the company.

Now, PC languages are getting into the act by providing version control software that enables programming departments to track versions of software. The version control tracks versions of distributed programs and keeps track of all source code that goes out to end users. Companies are seeing the need for such control on their PC software because so many data processing chores are being ported to the PC for client/server

> **caution**
>
> Speed and efficiency are great factors but don't forsake proper programming techniques if doing so means eeking out a microsecond or two of machine time. Clear code should be paramount in your coding. Computers are getting faster, not slower, so you know that your program will never run *more slowly* than it runs today. Some scientific and financial calculations, for example, get extremely complex. To clarify your code, you could break such calculations into several statements, storing intermediate calculation results along the way. Although it might be more efficient and execute a few microseconds faster if you combined all the calculations into one long expression, such expressions would later be difficult to debug or change if a problem arises. Therefore, unless a system's speed is critical (as might be the case in some medical or space exploration programs), don't make your code too tricky to be maintained later.

computing where the data may be stored on a networked mainframe but processed on the PCs connected to the mainframe. Such a distributed system of programs can get confusing so the version-tracking software keeps things in order.

When the programmers complete an application for a department, the programmer can use the version-control software to log every file related to the project. Software such as Visual Basic includes version control called *SourceSafe* as an option. Every time you save a source program, a dialog box such as the one in Figure 23.8 appears asking whether you want to add the program to the source code version control, meaning that you want to track the software in the version control system and assign a unique version number to the files in the project.

**FIGURE 23.8**

PC software requires version-control tracking just as mainframe software does.

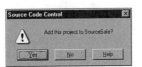

> **note**
>
> By requiring the proper authority, programming departments can help keep incorrect software out of the version library so that a user is not assigned the wrong program during the program's distribution.

Generally, not just anyone can, or should, add software to the version control system. Usually, a systems administrator or a DP security officer will control the adding of programs to version-tracking systems such as SourceSafe to maintain integrity and to make sure that all the software in the version-tracking system has been approved for storage there.

## Resource Editors

A Windows programming language brings its own requirements to the table. Tools exist to help the Windows programmer that were not needed in the DOS environment and that make no sense in the mainframe world.

One such tool is called a *resource* editor. A Windows resource is just about anything used in Windows. A resource might be an icon, a text

> **caution**
>
> The version control is *not* the same version-tracking values that you saw earlier in this chapter when compiling a program. Although you can assign major and minor version numbers to a compiled program, it is the source code that must be monitored with secure, version-control software.

string, a bitmap image, a menu, or a dialog box. As you work with programming languages, you will manipulate such resources. Resources appear in an application's project in a file that ends with the filename extension RES.

Several ways exist for you to use resources in your Windows applications. You can, for example, designate an icon to use for the end user's installation of your application. The user can click that icon to start the application. You might want to create your own icon. A tool called the *resource editor* can help you create and edit icons and other Windows resources. Visual Studio (Visual Basic's environment) contains a resource editor that appears as a dialog box, as shown in Figure 23.9, which lets you add, delete, and edit resources in your application's project.

## tip

One of the advantages of version control is that you can release a new version of an application and, if the user finds serious bugs, you can restore an older version of the software. The version tracking system will keep track of each version you release and will enable you to easily retrieve previous versions when needed.

**FIGURE 23.9**

The Visual Studio resource editor keeps track of your project's resources.

# Summary

This chapter was more technical and specific than many of the previous ones, but creating an installation script is rarely straightforward. By following along with the setup routines inside Visual Studio, you've seen how the Package and Deployment Wizard simplifies the creation of an installation script. Not only can you specify the files needed to install, but the wizard handles auxiliary files such as database and ActiveX files that your application needs. It also creates an uninstall program so that a user can remove the application from his system properly.

■ Many outlets for software distribution, including online downloading, exist today.

■ Windows applications are more than single files located in one folder.

- Your installation routine must ensure that all of your application's files, including the system files, are installed in their proper locations.

- Visual Basic's installation-development wizard creates an install and uninstall script that you can distribute along with your application.

- You must test your installation routine thoroughly to ensure that your users will have little trouble installing the software you write.

- Version control and resource editors are tools that help you, the software developer, create and maintain better programs.

## In This Chapter

- Data Processing and Other Departments
- Paying for the Data Processing Department
- Computer Jobs
- Job Titles
- Consulting

# 24

# The Programming Business

This chapter attempts to give you an idea of how companies program. The focus is on larger companies with big data processing staffs working on one or more mainframes and several micros, as well as supporting Web-based businesses. You will also learn about smaller companies and how they deal with programming staffs and other types of computer personnel. Companies must coordinate their programming efforts to make the best use of their resources. This doesn't mean that every program wanted by every person gets written.

Actually, the allocation of programming talent is one of the data processing manager's primary tasks. You will learn about the different types of jobs and how those people interface with one another. After this chapter, you will better understand the wording of the want ads for computer professionals, and you will get an idea of the experience needed to obtain different jobs in the computer industry.

- Data processing departments have job ranks, politics, and skills that you need to become familiar with.

- Companies use either the overhead or chargeback approach to paying for internal computer services.

- As a contract programmer, you can often enjoy benefits that full-time employees of the company do not enjoy.

- Several methods exist for you to bring your skills up to date with today's technology.

- Internet-related technology has opened the door for far more kinds of computer jobs than before the online world became so prevalent in daily lives.

# Data Processing and Other Departments

A company's data processing department often goes by several names. It is known as *DP, Data Processing, Information Services, Information Systems, IS,* and *MIS.* No matter what the company calls the computer department, it is commonly in the center of almost every major new project the company takes on. When a company expansion, acquisition, or merger is about to take place, the data processing department must prepare for the additional computing resources needed. When an engineering project begins, data processing supplies analysis programs for the engineers (although some engineering departments prefer to write their own programs and keep the central DP department in charge of the business side of the company). Whatever new direction a company takes, its data processing staff is usually involved in some way.

As Figure 24.1 shows, the data processing department writes programs for every other department in the company. Unless the company itself is a software-writing company (such as Symantec or Macromedia), the company's main focus is not going to be software development. The company has other objectives, but the computer department supplies the computer systems needed to keep the other departments working as effectively as they can.

**FIGURE 24.1**

The DP department writes programs for the rest of the company.

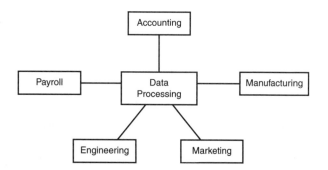

Such a corporate setup is natural. In the early years of business computing, the computer department was placed in the accounting department and governed by the accounting staff. The problem with putting the computer department under direct control of accounting is that accounting will tend to write computer systems it needs and the engineering, marketing, and upper-management departments might take a back seat. This doesn't mean that the accounting department would selfishly hoard the computer resources, but the accounting bias would be natural because part of the accounting department's own budget was set aside for the computer and its people.

It was realized in the late 1960s that the data processing department was not directly tied to any one department such as accounting, but instead, computer people worked for the entire company because they developed programs that the entire company used. Therefore, standalone computer departments started appearing on the company's organizational charts. Organizations began viewing their computer departments as individual cost centers that required their own budget and autonomy. Figure 24.2 shows how the typical data processing department fits into today's organizational charts. As you can see, the data processing department is located on the same level as accounting, payroll, engineering, and the rest of the departments.

**FIGURE 24.2**

The DP department ranks evenly with the company's other departments.

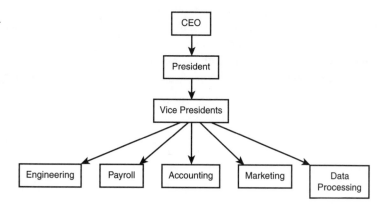

Despite the fact that the data processing department is now autonomous in most companies, that autonomy doesn't ensure proper allocation of computer resources. A data processing department's resources consist of the hardware, peripheral material such as paper and tapes, and people. The people are the most expensive resource in a data processing department. Their office space, desks, supplies, personal computer equipment, telephone, benefits, and payroll costs all add up to a tidy sum.

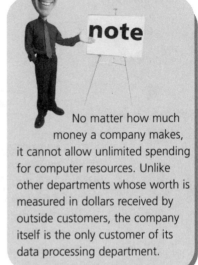

**note**

No matter how much money a company makes, it cannot allow unlimited spending for computer resources. Unlike other departments whose worth is measured in dollars received by outside customers, the company itself is the only customer of its data processing department.

# Paying for the Data Processing Department

Two approaches exist for budgeting data processing costs: the *overhead* approach and the *chargeback* approach. Overhead is the typical way in which other internal support departments are paid. The sales department's cost is paid for by goods sold (the commissions are commensurate with the sales). The engineering department's costs are paid for by breakthroughs made and eventually sold to the public. Unlike engineering and sales, the data processing department fits an internal niche, somewhat like the payroll department, in that it does nothing to generate outside revenue.

## Understanding the Overhead Approach

Most internal support departments such as DP are paid for with overhead funds. That is, each department's budget includes a little extra for overhead expenses (lights, desks, paper, telephones, faxes, copying, secretarial, and data processing use). By collecting some of each department's overhead budget, the company can pay for data processing resources.

The overhead method does not always work well. It is fine for departments such as accounting's general ledger group, but the data processing department's skills are more in demand than are those of other departments. Without checks and

**caution**

There isn't enough incentive with the overhead method to curb unreasonable data processing requests. Under this method, departments from all over the company will constantly hound the computer programmers for more programs.

balances of some kind, all the other departments will want programs written with little regard to cost (after all, they've already paid their share of the overhead expense). The computer department can't hire an unlimited number of programmers just because it receives endless requests for programs.

## Understanding the Chargeback Approach

For data processing, companies typically turn from the overhead approach to the chargeback approach. With chargeback, the data processing center is given no funds from the overhead account (which immediately lowers the overhead expenses for all the other departments). When a department needs a program written, that department requests the program from data processing. Data processing personnel estimate the cost of writing the program and send that estimate to the original department.

It is then up to the requesting department to accept or reject the charge for the programming. If the department wants the program badly enough, and it has the funds in its budget, that department's management can then transfer those funds to the data processing department's budget. DP then begins to work on the program.

One of the biggest advantages of the chargeback method is that a department cannot ask for the world unless it is willing to pay for it. Its own limited resources keep it from requesting more than it really needs.

The nice thing about chargeback is that the data processing department works like a miniature company within the company, supplying services as long as those services are paid for. The company doesn't have to worry about skyrocketing data processing costs; if the money is already in a department's budget, and that department wants to spend it on data processing, there is nothing wrong with that. The department will not have those funds to spend on other things, and departments have the right to determine how they spend their own budgets.

## The Contract Programmer's Role

Often, the data processing department hires contract programmers when the company's requests grow. If the DP department predicts that its workload will increase for a while, such as when another company is bought by the parent company, the data processing department hires contract programmers. A contract programmer is hired to program for a fixed time period. Whether the time is six months, a year, or longer is negotiable.

Generally, a contract programmer is paid a larger salary than a company employee doing the same work because the company doesn't have to pay for the contract programmer's benefits and retirement. There are software companies that hire programmers on a full-time basis, giving them benefits, and then hire them out to other companies who need contract programming. Don't rule out an opportunity for contract programming if you are looking for a job. The pay is good, the experience is better, and often a company eventually hires a contract programmer it uses if he turns out to be productive.

As a programmer, your career will include the reality of facing chargeback and overhead approaches. Your employer will always strive to keep overhead costs down, and if you work under the chargeback plan you will constantly be asked to stay billable, working on projects that are paid for by other departments. About 10% of your work time will be devoted to keeping track of your billable hours and overhead-related expenses. You'll want to be programming 100% of the time, but your employer will ensure that you keep track of your billable hours so that your time is paid for directly by other departments. This is the working reality of a programming career, even though you are considered a professional and are salaried instead of hourly. Unlike managers, financial workers, accountants, payroll department employers, and inventory personnel, none of whom worry about being billable, your programming life will constantly face the billable hours timesheet so that you can justify your position and be paid for directly by your projects.

If you have an interest in becoming a contract programmer, consider going to work for a company for a few years first to learn more about billing, company politics, and the pros and cons of contract programming from the other side. The only way to be able to help a company as a contract worker is to understand the business behind programming. The only way to understand the business behind programming is to go to work full time for a programming department. You will quickly learn where contract programmers can benefit such organizations and where the internal staff benefits.

## Computer Jobs

Several times a year, leading magazines and newspapers list the job outlook for the coming year, 5 years, and 10 years. For the last two decades, computer jobs have been high on the lists for the best job environments, pay, long-term stability, and so forth. That trend will continue for many years. Despite advancements, computer

> **tip**
>
> Many online sites provide job-seeking services. You can upload your résumé, explore available job titles, and match your skills to companies looking for outsourcing of those skills. Two of the largest online job market sites are http://www.Monster.com/ and http://www.dice.com/ where you can go and learn about thousands of jobs that are currently open.

technology is still in its infancy because there are a lot more programs to write than in the past.

Companies often allow data processing managers and personnel to work in more relaxed conditions than other departments. Whereas a company's accounting department reports in at 8:00 a.m., clocks out for exactly 60 minutes for lunch, and leaves at 5:00 p.m., its DP staff might not all arrive and leave at a uniform time.

Programmers, analysts, and computer technicians often need to pursue a problem or task until its conclusion, even if that means staying in the computer room for 20 hours straight. Programmers love to burn the midnight oil. As Chapter 2, "Anatomy of a Program," points out, programming is not a science yet, and it might never be one. A large part of programming reflects a person's style and involves a personal commitment to a project. There is a creative side to programming that programmers often find addictive. A programmer who drags in at 11:00 a.m. might be doing so because he stayed up until 4:30 a.m. trying to debug some code for the company.

DP managers understand that the creative spirit that programming brings often comes in spurts. When a programmer gets involved on a programming project, he spends more voluntary overtime than any other type of worker would consider. In addition, many companies allow their computer staff to work at home on a part-time or full-time basis, coming into work for meetings and group projects.

The atmosphere of the computer worker creates a relaxed attitude in many programming organizations.

**caution**

The Internet has changed some of the rules. Many *dot-coms* are now *not-coms* because of false expectations, sky-high price/earnings ratios, and unexpected drops in demand. Although the computer career path continues to look bright for most programmers, you must be careful of the companies you go to work for. New Internet companies simply don't have the historical foundation to ensure that they will stay around, whereas most traditional companies do. You might be wealthy with stock options in a short amount of time with a startup firm, but you take a real chance as a programmer with a startup technology company, such as an Internet or biotech firm, if the firm fails to stay in business.

# Job Titles

You should understand the kinds of jobs that are out there for programmers. Then when you look at the help wanted ads in newspapers, you'll have an idea of the qualifications and experience needed for the different jobs that are advertised.

The titles described in this section are fairly common in the computer industry, but they are not necessarily universal. Whereas the title for a job in one company might be Programmer Analyst, another company might give the same duties a title of Senior Programmer. The specific titles mentioned here, although open to change and interpretation, are common enough to describe most of the responsibilities and titles in most computer departments.

## Degrees and Certificates

Most computer jobs require some kind of degree or certification. Debate exists as to whether a two-year associate's degree or a four-year bachelor's degree is best. The four-year degree is always better in one respect: You are better grounded in the theory behind how computers work and will be able to learn new computer skills faster because of it. Nevertheless, a four-year degree keeps you out of the work force two years longer than a two-year degree, and two years is a long time in the rapidly changing field of computers.

A two-year programming degree simply doesn't give you enough time to learn much about foundational computing theory. In two years, a college will teach you as many hands-on skills as possible.

**note**

Another advantage of the programming field over many others is its equal opportunity. Because the business computer industry didn't really begin until the mid-1960s—when the idea of equal pay for equal work was coming into acceptance—equal opportunity was already a part of the computer industry. Many female, minority, and handicapped employees work in data processing departments, from the lowest-paid job to the highest, and the norm has always been for their jobs and pay to be equal to those of others among them.

You'll pick up one or two programming languages (as opposed to four or more in a four-year curriculum). However, you'll find that you can enter the programming marketplace at the same job rank and get paid just as much as someone with a four-year degree. The drawback to a two-year degree is that you will not progress through the ranks as fast as someone with a four-year degree.

Perhaps the best of both worlds is possible. You can get a two-year degree, go to work for a company in an entry-level programming job, and get the last two years part-time to finish a four-year degree (most four-year colleges give credit for classes taken for a two-year degree, with only a few exceptions here and there). Often a company will pay for or at least supplement its employees' continuing education.

Today, many computer professionals are partly, if not fully, self-taught. People are raised on computer technology from a young age now and can adapt well to programming. Many *hackers* (people who program as a hobby) become excellent programmers, especially in emerging technologies where schools have not tooled to handle the new languages well, such as Web-development systems, JavaScript, and Java. Companies often recognize the skill of the programmer as much or more than the programmer's schooling these days. If the skill is there, the skill outweighs an education many times.

## Certification

One of the newest credentials in the computing scene is not a degree at all. Instead of a degree, a technical certificate shows that you are well skilled in a specific area of computing. Microsoft, Novell, and several other companies offer certification training classes and testing sites.

> **tip**
>
> If you have the time and money to spare—and who doesn't (seriously, there are always scholarships, grants, and loans)—consider getting a second degree: either an additional two-year degree or a master's in a field other than programming. A second degree will augment your programming skills. In addition to understanding programming, you will be able to apply your programming skills more readily to an area such as accounting or engineering.

After you pass the certification test for a specific area, you are then certified by the corporation offering the certificate. Job applicants in the computing industry are in much greater demand if they are certified. Unlike a college degree, the certificate demonstrates a specific, measurable ability in a high-demand area of computing such as networking, Web services, or operating systems.

Certification does not stop when you get the certificate, either. Although continued education is costly, technology changes and you must change with it. You will have to refresh your certification regularly to update your skill set and to show your employers and potential employers that you have the ability to do what needs to be done.

## Data Entry

Some computer jobs don't require any programming skills. At the low end of the computer ranks falls the data entry clerk (often called data entry operators). A data entry clerk typically needs a high school diploma or its equivalent and some keyboarding skills. Except for those who have been with a company for a long time, a data entry clerk makes the lowest salary of any computer job in the company.

The life of a data entry clerk is simple: He sits in front of a computer screen typing data into the computer. Typically, a data entry clerk types on a terminal (keyboard and screen combinations) that is attached to a central computer, usually a mainframe, or that resides on a network. Eight hours a day, five days a week, the data entry department enters data.

A company's data entry requirements are massive. Payroll figures, sales figures, government figures, competing statistics, market trends, industry trends, projections—all must be factored into the company's working atmosphere. The larger the organization, the larger the data needs; some companies have hundreds of full-time data entry clerks.

At first glance, you might want to stay away from such a job. However, the data entry position can be a powerful first step into a computing career. Someone with little or no computer training who needs experience can begin as a data entry operator. While with the company, he can show a positive attitude, meet others within the company, and receive the typical benefits. If the clerk pursues the proper training, he can move into higher programming positions.

As mentioned earlier, a company will often pay for some or all of an employee's part-time education. Therefore, a data entry clerk with no programming background at all can take night classes to begin training in programming skills. After he finishes a degree or is trained adequately enough, the company can move him into an entry-level programming job. Such a person might never have been able to get a programming job if he had not started out in data entry.

## Types of Programmers

A person with programming knowledge will bypass the data entry job and move straight into a job related to programming. The first job title given to a new programmer hired fresh out of college (or one with little professional programming experience) is usually assistant programmer (also known as a junior programmer or programmer I). An assistant programmer is generally considered the entry-level job for anyone without experience as a programmer in another company.

A person typically doesn't remain an assistant programmer for more than six to eight months. The job is really a trial period so the company can determine the employee's work attitude, skills, and general benefit to the company. An assistant programmer does no new programming. Instead, he works on programs others have written, often doing routine program maintenance. During the trial period, an assistant programmer learns how the company operates, gets acquainted with other computer personnel, and generally learns the ropes of the company's working environment.

After a person stays in the assistant programmer role for a while, he is usually promoted to *programmer*, along with a small raise and a pat on the back. The programmer title means that the company expects good things in the coming years and has trust in the person. It is rare for a person to hold an assistant programmer title for several years and still be with the same company.

The programmer earns a respectable salary for someone with little experience. As mentioned earlier, the computer field pays well, and its titles tend to command higher pay when ranked with similar experience titles in other departments. Therefore, if a person graduates with a programming degree at the same time as someone with a different type of degree, and they both go to work for the same company, the programmer usually has a higher salary after the first year. Of course, this depends on many factors and doesn't always hold, but on average it does.

The programmer does little more than the assistant programmer. The programmer title is a little misleading. The programmer's primary job is to work on programs written by others, maintaining them and modifying them when the need arises. The programmer rarely gets to write a program from scratch for the first year or two.

After a year or two of success, the programmer's supervisor will begin to have the programmer write programs from scratch. Of course, the specifications of the program (the top-down design, output definition, and other documentation) will already be done, and the programmer only has to implement those specifications into a new program. After a while, the programmer's attitude and on-the-job learning can justify moving into a more advanced job with the title senior programmer (sometimes called a *programmer analyst*).

The senior programmer is responsible primarily for writing new programs after being given specifications to follow. The senior programmer doesn't have to worry much about maintaining older code because the new assistant programmers and programmers take care of that. (There is nothing wrong or unfair about maintaining programs, but when you train for writing programs, you cannot wait to get your hands on new programming projects.)

The senior programmer title usually commands a pay raise and maybe an office instead of having to share an office with an assistant programmer or programmer. A person is a senior programmer for a few years, writing code and getting to know the workings of the company, its users' needs, and the base of programs already in existence.

After a few years of success (the time is based on an individual's abilities, but two to three years is typical), the company will probably give that programmer the next higher programming title (along with a raise): *programmer analyst*.

A programmer analyst begins to work more closely on the front end of programming: program design. Chapter 2 explained a lot about the analysis and design steps that must take place before you can write a program. Although programmer analysts don't do a lot of design work, they work closely with those who do. By working with designers (whose jobs are described in the next section), supervisors can learn just how apt that programmer analyst will be at program design. The programmer analyst does more programming than analyzing, but he receives on-the-job training for the next step up the organizational ladder.

## Analysis and Design Staff

When you make it to the next level, *systems analyst*, you know you've made the big time. You'll probably never have to write another program again; instead, you'll analyze and design programs that others will write.

The systems analyst is the liaison between users and the other departments who need data processing work performed. The systems analyst talks to both the users and the programming staff. Users don't understand computer requirements; they only know what they want (or what they think they want). Users must work with the systems analyst to design the needed computer system. The systems analyst understands the needs of the programmers and the needs of the users in the company. The programmers might appear too technically oriented to the users; sometimes the users themselves don't even know what they want. The systems analyst must be able to produce the output definition and logic design through numerous conversations with the users.

**note**

Isn't it strange that you train for a long time to be a computer programmer and work hard at programming for several years, just so you don't have to program anymore? Actually, the programming experience is a must for the high-level systems analyst. Without the understanding that programming brings, you cannot design systems for others to program.

The job of the systems analyst is one of the most respected jobs in the computer industry. The systems analyst is paid a lot and often has high-level benefits available only to supervisory-level positions within the firm. Often, a person becomes a systems analyst and retires from that position instead of moving to another job. Some companies reward years of excellent performance by promoting a systems analyst to *senior systems analyst*. The senior systems analyst often does nothing different from the other systems analysts, however, and the new title is more of a "thank you" from the company than anything else.

---

**PROGRAMMING IN SMALLER COMPANIES**

In smaller programming departments, one person might wear lots of hats, but that person's job title doesn't accurately reflect the range of jobs performed.

For example, some companies have only two or three people in the entire computer department. All of them might program and also perform systems analysis and design duties. Smaller companies give you the opportunity to perform a wider range of programming tasks, improve your skills, and gain an understanding of the responsibilities of lots of job titles. Larger companies usually offer better benefits, pay, and job security, but it will take you longer to broaden your skills.

---

# Internet and Network-Related Jobs

The online world has created its own set of job positions, many of which overlap with those you've read about in this chapter. Programmers today often create Web pages by writing HTML code to format Web pages or by writing Java applets that work on pages sent to others, although the programmers who write programs for the Internet have their own specific titles, such as Web designer, Web master, HTML coder, and TCP/IP analyst (TCP/IP is an abbreviation for the communications protocol used by Internet programs).

The huge collection of networked computers generates its own set of jobs as well. You will see jobs with titles such as *LAN designer* and *WAN specialist*, as well as managers of those positions and technologies including security officers who patrol the network for unauthorized access. *LAN* is an abbreviation for *local area network*, a network that links two or more computers located in the same area, floor, or building. *WAN* is an abbreviation for *wide area network*, which is a network that spans more territory than the usual one-building network.

Because these positions are new, most companies link them to other positions. For example, a Java specialist might have the same corporate status and pay scale as a programmer or programmer analyst, although the Java specialist would concentrate on the online Java language only.

Demand plays a big role in the pay scales and corporate level of all computer-related jobs. For example, in the last half of the 1990s, the people with Internet-related skills received higher pay levels because of the need for that skill, although their corporate status might have been equal to a programmer analyst position.

# Management Possibilities

By the time a person has been a systems analyst for a few years, he understands the company and the data processing department very well. The systems analyst knows most of the users and all the computer people in the company because he has interacted with them for so long. A person at the systems analyst level might decide that he is ready to move into a management-level position.

The higher salaries offered in the computer field can be a mixed blessing. When you've been in data processing for a few years, your salary becomes much higher than that of others who have been with other departments for the same amount of time. A person who makes it to systems analyst and then decides that computers are no longer a challenge often finds it difficult to move to another position within that company. Companies rarely let people move to a position that requires a pay cut; such employees soon miss the money they were used to and start looking elsewhere for a job. Systems analysts find themselves locked into a job from which they cannot escape if they stay too long. Their only recourse when this happens is to move to a different company.

Often, a systems analyst decides that he is ready to move into management. One of the first management-level job titles in data processing is that of *supervisor*. Supervisors manage a small group of programmers and analysts, directing projects from a management point of view (making sure their people have adequate resources to do their jobs, are properly evaluated for raises, and so forth). Data processing departments normally prefer their supervisors to have data processing experience. That is why so many supervisors are promoted from within the ranks of systems analysts.

From a supervisory position, you might next move into a job called *data processing manager* and be responsible for several supervisors and their projects. The head manager of a data processing department is typically called the *director*. The director is usually even in rank with the vice presidents in other departments of the firm.

One of the advantages of moving into a supervisory or management position is that you can often move to non-DP departments within the company as a supervisor or manager. Before reaching a management position, your job rank and salary would make you overqualified for positions within other departments.

---

### "I WANT JOB SECURITY"

*Job security* is an overused term. Often you hear programmers jokingly talk about the cryptic code they write so that only they will be able to understand it. Modern programmers are only too aware of the fact that the better employers seek programmers who write clear, clean code, are more concerned with proper programming, and follow as many of the company's programming standards as possible.

Some people can write programs very quickly, but the spaghetti code they produce is unreadable for future maintenance. Don't fall into the trap of thinking that speed is more important than clear programs.

---

# Consulting

Many programmers find an enriching life as a computer consultant. Too many businesses and individuals buy a computer thinking all their problems will be solved, and they don't realize the amount of training that is often needed to use the computer effectively. There has been a growing niche for computer consultants over the last several years, and you might find success as a consultant yourself.

As a consultant, you can be a hero to your clients. So many times, computer consultants rush to help someone with a problem getting a report completed, only to find that the client is inserting a disk upside-down or forgetting to press the Online button on the printer. The computer is still a mystery to a vast number of people.

As a consultant, you can take on as much or as little work as you want. Many programmers moonlight as consultants, sometimes finding that their consulting business grows enough to do it full time. They might give up the benefits that a company can provide, but they like having full say over what they do.

Getting started as a consultant takes little more than word-of-mouth coverage. Offer to help your accountant, attorney, or anyone you know who uses a computer. Tell him that you'd like to start doing some consulting and that you'd be glad to give him an hour or two free of charge just to see how he likes your work (and how you like the work). Often, these initial free calls turn into a long-term proposition that is good for both you and your clients.

# Summary

You now have an understanding of computer departments and their people. There are many jobs in the computer industry, both for entry-level and advanced programmers. A computer job is a fun, well-respected, and needed occupation; you'll be glad you're a part of the computer industry. Understanding the job levels and job promotions can be confusing, especially because many companies follow a unique promotion and title scheme. Nevertheless, the general order of jobs that a programmer follows from the beginning to end of her career is similar across many companies. The online and networking worlds have increased the nature of jobs and improved demand to further complicate the industry and make the roles of programmers even more interesting.

- One of the most entry-level jobs available today is the data-entry clerk.
- Computer workers from the lowest levels can rise up the job ladder more easily in most cases than other staff.

■ Companies must pay for internal computer services. One method is to use chargeback where costs are incurred as a percentage of total cost of the department. The chargeback approach often brings better efficiencies to the use of the DP staff because a department's use of the DP staff is taken out of the department's funds for that year's budget.

■ As a contract or as a full-time programmer, you must adhere to the billing policies of the company and manage your hours for the proper payback to be accounted for.

■ From four-year schools, to certification, to self-study, the computer industry provides jobs for just about anyone with the skills to do those jobs.

## In This Chapter

- Will Programming Go Away?
- Training Never Stops
- From Beginner to Guru

**25**

# Your Programming Future

What's in store for you as a programmer? One thing is for certain and that's *change*. Change occurs rapidly in computing. The face of programming has changed dramatically since computers were first invented, and the rate of change is increasing. Today's programming tools were not even dreamed of 10 years ago. New languages such as JavaScript often crop up to handle new technology such as the Internet. This final chapter enables you to find resources that help you manage the change that's ahead.

- Programmers will always be needed.
- You should tap into resources that keep your skills up to date.

- Several good Web sites exist for the newcomer to programming as well as for the programming pros.
- Of the thousands of book titles, a few will specifically help you, the reader of this book, springboard to your next skill level.

# Will Programming Go Away?

As computer technology got more powerful in the 1980s and early 1990s, people began predicting the demise of programmers. As those predictions age, the demand for programmers keeps growing. The need for programming seems to be increasing at a rapid pace.

## Tools Go Out of Style, Programming Does Not

In the mid-1970s, the management information system (MIS) was going to be the answer to all computing needs. Each company would have an MIS in place, and all data needed by the company would be at each computer user's fingertips. Such data-filtering was to be so vast and efficient that ordinary and more specific programs would not be needed. The promise of MIS was not only over predicted but never materialized.

In the late 1980s, *Computer-Aided Software Engineering (CASE)* was going to replace programmers. Instead of having coders who knew one or more programming languages, programming teams would master CASE tools. CASE is like a program generator, only instead of helping programmers write programs, they help the DP staff create programs starting at the initial design level. A systems analyst can use CASE from the inception of a program request to the program's movement into production.

CASE is a massive program on the computer that the systems analyst can use for the initial output design, data definitions, logic definition (some CASE programs even draw flowcharts from a

**note**

The CASE products of the 1980s were not bad tools. The problems were due to the fact that CASE helped systems analysts and programmers make the same mistakes more quickly. Programming methods prior to object-oriented programming (OOP) suffered from difficult maintenance and documentation problems that OOP does not introduce. CASE could not eliminate the inherent problems that non-OOP programming contains. (OOP has its own set of problems as well, but it is viewed as an improvement over other traditional methods.)

description entered by the systems analyst), and program generation. CASE often produces code based on the analyst's logic definition, but heavy programmer intervention is needed to implement all but the most general of programs and to ensure the project's overall success.

CASE's proponents promised that CASE would revolutionize the programming environment and decrease the time and resources needed to produce a finished program. (Most of the newer programming advances promote quicker development time and easier maintenance as their primary goals.) The promises of CASE never materialized. Although it achieved limited success in some larger organizations, it never produced the advances in software development that were originally hoped.

> **tip**
>
> Think of CASE as a program that helps you and others design and write programs. CASE is good for handling the minute details throughout the system's development so you and the other programmers and systems analysts can work on implementing all the users' requests.

In recent years, programmer's tools have become more sophisticated, as you've seen throughout this text. Some even feel that wizard technology, such as the Visual Basic Application Wizard, will become so powerful that programming will become little more than answering a series of questions.

## The Changing Technology Requires Changing Programmers

The reason that programmers are needed more than ever is that computer technology keeps changing along with the programming tools. The early PCs brought new challenges to programs because of their lack of speed and high demand. As PCs got faster, they were networked to each other and to mainframes, creating the need for distributed client/server programs. Windows required much more effort to program than the simpler, text-based DOS mode. The Internet brought a new set of requirements for programmers.

Programming demand keeps increasing because the nature of computing keeps changing and becoming more complex. That trend will probably continue for years to come. Programming language developers are recognizing that new tools are needed not to replace programmers but to help them get their jobs done.

# Training Never Stops

A tremendous need for trainers exists in the programming field. As you learn more about programming, you should consider sharing your knowledge with others through training, consulting, writing, or teaching. You will find that your own programming skills improve when you teach them to someone else.

The need for training was never as apparent as it is now in virtually every programming department in the world. Programmers are often called on to train others who do not possess some needed skills. In-house training enables a company to limit its training costs and control the material being covered.

If you work as a contract programmer, you may be asked to use a new programming tool or language. As a contractor, you must adapt to the client's demands and use the tools the client uses. Although you cannot master every tool on the market, your knowledge base should be wide enough to adapt when needed. This requires extensive and constant learning on your part. The following sections describe some of the ways you can do so.

## Industry Periodicals

Read as many industry magazines as possible. Although periodicals such as PC magazines do not provide the in-depth coverage that books do, you will maintain your understanding of computer trends, both short-term and long-term. Even the ads in computer magazines help keep you up to date with current tools, languages, and hardware being used.

Stay informed with available jobs by scanning want ads, both in your local paper as well as newspapers in major metropolitan areas. If jobs are available, you know that the technology related to those jobs, such as Java programming, is currently a hot topic. Large bookstores often provide newspapers from major cities now but you can also check the Web for online newspapers. Most newspapers that are online provide free content and their classifieds are often included in the free materials.

## Books

Stay abreast of more in-depth knowledge with books. Today's bookstores are more friendly toward browsers than ever before with their good-tasting Java (and I don't mean the programming language!) and desserts. Check new titles frequently because computer books must be published often due to the changing technology. Often, bookstores provide monthly newsletters that highlight new technology trends.

Keep a library of your favorites and use your local library when possible. Libraries are notorious for stocking out-of-date computer books so stay on top of them with continued requests for titles you need. Scan Web sites such as Que Publishing (http://www.quepublishing.com) for new title listings (see Figure 25.1).

**FIGURE 25.1**

You can learn a lot and read books free on many publisher Web sites.

Now that you have a more solid foundation than almost any other beginning programmer has ever had, you are ready to direct your education toward more specific goals. You should now begin tackling a programming language in depth. Mastering a programming language takes time, and different people learn at different rates. Nevertheless, the biggest problem new programmers face is that they jump in too fast. After reading this book, you will not have that problem; you will be surprised at how well this book's concepts prepare you for your programming future, whether that future is just for fun or for a career.

- *Absolute Beginner's Guide to PC Upgrades*: This book explains the hardware associated with popular computers. If you've programmed only on larger computers, or you are one of the many who still are PC-phobic, this book will put you at ease and explain the essentials of PCs.

**tip**

Publishing Web sites are not all marketing oriented. You can learn a lot from their resources. For example, Que Publishing's Web site contains loads of free book offers, sample chapters, and often complete books online for your study. As an author, programmer, and speaker, I use Que's online site resources constantly so I practice what I preach. This is not intended as a plug for the company but a tip for you, the reader, to tap into.

- *Sams Teach Yourself HTML in 24 Hours, Sams Teach Yourself Visual Basic in 24 Hours, Sams Teach Yourself Java in 24 Hours,* and *Sams Teach Yourself C++ in 24 Hours*: These books are the perfect next step from this book to take you more deeply into the language of your choice.

- *JavaScript 1.5 by Example* introduces you to writing scripts for the Web, using the most current version of JavaScript.

- *Sams Teach Yourself Visual Basic in 21 Days, Sams Teach Yourself C in 21 Days,* and *Sams Teach Yourself C++ in 21 Days*: These books take you far into the languages to prepare you for your career or hobby.

- *C by Example* and *Java 2 by Example* explain how to enhance your programming foundation with more extensive languages.

- *Moving from C to C++*: Written for C programmers and designed to take the C programmer into the OOP-based world of C++.

- *Visual Basic Unleashed* and *Visual C++ Unleashed*: These books assume some familiarity with the respective languages and dig deep into the language to provide you with a comprehensive reference and study aid.

- *Korn Shell Programming by Example* and *Sams Teach Yourself Shell Programming in 24 Hours* are good introductions to how to do shell scripting in the Unix/Linux environment.

Computer books are known for their series approach. For example, the *Sams Teach Yourself in 24 Hours* series is designed to teach you the basics of a subject in as little time as possible. The *Sams Teach Yourself in 21 Days* series is also designed to teach a topic to a newcomer, but the topic is taught in more depth because of the added time. As you browse the bookshelves, you'll also see special editions of books from several series, such as the *Sams Teach Yourself More* books designed to add content to earlier books in the series. In addition to the highly successful *Sams Teach Yourself* series, you'll want to use the *Unleashed* books to master the advanced aspects of a programming language. Other series are targeted to specific needs of the programmer.

## The Classroom and the Web

The need for classroom training cannot be stressed enough. Plenty has been said throughout this book about training but the term "classroom training" is changing almost as fast as computer technology. The classroom now can be your office because of the large number of courses now offered online, not only through the traditional outlets such as universities but from companies, individuals, and vendors who know the importance of keeping a well-informed public. The Internet-based learning resources offer low-cost alternatives to the physical classroom and some sites, such as `http://www.BarnesAndNoble.com/`, provide free online courses.

Many online sites target you, the programmer. An incredible number of sites now provide extensive training for absolutely no price whatsoever. Given the importance of online programming, you should monitor the WebMonkey site (`http://www.WebMonkey.com/`) for the latest online programming technology explained in depth but with humor and simplicity.

Specialty sites are now appearing that attempt to be all things to all computer programmers...and they basically are. One of the best examples of such a site is InformIT.com (`http://www.InformIT.com/`). The way it attempts to be all things is by providing training, online articles and books, the latest in industry news, interviews by industry observers, movers, and shakers, and provides e-mail services to keep you abreast of new postings regularly.

Whereas many sites are becoming more specific, a megasite such as InformIT.com (see Figure 25.2) is a site you will want to bookmark as a reference site when you want to dig deep into a technology and read what the insiders have to say. The download libraries are full of software, training materials, and news.

The training materials on such sites are massive, not only in their content but in their approach. For example, InformIT.com provides several ways you can learn, including

- Self-paced courses
- Instructor-led courses where you can interact with an instructor via e-mail and chat
- Classroom courses where you view materials online with others with whom you can converse in chat sessions
- Quick studies where you can get the basics of a topic quickly and then select more depth as you go

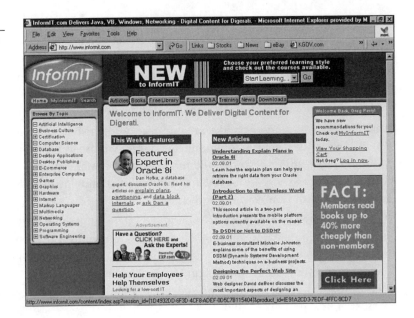

# From Beginner to Guru

As you can see, your own computer training should not stop. The computer industry changes rapidly. The skills you have today can be obsolete in five years, so part of your job is to continue your own training. It is incumbent upon you to stay up with current trends if you want to secure your computer position in the future.

---

### INDUSTRY STANDARDS

Not every new breakthrough in computer hardware and software becomes an industry standard. You do not have to be on the "bleeding edge" of technology (a programmer's pun describing very new and unproved technology), learning everything there is to learn. You do not even have to be on the leading edge of computer programming innovations. For instance, object-oriented programming is now considered by the industry to be the best way to program, but many programmers haven't learned how to program with objects. They may or may not have to do so, depending on where their jobs take them and the language they must master in their companies. The future seems to be heading toward using OOP languages in most situations, however. There is rarely a need to stay on top of the latest trends, because today's breakthrough might be tomorrow's flop.

You will find your own niche in the computer field. Specialization is almost a must these days. It is very difficult to master everything. Some people choose to specialize in networking, Internet programming, Web page design, object-oriented programming, or graphical user interfaces. As you learn more about programming, you will find the area that best fits your own interests.

# Summary

Programming tools go far beyond just the languages themselves. Throughout this text, you've seen examples of languages and programming tools that help you be a better programmer. This chapter showed you additional tools that programmers—especially Windows programmers—can use to become more productive.

Every month, take a trip to your local library or bookstore to scan the shelves for the latest computer magazines. Try to read one good computer book every month or two. Every six months, research a new topic of computer programming to improve your skill levels. Most computer people find that self-study is not a job they balk at; the field of programming is exciting. It never gets old. The innovations everywhere you look are always exciting and hold promise of powerful computing power in the future.

After you've mastered programming, what's next? Keep mastering! Continuing education is almost as vital in the field of computers as it is in the medical profession. Rapidly changing computer technology requires that a programmer stay on top of current trends by reading books and magazines and taking courses when possible. Share your knowledge with others to help improve the programming community and reduce the backlog that the industry faces. Knowledge shared is knowledge improved.

- Computer technology changes rapidly and so will your skills.
- You cannot learn everything about programming so you should specialize. Locate a topic that interests you and master that topic.
- Plenty of magazines, newspapers, books, and Web sites are available to keep you abreast of trends and skills needed.
- Do not jump on the bandwagon too quickly when a new technology appears. Some, such as VBScript, do not take hold as well as others (such as JavaScript). Give new technologies time to mature and gain acceptance before you spend too much time mastering the topic. But don't ignore new technologies! Learn an overview of whatever you can, understand what new technologies are trying to accomplish, and stay informed so you'll know what to master when it's time to do so.

# Index

## Symbols

**&lt;a&gt; HTML tag, 282-283**

**&lt;a href&gt; HTML tag, 282-283**

**& (ampersand)**
bitwise and operator (C), 213
concatenation operator, 120-122
data type suffix character, 114
Visual Basic Caption property, 98

**' (apostrophes), Visual Basic remarks, 102-103**

**\* (asterisk)**
math operator, 120
multiplication operator, C, 213

**@ (at sign), data type suffix character, 114**

**&lt;b&gt; HTML tag, 278**

**&lt;body&gt; HTML tag, 277**

**&lt;br&gt; HTML tag, 278**

**{ } (braces), Java, 316**

**^ (caret), math operator, 120**

**(&gt; or =) comparison operator, 123**

**(&gt;) comparison operator, 122**

**(&lt;&gt;) comparison operator, 123**

**2's complement, binary arithmetic, 45**

**= (equal sign), assign comparison operator (C), 213**

**= (equal to) comparison operator, 122**

**== (equal to) relational operator, C, 225**

**! (exclamation mark), data type suffix character, 114**

**&lt;&lt; (extraction operator), C++, 230-231**

**&lt;font size&gt; HTML tag, 279-280**

**/ (forward slash)**
division operator, C, 213
HTML tags, 265
math operator, 120

**&lt;h&gt; HTML tag, 278-279**

**&lt;head&gt; HTML tag, 277**

**&lt;!—&gt; HTML comment tag, 277**

**&lt;html&gt; HTML tag, email hyperlinks, 277**

**&lt;i&gt; HTML tag, 278**

**&lt;img src&gt; HTML tag, 280**

**#include statement (C), 215**

**&lt; (less than) comparison operator, 122**

**&lt;= (less than or equal to) comparison operator, 123**

**- (minus sign)**
math operator, 120
subtraction operator, C, 213

**!= (not equal to) relational operator (C), 213, 225**

**(::) operator (C++), 237**

**&lt;p align&gt; HTML tags, 278**

**. (period)**
accessing object members (C++), 235
referencing data structure items, 209

**+ (plus sign)**
addition operator, C, 213
concatenation operator, 122
math operator, 120

**# (pound sign)**
data type suffix character, 114
date/time literals, 113
preprocessor directives (C), 215

**; (semicolon), C statements, 214, 223**

**; (semicolon), Java, 316**

**(") String data type, 113**

**&lt;title&gt; HTML tag, 277**

**&lt;u&gt; HTML tag, 278**

**\* (wildcard character), Java import command, 316**

## A

**&lt;a href&gt; HTML tag, 282-283**

**About boxes, 183**

**abstraction (C++ objects), 228**

**accessing members (C++ objects), 235**
member functions, 236
*overloading operators, 239-240*

**accumulators, 198-199**

**Active Server Pages (ASP), 269-270**

**ActiveX**
controls, 187, 266-267
documents, 191-192

**ActiveX, Windows Scripting Host (WSH) language, 257**

**ADA language, 58**

**AddItem method (Visual Basic list boxes), 151**

**algorithms, 197-198**
counters/accumulators, 198-199
data structures, 208-210
*grouping data, 208-209*
*referencing items, 209-210*
nested loops, 203-204
searching arrays, 204-205
*binary searches, 206-208*
*random-access file control, 205*
*sequential searches, 205-206*
sorting data, 201-203
swapping values, 200-201

**alphanumeric data, 112**

**American Standard Code of Information Interchange. See ASCII table**

**ampersand (&)**
bitwise and operator (C), 213
concatenation operator, 120-122
data type suffix character, 114
Visual Basic Caption property, 98

**analysts/design staff, 384**

**analyzing programs, profilers, 368-369**

**anchor tags (HTML), 282-283**

**And logical operator (VB), 130. *See also* decision making (VB)**

**APL language, 58**

**apostrophes ('), Visual Basic remarks, 102-103**

**applets (Java), 307. *See also* Java**
appearance in HTML documents, 308
bytecode, 309-310
creating, 311
Listing 20.1, simple Java applet, 315
*code explanation, 316-318*
security, 311-312
<APPLET> tag, 308

**<APPLET> HTML tag, 308**

**Application Wizard (VB), 180-184**
creating an application, 180-184
Internet applications, 184-185
*creating an application, 185-187*
*default URLs (uniform resource locators), 185*
*running sample applications, 187-188*
profiles, 181

**applications, Internet. See Internet applications**

**arithmetic, binary arithmetic, 44-47**

**arrays**
searching, 204-205
*binary searches, 206-208*
*random-access file control, 205*
*sequential searches, 205-206*
subscripts, 199
totaling with accumulators, 199

**artificial intelligence, 27**

**ASCII table (American Standard Code of Information Interchange), 42**

**ASP (Active Server Pages), 269-270**

**assemblers, 48-49**

**assign (=) relational operator (C), 213**

**assignment statements, 117**

**asterisk (*)**
math operator, 120
multiplication operator, C, 213

**asterisk (*) wildcard character, Java import command, 316**

**at sign (@), data type suffix character, 114**

## B

**Barnes & Noble Web site, 395**

**BASIC languages**
history, 66-70
*QuickBASIC, 69-70*
*Visual Basic, 71-72*
Listing 4.2, 67-68
QuickBASIC, Listing 4.3, 69-70
Visual Basic. *See* Visual Basic

**batch language, 244-247**
.bat file usage, 244-245
common commands, 246
Job Control Language (JCL), 245
Listing 15.1, printing a directory listing, 246-247
wildcard characters, 247

**behavior (C++ objects), 235-238**

**Beowulf clusters, 18**

**Beowulf Web site, 18**

**beta testing, 352-353. *See also* testing**

binary arithmetic, 44-47

binary digits (bits), 42

binary equivalents of numbers, 45-46

binary searches (arrays), 206-208

bits, 42

bitwise operators (C), 213

blocks, 127
  loops. *See* loops

books, 392-394

Boolean data type, 111

BorderStyle property, Line control (VB), 145-147

bottom-up design, 33

braces ({ }) (Java), 316

Brady Games Web site, 293

branching, 347
  decision, 348-350

breakpoints, 354

browsers, 263

bubble sorts, 201-203

bugs, 30-31
  debugging, 30-31, 353-355

button rollover effect
  DHTML, 290-293
  JavaScript, 328-331

buyers, computers, 10-11

Byte data type, 111

bytecode (Java), 309-310

bytes, 42

# C

C, 211-213. *See also* C++
  #include statement, 215
  ; (semicolon), 214, 223
  comments, 216-217
  control statements, 224-226
  conversion characters, 218-219
  data, 215-216
  declaring variables, 217
  function procedures, 214
  functions
    *built-in, 217-218*
    *main( ), 214-215, 222-223*
    *printf( ), 218-219, 221-222, 230*
    *scanf( ), 220-222*
    *writing functions, 222-223*
  header files, 215
  history, 63-64
  if statements, 225
  keyboard input (scanf( ) function), 220-222
  keywords, 212
  Listings
    *13.1, sample small program, 214*
    *13.2, input/output, 221*
    *13.3, main( ) function, 222-223*
  loops, 225-226
  main( ) function, 214-215, 222-223
  null zero character, 219-220
  operators, 212-213, 224
    *compound assignments, 224*
    *math, 212-213*
    *relational, 225*
  preprocessor directives, 215
  programs, sample small program, 214
  strings, 219-220
  versus C++
    *comments, 229-230*
    *I/O, 230-231*
    *name differences, 230*

C# language, 271

C++, 227-228. *See also* C language
  (::) operator, 237
  (>)(>) (insertion operator), 230-231
  << (extraction operator), 230-231
  . (dot operator), 235
  comments, 229-230
  functions, prototypes, 236
  history, 65
  I/O, 230-231
  input, 231
  int keyword, 233
  multiple inheritance, 65
  objects, 228-233
    *abstraction, 228*
    *accessing members, 235*
    *adding behavior, 235-238*
    *cin, 231*
    *class scope, 238-239*
    *classes, 228*
    *constructors, 237*
    *cout, 230*
    *declaring classes, 233-236*
    *declaring variables, 234-235*
    *destructors, 237*
    *inheritance, 229, 240*
    *libraries, 240*
    *member functions, 236-240*
    *messages, 229*
    *overloading operators, 239-240*
    *polymorphism, 229, 240*
    *reuse, 229, 232*
    *terminology, 229*
  OOP (object-oriented programming), 227
    *advantages, 239-240*
  operators, overloading, 239-240
  output, 230-233
  versus C
    *comments, 229-230*
    *I/O, 230-231*
    *name differences, 230*

calculations, binary arithmetic, 44-47

calculator applications (VB). *See* interest rate calculator application (VB)

Call Stack dialog box (VB), 355

card-punch machines, 49

careers. *See* programming industry; jobs

caret (^), math operator, 120

CASE (Computer-Aided Software Engineering), 390-391

case sensitivity, Java, 315

Case statement, Visual Basic Select Case statement. *See* Select Case statement (VB)

cash flow interest calculations, 161

catch keyword (Java exception handling), 320-321

certificates/degrees, 380-381

CGI (Common Gateway Interface), 325
  programming, 309

character string data, 50

chargeback payment approach (data processing departments), 377

chips, 16. *See also* integrated circuits (IC)

cin object (C++), 231

classes (C++ objects), 228
  declaring, 233-236
  libraries, 240
  scope, 238-239

Click event
  Visual Basic, 98
  Visual Basic command buttons, 173-174

COBOL language, 52-55

code
  blocks, 127
    *loops. See loops*
  bytecode (Java), 309-310
  compiled, 67
  debugging, 353-355
  interpreted, 67
  listings. *See* listings

modules, Visual Basic, 175-177

program design, 36

pseudocode, 342-343

source code. *See* source programs

spaghetti code, 351

testing, 352-353

Visual Basic, modules, 175-177

Visual Basic interest rate calculator application
  *Compute Interest calculation, 171-173*
  *error checking, 173-178*
  *Exit command button, 173-174*

color, setColor() method (Java), 318

command buttons, Visual Basic programs, 97-98

commands, HTML. *See* tags, HTML

comments
  C language, 216-217
  C++ versus C, 229-230
  HTML, 277
  JavaScript, 331

Common Gateway Interface (CGI), 325
  programming, 309

comparing languages, 72-73

comparison operators, 122-124
  If statements, 126

comparisons, Visual Basic. *See* decision making (VB)

compiled code, 67

compilers, 29
  COBOL. *See* COBOL language

compiling
  Java, 309-311
  Windows programs, 359-361

CompuServe PPP script file, 255-256

Computer-Aided Software Engineering (CASE), 390-391

computers, 6-7
  buyers, 10-11
  data, 6
  data storage
    *ASCII table, 42-44*
    *switches, 42*
  hardware, 11-12. *See also* hardware
  history, 14-16
    *card-punch machines, 49*
    *first programs, 47-48*
    *keyboards, 48-49*
    *languages. See languages, history*
    *shared-program concept, 47-48*
  mainframes, 18-19
  microcomputers, 19. *See also* PCs (personal computers)
  minicomputers, 19
  myths, 7
    *programming, 8-9*
  PCs (personal computers), 16, 19
  programming, 7
  programs, 7
  software, 12. *See also* software
  speed, 17
  supercomputers, 17-18
  users, 10
    *costs, 13*

concatenating operators, 121-122

constructors (C++ objects), 237

constructs, structured programming, 347

consulting jobs, 387

continuing education
  books, 392-394
  industry magazines, 392

online classes, 394-396
training, 391-392

**contract programmers (data processing departments), 377-378**

**control statements (C), 224-226**

**controls**
ActiveX, 187, 266-267
*ActiveX documents, 191-192*
focus, 163-166
Visual Basic. *See also* Visual Basic, controls
*control arrays, 167-168*
*copying, 167*
*grouping (control arrays), 167-168*
*Internet controls, 188-190*

**conversion characters, C language, 218-219**

**copying controls (VB), 167-168**

**costs**
computer users, 13
hardware, 11

**counters, 198-199**

**cout object (C++), 230**

**curly braces ({ }) (Java), 316**

**Currency data type, 111**

## D

**data, 6**
alphanumeric, 112
assignment statements, 117
binary arithmetic, 44-47
binary equivalents of numbers, 45-46
C language, 215-216
character strings, 50
data entry, 13
GIGO (garbage-in, garbage-out), 13

grouping, data structures, 208-209
literals, 112-114
processing procedures, 14
sorting, 201-203
storage
*ASCII table, 42-44*
*switches, 42*
structures, 208-210
swapping, 200-201
variables, 114-117
*Dim statement, 114-117*
*name prefixes, 115-116*
*placeholders, 115*
*storing data in variables, 117-119*

**data entry**
error checking, Visual Basic, 174-178
jobs, 381-382

**data processing, data processing departments, 374-376**
chargeback payment approach, 377
contract programmers, 377-378
overhead payment approach, 376-377

**data processing managers, 386**

**data types, 111-113**
suffix characters, 113-114

**databases, DHTML database manipulations, 287**

**Date data type, 112**
# (pound sign), 113

**debugging, 30-31, 353-355**
breakpoints, 354
watch variables, 354

**Decimal data type, 112**

**decision (structured programming), 348-350**

**decision making (VB), 126-127**
Else statements, 127-129
If statements, 126-127
mutually exclusive statements, 128
nesting If...Else statements (ElseIf), 131
Select Case statements, 131-134

**declaring**
object classes (C++), 233-236
object variables (C++), 234-235

**declaring variables, C language, 217**

**defining. *See* declaring**

**degrees/certificates, 380-381**

**deploying programs, Windows programs, 361-366**

**designing programs, 31-36**
code, 36
defining output, top-down design, 35
logic, 36
output, 33-36
*bottom-up design, 33*
*top-down design, 33-34*

**desk checking, 352. *See also* testing**

**destructors (C++ objects), 237**

**DHTML (Dynamic HTML), 285-287**
automatic font/color adjustments, 287
button rollover effect, 290-293
database manipulations, 287
Document Object Model (DOM), 289
example DHTML page, 287-288
help systems, 287

javascript keyword, 291
Listing 18.1, rollover scriptlet, 291
menus, 286
Netscape/Microsoft support, 290
scriplets, 289
*example usage, 290-293*

**Dice Web site, 378**

**Dim statement, 114-117**

**distributing applications, 357-358**
network installations, 367-368
profilers, 368-371
resource editors, 370-371
setup routines, testing, 361-367
uninstalling applications, 368
Windows programs, 358-359
*compiling, 359-361*
*deploying, 361-366*
*testing setup, 367*

**distributing the processing, 16**

**Do Until loops (VB), 137-139**

**Do While loops (VB), 135-137**

**Document Object Model (DOM), DHTML, 289**

**Document Type Definitions (DTD), XML, 298**
defining, 301-304

**DOM (Document Object Model), DHTML, 289**

**DOS, batch language.** *See* **batch language**

**dot-coms, working for, 379**

**Double (double-precision) data type, 112**

**downtime, 18**

**drawing**
lines, Visual Basic Line control, 145-147
picture boxes, Visual Basic Picture Box control. *See* Picture Box control (VB)
shapes, Visual Basic Shape control. *See* Shape control (VB)

**drawString() method (Java), 318**

**DTD (Document Type Definition), XML, 298**
defining, 301-304

**Dynamic HTML.** *See* **DHTML**

### E

**education**
continuing education
*books, 392-394*
*industry magazines, 392*
*online classes, 394-396*
*training, 391-392*
degrees/certificates, 380-381

**Else statement (VB), 127-129**
nesting If...Else statements (ElseIf), 131

**email hyperlinks (HTML), 283**

**empty (null) strings, VB If statements, 127**

**empty strings, 113**

**encapsulation, 189**

**equal sign (=) assign relational operator (C), 213**

**equal to (=) comparison operator, 122**

**equal to (==) relational operator (C), 225**

**error checking, Visual Basic, 173-178**

**errors.** *See* **bugs**

**event handling, JavaScript, 328-331**

**events, Visual Basic, Click, 98**

**events (Windows), 90-91**

**exception handling, Java, 318-321**
catch keyword, 320-321
throws keyword, 319-320
try keyword, 320-321

**exclamation mark (!), data type suffix character, 114**

**exe files, 366.** *See also* **setup routines**

**executable content (Java), 307-309**
multiplatform, 309-310

**expressions, 117-118**
operators. *See* operators

**Extensible Markup Language.** *See* **XML**

**extraction operator (<<), C++, 230-231**

### F

**F5 function key (Visual Basic), 78**

**FillStyle property, Shape control (VB), 148-149**

**flowcharts, 336-342**
examples, 339-342
rules, 338-339
structured programming
*decision, 350*
*looping, 351*
*sequence logic, 347-348*
symbols, 336-338
templates, 336

**focus (Windows), 163-166**

**For loops (VB), 139.** *See also* **loops**
Listing 8.7, a For loop, 139
Listing 8.7, a For loop adding numbers 1 to 10, 139

Listing 8.8, a For loop adding numbers 1 to 100, 141
nested, 203-204
Visual Basic, 139-141

**For...Next loop (Visual Basic), 270**

**Form Layout window (Visual Basic), 86**

**Form window (VB).** *See* **Visual Basic, Form window**

**forms, defined, 83**

**FORTRAN language, 50-52**

**forward slash (/) division operator (C), 213**
HTML tags, 265
math operator, 120

**free form languages, 62**

**function procedures (C), 214**

**functions**
C
*built-in, 217-218*
*main ( ), 214-215, 222-223*
*printf( ), 218-219, 221-222, 230*
*scanf( ), 220-222*
*writing functions, 222-223*
C++ prototypes, 236
getAge(), 239
LoadPicture(), 156
versus methods (JavaScript), 328
Visual Basic, 173
*InputBox(), 107-108*
*MsgBox(), 104-106*

**future of programming, 390-391**

**G**

**getAge() function, 239**

**GIGO (garbage-in, garbage-out), 13**

**global variables (C), 217**

**GOTO statements, 347**

**graphics**
HTML, 280-282
Line control (VB), 145-147
*drawing lines, 146-147*
*properties, 145-147*
Picture Box control (VB). *See* Picture Box control (VB)
Shape control (VB). *See* Shape control (VB)

**greater than () comparison operator, 122**

**greater than < relational operator (C), 213**

**greater than (>) relational operator (C), 225**

**greater than or equal to (<=) relational operator (C), 213**

**greater than or equal to (>=) relational operator (C), 225**

**greater than or equal to () comparison operator, 123**

**grouping data, data structures, 208-209**

**H**

**handling events, JavaScript, 328-331**

**handling exceptions, Java, 318-321**
catch keyword, 320-321
throws keyword, 319-320
try keyword, 320-321

**hardware, 11-12**

**header files (C), 215**

**help, DHTML Web site help systems, 287**

**Help menu (Visual Basic), 87**

**high-level languages, 50.** *See also* **languages**

**hotkeys, Visual Basic forms, 162-163**

**HTML, 264-266, 273-276**
Active Server Pages (ASP), 269
code, whitespace, 277
commands. *See* HTML, tags
comments, 277
Dynamic HTML. *See* DHTML
formatting
*graphics, 280-282*
*text, 277-280*
*Web pages, 276-277*
hyperlinks, 282-283
Java applets, 308. *See also* Java
listings
*16.1, sample Web page, 264*
*17.1, general HTML format, 276*
*17.1, simple HTML commands, 274*
*17.3, <h> tag, 279*
*17.4, <font size> tag, 279-280*
*17.5, img src tag, 281*
sample Web page, 264-265
simple Web page code, 274-275
tags, 265
*<!—>, 277*
*<> (angle brackets), 265*
*<a href>, 282-283*
email hyperlinks, 277, 283
*<a>, 282-283*
*<APPLET>, 308*
*<b>, 278*
*<body>, 277*
*<br>, 278*
*<font size>, 279-280*
*<h>, 278-279*
*<head>, 277*
*<html>, 277*
*<i>, 278*
*<img src>, 280-281*
*<p align>, 278*
*<title>, 277*
*<u>, 278*
*/ (forward slash), 265*
case, 277

*How can we make this index more useful? Email us at indexes@quepublishing.com*

*metatags, 277*
*script>, 325*
*<a href>, DHTML scriptlets, 289*
*<script>, 293*
viewing Web page source code, 275
writing code
*text editors, 276*
*WYSIWYG (What You See Is What You Get) editors, 274*
**HTML (Hypertext Markup Language), 66, 191-192**
**HTTP (Hypertext Transfer Protocol), 185**
**hyperlinks (HTML), 282-283**
**Hypertext Markup Language (HTML), 66, 191-192**
**Hypertext Transfer Protocol (HTTP), 185**

## I

**I/O, 232. *See also* input and output**
C++ versus C, 230-231
**IBM, PL/I language, 55-57**
**IC (integrated circuits), 16. *See also* chips**
**icons, creating with resource editors, 370-371**
**If statement (VB), 126-127**
comparison operators, 126
Else statements, 127-129
Listing 8.1, If...Else statement, 129
Listing 8.2, nested If...Else statement with ElseIf, 131
logical operators, 129-131
nesting If...Else statements (ElseIf), 131
**if statements (C), 225**
**images. *See* graphics**
**import command (Java), 316**
**include (#include) statement (C), 215**
**industry standards, 396**
**InformIT.com Web site, 395-396**
**inheritance, multiple, 65**
**inheritance (C++ objects), 229, 240**
**init() method (Java), 317**
**initializing Visual Basic list boxes, 151**
**input**
C++ versus C, 231
data entry, 13
scanf( ) function (C), 220-222
**input boxes, Visual Basic, 103-104, 107-108**
**insertion operator (>>), C++, 230-231**
**int keyword (C++), 233**
**Integer data type, 112**
**integrated circuits (IC), 16. *See also* chips**
**interest rate calculator application (VB), 160**
adding labels/text boxes, 165-171
Compute Interest command button
*adding to form, 171*
*calculation code, 171-173*
creating the form, 161-163
*adding hotkeys, 162-163*
*adding labels/text boxes, 162*
*focus, 163-165*
*Form window position, 163*
*positioning Form window, 161-163*
*tab order, 165-166*
defining output, 160-161
error checking, 173-178
Exit command button
*adding to form, 171*
*calculation code, 173-174*
*Unload statement, 174*
**Internet**
jobs, 385
online job market sites, 378
**Internet applications, 259-260**
Active Server Pages (ASP), 269-270
ActiveX controls, 266-267
connections to the Internet, 260-262
*point-to-point (PPP), 261-262*
HTML, 262
HTTP (Hypertext Transfer Protocol), 185
Microsoft .NET technology, 270-271
online service protocol scripts, 254-257
packet transfer, 262-264
scripting, 267-268
*JavaScript. See JavaScript*
*VBScript, 267-268*
URLs (uniform resource locators), 185, 263
Visual Basic
*ActiveX documents, 191-192*
*HTML (Hypertext Markup Language), 191-192*
*Internet controls, 188-190*
*VBScript, 192*
Visual Basic Application Wizard, 184-185
*creating an application, 185-187*
*default URLs (uniform resource locators), 185*
*running sample application, 187-188*
Web browsers, 263
Web pages, 262-263
**Internet Explorer, DHTML support, 290. *See also* Web browsers**

**interpreted code, 67**

**intranet applications, 184.** *See also* **Internet applications**

## J

**Java, 305-307**
; (semicolon), 316
applets, 307
*appearance in HTML documents, 308*
*creating, 311*
*<APPLET> tag, 308*
bytecode, 309-310
case sensitivity, 315
coding principles, 315-316
compiling, 309-311
drawString() method, 318
exception handling, 318-321
*catch keyword, 320-321*
*throws keyword, 319-320*
*try keyword, 320-321*
executable content, 307-309
*multiplatform, 309-310*
import command, 316
init() method, 317
Listing 20.1, simple Java program, 315
*code explanation, 316-318*
paint() method, 317-318
resize() method, 317
sample program, 314-315
security, 311-312
setColor() method, 318
Sun Microsystems Web site, 312
viewing Java Web pages with Web browsers, 310-312
Visual J++, 312-314
whitespace, 316

**JavaScript, 267, 323-326**
button rollover effect, 328-331
comments, 331
event handling, 328-331

Listing 21.1, button rollover effect, 328-330
looping, 331
methods versus functions, 328
objects, 326-328
scriptlets, 289
*example usage, 290-293*
scriptlets, viewing source code, 325
statements, 331
<script> tag, 325

**javascript keyword (DHTML), 291**

**JCL (Job Control Language), 245**

**Job Control Language (JCL), 245**

**jobs, 378-379.** *See also* **programming industry**
analysts/design staff, 384
consulting, 387
contract programmers (data processing departments), 377-378
data entry, 381-382
degrees/certificates, 380-381
dot-coms, 379
equal opportunity, 380
Internet/Web positions, 385
job security, 386
job titles, 379-380
management, 385-386
network-related positions, 385
online job market sites, 378
programmers, 9-10, 24, 382-385
small companies, 385
trainers, 391-392
working conditions, 3

## K

**keyboard input**
C++ versus C, 231
scanf( ) function, C, 220-222

**keyboard shortcuts.** *See* **shortcut keys**

**keyboards**
card-punch machines, 49
history, 48-49

**keywords (C), 212**

**Knuth, Dr. Donald, 209**

## L

**labels**
Visual Basic forms, adding, 165-171
Visual Basic programs, 96-97

**languages, 27-29, 36-37**
ADA, 58
APL, 58
BASIC, history, 66-70
batch. *See* batch language
C. *See* C
C#, 271
C++. *See* C++
COBOL, 52-55
comparing, 72-73
compilers, 29
DHTML (Dynamic HTML). *See* DHTML
FORTRAN, 50-52
free form, 62
history, 27-29
*binary arithmetic, 44-47*
*ADA, 58*
*APL, 58*
*ASCII table, 42-44*
*assemblers/translators, 48-49*
*BASIC, 66-70*
*C, 63-64*
*C++, 65*
*COBOL, 52-55*
*first programs, 47-48*
*FORTRAN, 50-52*
*high-level languages, 50*
*keyboards, 48-49*
*low-level languages, 49-50*
*mnemonics, 48-49*

*How can we make this index more useful? Email us at indexes@quepublishing.com*

*Pascal, 62-63*
*PL/I, 55-57*
*QuickBASIC, 69-70*
*RPG, 57-58*
*switches, 42*
*Visual Basic, 71-72*
HTML (Hypertext Markup
Language), 66. *See* HTML
Java. *See* Java
JavaScript. *See* JavaScript
Job Control Language (JCL),
245
macro. *See* macro languages
PL/I, 55-57
QuickBASIC, history, 69-70
RPG, 57-58
scripting. *See* scripting
scripting languages, 66
self-documenting languages,
52
syntax, 28
translators. *See* languages,
compilers
Visual Basic. *See* Visual Basic
Visual Basic for Applications.
*See* VBA
Visual J++, 312-314
Windows Scripting Host
(WSH), 254-257
XML. *See* XML (Extensible
Markup Language)

**LANs (local area networks),
385**

**left angle bracket (<), HTML
tags, 265**

**less than < comparison oper-
ator, 122**

**less than < relational opera-
tor (C), 225**

**less than or equal to (>=)
relational operator (C), 213**

**less than or equal to (<=)
comparison operator, 123**

**line breaks, Web pages, 278**

**Line control (VB), 145-147**
drawing lines, 146-147
properties, 145-146
*BorderStyle, 146-147*

**links (HTML).** *See* **hyperlinks**

**List control (VB), 151-152**

**listings**
accumulator, totaling an
array, 199
Active Server Pages (ASP),
269
BASIC sample program,
67-68
batch language, printing a
directory listing, 246-247
bubble sort, 202-203
C
*input/output, 221*
*main( ) function, 222-223*
*sample small program,
214*
COBOL sample program,
53-55
counter (number-guessing
game), 198-199
DHTML rollover scriptlet, 291
FORTRAN sample program,
51-52
HTML
*<font size> tag, 279-280*
*<h> tag, 279*
*general HTML format, 276*
*img src tag, 281*
*sample Web page, 264*
*simple HTML commands,
274*
Java program, 315
*code explanation,
316-318*
JavaScript button rollover
effect, 328, 330
Pascal sample program, 63
PL/I sample program, 56-57
PPP connection script file,
255-256
QuickBASIC  sample pro-
gram, 69-70

RPG sample program, 57-58
searching arrays
*binary search, 207-208*
*sequential search,
205-206*
VBScript example, 267-268
Visual Basic
*changing form shape
according to list box
selection, 152*
*changing list box patterns,
152*
*Do While loop, 136*
*ErrorCheck( ) function,
176-177*
*For loop, 139*
*For loop adding numbers
1 to 10, 139*
*For loop adding numbers
1 to 100, 141*
*If...Else statement, 129*
*initializing list boxes, 151*
*interest calculation com-
mand button procedure,
172*
*LoadPicture() function,
156*
*nested If...Else statement
with ElseIf, 131*
*placing a caption on a
form, 119*
*Select Case statements,
comparing multiple val-
ues, 132*
*Select Case statements,
conditional comparisons,
133*
*Select Case statements,
using a range to com-
pare grouped values,
134*
*terminating a program,
153*
XML
*DTD and corresponding
code, 303-304*
*well-formed XML file, 299*
**literals, 112-114**

**LoadPicture() Function (VB),
156**
VB Picture Box control,
155-156

**local area networks (LANs),
385**

**logic**
flowcharts. *See* flowcharts
program design, 36

**logical operators, If state-
ments, 129-131**

**Long data type, 112**

**looping**
JavaScript, 331
structured programming,
349-351

**loops**
C, 225-226
infinite loops, 135
nested loops, 203-204
Visual Basic, 135-141
*Do Until, 137-139*
*Do While, 135-137*
*For, 139-141*
*For loop adding numbers
1 to 10, 139*
*For loop adding numbers
1 to 100, 141*

**loops (Visual Basic),
For...Next, 270**

**low-level languages, 49-50.**
*See also* **languages**

# M

**macro languages, 248-251**
advantages, 248-249
recording macros, 249-250
VBA (Visual Basic for
Applications), 252. *See also*
VBA

**magazines, 392**

**mailto hyperlinks (HTML),
283**

**main( ) function (C), 214-215,
222-223**

**mainframes, 18-19**
EBCDIC table, 43

**maintenance**
debugging, 353-355
flowcharts, 336-342
*examples, 339-342*
*rules, 338-339*
*symbols, 336-338*
*templates, 336*
pseudocode, 342-343
structured programming. *See*
structured programming
testing, 352-353

**math, binary arithmetic,
44-47**

**math operators, 119-122**
C, 212-213
concatenating, 121-122
operator precedence,
120-121

**members (C++ objects)**
accessing, 235
member functions, 236
*overloading operators,
239-240*

**memory, random-access file
control, 205**

**menus, Web sites (DHTML),
286**

**message boxes, Visual Basic,
103-106**

**messages (C++ objects), 229**

**metatags (HTML), 277**

**methods, 151**
versus functions (JavaScript),
328

**microcomputers, 19.** *See also*
**PCs (personal computers)**

**microprocessors, 16**

**Microsoft**
.NET technology, 270-271
DHTML support, 290
QuickBASIC language, 69-70
VBA (Visual Basic for
Applications). *See* VBA
Visual Basic. *See* Visual Basic
Web sites, 78

**Microsoft Excel, VBA (Visual
Basic for Applications) functionality, 252-254**

**Microsoft Internet Explorer,
263.** *See also* **Web browsers**

**Microsoft Word, recording
macros, 249-250**

**minicomputers, 19**

**minus sign (-)**
math operator, 120
subtraction operator (C), 213

**Miscrosoft, Visual J++,
312-314**

**mnemonics, 48-49**

**modules, Visual Basic,
175-177**

**Monster.com Web site, 378**

**Mosaic Web browser, 263.**
*See also* **Web browsers**

**mouse clicks, Click event
(Visual Basic), 98**

**mouse rollover effect
(DHTML), 290-293**

**mouse rollover effect
(JavaScript), 328-331**

**MsgBox() function (Visual
Basic), 104-106**

**multiple inheritance, 65**

**mutually exclusive state-
ments, 128**

# N

**named constants (Visual
Basic), 97**

**named literals (Visual Basic),
97**

**nested loops, 203-204**

**nesting If...Else statements (VB), 131**

**NET (.NET) technology, 270-271**

**Netscape Navigator.** *See* **Web browsers**

**networking, 16**

**networks**
  jobs, 385
  software installations, 367-368

**not equal to (!=) relational operator (C), 213, 225**

**not equal to () comparison operator, 123**

**Not logical operator (VB), 130-131.** *See also* **decision making (VB)**

**null (empty) strings, VB If statements, 127**

**null zero character, C strings, 219-220**

**numbers**
  binary arithmetic, 44-47
  binary equivalents, 45-46

### O

**Object data type, 112**

**object-oriented programming (OOP), 26, 65, 222.** *See also* **C++**
  advantages, 239-240

**objects.** *See also* **data, structures**
  JavaScript, 326-328
  models, 255
  scalable, 267

**objects (C++), 228-233**
  abstraction, 228
  adding behavior, 235-238
  cin, 231

classes, 228
  *declaring, 233-236*
  *libraries, 240*
  *scope, 238-239*
  constructors, 237
  destructors, 237
  inheritance, 229, 240
  members
    *accessing, 235*
    *member functions, 236, 239-240*
  messages, 229
  polymorphism, 229, 240
  reuse, 229, 232
  terminology, 229
  variables, declaring, 234-235

**online service protocol scripts, 254-257**

**OOP (object-oriented programming), 65, 227.** *See also* **C++**
  advantages, 239-240

**operating systems, Unix, 64**

**operators, 119**
  C, 212-213, 224
    *compound assignments, 224*
    *math, 212-213*
    *relational, 225*
  C++, overloading, 239-240
  comparison operators, 122-124
    *If statements, 126*
  logical operators, If statements, 129-131
  math operators, 119-122
    *concatenating, 121-122*
    *operator precedence, 120-121*

**Or logical operator (VB), 130.** *See also* **decision making (VB)**

**outlines, defined, 180**

**output**
  batch language, 246-247
  C++, 232-233
  C++ versus C, 230-231

printf( ) function (C), 218-222, 230
  program design, 33-36

**output buffer, 231**

**overhead payment approach (data processing departments), 376-377**

**overloading operators (C++), 239-240**

### P

**Package and Deployment Wizard (Visual Studio)**
  deploying applications, 361-366
  uninstalling applications, 368

**packet transfer, Internet applications, 262-264**

**paint() method (Java), 317-318**

**parallel testing, 353.** *See also* **testing**

**Pascal language, 62-63**

**patterns, list boxes (Visual Basic), 152**

**PCs (personal computers), 16-19**

**period (.)**
  accessing object members (C++), 235
  referencing data structure items, 209

**personal computers (PCs), 16-19**

**petabytes, 18**

**Picture Box control (VB), 154-155**
  file types, 156-157
  LoadPicture() function, 155-156
  properties, 155-156
  setup, 155-156

**PL/I language, 55-57**

**placeholders, variables, 115**

**platforms, defined, 264**

**plus sign (+)**
addition operator (C), 213
concatenation operator, 122
math operator, 120

**point-to-point (PPP) Internet connections, 261-262**

**polymorphism (C++ objects), 229, 240**

**pound sign (#)**
data type suffix character, 114
date/time literals, 113
preprocessor directives (C), 215

**PPP (point-to-point) Internet connections, 261-262**

**preprocessor directives (C), 215**

**printf( ) function (C), 218-219, 221-222, 230**

**printing.** *See also* **output**
batch language, 246-247
C++ versus C, 230-231

**procedures, function procedures (C), 214**

**profilers, 368-369**

**programmer analysts, 383**

**programmers, 22, 382-385**
continuing education
*books, 392-394*
*industry magazines, 392*
*online classes, 394-396*
need for, 9-10, 24

**programming, 7**
designing programs, 33-36
*defining output, 33*
*output, 34*
errors. *See* bugs
future of programming, 390-391
history
*card-punch machines, 49*
*first programs, 47-48*

*keyboards, 48-49*
*languages. See languages, history*
*shared-program concept, 47-48*
languages. *See* languages
mnemonics, 48-49
myths, 8-9
object-oriented, 26
object-oriented programming (OOP), 65
program design, 31-36
*code, 36*
*logic, 36*
*output, 33-36*
programs design, output, 35
structured, 26
structured programming. *See* structured programming

**programming industry**
data processing departments, 374-376
*chargeback payment approach, 377*
*contract programmers, 377-378*
*overhead payment approach, 376-377*
jobs, 378-379
*analysts/design staff, 384*
*consulting, 387*
*data entry, 381-382*
*degrees/certificates, 380-381*
*dot-coms, 379*
*equal opportunity, 380*
*Internet/Web positions, 385*
*job security, 386*
*job titles, 379-380*
*management, 385-386*
*network-related positions, 385*
*online job market sites, 378*
*programmers, 382-385*
*small companies, 385*
*trainers, 391-392*
*working conditions, 379*

**programs, 7, 24-26.** *See also* **software**
analyzing, profilers, 368-369
applets. *See* applets (Java)
ASCII table, 42-44
assemblers, 48-49
binary arithmetic, 44-47
branching, 347
C
*#include statement, 215*
*main( ) function, 214-215, 222-223*
*sample small program, 214*
COBOL program sample, 53-55
code listings. *See* listings
companies' need for programs, 22
debugging, 353-355
designing, 31-36
distributing. *See* distributing applications
errors. *See* bugs
file size, 346
flowcharts, 336-342
*examples, 339-342*
*rules, 338-339*
*symbols, 336-338*
*templates, 336*
FORTRAN program sample, 51-52
history
*first programs, 47-48*
*shared-program concept, 47-48*
instructions, 24-26
Java, 314-315
*coding principles, 315-316*
languages. *See* languages
maintenance. *See* maintenance
methods of obtaining programs, 22
obtaining, 22
*advantages, 22-23*
*disadvantages, 22-23*
PL/I program sample, 56-57

RPG program sample, 57-58
Shape control application (VB), 150-154
  *changing form shape according to list box selection, 152*
  *changing list box patterns, 152*
  *form properties and values, 153-154*
  *initializing list boxes, 151*
  *terminating the program, 153*
shells, 180
source programs. *See* source programs
structured programming. *See* structured programming
terminating, Visual Basic (Listing 9.4), 153
testing, 352-353
version controllers, 369-371
Visual Basic
  *Application Wizard. See Application Wizard (VB)*
  *interest rate calculator. See interest rate calculator application (VB)*
  *resource files, 182*
  *simple program, 78-81*
whitespace, 62
Windows programs, 90-91. *See also* Visual Basic

**Project Explorer window (Visual Basic), 86**

**projects (Visual Basic), 80**

**properties, Visual Basic. *See* Visual Basic, properties; Visual Basic, Properties window**

**Properties window (Visual Basic), 87**

**protocols, online service scripts, 254-257**

**prototypes (C++ functions), 236**

**pseudocode, 342-343**
  structured programming
  *decision, 349*
  *looping, 349*
  *sequence logic, 348*

## Q

**Que Publishing Web site, 392-393**

**QuickBASIC language**
  history, 69-70
  Listing 4.3, 69-70

**quotation marks (), String data type, 113**

## R

**recording macros, 249-250**

**records, 208. *See also* data, structures**

**relational operators (C), 225**

**Rem statements, 102**

**remarks, 68**
  Visual Basic, color coding, 152
  Visual Basic programs, 101-103

**resize() method (Java), 317**

**resource editors, 370-371**

**resource files, 182**

**reuse (C++ objects), 229, 232**

**right angle bracket (>), HTML tags, 265**

**rollover effect**
  DHTML, 290-293
  JavaScript, 328-331

**RPG language, 57-58**

## S

**scalable objects, 267**

**scanf( ) function (C), 220-222**

**scope (C++ object classes), 238-239**

**scriplets, 289**
  example usage, 290-293

**scripting, 254**
  Internet applications, 267-268
    *JavaScript. See JavaScript*
    *VBScript, 267-268*
  Listing 15.2, PPP connection script file, 255-256
  online service protocols, 254-257
  WSH (Windows Scripting Host), 254-257
  <script> tag, 325

**scripting languages, 66**
  VBScript, 192

**scriptlets, viewing source code, 325**

**<script> HTML tag, 293, 325**

**searching arrays, 204-205**
  binary searches, 206-208
  Listing 12.4, binary search, 207-208
  Listing 12.4, sequential search, 205-206
  random-access file control, 205
  sequential searches, 205-206

**security, Java, 311-312**

**Select Case statement (VB), listings, 131-134**

**self-documenting languages, 52**

**semicolon (;)**
  C statements, 214, 223
  Java, 316

**sequence (structured programming), 347-348**

**sequential searches (arrays), 205-206. *See also* searching, arrays**

**setColor() method (Java), 318**

**setup routines**
generating, 361-366
testing, 367

**Shape control (VB), 144**
properties, 148-149
*FillStyle, 148-149*
*Shape property, 149*
sample application, 150-154
*changing form shape*
*according to list box*
*selection, 152*
*changing list box patterns,*
*152*
*form properties and val-*
*ues, 153-154*
*initializing list boxes, 151*
*terminating the program,*
*153*

**Shape property, Shape con-**
**trol (VB), 149**

**shells (programs), 180**

**shortcut keys**
adding hotkeys to Visual
Basic forms, 162-163
Visual Basic, F5 (compile and
run), 78

**Single data type, 112**

**slashes, forward slash (/)**
division operator (C), 213
math operator, 120

**software, 12.** *See also* **pro-**
**grams**
installing across networks,
367-368
legalities, 12
uninstalling, 368
version controllers, 369-371

**software distribution.** *See*
**distributing applications**

**sorting data, 201-203**
bubble sorts, 201-203
Listing 12.3, bubble sort,
202-203

**source code, 29**

**source programs, 29**

**SourceSafe version control**
**(VB), 370**

**spaghetti code, 351**

**speed, analyzing with profil-**
**ers, 368-369**

**statements**
JavaScript, 331
Rem, 102

**String data type, 112-113**
defining strings, 116
empty strings, 113

**strings**
C, 219-220
null (empty) strings, VB If
statements, 127

**structured programming, 26,**
**344-346**
constructs, 347
decision, 348-350
looping, 349-351
sequence, 347-348

**structures.** *See* **data, struc-**
**tures**

**subroutines, 119**

**subscripts (arrays), 199**

**Sun Microsystems, Inc., 312**

**supercomputers, 17-18**

**swapping data, 200-201**

**switches, 42**

**syntax, 28**
errors. *See* bugs and debugging

**systems analysis and design,**
**22**

**systems analysts/design staff,**
**384**

**T**

**tab order, Visual Basic forms,**
**165-166**

**tags**
HTML, 265
*<!—>, 277*
*<> (angle brackets), 265*
*<a href>, 282-283*
email hyperlinks, 283
*<a>, 282-283*
*<b>, 278*
*<body>, 277*
*<br>, 278*
*<font size>, 279-280*
*<h>, 278-279*
*<head>, 277*
*<html>, 277*
*<i>, 278*
*<img src>, 280-281*
*<p align>, 278*
*<title>, 277*
email hyperlinks, 277
*<u>, 278*
*/ (forward slash), 265*
*<APPLET>, 308*
*case, 277*
*metatags, 277*
*<script>, 325*
*<a href>, DHTML*
*scriptlets, 289*
*<script>, 293*
XML. *See* XML

**temporary variables, 201**

**teraflops, 18**

**terms (investments), 173**

**testing, 352-353**
setup routines, 367

**text boxes, Visual Basic**
**forms, 165-171**

**text formatting (HTML),**
**277-280**

**throws keyword (Java excep-**
**tion handling), 319-320**

time data. *See* Date data
   type

ToolTips, Visual Basic controls, 99-100

top-down design, 33-36

training, 391-392
   books, 392-394
   industry magazines, 392
   online classes, 394-396

translator programs/assem-
   blers, 48-49

translators. *See* compilers

try keyword (Java exception
   handling), 320-321

twips (Visual Basic), 83

## U

uniform resource locators
   (URLs), 185, 263

uninstalling applications, 368

Unix operating system, 64

Unload statement (VB), 174

URLs (uniform resource locators), 185, 263

users, computers, 10
   costs, 13

## V

validating XML code, 300-301

variables, 114-117
   C++ objects, declaring,
      234-235
   declaring, C language, 217
   Dim statement, 114-117
   name prefixes, 115-116
   placeholders, 115
   storing data, 117-119
   swapping, 200-201
   temporary variables, 201
   watch variables, 354

Variant data type, 112
   declaring, 117

VB. *See* Visual Basic

VBA (Visual Basic for
   Applications), 251-254
   macros, 252
   Microsoft Excel application,
      252-254
   object models, 255

VBScript, 192, 267-268
   Listings 16.2, VBScript exam-
      ple, 267-268
   scriplets, 289

version controllers, 369-371

Visual Basic, 77-80
   ampersand (&), Caption
      property, 98
   apostrophes ('), remarks,
      102-103
   Application Wizard. *See*
      Application Wizard (VB)
   Call Stack dialog box, 355
   code, modules, 175-177
   comparison operators. *See
      also* Visual Basic, decision
      making, 122-126
   controls, 91, 99-101, 145
      *adding labels/text boxes,
         165-171*
      *Alignment property, 97*
      *command buttons, 97-98*
      *common tools, 100-101*
      *control arrays, 167-168*
      *copying, 167*
      *example usage, 96-98*
      *focus, 163-166*
      *grouping (control arrays),
         167-168*
      *Internet controls, 188-190*
      *Label control, 96-97*
      *Line, 145-147*
      *List, 151-152*
      *Picture Box. See Picture
         Box control (VB)*
      *placing on Form window,
         91-93*

   *setting properties, 87,
      93-98*
   *Shape. See Shape control
      (VB)*
   *toolbox, 84-86*
   *ToolTips, 99-100*
   data, 111
      *assignment statements,
         117*
      *data type suffix charac-
         ters, 113-114*
      *data types, 111-113*
      *Dim statement, 114-117*
      *literals, 112-114*
      *placeholders, 115*
      *specifying values, 112-114*
      *storing data in variables,
         117-119*
      *variables, 114-117*
   debugging, 355
   decision making, 126-127
      *Else statements, 127-129*
      *If statements, 126-127*
      *mutually exclusive state-
         ments, 128*
      *nesting If...Else statements
         (ElseIf), 131*
      *Select Case statements,
         131-134*
   environment, 80-82
      *code window, 78-79*
      *Form Layout window, 86*
      *Form window, 83-85*
      *forms, 83*
      *menu bar, 82-83*
      *New Project window, 81*
      *output window, 79-80*
      *Project Explorer (project)
         window, 86*
      *Properties window, 87*
      *toolbar, 82-83*
      *toolbox, 84-86*
      *twip measurements, 83*
   events, 90-91
      *Click, 98*
      *controlling. See also Visual
         Basic, controls*
      *event procedures, 91*

expressions, 117-118
  operators. *See Visual Basic, operators*
F5 function key, 78
Form window, 83-85
  activating forms, 86
  placing controls, 91-93
  resizing, 91-92
  setting startup position, 161-163
  size, 83
forms
  adding command buttons, 171
  adding labels/text boxes, 165-171
  captions, 119
  changing form shape according to list box selection (Listing 9.3), 152
  hot keys, 163
  hotkeys, 162-163
  interest rate calculator sample form, 161-162
  Unload statement (VB), 174
functions, 173
  InputBox(), 107-108
  MsgBox(), 104-106
graphics
  Line control, 145-147
  Picture Box control. See Picture Box control (VB)
  Shape control. See Shape control (VB)
Help, 87
history, 71-72. See also BASIC languages, history
input boxes, 103-104, 107-108
Internet applications. See also Application Wizard (VB)
  ActiveX documents, 191-192
  HTML (Hypertext Markup Language), 191-192
  Internet controls, 188-190
  VBScript, 192

Listings
  7.1, placing a caption on a form, 119
  8.1, If...Else statement, 129
  8.2, nested If...Else statement with ElseIf, 131
  8.3, Select Case statements, comparing multiple values, 132
  8.3, Select Case statements, conditional comparisons, 133
  8.4, Select Case statements, conditional comparisons, 133
  8.5, Select Case statements, using a range to compare grouped values, 134
  8.6, Do While loop, 136
  8.7, For loop, 139
  8.7, For loop adding numbers 1 to 10, 139
  8.8, For loop adding numbers 1 to 100, 141
  9.1, initializing list boxes, 151
  9.2, changing list box patterns, 152
  9.3, changing form shape according to list box selection, 152
  9.4, terminating a program, 153
  9.5, LoadPicture() function, 156
  10.1, interest calculation command button procedure, 172
  10.2, ErrorCheck( ) function, 176-177
logical operators, 129-131
loops, 135-141
  Do Until, 137-139
  Do While, 135-137
  For, 139-141
  For...Next, 270
message boxes, 103-106

methods, 151
named constants, 97
named literals, 97
operators, math operators, 119-122
programming, basic programming steps, 80-81
programs
  adding code, 110-111
  adding controls, 96-98
  Application Wizard. See Application Wizard (VB)
  compiling/running, 78-79
  design-time state, 84
  developing a simple application, 96-99
  focus, 163-166
  interest rate calculator. See interest rate calculator application (VB)
  projects, 80
  remarks, 101-103
  resource files, 182
  simple program, 78-81
  terminating (Listing 9.4), 153
properties
  Alignment property, 97
  Line control, 145-147
  Shape control, 148-149
Properties window, 87
  setting control properties, 93-95
Rem statements, 102
remarks, 101-103
  color coding, 152
screen elements. See Visual Basic, environment
shortcut keys, F5 (compile and run), 78
SourceSafe version control, 370
subroutines, 119
Swap command, 200. See also swapping data
tools. See Visual Basic, controls
Visual Studio. See Visual Studio

*How can we make this index more useful? Email us at indexes@quepublishing.com*

Windows programs, 90-91
wizards. *See* Application
  Wizard (VB)

**Visual Basic controls, 100**

**Visual J++, 312-314**

**Visual Studio, 359**
compiling programs, 359-361
deploying programs, 361-366
resource editor, 371
uninstalling applications, 368

# W-Z

**WANs (wide area networks),
385**

**watch variables, 354**

**Web browsers, 263**
DHTML support, 290
viewing HTML source code,
  275
viewing Java Web pages,
  310-312

**Web jobs, 385**

**Web pages, 262-263.** *See also*
**Internet applications; HTML
(Hypertext Markup
Language)**
DHTML features. *See* DHTML
general HTML format,
  276-277
graphics, 280-282
hyperlinks, 282-283
line breaks, 278
sample Web page HTML, 264
security, Java, 311-312
simple Web page, 274-275
text formatting, 277-280
viewing HTML source code,
  275

**Web sites**
Barnes & Noble, 395
Beowulf, 18
book publisher sites, 392-393
Brady Games, 293
DHTML features. *See* DHTML
Dice, 378

InformIT.com, 395
Java, 312
Microsoft, 78
Monster.com, 378
online classes, 394-396
online job market sites, 378
WebMonkey, 395

**WebBrowser control (VB),
185-189**

**WebMonkey Web site, 395**

**whitespace**
HTML code, 277
Java, 316

**whitespace (programs), 62**

**wide area networks (WANs),
385**

**wildcard characters, batch
language, 247**

**Windows**
Clipboard, copying Visual
  Basic controls, 167
distributing applications,
  358-359
    *compiling, 359-361*
    *deploying, 361-366*
    *testing setup routines,
      367*
focus, 163-166
object models, 255
programs, 90-91
resource editors, 370-371
Visual Basic. *See* Visual Basic

**Windows Scripting Host
(WSH) language, 254-257**

**wizards.** *See* **Application
Wizard (VB)**

**WSH (Windows Scripting
Host) language, 254-257**

**WYSIWYG (What You See Is
What You Get) HTML edi-
tors, 274**

**XML (Extensible Markup
Language), 295-297**
code requirements, 298
cross-platform capability,
  297-298
Document Type Definitions
  (DTD), 298
    *defining, 301-304*
importance of XML, 296-297
Listings
    *19.1, well-formed XML
      file, 299*
    *19.2, DTD and corre-
      sponding code, 303-304*
validating code, 300-301
well-formed XML code example, 298-300

# informIT

**www.informit.com**

## Your Guide to Information Technology Training and Reference

**Que** has partnered with **InformIT.com** to bring technical information to your desktop. Drawing on Que authors and reviewers to provide additional information on topics you're interested in, **InformIT.com** has free, in-depth information you won't find anywhere else.

## Articles

Keep your edge with thousands of free articles, in-depth features, interviews, and information technology reference recommendations – all written by experts you know and trust.

## Online Books

Answers in an instant from **InformIT Online Books'** 600+ fully searchable online books. Sign up now and get your first 14 days **free**.

POWERED BY

## Catalog

Review online sample chapters and author biographies to choose exactly the right book from a selection of more than 5,000 titles.